Second Edition

Education for Sexuality

CONCEPTS AND PROGRAMS FOR TEACHING

JOHN J. BURT

Professor and Chairman, Department of Health Education, University of Maryland

LINDA BROWER MEEKS

Assistant Professor of Health Education, Division of Health, Physical Education and Recreation, The Ohio State University

ILLUSTRATIONS BY JAMES C. BROWER

W. B. SAUNDERS COMPANY · Philadelphia · London · Toronto

The illustrations shown below and throughout this text are archaic symbols of the family. Those symbols in the book which are not reproduced below are the artist's concept based on these classic motifs.

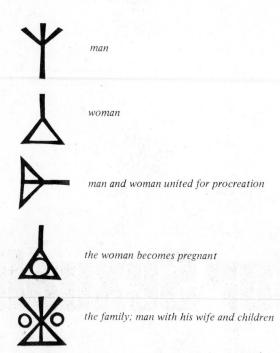

man

woman

man and woman united for procreation

the woman becomes pregnant

the family; man with his wife and children

W. B. Saunders Company: West Washington Square
Philadelphia, PA 19105

1 St. Anne's Road
Eastbourne, East Sussex BN21 3UN, England

1 Goldthorne Avenue
Toronto, Ontario M8Z 5T9, Canada

Library of Congress Cataloging in Publication Data

Burt, John J.

Education for sexuality.

Abridged and rev. ed. published in 1973 under title: Toward a healthy sexuality.

1. Sex instruction. I. Meeks, Linda Brower, joint author. II. Title. [DNLM: 1. Sex education. HQ56 B973e]

HQ57.3.B86 1975   612.6'007   74-4555

ISBN 0-7216-2204-6

Listed here is the latest translated edition of this book together with the language of the translation and the publisher.

Spanish (2nd Edition)—
NEISA,
Mexico City,
Mexico

Education for Sexuality

ISBN 0-7216-2204-6

Last digit is the print number: 9 8 7 6 5 4

*For their constant reassurance
that the American family
is not a dying institution,
we dedicate this book to:*

ANN, EME, KEITH, and JOE

and

JIM, ELSIE, BETH, MARGARET, WILLIAM,
SANDY, LARRY, JACK, and KRISTEN

Preface to the SECOND EDITION

During the five years that have elapsed since the publication of the first edition of *Education for Sexuality*, a number of important social and legal changes relating to human sexuality have occurred. These changes, together with numerous advances in our knowledge of sexuality, have necessitated a major revision of the First Edition.

The Supreme Court's decision that abortion is a matter between a woman and her physician touched off an explosion in the number of legal abortions in the United States and made an entire chapter on this topic appropriate. Equally important from a social viewpoint was a decision by experts in psychiatry to remove homosexuality from the list of "psychological maladies." This revised position has necessitated a major revision of the homosexuality chapter. The past five years were also permeated by a widespread interest in alternative sexual life styles. In view of this interest, the Second Edition includes a new chapter entitled "Intelligent Choice of a Sexual Life Style." The intensified women's liberation movement constitutes another social development of major interest. This movement and its challenge to "old ways of thinking about female sexuality" have effected a revision of some of the material included in the First Edition. Finally, recent advances in the biomedical aspects of human sexuality have been incorporated into several chapters, with contraception and venereal diseases receiving the most attention.

The Second Edition, like its predecessor, is a textbook for teachers. The first three sections of the book are designed to acquaint the teacher or future teacher with basic information and concepts related to sexuality. In Section Four, the scope and sequence of the sex education curriculum for elementary, junior, and senior high school are presented. The curriculum includes detailed teaching units for the various grade levels, together with the most recent list of supplementary materials. In addition, the book includes an Atlas of Human Sexuality (especially designed for easy reproduction on transparencies for use with the overhead projector), a Glossary of Terms, and additional readings.

Education for Sexuality was conceived, written, and designed by teachers for teachers.

JOHN BURT

LINDA MEEKS

ACKNOWLEDGMENTS

We are most grateful to our editor, Wallace Pennington, for the many helpful suggestions that attended the preparation of the second edition.

We are also grateful to Lorraine Battista for her extra efforts in designing this edition.

For permission to include some of his work, we are also indebted to Harrison Evans.

CONTENTS

TABLES

SECTION

1

INTRODUCTION TO SEX EDUCATION

CHAPTER ONE

Sex Education as Education for Love

Love is the only satisfactory answer to the problem of human existence.

Eric Fromm
The Art of Loving

It is one of the greatest achievements of Western civilization that it has succeeded in culturally linking the physical drive of sexuality with the emotion of love, which Westerners today consider the most 'noble' of emotions. This linking is not 'natural.' It is, rather, a cultural discovery.

Paul Bohannan
Love, Sex, and Being Human

Assuming good health for yourself and others, what is the one situation that you would least like to encounter in life? Whether you are a college student or a college professor, a middle-aged adult or a retired senior citizen, a wealthy individual or a prisoner hardened to physical brutality, the answer to this question is likely to be the same: "I would dread social isolation most." Fortunately, complete social isolation is not a realistic threat for most of us, and the current population explosion makes this even less likely in the future. On the other hand, each of us fights a personal battle, attempting to overcome our feelings of aloneness in the midst of a world of billions. In fact, history is a record of man's struggle with his "aloneness problem" — his attempts to gain recognition and appreciation, his attempts to belong, his attempts to be more than just chemical and physical processes, and his attempts to find himself.

A study of the history of man's struggle with his problem of aloneness reveals that the time-tested antidote for feelings of estrangement is the establishment of deep and lasting relationships with other human beings. One can obtain many worthy guidelines for establishing such relationships from older members of the family, from religion, from schools, and even from public law. In time, one also learns by trial and error.

In his attempts to establish deep and abiding relationships that will prevent, relieve, or counteract feelings of aloneness, man is limited to three categories of relationships: male-female relationships, male-male relationships, and female-female relationships. In turn, each of these relationships may be maintained on a psychic basis (no physical expression) or they may involve physical expressions of love. When the male-female relationship includes physical expression or desire for physical expression, it is termed a heterosexual relationship; when male-male or female-female relationships involve physical expression or desire for expression, they are termed homosexual relationships. But whether the relationship is maintained on a purely psychic, a heterosexual, or a homosexual basis, the motivation is the same—to prevent, relieve, or counteract feelings of aloneness.

Psychiatry suggests that deep and abiding social relationships capable of serving as antidotes for aloneness must be permeated by love. It further suggests that those social relationships not attended by love are likely to accentuate feelings of aloneness. Accordingly, love becomes the major weapon against man's major problem.

Dr. Erich Fromm, a world-famous psychoanalyst, expresses it this way: "Love is the only satisfactory answer to the problem of human existence." And there is great wisdom in the biblical statement that he who has not love is but a noisy gong or a clanging cymbal (i.e., the world is filled with noisy gongs and clanging cymbals trying to find themselves).

Since sexual relationships are intimate forms of social relationships, it seems entirely appropriate to begin this book with a discussion of that commodity essential to all social relationships that are worthy—love. Indeed, Paul Bohannan[1] writes: "It is one of the greatest achievements of Western civilization that it has succeeded in culturally linking the physical drive of sexuality with the emotion of love, which Westerners today consider the most 'noble' of emotions. This linking is not 'natural.' It is, rather, a cultural discovery." In view of this, the authors are of the opinion that the primary goal of sex education should be the integration of human love and human sexuality. Achievement of this goal, however, is rendered difficult by the fact that definitions of love are variable and apparently ever-changing.

DEFINITIONS OF LOVE

It is, of course, the prerogative of any writer or group to define terms "as they think suitable." However, the ambiguities created by several definitions of a single word must be "brought into the open" and not played upon. In this regard it should be noted that historically man has used the word love in at least two senses. In the first sense love is exclusive—directed toward one person. The Greeks

---

[1] Paul Bohannan, *Love, Sex and Being Human,* Doubleday and Company, New York, 1969, p. 85.

termed this kind of love *eros.* In the second sense love is directed toward all people—a more general love of mankind. The Greek word for this type of love was *agape.* In the Christian era it became brotherly love.

These two senses of the word *love* frequently render its use ambiguous because the motivations for erotic love and humanitarian love may be the same or they may be different. Differences are highly important in terms of the effectiveness of the relationship in overcoming human estrangement. Fromm[2] points out:

> If the desire for physical union is not stimulated by love, if erotic love is not also brotherly love, it never leads to union in more than an orgiastic, transitory sense. Sexual attraction creates, for the moment, the illusion of union, yet without love this union leaves strangers as far apart as they were before—sometimes it makes them hate each other, because when the illusion has gone they feel their estrangement even more markedly than before.

When the authors suggest that the goal of sex education should be the integration of love and sexuality, the reference is to *agape* (brotherly love, true love, or deep love). A complete discussion of this type of love is beyond the scope of this or perhaps any book, but summary answers to three questions will be attempted:

1. What is the nature of love?
2. How is love practiced?
3. Why is love important?

WHAT IS THE NATURE OF LOVE?

In contrast to popular opinion, there is much common agreement about the nature of love (*agape* type). Surveys of college students by the authors and by others reveal that the majority agree on the nature of love.[3] Four definitions or descriptions of love will serve to indicate areas of agreement.

Alexander Magoun[4] has defined love this way:

> Love is the passionate and abiding desire on the part of two or more people to produce together the conditions under which each can be and spontaneously express his real self; to produce together an intellectual soil and an emotional climate in which each can flourish [that is] far superior to what either could achieve alone.

Paul Bohannan[5] notes that love is not selfless:

> Like "life" in general, love embodies what appears to be a contradiction: the satisfaction of the self through the satisfaction of the needs and desires of others.
>
> Far from being selfless, love provides a double satisfaction—even a triple satisfaction—to the self: once to the self because you can love and are loving; once to the self when love is reciprocated and you are loved; and once to the self because you know that, since you are loving and being loved, you must have a lovable self. When it is all there, you are well and truly "locked in." Nobody wants out.

[2] Eric Fromm, *The Art of Loving,* Bantam Books, Inc., New York, 1963, p. 46. (First published by Harper and Row, 1956.)

[3] William M. Kephart, *The Family, Society and the Individual,* Houghton Mifflin, Boston, 1961, p. 321.

[4] F. Alexander Magoun, *Love and Marriage,* Harper and Row, New York, 1948, p. 4.

[5] Bohannan, *op. cit.,* p. 88.

Dr. Joseph Trainer[6] comments on the ability to love:

The ability to love is the capacity to escape the self-containment of one's own ego and seek instead to nourish another. A person with this ability well developed is able to give love freely to someone else. In its best example it is like a floodlight. The more energy put into it, the more people it can light or warm. In turn, more light and warmth shed back on the giver, and it is characteristic of those with this ability to be as able to receive as to give. In their general relation to the world, they are giving, outgoing, friendly people, those who reach out automatically to the world around them.

About love First Corinthians states:

Love is patient and kind; love is not jealous or boastful; it is not arrogant or rude. Love does not insist on its own way; it is not irritable or resentful. . . .

These definitions and descriptions of love have a central theme: to love is to be in an active state of concern about those whom one loves; in turn, this state of concern provides a climate in which both the loved and the lover can flourish.

HOW IS LOVE PRACTICED?

In the practice of love the lover uses his talents to express his concern for the loved one. Fromm[7] expresses it this way:

What does one person give to another? He gives of himself, of the most precious he has, he gives of his life. This does not necessarily mean that he sacrifices his life for the other—but that he gives him of that which is alive in him; he gives him of his joy, of his interest, of his understanding, of his knowledge, of his humor, of his sadness—of all expressions and manifestations of that which is alive in him.

WHY IS LOVE IMPORTANT?

Motivation for human behavior is a function of the entire nervous system, not of any particular portion. However, two components appear to dominate behavior in man. First, there remains in him, as a part of his evolutionary heritage, an old brain. This is his animal brain which appears to be concerned with the affective nature of sensory sensations—pleasure and pain. Anatomically, it is referred to as the hypothalamus. If electrodes are implanted in certain pleasure centers of the old brain in such a way that an experimental animal can stimulate his own hypothalamus ad libitum, the animal may initiate stimulation as often as 4000 times per hour—forfeiting opportunities for food and other distractions. By further experimentation the principal centers for pain, punishment, and escape have also been located in the hypothalamus.

A second part of man's brain is found to cover the first like a skull cap. This appears to be his thinking and reasoning brain, his most recently evolved brain, and the factor that differentiates him most from lower forms of animal life. It is termed the cerebral cortex.

Most of us seem to have an almost constant struggle between the old and new brain. The old brain says, "Satisfy your needs and appetites right now and never mind the consequences to others." It is completely self-centered. But the cortex

---

[6] Joseph Trainer, *Physiologic Foundations of Marriage Counseling*, C. V. Mosby, St. Louis, 1965, p. 10.

[7] Fromm, *op. cit.*, p. 20.

says: "If we only satisfy our own chemical and physical processes, then we are not too different from a plant, a tree, or a bacterium." This description of the self is not acceptable to the cortex, which appears to be very sensitive about worth-whileness. Perhaps this is because the cortex is the anatomical part of us that is more than just a chemical or physical process. It can reason. Or, put another way, if humans were only chemical and physical processes, there would be little need for a cerebral cortex. We sometimes refer to individuals whose cerebral cortices have been damaged as vegetables. While this is unkind, it is, nevertheless, rather descriptive. It must be noted, therefore, that the cortex has a vested interest when it comes to being more than a vegetable, that is, when it comes to human worth-whileness.

The desire to be more than just a series of chemical and physical processes or to be more worthwhile is the motivation for love. As we have seen, love is the ability to escape self-containment; therefore, love is the business of the cerebral cortex. It is not a passion of the old brain since the latter is completely self-con-tained. The decision to love is then a cortical decision to do something more than just spend seventy-two years (human life span) satisfying one's chemical and physi-cal processes. It is the decision to help others, to be worthwhile, and thereby add to the happiness of others as well as to one's personal happiness.

Love is the only satisfactory answer to human existence because without love man is nothing more than his chemical and physical processes—a parasite de-pending on something else for existence or support without making a useful or adequate return. Unless man can escape self-containment (parasite state) by doing something for others and thus feeling worthwhile, his cerebral cortex is offended. Human dignity is lost. He remains a lower animal.

Loss of human dignity is a very traumatic experience for the cerebral cortex. Having become "thingified" or reduced to animalistic functions like the old brain, the cortex frequently reacts in a defensive and immature way. It may even suggest suicide. Some examples may help to bring the problem into clear focus. A well-known and beautiful motion picture star may feel "thingified" because of her ac-ceptance only as a sex symbol and not as a total person. Suicide may be the final decision of her offended cortex. In like manner, a victim of a long-term illness may consider himself a burden to others and no longer of individual worth, or a person who has exploited others for individual gain may in time come to consider himself useless. The available records show that in the United States, approximately 56 people per day commit suicide. All these result from feelings by the cortex of not being worthwhile or of no longer being worthwhile.

As another possibility, an offended cortex may suggest withdrawal into men-tal illness. It is interesting that the number of people in the United States who ex-hibit this condition exceeds the number of college graduates. A less drastic sug-gestion of the cortex might be temporary escape with drugs, alcohol, obsession with work, or even war.

In summary, the newly evolved cerebral cortex has an innate desire to be worthwhile, to be more than a chemical and physical process, to escape self-containment, and to be a part of something more lasting. Thus, the need to be loved and to love has evolved.

But love did not evolve as a selfless attribute. Too many people have the mistaken notion that to love is to be self-sacrificing, and this attitude prevents them from being loving people. To give of what is alive in one's self, to express one's talents, and to contribute freely to mankind should not be viewed as a sacrifice for others but rather as a necessity for personal sanity. To love is to reap a personal gain. It appears to be the only satisfactory answer to human existence.

INTEGRATION OF LOVE AND SEXUAL BEHAVIOR

The highly developed cerebral cortex of the human being provides him with a unique facility: the ability to profit from the compromises and mistakes of history. This human capacity is of great importance to the sex educator because he presupposes that mistaken sexual behavior can be identified and that this behavior can be improved.

An examination of the history of sexual behavior reveals that the most recurrent mistake and the one most destructive of human happiness has been man's failure to integrate love and sexual behavior. For example, in the twelfth century love was viewed as the spiritualization and sublimation of carnal desire; consequently love between man and wife was considered impossible. During this period in history, marriages were arranged on a rational or materialistic basis, and unfulfilled love desires were channeled into codes and causes that man pursued. In time, this concept of psychic love (without physical expression) was recognized as being mistaken; it gradually gave way to the Romantic movement. Hugo G. Beigel[8] writes: " . . . the Romanticist rebelled against the progressing dehumanization, the all-devouring materialism and rationalism, and sought escape from these dangers in the wonders of the emotions." The Romanticists, therefore, were able to profit by the mistakes of earlier centuries: specifically, the Romantic movement was responsible for love's dropping its cloak of sublimation. But learning is a slow process and the notion that love and marriage were irreconcilable continued; i.e., until the end of the eighteenth century, romantic love was carried on outside marriage.

Approximately seven hundred years were required for the Western world to bridge the twelfth century schism between love and marriage, for it wasn't until the nineteenth century that love was considered a prerequisite to marriage. And even then love and sex remained somewhat dissociated; i.e., sex as an expression of love or for any reason other than reproduction was considered sinful. It was finally the twentieth century that bravely claimed that sex was for pleasure as well as reproduction and that both aspects belonged within a marriage based on love.

Thus the recommendation that love and sexual behavior should be integrated results from the experiences and mistakes of many people of many ages. The relevance of this conclusion for today's world is attested by the observation that deviations from this concept are continually being recognized as mistaken behavior (behavior that is not in the best interest of either the individual or society).

For example, 200 of Sweden's most prominent physicians recently met with the king's personal physician to discuss problems associated with human sexuality

---

[8] Hugo G. Beigel, "Love: Courtly, Romantic, and Modern." In *Selected Studies in Marriage and the Family,* edited by Robert F. Winch and Robert McGinnis, Henry Holt, New York, 1953, p. 350.

in that country. The conference concluded by asking the nation to reconsider its free-and-easy sex morals.

More recently in the United States, Dr. William Masters and Virginia Johnson noted that the pendulum may have swung too far toward sex without commitment. They further commented that now may be the time to return sex to the domain of the family.[9]

A further example of the ability of the cerebral cortex to profit by the mistakes of history comes from the Soviet Union. This country concluded that its experiences with free love represented mistaken sexual behavior. Their publication, *Soviet Education,* concedes the mistake in these words: " . . . such practices [free love] necessarily lead to a laxity and vulgarization of relationships unworthy of man, cause difficult personality problems, unhappiness and disruption of the family, making orphans of the children." Today, in fact, the Soviets condemn in other cultures sexual behavior they once defended in their own.

SEX EDUCATION AS EDUCATION FOR LOVE

Eric Fromm[10] has skillfully dissected love into four constituent parts:

1. Labor—meaning that one is willing to work for and give of one's self for those whom he loves.
2. Responsibility—meaning that one constantly evaluates the consequences of his behavior as it relates to others and stands prepared to help when needed by those he loves.
3. Respect—meaning that one refrains from exploitation of others; avoids co-action in which one is benefited at the expense of the other.
4. Understanding—meaning that one tries to "place himself in the shoes of another."

Sex education as education for love thus attempts to render clear these four constituents of love as they relate to sexual behavior.

Labor. With respect to this component, sex education has one major function: to point out again and again the inconsistency in behavior of those who say they love but are unwilling to give of themselves for the person they profess to love and to expose differences between real love and erotic or romantic love.

Responsibility. Sex education should provide the knowledge that will enable the student to evaluate and effectively handle the consequences of his sexual behavior. Thus, a major portion of this book is designed to acquaint the reader with the biological, sociocultural, psychological, and physical consequences of various types of sexual behavior.

Respect. In the total realm of interpersonal relationships there is probably no greater temptation to exploit another human being than in the area of sexual behavior. Accordingly, this book includes chapters devoted to the ethical aspects of human sexuality.

---

[9] *Newsweek,* May 14, 1973.
[10] Fromm, *op. cit.,* p. 22.

Understanding. Sex education, to be effective, should constantly remind the student that mature love must be sensitive not only to the wishes and desires of the other person but also, whenever possible, to the motivations that underlie these wishes and desires. Put another way, mature love suggests that you try to "put yourself in the shoes of the other sex" and thus gain a better understanding of sexuality as viewed from the opposite side. Such understanding is best developed through carefully planned sex education that begins with parents and is a part of the curriculum at every age or grade level. Such a program constitutes the second half of this book.

SEX VERSUS SEXUALITY

A systematic and orderly body of knowledge about the biological aspects of sex and reproduction has been available for many years. However, this body of knowledge has not been accepted in the school curriculum because somehow "it didn't seem right to talk about sex as a chemical and physical process." In the past, therefore, reproductive physiology has been a kind of mystery for the average student, and parents have been happy to keep it that way. Even medical schools only went as far as to teach the basic knowledge about childbirth and contraception. And even today one hears the comment that Masters and Johnson[11] were only studying chemical and physical process (the intent of the statement being to convey the message that such studies do not dignify sex but are only of physiological interest). It would thus appear that if sex education is to enjoy widespread acceptance, it must be more than just a course in biology—it must be education for love. But since love is most effectively practiced in full view of biological consequences, sex education cannot ignore detailed biological facts. Thus, we need a term that includes the biological aspects of sexual behavior and yet one that also includes other aspects of sex-linked behavior. To this end, the word *sexuality* was coined.

With regard to this word, Dr. George Berry, former Dean of Harvard Medical School, writes: "Its use . . . to connote the totality of being and the expression of maleness or femaleness, in place of the word 'sex' with its implied restriction to an act, appears to be the touchstone that is freeing people to contemplate this universal characteristic of life with greater openness and composure, and in much greater depth, than has heretofore been possible." Thus, sexuality becomes a tent that encloses the biological, psychological, sociocultural, and ethical aspects of human sexual behavior. It is recommended that sex education be approached in this context.

GETTING STARTED IN SEX EDUCATION

If you experience a feeling of inadequacy or apprehension as you ponder teaching your first class in sex education, don't despair—your feelings are not justified. Chances are that you already know more about sexuality than you do

---

[11] William Masters and Virginia Johnson, *Human Sexual Response,* Little, Brown and Co., Boston, 1966.

about astronomy, meteorology, electricity, or other topics that stimulate student discussion. You would not be embarrassed to look up an answer to a question related to one of these latter topics or to obtain a book written for the comprehension level of your class. Why not adopt the same attitude toward sexuality in the classroom?

The key to a relaxed and effective approach to sex education is confidence on the part of the teacher. There are two steps in the attainment of such confidence:

Step One: Confidence Through Knowledge

Knowledge is the basic antidote for fear. Thus the first step is acquisition of the biological, sociological, and psychological knowledge that attends sexuality. Biological knowledge takes the mystery out of human sexuality and helps you to deal with the topic as you would with other functions of the human body. Sociological data provide you with a knowledge of how people use their sexuality, and psychology attempts to help you with the question, why do people behave the way they do sexually? As you study the chapters that follow, your confidence will leap upward as you increase your knowledge of sexuality, of how it is used, and of why it is used in these ways.

Step Two: Confidence Through Philosophical Assurance

Although knowledge greatly increases your confidence, it is not enough. Complete confidence can be gained only by a feeling of "what I am doing is really right." And such a feeling can come only when you have developed a sound philosophy and have related sexuality to that philosophy. This, of course, is a step that you must take for yourself, but the philosophical positions presented in this book may serve as a catalyst.

SECTION
2

THE BIOLOGICAL ASPECTS OF HUMAN SEXUALITY

CHAPTER TWO

The Biological Male

To understand the male we must dissect him not only with the scalpel of the anatomist, but also with the more blunt tools of psychology and sociology. This chapter, however, is limited to the biological aspects of maleness.

THE MALE REPRODUCTIVE SYSTEM

Gonads

Very early in prenatal life special sex cells are set aside from the other cells of the body.

These cells organize into a group of cells known as gonads.

The gonads develop into testes in the male and ovaries in the female.

Testes

The testes begin to evolve about the seventh or eighth week of prenatal development.

Early development of the testes

Initially, they develop in the abdominal cavity at a level just below the upper border of the hip bone.

During the eighth and ninth months of fetal life, the testes leave their position in the abdominal cavity and start to move downward.

Descent of the testes

They are guided through a tunnel-like passageway in the abdominal cavity into a sac-like container outside the body cavities (Fig. 1).

The tunnel is the inguinal canal; the sac is the scrotum.

After the testes pass through the inguinal canal, this tunnel closes to prevent other tissues from descending into the scrotum.

Thus the inguinal canal is partly or totally obliterated in 80 per cent of infants over two months of age.

Among fully mature infants, the testes are found in the scrotum at birth in 96 per cent of the cases.

For the prematurely born, the corresponding figure is 70 per cent. But among those born with undescended testes, 50 per cent descend normally after birth.

If the inguinal canal fails to close or for some reason opens again, some of the other contents of the abdominal cavity may pass into this tunnel-like passageway. An unclosed inguinal canal can also lead to the return of one or both testes to the abdominal cavity.

Descent of Testes

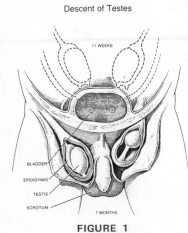

11 WEEKS

BLADDER
EPIDIDYMIS
TESTIS
SCROTUM
7 MONTHS

FIGURE 1

Hernia

Protrusion of the contents of one of the body's cavities through an abnormal opening in the cavity wall is termed herniation (Fig. 2). Hernia may occur anywhere in the body, but the male is especially susceptible to hernia through the inguinal canal.

In inguinal hernia a loop of intestine sometimes descends through the inguinal canal. Such cases are potentially hazardous because of the possibility of strangulation of the blood supply to the intestine. For this reason, hernia usually requires surgical correction.

Hernia

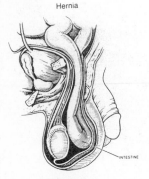

INTESTINE

FIGURE 2

Functions of the scrotum

The scrotum has two main functions:

1. To contain the testes.
2. To regulate temperature.

The testes are located in the scrotum because sperm cannot be effectively produced at body temperature. Sperm are most effectively produced when the temperature in the testes is 1.5 to 2° C. below body temperature. Thus temperature is a critical factor for normal function of the testes.

Cremasteric muscles

The scrotum has two major mechanisms for regulating temperature:

1. It contains many sweat glands and sweats freely.
2. It contains muscles (cremasteric muscles) that contract and bring the testes closer to the body to increase temperature and

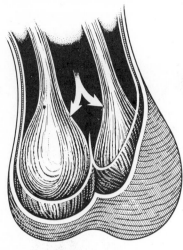

FIGURE 3

relax to lower the testes away from the body and thus reduce temperature (Fig. 3).

If the testes do not descend into the scrotum, sperm cannot be produced; and the male is sterile.

The medical name for the condition in which the testes do not descend is cryptorchidism. In this condition, it is possible to relocate the testes by surgery and thus render the male fertile.

Immersion of the testes into very hot water may produce temporary sterility, but this seems to be a transitory effect. On the other hand, enclosing the scrotum in ice for one-half hour daily may increase the sperm count by 10 per cent in some males.

Fever

It should be noted, however, that after a prolonged fever, sperm production may be reduced for as long as two months.

Occupation

Also, occupations that cause the scrotum to be bound up close to the body for many continuous hours may impair sperm production, e.g., long distance truck driving.

Men working near blast furnaces have a high incidence of defective spermatogenesis.

Continual compression of the testes by tight underwear (knitted briefs) or athletic supports definitely reduces the output of sperm.

Testes

The two testes are approximately equal in size (2 X 1 X 1¼ inches). Usually, the left testis hangs somewhat lower than the right. The weight of the testes tends to lessen in old age.

Function of the testes

The two major functions of the testes during the normal sequence of male growth and development are:

1. To produce male sex hormones.

2. To produce sperm.

Both these functions remain dormant during the early years of male life.

Physiologists are not sure just how the two functions of the testes are initiated, but the available evidence suggests that it happens this way:

Hormonal stimulation

At approximately ten years of age the hypothalamus releases a poorly identified hormone, which flows through a special system of blood vessels to the anterior pituitary gland.

The anterior pituitary gland, in turn, sends out "gonad stimulating hormones" called gonadotropic hormones. These gonadotropic hormones pass by way of the circulatory system to the testes where they stimulate male sex hormone and sperm production.

Hormones and their importance

Hormones play a very important role in human sexuality. Indeed, hormones are the direct cause of anatomical maleness and femaleness.

Their medicinal uses as contraceptives, as promoters of fertility, and as therapy for the aging make them a contender for honors in the view of the sexologists.

Male hormones

In the male we shall limit our discussion to three hormones: two that come from the pituitary gland to stimulate the testes and one that is produced by the testes when they are stimulated by the first two.

FSH

Seminiferous Tubules and Interstitial Cells

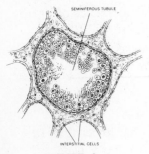

SEMINIFEROUS TUBULE

INTERSTITIAL CELLS

FIGURE 4

The first pituitary secretion is called follicle stimulating hormone (FSH). This hormone stimulates sperm production in the male and maturation of ova in the female.

The name FSH seems a bit inappropriate when referring to the male (follicles are found in ovaries). The explanation for the name is that the hormone was discovered first in the female. Thus, maturation of both sperm and ova is initiated by the same hormone—FSH.

Specifically, FSH is responsible for the conversion of primary spermatocytes into secondary spermatocytes.

Spermatogenesis cannot proceed in the absence of FSH.

ICSH

A second hormonal telegram from the pituitary gland instructs the testes to produce male sex hormone. This hormone is called interstitial cell-stimulating hormone (ICSH).

The name is derived from the fact that this hormonal substance stimulates a special group of cells in the testes called interstitial cells (Fig. 4).

Results

The testes, under orders from the pituitary via its messengers, FSH and ICSH, produce male sex hormones and sperm.

Testosterone

After pituitary stimulation, the testes produce testosterone—the primary male sex hormone.

When testosterone is released into the blood it effects many changes.

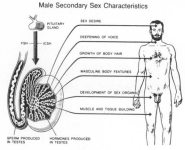

Male Secondary Sex Characteristics

FIGURE 5

We have already seen that it is responsible for primary sex characteristics in the male (i.e., the male reproductive system proper). In addition, testosterone is responsible for the male secondary sex characteristics (Fig. 5).

1. Longer and heavier bones.

2. Larger muscles.

3. Thicker and tougher skin.

    A. This overgrowth of skin during adolescence may close over the openings of sebaceous glands (oil glands), causing pimples.

4. Deep voice.

5. Distribution of body hair.

6. Development of pubic hair with a triangular border.

7. Baldness in later life.

8. Increased metabolism.

Sex hormones and physical performance

Because male sex hormones may increase weight, endurance, and aggressiveness, some athletic coaches have attempted to use them to improve performance.

There are two reasons why this practice should be avoided:[1]

1. There is no evidence that hormones actually improve performance.

2. The hormonal pills used for this purpose may cause:

    A. Shrinking of the testicles.

    B. Loss of sex drive.

    C. Dizziness.

    D. Muscle aches.

    E. Liver damage.

Spermatogenesis

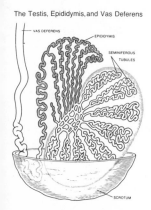

The Testis, Epididymis, and Vas Deferens

FIGURE 6

Sperm production occurs in some 300 sections of microscopic tubes located in the testes and known as seminiferous tubules (Fig. 6). Uncoiled, this network of tubes would extend over a mile.

These seminiferous tubules are stimulated to produce sperm by FSH, but final maturation of the immature sperm also requires testosterone.

Spermatogenesis begins at about 12 years of age, but first ejaculation of mature sperm usually occurs at about 13 years and ten months.

---

[1] Statement by The Joint Committee on the Medical Aspects of Sports, American Medical Association.

The process of spermatogenesis

Sperm Development

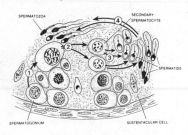

FIGURE 7

The spermatogonium is the earliest form in the development of a mature spermatozoon (Fig. 7).

The spermatogonium develops in the cells lining the outer wall of the seminiferous tubules.

As these cells grow they move toward the center of the tubules.

As the spermatogonium grows it moves into the first stage of sperm development: a primary spermatocyte (Fig. 7[1]). The primary spermatocyte then divides to form two secondary spermatocytes (Fig. 7[2]).

As the developing sperm move toward the center of the seminiferous tubules, the secondary spermatocytes divide into two spermatids (Fig. 7[3]).

The spermatid, in turn, reorganizes its nucleus to form a compact head and becomes a mature spermatozoon (Fig. 7[4]).

It is thought that special cells located in the seminiferous tubules secrete nutritional substances for the developing sperm. These cells are called sustentacular cells.

In summary, spermatogenesis is a process whereby small cells contained in the lining of the seminiferous tubules are stimulated by hormonal substances to grow into mature sperm that are released into tube-like passageways.

Sperm formation requires approximately 74 days and is not affected by sexual activity.

Factors that affect spermatogenesis

Stress

Stress will reduce spermatogenesis.

Studies during wartime have demonstrated that bomber crews flying six to eight hour strikes for 50 missions became relatively infertile.

Altitude

High altitude also appears to reduce spermatogenesis: the Andean miners have for many years made a trip down the mountain to reproduce.

Radiation

Radiation may inhibit or completely block spermatogenesis.

Ejaculation

After their production in the testis sperm must pass through the penis and into the female vagina in order to fertilize the ovum. The physiological mechanism by which this is accomplished is termed ejaculation.

During ejaculation, sperm pass through four successive structures:

1. Epididymis.
2. Vas deferens.

3. Ejaculatory duct.

4. Urethra.

Along the way sperm are joined or preceded by chemical contributions of three glands:

1. Seminal vesicles.

2. Prostate gland.

3. Bulbourethral gland (Cowper's gland).

The epididymis

The epididymis is a comma-shaped structure found on the posterior side of the testes (Fig. 6).

The upper end of the comma, which surmounts the testis like a helmet, is called the head.

The lower end of the comma is the tail of the epididymis.

After the production phase, sperm pass into the epididymis where a small quantity is stored.

Most sperm, however, are stored in the vas deferens.

The vas deferens

The vas deferens emerges from the tail of the epididymis (Fig. 6).

They course (one from each testis) for approximately 45 centimeters to enter the ejaculatory duct.

Seminal vesicles

The vas deferens thus functions as a passageway for sperm.

The vas deferens is joined en route by a duct from the seminal vesicles (Fig. 8).

During ejaculation the seminal vesicles (one on each side of the body) add fluid secretions.

The primary constituent of seminal fluid is fructose, a simple sugar that provides nutrition for sperm.

At one time, it was thought that sperm were stored in the seminal vesicles. This is not true.

It has also been commonly held that the intensity of male sex drive is related to the degree of distention of the seminal vesicles. But the currently available evidence does not appear to be sufficient to either confirm or deny this claim.

It would appear, however, that the greater the amount of seminal fluid in the seminal vesicles at the time of ejaculation, the more satisfying the orgasmic experience.

Thus, in multiple ejaculations during a short period of time, the first is more satisfying than subsequent climaxes.

This correlates well with the lower volume of semen observed in multiple ejaculations.

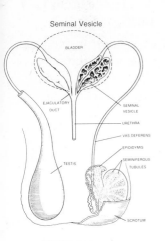

Seminal Vesicle

BLADDER

EJACULATORY DUCT

SEMINAL VESICLE

URETHRA

VAS DEFERENS

EPIDIDYMIS

SEMINIFEROUS TUBULES

TESTIS

SCROTUM

FIGURE 8

Ejaculatory duct

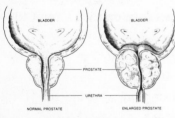

Prostate and Bulbourethral Glands

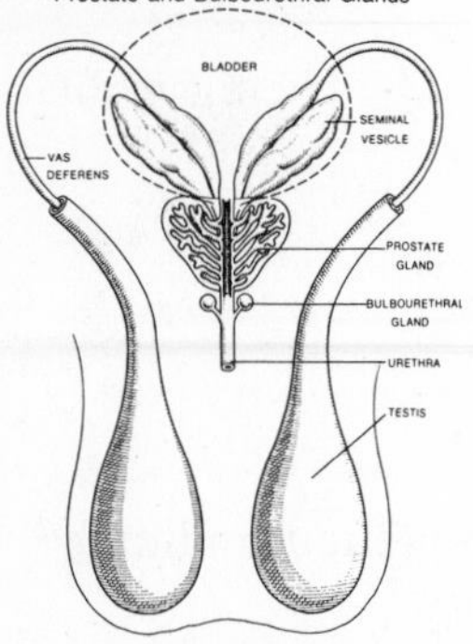

FIGURE 9

The duct that leaves the seminal vesicles joins with the vas deferens to form one common duct known as the ejaculatory duct (Fig. 9).

It is a short straight tube that passes into the prostate gland to open into the urethra.

The prostate gland

The prostate gland is made up of glandular tissue (Fig. 9).

It is pyramidal and lies just beneath the bladder.

The prostate gland produces several chemical substances thought to aid sperm in their attempt to fertilize an ovum.

Probably the most important role of prostatic fluid is to neutralize the acid vagina.

Normally, the vagina exhibits high acidity, which is not conduciv to sperm longevity or movement.

Immediately following ejaculation, the acidity of the vagina is neutralized by the semen.

The prostate in disease

Prostatic Hypertrophy

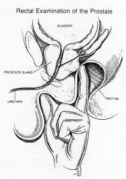

NORMAL PROSTATE   ENLARGED PROSTATE

FIGURE 10

Rectal Examination of the Prostate

FIGURE 11

Because of its anatomical position surrounding the urethra, enlargment of the prostate may block urination (Fig. 10).

The prostate gland is also a frequent site of cancer in the male. In fact, among men over 50 years of age cancer of the prostate is one of the leading causes of cancer death. Fewer than one man in ten survive this disease. Thus, early detection is extremely important.

In the early stages of cancer of the prostate, hard lumps can be detected (in the same way that lumps may indicate cancer of the breast).

These lumps are detectable during rectal examination (Fig. 11).

With regard to cancer of the prostate, Dr. Nathaniel Shafer, a New York specialist in internal medicine, writes:

> Many of these deaths are unnecessary. According to estimates, a simple five or ten second rectal examination would allow for over 50 per cent of the cases to be discovered at a stage when they could be cured. However, because of social inhibitions and prudishness, a rectal examination is not performed as frequently and as routinely as it should be.

The following signs may accompany cancer of the prostate:

1. Loss in force in the urinary stream.

2. Dribbling.

3. Frequency of urination.

4. Blood in the urine.

5. Passing urine at night.

Removal of the prostate

Removal of the prostate gland may render the male sterile, but it usually does not diminish a male's sexual ability.

Sterility results for two reasons:

1. Retrograde ejaculation—meaning that in prostatic surgery the valves that regulate the passageway to the bladder are damaged and as a consequence ejaculation during the sex act is into the bladder.

2. To prevent spread of infection, the vasa deferentes are usually cut and tied during prostatic surgery. This blocks the normal passageway for sperm.

The occurrence of sterility following prostatectomy varies considerably with the surgical approach used. Newer methods of irradiation almost never render the patient sterile.

The bulbourethral glands

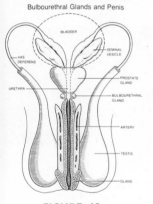

Bulbourethral Glands and Penis

FIGURE 12

The bulbourethral glands are two small glands that open by excretory ducts into the urethra (Fig. 12).

Their function is to produce a fluid that lubricates the urethra. The secretion is alkaline in nature and neutralizes the urethra before sperm pass.

Urination acidifies the urethra.

The secretions of the bulbourethral glands are often referred to as precoital fluid. Although these secretions usually precede ejaculation, they may contain spermatozoa and thus effect pregnancy.

The penis

The penis is composed of three cylinders, each containing erectile tissue (sponge-like tissue that can fill with blood to cause erection) (Fig. 12).

These three cylinders are bound together with connecting tissue, giving the outward appearance of one cylinder.

This cylinder ends in a cone-like expansion called the glans penis.

A circular fold of skin called the foreskin (prepuce) is reflected over the glans.

A number of small glands are located in the foreskin (preputial glands) and discharge their secretions onto the glans.

Smegma Secretion

The accumulation of these secretions on the glans is called smegma (Fig. 13).

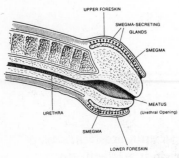

UPPER FORESKIN

SMEGMA-SECRETING GLANDS

SMEGMA

MEATUS
(Urethral Opening)

URETHRA

SMEGMA

LOWER FORESKIN

FIGURE 13

Circumcision

Circumcision

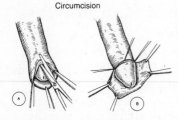

A

B

C

D

FIGURE 14

Circumcision or removal of the foreskin is recommended by many physicians as a hygienic means of avoiding the accumulation of smegma—a waxy substance (Fig. 14).

The value of circumcision is further suggested by the observation:

1. That women married to circumcised men tend to have a lower incidence of cancer of the cervix.

2. That circumcised men have a lower incidence of cancer of the penis.

Statistical relationship to cancer

These observations are primarily statistical and there is little evidence as to a cause and effect mechanism.

It is interesting to note, however, that horse smegma causes cancer in mice.[2]

Nevertheless, there are some physicians who feel that circumcision should not be routinely performed—that the only thing to recommend it is tradition. Historically, circumcision has been customary for many centuries; the Egyptians practiced it even before the Hebrews made it part of their religious customs.

Penis size

Many males worry unnecessarily about the size of the penis.

This worry stems from the mistaken notion that a large penis is necessary for adequate sexual function.

---

[2] A. Plaut and A. C. Kohn-Speyer, "Carcinogenic Action of Smegma." *Science,* 104:39, 1949.

This worry can be eliminated by the knowledge that the female vagina stretches to accommodate any size penis.

From a statistical standpoint, the following standards for the erect penis have been reported:

	Length	Diameter
Small	3½ inches	1 inch
Average	6 inches	1½ inches
Large	More than 8 inches	2 inches

It should further be pointed out that it is primarily the labia and clitoris that are excitable in the female, so penis size is not an important factor.

It is generally impossible to enlarge the size of the adult penis, either by operative procedure or hormonal treatment.

Injection of a substance such as silicone may completely destroy the capacity for erection.

Captive penis

Captive penis (penis trapped in the vagina) occurs in animals but not in humans.

For example, there is a bone in the penis of the male dog that allows insertion into the vagina before erection.

When erection occurs, the head of the penis enlarges inside the female vagina.

The vagina swells and thus prevents the male dog from withdrawing until ejaculation occurs and erection of the penis subsides.

Although many humans have deep seated fears of captive penis, there is not one authentic case on record.

And only seven scientifically documented cases of bones in human penises have been reported since 1884.

Urethra

Male Reproductive System (Side View)

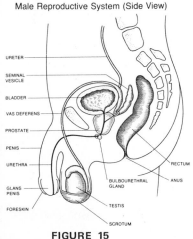

URETER
SEMINAL VESICLE
BLADDER
VAS DEFERENS
PROSTATE
PENIS
URETHRA
GLANS PENIS
FORESKIN
RECTUM
BULBOURETHRAL GLAND
ANUS
TESTIS
SCROTUM

FIGURE 15

The urethra is a tube-like passageway extending from the bladder through the prostate gland where it is joined by the ejaculatory duct (Fig. 15).

From the prostate gland the urethra passes through the penis to open to the outside.

It serves as a common outlet for sperm and urine.

Prior to the passage of sperm, the acid urethra is neutralized by fluids from the bulbourethral gland.

During ejaculation, the opening from the bladder is normally closed off by a nervous reflex. If it is not closed off, as happens in disease, ejaculation is into the bladder.

Male reproductive role

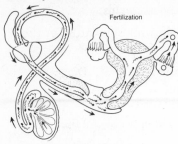

FIGURE 16

Erectile Tissue

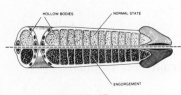

FIGURE 17

The male reproductive role is two-fold:

1. Production of sperm.

2. Transfer of these sperm to the female reproductive system.

To accomplish the latter function, the penis becomes erect, is inserted into the vagina, and sperm are ejaculated (Fig. 16).

Erection occurs when the erectile tissue of the penis becomes engorged with blood (Fig 17).

The reaction of the excited nerve fibers causes the arteries of the penis to distend, allowing blood to rush into the cylinders; a simultaneous constriction of the veins prevents this blood from escaping.

The erectile tissues thus fill with blood, and the penis becomes erect.

The male sexual response will be discussed in more detail later.

Ejaculation

The male ejaculate averages 3 milliliters in quantity and is called semen.

Semen thus contains:

1. Sperm.

2. Secretions from the seminal vesicles.

3. Secretions from the prostate gland.

The sperm constitute only a small portion of the semen.

Sperm size

Structure of a Sperm

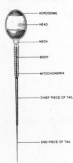

FIGURE 18

Mature sperm are very small. In fact, if all the sperm responsible for producing the entire world population were brought together, their bulk would be about one-half that of an aspirin tablet (Fig. 18).

The head of the sperm is approximately 5 microns long, the middlepiece 5 microns, and the tail 30 to 59 microns (1 micron = .001 millimeters).

By contrast, the ovum is about 130 to 140 microns in diameter.

X-bearing (female producing) sperm are thought to have larger, oval-shaped heads, whereas Y-bearing (male producing) sperm have smaller and longer heads.

Number

Each milliliter of semen contains approximately 120 million sperm.

However, even in the normal male the sperm may vary from 35 to 200 million per milliliter.

But the average male ejaculate of 3 milliliters contains approximately 360 million sperm.

With regard to fertility, the following values have been established:

At least 60,000,000/ml. = normal fertility

40 to 60,000,000/ml. = fair fertility

20 to 40,000,000/ml. = fertility possible

10 to 20,000,000/ml. = conception barely possible

Less than 10,000/ml. = conception unlikely but not impossible.

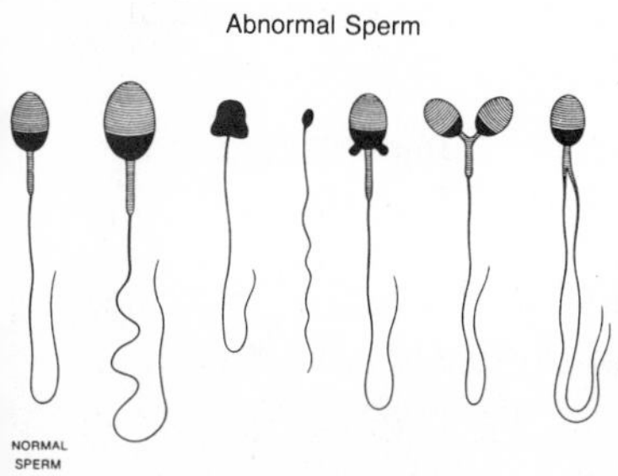

However, men with sperm counts of only a few million per milliliter have impregnated their wives.

Also, if more than 25 per cent of the sperm are defective, the male is likely to be sterile even though the total count is normal (Fig. 19).

The reasons for diminished fertility with a low sperm count or defective sperm are not clear, since only one sperm is required for fertilization.

A currently popular theory suggests that many sperm are required to assist the one that finally fertilizes the egg.

According to this theory, each sperm carries a small enzyme bomb in its head—the bomb is known as the acrosome.

When the acrosome comes near the vicinity of the ovum it is thought to explode.

The enzyme thus released (hyaluronidase) has the ability to separate cells that are cemented together.

As it happens, the expelled ovum carries several layers of cells attached firmly to its surface.

These cells must be removed before a sperm can reach the ovum.

Hyaluronidase secreted in the semen or released from the acrosomes of the sperm heads is believed to cause these extra cells to break away from the ovum.

It is thought that the sterility associated with low sperm counts is due to a lack of hyaluronidase.

Physiology of sperm

Because of the importance of sperm in human reproduction, we will examine them in more detail (Fig. 18).

After formation in the testes, sperm pass into the epididymis.

Here they develop motility and the ability to fertilize.

This is completed about 18 hours after they enter the epididymis.

A small quantity of sperm may be stored in the epididymis, but most are stored in the vas deferens.

Sperm exhibit little movement in storage.

Abnormal Sperm

NORMAL SPERM

FIGURE 19

This is probably because their metabolic processes secrete large quantities of carbon dioxide into the surrounding fluids, making them acidic in nature.

Sperm live in storage for 30 to 60 days. If ejaculation does not occur during this time interval, sperm degenerate and are replaced by new ones.

Dislike for an acid medium

Sperm do not move well in an acid medium.

Sperm stored in the genital ducts maintain their fertility for 42 days or longer.

Sperm that have been ejaculated into the female vagina are thought to have an effective life of about 72 hours.

Seven days later

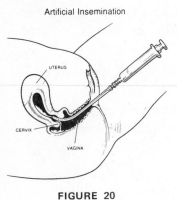

Artificial Insemination

UTERUS

CERVIX

VAGINA

FIGURE 20

However, sperm have been found alive in the vagina seven days after ejaculation. Their effectiveness after seven days is a matter for further research.

Sperm frozen after ejaculation can be maintained in an effective state for a number of years (to be used for artificial insemination—Figure 20).

Recent research,[3] however, indicates that the process of freezing and thawing reduces by half the motility of spermatozoa in a specimen.

It is further demonstrated that less than 20 per cent of the initial motility remains after five years in storage.

The price of prize bulls offers good testimony to the effectiveness of artificial insemination in the livestock industry.

Production independent of use

Sperm production seems to be quite independent of sexual activity.

The fertilizing capacity of successive ejaculations is thought to decline because of the inclusion of immature sperm.

Prolonged rest

Lowered fertility may also accompany prolonged sexual rest because of the inclusion of senile spermatozoa (spermatozoa that have lost their effectiveness because of aging).

Following ejaculation, sperm are able to travel at a rate of approximately 1 to 5 millimeters per minute.

Sperm tend to travel in a straight line, but the direction is purely random.

Their activity is greatly enhanced in neutral or slightly alkaline environments.

Acid reduces activity and kills sperm.

---

[3] K. D. Smith and E. Steinberger, "Survival of Spermatozoa in a Human Sperm Bank," *J.A.M.A.*, 223:774, 1973.

Sperm migration

The migration of sperm once they have entered the female body has been difficult for scientists to study, especially in the human.

Thus, neither the time interval nor the mechanism for travel is well understood.

Following the observation by microscope that sperm were motile, it became commonly held that sperm traveled to the Fallopian tubes by means of their own propellant activity.

However, more recent observations suggest that other factors are involved.

Rate of travel

For example, nonmotile (inability for self-movement) and motile sperm seem to move at the same rate of speed.

Secondly, sperm reach the Fallopian tube much faster than can be explained on the basis of their propellant activity.

Cows

Observations on cows indicate that sperm pass from the cervix to the far end of the Fallopian tubes in two minutes.

A unique experiment

And in a unique experiment reported by Dr. Boris B. Rubenstein and others (*Fertility and Sterility* 2:15, 1951), sperm placed in the vagina prior to an operation were found to ". . . migrate through the cervix, fundus, and Fallopian tubes of women within thirty minutes after their introduction. . . ."

One reasonable hypothesis to explain the rapid movement of sperm suggests that the stimuli of mating or artificial insemination cause release of a hormonal substance (oxytocin) that increases uterine contractions.

Male sterilization

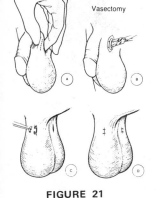

FIGURE 21

Vasectomy is becoming increasingly popular as a means of birth control—approximately 45,000 cases per year.

This is a simple surgical procedure in which the vas deferens is cut and tied off (Fig. 21).

Vasectomy is discussed in more detail in Chapter Six (Contraception).

Currently there is no evidence that vasectomy interferes with sexual activity in any way. And most men return to normal sexual activity within two weeks.

Approximately 98 per cent of vasectomized men report the same or increased frequency of sexual intercourse.

Greater promiscuity

There is no evidence to support the claim that vasectomy leads to greater promiscuity among men.

Male climacteric

Sudden removal of testicular hormone causes most males to lose some of their vigor, spontaneous energy output, and sense of well-being.

Also, experiments with rats clearly indicate that castration reduces spontaneous activity of these animals to a very low level.

Since testicular hormones wane with aging, some males suffer a condition that is analogous to the menopause of the female.

This may involve hot flashes, fatigue, nervousness, and loss of pep.

The male climacteric, however, is somewhat rare.

Frequently, the symptoms attributed to diminished testicular hormones are due to other factors associated with aging.

Indeed, many patients receive as many benefits from placebos (fake pills) as from testosterone.

Eunuchism

A eunuch is one who has a complete loss of testicular function due to castration or for other reasons.

If this occurs prior to puberty, the secondary sex characteristics do not develop.

If it occurs after puberty, the secondary sex characteristics may exhibit regression.

Following castration, sexual desire decreases but is not totally diminished. Erection and ejaculation can still occur.

There are cases of men participating actively in sexual intercourse 15 years after castration.

Sexual life of the male

The average age of first ejaculation is 13 years and ten months.

Ejaculation has been observed at eight years of age, but this is rather unusual.

Indeed, only 25 per cent of the male population has experienced ejaculation by age 12.

The adult achieves an average of three orgasms per week.

The frequency of orgasm is highest between 15 and 30. After 30 there is a gradual decline into old age.

But active sex life for 70 per cent of the population continues past the age of 70 years.

Sex and athletic performance

Analysis of the content of semen indicates that it contains less than nine calories per milliliter.

Hence, it seems very unlikely that the sex act represents a drain on energy stores!

CHAPTER THREE

The Biological Female

> *. . . hitherto woman's possibilities have been suppressed and lost to humanity, and . . . it is high time she be permitted to take her chances in her own interest and in the interest of all.*
>
> Simone de Beauvoir
> The Second Sex

A major goal of sex education is that femaleness should be understood and appreciated by both sexes. This chapter discusses only the physiological aspects of femaleness, but a careful study of this information may be helpful in eliminating some of the misconceptions, superstitions, and mysteries that attend female sexuality.

THE FEMALE REPRODUCTIVE SYSTEM

Ovaries

Very early in the development of a new individual special sex cells are organized into a group of cells known as a gonad.

As we learned in the previous chapter, gonads have the capacity to develop into either ovaries or testes, depending upon hormonal stimulation.

In the male, testosterone usually causes the testes to start to evolve by the seventh to eighth week following conception.

31

In the normal female child the gonads begin to evolve into ovaries by the tenth or eleventh week.

Early location

In the embryo, the ovaries, two in number, develop high in the abdomen, near the kidney.

Prior to birth, however, they move downward to the brim of the pelvis.

Size and form

As found in the pelvis, the ovary resembles an almond in shape (Fig. 22).

It is about 1 inch wide, 1½ inches long, and one-quarter of an inch thick.

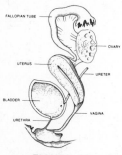

Female Reproductive System
Side View

FALLOPIAN TUBE

OVARY

UTERUS

URETER

BLADDER

VAGINA

URETHRA

FIGURE 22

Appearance

In the young woman it is smooth and pink; in the older woman it is shrunken, wrinkled, and gray.

And because of repeated discharges of ova through its surface, its outward appearance becomes puckered by the formation of scars.

Function

The ovaries, in their location in the pelvis, have a dual responsibility:

1. To produce ova.

2. To secrete hormones.

Primary follicles

At birth the ovary contains many small sac- or pod-like structures that contain immature ova.

These pod-like structures are called primary follicles (also called primordial follicles).

An estimated 200,000 to 400,000 of these primary follicles are found in each ovary at birth.

It has been claimed that additional primary follicles are formed throughout the reproductive life of the female, but the consensus among scientists is that all the follicles are present at birth.

Many of the original follicles degenerate between birth and puberty.

375 mature follicles

During the reproductive life of the female, approximately 375 of these primary follicles develop enough to expel ova.

The remaining follicles degenerate.

Thus, the ovary contains approximately 400,000 primary follicles at birth, and 10,000 at puberty; by the age of 50 most of them have disappeared.

Puberty

At the age of approximately eight years, the pituitary gland sends a hormonal messenger to the ovary indicating that plans should be made to remodel the female reproductive system.

Between the ages of 11 and 14 years the pituitary gland sends a more forceful message indicating that it is time to carry out these plans.

The remodeling period is known as puberty.

During puberty the ovaries, in response to stimulation by the pituitary gland, release the female sex hormone, estrogen, into the circulatory system.

Estrogen, in turn, is responsible for the development of the primary and secondary sexual characteristics of the female.

Primary sexual characteristics

Growth of the
Female Reproductive System

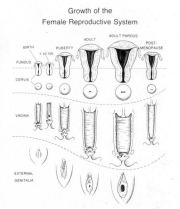

FIGURE 23

Under the influence of estrogen, the Fallopian tubes, uterus, and vagina (involved in the development of the primary sexual characteristics) all increase in size and physiological maturity (Fig. 23).

In this way, the reproductive system is made ready for reproduction.

Secondary sexual characteristics

Female Secondary Sex Characteristics

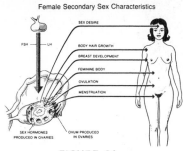

FIGURE 24

Breast Development and Alteration

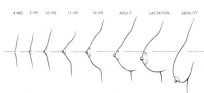

FIGURE 25

The secondary sexual characteristics produced by estrogen include (Fig. 24):

1. Deposition of fat in the breasts accompanied by development of an elaborate duct system (Fig. 25).

2. Broadening of the pelvis and changes from a narrow funnel-like outlet to a broad oval outlet.

3. Development of soft and smooth skin.

4. Deposition of fat in buttocks and thighs.

5. Development of pubic hair with a flat upper border (a triangular border is characteristic of the male).

6. Early uniting of the growing end of long bones with the bone shaft—also caused by estrogen. In the absence of estrogen females usually grow several inches taller than normal.

Physiological changes during puberty

Concurrent with its anatomical remodeling, the female reproductive system also exhibits important physiological changes during puberty.

These changes initiate:

1. Ovulation.

2. Menstruation.

Ovulation

The release of a mature ovum from the ovary is termed ovulation.

Prior to ovulation, however, the primary follicles present in the ovary at birth must undergo several changes.

To understand these changes, we must examine the primary follicle in more detail.

The nature of the primary follicle

Immature ova are surrounded by a thin layer of cells usually termed follicular cells.

These follicular cells, together with the immature ovum that they surround, constitute the primary follicle.

The primary follicles are stimulated to grow and reach maturity by two pituitary hormones.

FSH and LH

In sequence, these hormones are FSH (follicle stimulating hormone) and LH (luteinizing hormone).

When the release of FSH or LH is inhibited by disease or by oral contraceptives, ovulation does not occur.

FSH is responsible for the early growth of immature ova and the enlargement of the primary follicle.

The primary follicle enlarges because of an accumulation of fluids.

The process is similar to the formation of a blister.

A cycle begins

Following hormonal stimulation, 15 to 20 immature follicles start to grow each month.

Usually only one of these balloons outward into full maturity.

The one follicle that reaches maturity is called the Graafian follicle.

A stigma

The surface of the swelling Graafian follicle exhibits a small dot or nipple-like protrusion called the stigma.

Simultaneous with development of the stigma, the pituitary gland increases its output of LH.

LH, in turn, causes disintegration of the stigma and rupture of the Graafian follicle.

The ovum thus escapes from the Graafian follicle.

The other primary follicles that started to grow but lost out in the race to become the Graafian follicle degenerate.

A new ovum

The newly released ovum is a very fragile structure and requires careful handling.

In fact, even under the very best conditions it can only be fertilized during the first 12 to 24 hours after it is released.

So rather than "throw out the ovum to fend for itself," the follicular cells continue to exhibit responsibility.

To aid the ovum, the follicular cells that remain in the ovary are transformed into a temporary endocrine gland by the action of LH.

This yellow glandular body, formed in the ovary from the follicular remains, is called the corpus luteum (yellow body).

To prepare the female reproductive system for the reception of the ovum, the corpus luteum secretes two important hormones:

1. Estrogen.

2. Progesterone.

Prior to an examination of the effects of these hormones, however, it is necessary to review some other features of the female reproductive system.

Fallopian tubes

The first structure we will examine is the Fallopian tube, named after its Italian discoverer, Gabriel Fallopius (Fig. 22).

The Fallopian tubes are trumpet-shaped structures lying in close proximity to the ovaries and extending to the corners of the uterus.

These 3 to 5 inch tubes are also known as "uterine tubes" or "oviducts."

How the ovum gets into the Fallopian tube

Entrance of the ovum into the Fallopian tube has been a difficult mechanism to investigate, and scientists still do not completely understand the process.

However, experiments with rabbits and monkeys and x-ray studies of women suggest that it happens this way:

At the time of ovulation, the musculature of the Fallopian tube and the ligaments by which it is suspended tend to draw the flaring end of the tube and the ovary together.

Contractions of the muscular walls of the Fallopian tube create a suction that directs the ovum into the tube.

The process is further aided by the constant beating of hair-like projections found on the inner surfaces of the Fallopian tubes.

These projections are called cilia, and their beating action creates a constant current into the uterus.

Ordinarily, ova from the right ovary enter the right Fallopian tube and those from the left enter the left tube.

However, there are numerous cases on record to support the observation that cross-over occurs (e.g., the left tube may move over to pick up an ovum from the right ovary).

The ovum in transport

When the Graafian follicle ruptures, the discharge contains more than just the ovum.

The ovum is surrounded by many follicular cells called cumulus cells.

The cilia serve to partially separate the ovum from the cumulus cells as the mass passes through the Fallopian tube.

Contraction of Fallopian tubes

Once inside the tube, the ovum and its cumulus are transported by the peristaltic contractions of the tube itself.

Movement through the Fallopian tube takes place at a leisurely pace. The ovum arrives at the uterus three to seven days later.

This time interval allows the corpus luteum to direct some last minute remodeling in the uterus.

Where fertilization occurs

Fertilization of the ovum usually occurs in the upper third of the Fallopian tube.

Although this places an extra burden on the sperm in terms of travel, it is necessitated by the fact that the ovum must be fertilized during the first 12 to 24 hours or not at all.

Nutrition

Progesterone from the corpus luteum initiates secretion of glands in the walls of the Fallopian tubes.

These secretions provide important nutrition for the ovum as it passes through the Fallopian tubes.

A silent trip

Ordinarily the female is unable to perceive ovulation.

In a few women, however, a slight pain may accompany ovulation. This is often referred to as mittelschmerz ("middle pain" in German).

It is a transitory irritation caused by the small amount of blood and fluid released at the site of the ruptured follicle.

The uterus

The uterus or womb is a hollow muscular pouch located in the pelvic cavity between the bladder and the rectum.

This reproductive organ resembles a pear. It is about 3 inches long and 2 inches wide at the top, narrowing down to the cervix or neck where it is normally about ½ to 1 inch in diameter.

Size of the uterus

The size of the uterus, however, varies with age and physiological state (Fig. 23):

1. At birth the uterus is large owing to a small amount of estrogen that passes from the mother.
2. During childhood the uterus is smaller because it lacks this hormonal stimulation.
3. At puberty, estrogen signals the uterus to grow, and it reaches adult dimensions.
4. After childbearing, the uterus reaches its largest dimension.

Anatomical divisions of the uterus

The uterus is divided into three anatomical parts:

1. Corpus or body.
2. Isthmus.
3. Cervix.

Corpus

The corpus or body is the upper muscular division of the uterus.

It is dome shaped, the anterior surface being almost flat and the posterior surface being convex.

The corpus is able to expand in the pregnant state because of its muscular layers.

Isthmus

Below this muscular division is the constricted area of the uterus, the isthmus.

The isthmus lengthens and thins out during pregnancy.

It aids the corpus in causing enlargment of the womb for the growing embryo.

Cervix

If the uterus were an upside-down milk bottle, the neck of the bottle would be the cervix.

During pregnancy the cervix retains the growing embryo.

Uterine layers

In addition to the three anatomic divisions of the uterus, there are two uterine layers:

1. Myometrium.
2. Endometrium.

Myometrium

The muscular layer of the uterus is called the myometrium.

It consists of many interweaving fibers.

Arteries and veins lie between the muscle fibers, giving rise during pregnancy to a spongy appearance known as stratum vasculare.

When pregnancy is over, the arteries are kept from hemorrhaging by the constriction of these muscle fibers.

Endometrium

The innermost layer of the uterus is known as the endometrium.

It is a soft tissue richly supplied with blood vessels.

It is about 3 to 4 millimeters in thickness.

This lining grows each month and is prepared to serve as a home for the fertilized egg.

Preparation for implantation

If the ovum is fertilized, it must establish a more permanent connection with the mother's reproductive system.

This connection must be established in the uterus if the fertilized ovum is to develop into a full-term baby.

Ectopic pregnancy

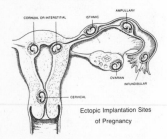

Ectopic Implantation Sites
of Pregnancy

FIGURE 26

Occasionally implantation takes place in the Fallopian tube; but because of a shortage of space at this location, such an implantation must be surgically removed (Fig. 26).

The incidence of this condition, termed ectopic pregnancy, is estimated to be in the region of 1.0 per cent.

Normally, however, the fertilized ovum will implant itself in the lining of the uterus.

Normal implantation

Preparation of the endometrium for reception of a fertilized egg is accomplished by estrogen and progesterone in the following way:

At the beginning of each new menstrual cycle, only a very thin layer of endometrial cells remains.

The others were shed at the time of the last menstrual flow.

Immediately following menstruation the endometrium begins a three-stage rebuilding process.

Proliferative or estrogen phase

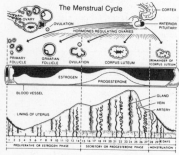

FIGURE 27

The first phase is called the proliferative phase or estrogen phase (Fig. 27).

To proliferate means to grow by the rapid production of new cells.

And that is exactly what happens to the lining of the uterus when it is stimulated by estrogen during the early days of the menstrual cycle.

By the time of ovulation, the endometrial lining of the uterus has attained a thickness of 2 to 3 millimeters.

The secretory or progestational phase

The second stage of rebuilding is termed the secretory or progestational phase (Fig. 27).

This phase is initiated by progesterone from the corpus luteum.

The corpus luteum also secretes additional amounts of estrogen.

Acting together, these hormones:

1. Cause further growth of the cells in the endometrium.

2. Increase the blood supply in the lining of the uterus.

3. Cause the glands that have developed in the lining of the uterus to secrete endometrial fluid.

The endometrium reaches a thickness of 4 to 6 millimeters during this stage.

Function of the secretions

From the time of fertilization until implantation, the secretions of the Fallopian tubes and uterine glands provide nutrition for the ovum.

Inhibition of FSH and LH

In addition to preparing the endometrium, estrogen and progesterone have other effects:

They inhibit further release of FSH and LH so that no new primary follicles start to mature.

Specific actions of progesterone

Progesterone inhibits the myometrium, thus preventing contraction. This is a precautionary measure to protect an implanted ovum from expulsion.

It also stimulates the development of ducts in the mother's breasts to make them ready to nourish the newborn.

Progesterone level during pregnancy

In order that these important functions be continued, progesterone is maintained at a high level during pregnancy.

To do this, the corpus luteum is maintained during the early stages of pregnancy by hormones released by the developing embryo.

In the later stages of pregnancy, progesterone is secreted in large quantities by the placenta.

The placenta is a membrane that connects the baby to the mother. It will be discussed in connection with pregnancy in a later chapter.

Menstruation

If fertilization fails to take place, phase three of the recurrent female cycle is initiated (Fig. 27).

By way of review, the proliferative or estrogen phase is responsible for the early growth of the endometrium; the secretory or progesterone phase completes endometrial growth and initiates secretion; and the final or menstrual phase takes off the "endometrial wall paper" in order that the cycle can start again.

The menstrual phase, like the proliferative and secretory phases, is under hormonal control.

And it is the corpus luteum that is most responsible for this phase.

Degeneration of the corpus luteum

Immediately following ovulation, follicular cells quickly develop into a corpus luteum.

The corpus luteum persists in an active form for 10 to 12 days.

During this time it secretes estrogen and progesterone to make the endometrium receptive for a fertilized ovum.

If fertilization does not occur, the corpus luteum begins to degenerate and is replaced by connective tissue.

Approximately two days before the end of the normal female cycle, the secretion of estrogen and progesterone decreases sharply as the corpus luteum becomes inactive.

Decreased secretion of estrogen and progesterone is thought to cause menstruation in the following way:

Cells die

When hormonal stimulation of the endometrial cells stops, these cells shrink to approximately 65 per cent of their previous size.

Then approximately 24 hours prior to menstruation, the blood vessels to the lining of the uterus are closed off.

In the absence of a blood supply the lining of the uterus dies.

Gradually this dead layer of cells separates from the rest of the uterus.

The dead tissue, together with a small quantity of blood in the uterine cavity, initiates uterine contractions.

Menstrual flow

Lining of the Uterus in Three Stages

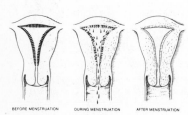

BEFORE MENSTRUATION   DURING MENSTRUATION   AFTER MENSTRUATION

FIGURE 28

These contractions expel the contents of the uterus as the menstrual flow (Fig. 28).

During menstruation approximately 35 milliliters of blood, 35 milliliters of fluid, and the lining of the uterus are expelled.

The uterus develops a new lining, and bleeding stops about five days after the onset of menstruation.

The menstrual flow marks the end of the three-phase female cycle.

Menarche to menopause

Menarche is the term used to describe the first menstrual cycle; menopause marks the last cycle.

Menorrhagia

An abnormally large menstrual flow is termed menorrhagia.

Possible causes of menorrhagia include:

1. Diseases.

2. Endocrine disorders.

3. Abnormalities of the sexual organs.

Excessive bleeding should be reported to a physician.

Amenorrhea

Amenorrhea is the absence of menstruation.

If menstruation has never occurred, the condition is called *primary* amenorrhea; if it has occurred but ceases before the normal age for menopause, the condition is *secondary* amenorrhea.

Primary amenorrhea may result from:

1. Malformed or underdeveloped female organs.

2. Glandular disorders.

3. General poor health.

4. Emotional factors.

Secondary amenorrhea is normal during pregnancy and while the mother is nursing.

It may occur sporadically during the first and last months of a woman's childbearing years.

If amenorrhea persists, medical assistance is indicated.

Scanty menstruation

At times the menstrual flow is so slight that it amounts to little more than staining. This slight staining is termed "scanty menstruation." Scanty menstruation is also caused by:

1. Malformed or underdeveloped female organs.

2. Glandular disorders.

3. General poor health.

4. Emotional factors.

A frequent cause of scanty menstruation is anemia, a condition in which there is a reduction in the number of red blood cells.

Scanty menstruation should be reported to one's physician.

Irregularity

Irregular menstrual periods may be the result of a harmless change in nature's timing. If this is the case, the irregularity will soon be corrected.

On the other hand, irregularity may result from a disease in some part of the body, such as the thyroid gland or ovary.

Most important, irregularity can be a sign of cancer.

When irregularity persists, a physician should be consulted.

Dysmenorrhea

It is not unusual for a woman to experience mild discomfort at the onset of her menstrual period.

Because of great individual differences in response to discomfort, there is no clear demarcation between menstrual discomfort and menstrual pain.

Thus, painful menstruation is largely a subjective matter.

However, if a woman's menstrual cramps do not yield to mild pain killers or if such cramps prevent a normal social life, a condition called dysmenorrhea is diagnosed.

Dysmenorrhea is thus another term for painful menstruation.

Causes of dysmenorrhea

Dysmenorrhea may be caused by:

1. Inflammation.
2. Constipation.
3. Psychological stress.
3. Other factors.

Actually, the causes of dysmenorrhea are poorly understood by medical investigators.

Organic causes

In the past there was a tendency to believe that cramps were always due to some organic cause.

For example, dysmenorrhea was usually attributed to the fact that the cervix was too narrow and needed to be stretched.

Some believed that dysmenorrhea was caused by abnormal positioning of the uterus.

Operations were frequently performed to correct this, but in most cases the pain was not relieved.

In general, dysmenorrhea cannot be accounted for by any organic disorder and is therefore functional.

It occurs most often in young girls or in women who are unmarried but rarely in women who have had children.

In many cases there is conclusive evidence that it is caused by emotional factors.

Menstrual protection is best understood after a discussion of the external anatomy of the female. Thus, a discussion of this important matter will be delayed until the end of the following section.

The vagina and external female genitalia

Although proportionately greater tasks are assigned to the ovaries and uterus, the vagina and external female genitalia are more than idle bystanders in female reproductive physiology.

Vagina

The vagina is a 3 to 4 inch muscular tube extending from the cervix of the uterus to the external genitalia.

It is situated behind the bladder and in front of the rectum; its axis forms an angle of approximately 90 degrees with that of the cervix.

The vaginal tube is 6 to 7 centimeters along its front wall and 9 centimeters along its back wall.

The vaginal wall has three layers:

1. A top mucous layer with numerous blood vessels.

2. A muscular layer (Fig. 29).

3. An elastic fibrous layer.

Vaginal Muscles

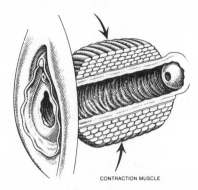

CONTRACTION MUSCLE

FIGURE 29

A potential space

The vagina can best be described as a "potential space."

In its normal unstimulated state the walls of the tube are in almost direct contact with each other.

These soft "collapsed" walls open when something is forced through the vaginal tube.

It can extend to four or five times its normal size to facilitate childbirth.

Adjustable size

The vagina also extends to adapt to the size of the penis during intercourse.

It should be noted that the normal female vagina adapts to any size penis. Thus, worry over anatomical misfits, like most sexual anxieties, is senseless.

It should also be pointed out that the inner two thirds of the vagina are practically without sensation.

The walls of the vagina are kept moist by secretions from the uterus and by a "sweating phenomenon" in which the walls of the vaginal barrel pass droplets of mucoid material.

There are numerous folds in the vaginal canal. These folds tend to smooth out as the female bears children and ages.

Functions of the vagina

The vagina serves as:

1. The female organ of intercourse.

2. A passageway for the arriving male sperm.

3. A canal through which the baby is born.

4. A passageway for the menstrual flow.

Hymen

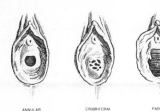

The Hymen

ANNULAR
HYMEN

CRIBRIFORM
HYMEN

PAROUS
INTROITUS

FIGURE 30

The hymen or maidenhead is a thin membrane that stretches across the opening of the vagina (Fig. 30).

It varies in thickness and extent, and is sometimes absent.

In the center of the hymen is a circular perforation.

It is through this perforation that the menstrual flow leaves the vagina and that the tampon or internal protection is inserted.

In rare cases there is no central perforation, and the menstrual flow is blocked. Medical assistance is indicated in this situation.

Virginity

Virginal Pregnancy

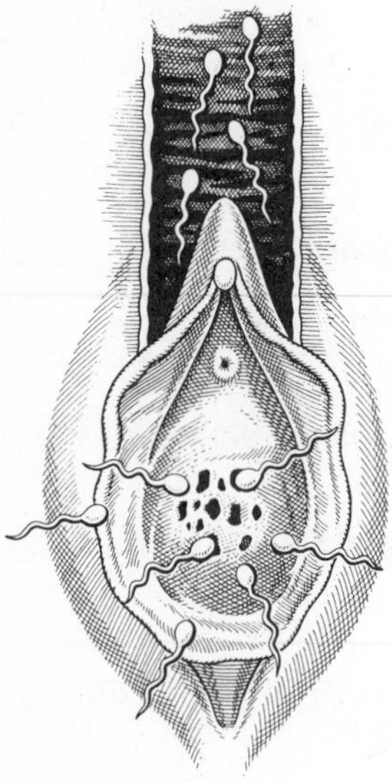

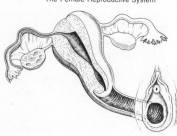

FIGURE 31

Contrary to popular belief, the absence of the hymen is not a sign that a girl is no longer a virgin, nor is the presence of the hymen an absolute sign of virginity.

Women have been known to come to the delivery of their first child with an intact hymen (Fig. 31). On the other hand, virginal women have been known to have a poorly developed or broken hymen.

If the hymen is present it will usually rupture and tear at several points during the first coitus.

The amount of bleeding accompanying the coital tearing varies.

Generally there is a slight bleeding if the hymen is intact at the first coitus; however, this again is not an absolute sign of virginity.

In rare cases the hymen is resistant to coital tearing and must be surgically divided before intercourse can take place.

To avoid difficulty during the first sexual intercourse, the physician frequently ruptures the hymen at the time of the premarital examination.

External female genitalia

The Female Reproductive System

FIGURE 32

The term vulva or pudendum as generally applied includes all the female external genitalia (Fig. 32). They consist of the:

1. Mons veneris.
2. Labia majora.
3. Labia minora.
4. Clitoris.
5. Vestibule of the vagina.
6. Bulb of the vestibule.
7. Greater vestibular glands.

Mons veneris

The fatty cushion resting over the front surface of the pubic bone is called the mons veneris. Interestingly, the term mons veneris is Latin for "mountain of love."

This fatty cushion serves largely as a protective cushion protecting the female reproductive organs.

At puberty, kinky hair covers the mons veneris in a triangular fashion, its base corresponding to the upper margin of the pubic bone.

Labia majora

The labia majora are large heavy folds of skin surrounding the external opening of the vagina.

Each labium has two surfaces:

1. An outer, pigmented surface covered with strong thick hairs.

2. An inner, smooth surface with large sebaceous follicles.

The labia majora are richly supplied with blood vessels, which become engorged with blood during sexual excitement.

Labia minora

The labia minora are two smaller folds of skin situated between the labia majora.

They extend from the clitoris backward for about 4 centimeters on either side of the vaginal opening.

The anterior labia minora is divided into two portions:

1. An upper portion, which forms a fold overhanging the glans of the clitoris.

2. A lower division, uniting below the clitoris to form the frenulum of the clitoris.

Clitoris

Female External Genitalia

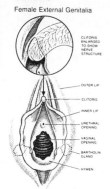

CLITORIS ENLARGED TO SHOW NERVE STRUCTURE

OUTER LIP

CLITORIS

INNER LIP

URETHRAL OPENING

VAGINAL OPENING

BARTHOLIN GLAND

HYMEN

FIGURE 33

Projecting between the labia minora is the small cylindrical body known as the clitoris (Fig. 33).

The clitoris is richly supplied with blood vessels, and the pudendal nerve supplies it with sensory fibers.

Thus, the clitoris serves as a receptor and transmitter of sexual stimuli.

However, the clitoris does not respond to sexual stimulation with a rapidity equal to that of penile erection. This is a physiological misconception resulting from the assumption that the penis and the clitoris are alike.

The size and location of the clitoris are not very important elements of the sexual response. Most important in sexual excitement is the stimulation of the entire external female genitalia.

Vestibule of the vagina

The vestibule is a space between the labia minora into which open the urethra, the vagina, and the ducts of Bartholin's glands.

The urethra opens into the floor of the vestibule, midway between the glans of the clitoris and the vaginal opening.

Bulb of the vestibule

The bulb of the vestibule consists of two elongated masses of erectile tissue, one on either side of the vaginal opening.

Each bulb is filled with a convoluted mass of veins.

Greater vestibular glands (Bartholin's glands)

The greater vestibular or Bartholin's glands are bean-shaped glands found behind the posterior part of each vestibular bulb.

Each gland is about 5 millimeters in its greatest dimension.

The ducts from these glands empty into the posterior part of the vestibule approximately in the middle of the labia minora.

Traditionally, Bartholin's glands have been presumed to provide lubrication for painless penetration of the vagina.

However, on the basis of their research, Masters and Johnson[1] conclude: "Under observation . . . there never has been sufficient secretory material produced to accomplish more than minimal lubrication of the vaginal introitus."

It is now thought that Bartholin's glands are associated with creating a genital scent.

Menstrual protection

The two products commercially produced to absorb the menstrual flow are:

1. Sanitary pads or napkins.
2. Tampons.

The sanitary pad or napkin is made of gauze and filled with an absorbent material.

It is supported in the back and front by a narrow belt.

One of the disadvantages of the sanitary pad is that when soaked the pad can irritate the inside surface of the thighs.

Tampons

The tampon is a roll of absorbent material about as big as your little finger.

It comes in a thin cardboard tube with a string attached to the cotton plug.

The cotton end is placed inside the vagina through a small perforation in the hymen; the string end is left hanging for later removal of the tampon.

Safety of tampons

One question that usually comes to the mind of teenage girls beginning to menstruate involves the safety of the tampon.

There are many fears and misconceptions that should be abandoned.

---

[1] William Masters and Virginia Johnson, *Human Sexual Response,* Little, Brown and Company, Boston, 1966, p. 44.

One popular misconception is that the vagina of virginal women is too small to use commercial tampons.

A study of 100 girls aged 12 to 19 and 174 freshmen nursing students aged 17 to 25 was conducted to determine the size of the opening at the entrance of the vagina.

Of the two groups 91 per cent were of sufficient diameter to use regular absorbing size, commercially available tampons.

A study of the size of hymenal openings

Since the average hymenal opening is 3/4 to 7/8 inch in diameter and most tampons are slightly larger than 1/2 inch in diameter, there is little difficulty in inserting the tampon.

There is also a distinct advantage in tampon insertion.

Once the tampon is securely in place, it absorbs the menstrual flow, and thus the absorbent tampon is larger than the tampon originally inserted.

Thus, upon removal, the now larger tampon slightly stretches the hymenal opening. This slight stretching aids the doctor in obtaining a Papanicolaou (pap″ ah-nik″ o-la′ $\overline{oo}$) smear in an examination for cancer; it also makes the first coitus easier.

Tampons also have other advantages.

Odor

The formation of a distinctive odor of menstrual fluid is dependent upon the menstrual fluid's being exposed to air.

With the usage of tampons, the flow does not come in contact with air, and hence, there is no odor.

Chafing

Because sanitary napkins chafe and become soaked and malodorous, tampons represent the best protection for athletes.

It has been thought in the past that athletic women, especially swimmers, should not use tampons because they would not afford complete protection.

Bathtub experiments have demonstrated that tampons prevent any blood loss during swimming.

Athletics and menstruation

Another popular misconception is that exercise during menstruation is attended by congestion, dysmenorrhea, and a diminution in athletic performance.

A study done at the Tokyo Olympics of 66 women athletes throws an interesting light upon this topic. The study revealed that training and competition did not significantly alter the course of the menstrual cycle.

The following results were obtained regarding physical performance during menses:

1. 70 per cent retained normal performance.

2. 15 per cent did better.

3. 15 per cent did worse.

Further studies were done to examine the effect of childbearing on performance.

The 13 mothers who took part in the Tokyo Olympics claimed that they became stronger, had greater stamina, and were more balanced in every way after motherhood.

Female climacteric

The climacteric is a term used to describe the symptoms that attend the waning production of estrogen that occurs as the woman grows older.

The word climacteric is Greek in origin and means "rung of the ladder."

The symptoms that are collectively termed the climacteric may be present for a number of years. Put another way, ovarian function does not suddenly stop but exhibits a gradual decrease for a variable length of time.

The menopause is a dramatic incident that occurs during this time span.

Thus, the symptoms of the climacteric both precede and follow the menopause.

Signs and symptoms of climacteric

The oncoming climacteric is first signaled by a menstrual cycle that does not include ovulation.

In this situation, progesterone would not be produced, since no corpus luteum was formed.

Thus, the lining of the uterus would persist in the estrogen (proliferative) phase when it should have moved into the secretory phase.

Irregularity

As estrogen production diminishes the menstrual cycles become irregular.

Then amenorrhea may occur for two or three months, followed by a menstrual flow that may be excessive and prolonged.

In most cases menstruation does not suddenly stop without warning.

Menopause is generally preceded by noticeable changes in the menstrual pattern.

Menopause

Menopause is the term applied to cessation of periodic bleeding.

It usually occurs between the ages of 47 and 59 years.

The average woman today reaches menopause at approximately 50 years of age.

This is slightly higher than the figure reported in the older literature.

There is every reason to suggest that with good nutrition and health menopause will be further delayed.

Diminishing estrogen

Also occurring at this time as a result of diminishing estrogen production are the following:

1. Atrophy of the primary sexual glands:
    A. The clitoris becomes smaller.
    B. The labia are reduced in size.
    C. Degenerative changes occur in the vaginal wall.
2. Changes in the secondary sex characteristics:
    A. There is a loss of pubic hair.
    B. Hair on the head becomes sparse.
    C. Hair may grow on the upper lip and chin.
    D. The breasts droop because of a loss of elasticity.
    E. The skin tends to wrinkle because it loses its elasticity.
    F. The bones become brittle.
3. Disturbances of general physiology:
    A. Hot flashes may occur.
    B. Headaches and insomnia may become frequent.
4. Libido may de decreased or increased:
    A. Sex drive generally diminishes with aging.
    B. But some women exhibit an exaggerated need for sexual gratification at this time of life.
5. Psychosomatic symptoms may occur:
    A. Nervousness.
    B. Apprehension.
    C. Decrease in ability to concentrate.
    D. Irritability.
    E. Depression.

Treatment

Most healthy and well adjusted women pass through the menopause with a minimum of difficulty.

Only about 20 per cent require medical therapy.

Effective treatment is usually composed of the administration of estrogen and psychological reassurance.

Misconceptions

The climacteric does not cause the female to become:

1. Unattractive.
2. Obese.
3. Mentally disturbed.
4. Sexually disinterested.

CHAPTER FOUR

Human Sexual Response

The early American devoted most of his time to the tasks of obtaining food, clothing, and shelter. Pleasures were necessarily minimal and in most cases were even considered sinful (Puritanism). However, advances in technology soon obviated routine physical tasks and enhanced production of essential goods to such a level that adequate food, clothing, and shelter became commonplace. Today production techniques have become so sophisticated that only a small portion of the total population is required to produce the needed goods. And we are rapidly becoming a nation of consumers. Indeed, it is estimated that in the very near future 20 per cent of the population will be able to produce all the goods needed. Unconstrained by the technical tasks that previously attended production, most of the population will be at liberty to take part in other types of activity.

History suggests that when man's energies and thoughts are no longer depleted by essential tasks, his attentions may meander toward pleasure seeking. But despite its seeming simplicity, pleasure seeking is one of the most difficult tasks that man has ever tackled. It is rendered difficult by lack of criteria to judge success. How does one know when he is being successful in his pleasure seeking? Initially, man is almost certain to judge his pleasures by the same standards that he previously judged production. Thus, man asks about his pleasures: Am I doing as well as I should? Would I accumulate more pleasure if I invested in another activity? Would my profits increase if I used another method? In the absence of satisfactory answers to these questions, pleasure seeking has been something of a disappointment in recent times.

It is significant to realize that the history of American sexuality closely parallels our transition from a society of producers to a society of consumers. The early American was reluctant to admit that sex served any function other than procreation. He no doubt discovered that sexual intercourse could be fun, but he never "let on." And even to this day many people feel guilty when they view sex as being for fun.

If we could disregard our historical past and tell the younger generation about the sex act "the way it really is," our presentation might go something like this:

From a biological point of view, sexual intercourse serves two functions: procreation and the production of pleasurable sensation. It is important to note that the reproductive and pleasure functions are not physiologically dependent but may be fulfilled separately. For example, a male with a transected spinal cord could impregnate his wife but would perceive no pleasure from the act. Or a woman could experience an orgasm from stimulation of erogenous areas other than those directly associated with the reproductive system. In addition to physiological independence, the development of highly effective contraceptive techniques has made it possible for twentieth century man to separate almost completely the procreative and recreative aspects of sex.

Our presentation might continue: The adult society is rapidly dissociating sex and procreation and more emphasis is being placed on the pleasurable aspects. Nelson Foote puts it this way: "The view that sex is fun can . . . hardly be called the invention of immoralists; it is every man's discovery." People who are honest with themselves readily admit that giving or receiving pleasure is the major motivation for participation in the sex act. And the higher we go in the animal kingdom, the greater the concern for the simultaneous giving and receiving of pleasure.

In keeping with this approach to sex education, a rather progressive high school teacher began her first sex education class by "telling it like it is." She said, "Sex is for fun and reproduction and in that order." The next day she was looking for a new job. Despite this occurrence, the facts remain: twentieth century American society is focusing on consumption more than on production. Much of the emphasis on consumption is motivated by pleasure seeking, and sex ranks high on man's list of pleasures. It is not surprising, therefore, that more and more people are seeking help (from books, counselors, physicians, and others) to qualitatively enhance their sexual experiences.

A discussion of the problems that attend sexual inadequacy is beyond the scope of this book, but an understanding of the basic human sexual response should be a part of any sex education program. In fact, such an understanding would eliminate many cases of sexual inadequacy. This chapter attempts to provide such an understanding.

Prerequisites for heterosexual response

Dr. Charles W. Lloyd[1] of the Worcester Foundation of Experimental Biology lists four prerequisites for normal heterosexual response:

1. Functional integrity of those areas of the central nervous system that are involved.

2. Adequate genital structures.

---

[1] Charles W. Lloyd, "Sexual Response." In *Human Reproduction and Sexual Behavior,* edited by Charles W. Lloyd, Philadelphia, Lea & Febiger, 1964.

3. Appropriate hormonal stimulation of the genitalia.

4. A psychological environment that is conducive to sexual response.

Role of the nervous system

Sexual activity, like most human activities, is highly dependent upon the central nervous system.

The central nervous system is made up of the brain and spinal cord.

The brain, in turn, is subdivided into many parts.

A knowledge of all these parts is not essential to an understanding of the human sexual response. However, a few basic concepts are required.

As we have seen, the cerebral cortex is man's thinking-reasoning brain, his most highly evolved brain.

Without the cortex he operates in much the same way as a lower animal.

It is interesting to note, however, that decorticated (cerebral cortex removed) animals are capable of almost normal sexual behavior.

For example, a decorticated cat given estrogen to bring her into heat exhibits:

1. Courtship: playful rubbing and sexual crouching.

2. Reaction after vaginal stimulation: rubbing, licking, squirming, and rolling.

Thus, sexual behavior occurs at a brain level lower than that of the thinking and reasoning brain.

This does not mean that the intact cerebral cortex does not affect sexual behavior. Indeed, the cerebral cortex greatly accentuates response in the human.

Nevertheless, it would appear that sexual behavior is integrated at a level below that of the cerebral cortex.

Put another way, it takes no brains to copulate!

Ruch and Patton in their book, *Physiology and Biophysics,*[2] conclude that the basic elements of sexual behavior are located in the hypothalamus.

This is not unexpected, since most of the "automatic" functions of the nervous system are governed by the hypothalamus.

Some sexual functions may be directed from an even lower level.

For example, in the male, erection and ejaculation are regulated by the spinal cord.

---

[2] Theodore C. Ruch and Harry D. Patton, *Physiology and Biophysics,* W. B. Saunders Company, Philadelphia, 1973, Ed. 20.

In rats, rabbits, and guinea pigs, erection and ejaculation can easily be accomplished by electrical stimulation of the cord.

Also, genital stimulation can cause erection and ejaculation in the human male with a transected spinal cord. Although these men can feel no sensation, they are capable of impregnating their wives.

Adequate genital structures

Certain genital structures are prerequisites for normal sexual relations.

Male

The male must have a penis, but testicles are not entirely necessary.

Cutting the vas deferens does not affect the sexual response.

In the absence of a prostate gland, the ejaculate is likely to pass into the bladder. However, this does not impair sexual sensation.

Female

A vagina is required for normal performance of the sexual act.

However, a vagina is not required for female orgasm. Some women attain orgasm during anal intercourse.

Although the clitoris is the most consistently erotic area of the female, it is not essential to sexual orgasm.

Hormonal stimulation of genitalia

Male

Testicular hormones are not absolutely essential to male sexual performance.

Dr. Lloyd[3] states:

> The preadolescent or hypogonadal male can engage in heterosexual activity, albeit without the intensity of satisfaction to himself or his partner that would be achieved if full androgenic stimulation had taken place.
>
> The sensitivity and the size of the penis and other secondary sexual tissues are enhanced by the presence of androgen.

On the other hand, the castrated male does not necessarily lose his sexual ability.

Indeed, castrated males have participated in heterosexual intercourse 15 years after castration!

Female

Estrogen is important in the development of the size and sensitivity of the erogenous structures of the female.

However, an orgasmic response sometimes occurs in the preadolescent.

Once the female erogenous structures have fully developed, the

---

[3] Lloyd, *op. cit.*

removal of sex hormones seems to have little effect on the sex drive.

Psychological environment

Both male and female sexual responses are greatly modified by the psychological environment.

Indeed, it seems clear that the most important factor affecting female sexual response is the attitude of the female toward her male partner.

An unfavorable psychological environment is a far more frequent cause of sexual inadequacy than poorly developed genital structure, lack of hormonal stimulation, or disturbances of the nervous system.

Physiology of the human sexual response

Although the sexual experience may be modified by many factors, it is ultimately a series of physiological events.

The intensity of the physiological response is attested by marked increases in heart rate, respiratory rate, and blood pressure.

Masters and Johnson

Until recently, little was known about the physiological response of the reproductive system to sexual stimulation.

To fill this void in our knowledge of sexuality, William Masters and Virginia Johnson published the results of several years of work in a book entitled *Human Sexual Response*.[4] The teacher is referred to this excellent book for a detailed account of the physiology of the human sexual response. Only the highlights can be included here.

A sequence of events

The physiological responses that attend the human sexual response appear to follow an orderly sequence.

For purposes of simplicity, Dr. Masters and his colleagues have divided these responses into four phases:

1. Excitement phase.
2. Plateau phase.
3. Orgasmic phase.
4. Resolution phase.

The excitement phase

The excitement phase begins with the initial sexual stimulation, ranges from a few minutes to as long as several hours, and ends by passage into the plateau phase.

Male

In the male, the excitement phase consists of erection of the penis secondary to the engorgement of erectile tissue with blood.

The testes are also elevated toward the body in this phase.

---

[4] William Masters and Virginia Johnson, *Human Sexual Response*, Little, Brower and Company, 1966.

Female

Corresponding changes in the female include:

1. Erection of the nipples and enlargement of the breasts.
2. Vaginal lubrication (10 to 30 seconds after stimulation).
3. Enlargement of both the length and diameter of the vaginal barrel.
4. Increase in the length and diameter of the clitoral shaft may occur.

The changes that occur during the excitement phase make heterosexual intercourse possible:

1. The erect penis can be inserted into the vagina.
2. The vagina enlarges to accommodate the penis and produces a lubricating fluid to facilitate intercourse.

The plateau phase

During the plateau phase tension builds for the leap into orgasm.

Male

Further changes in the male include:

1. An increase in the circumference of the penis, especially the glans.
2. Secretions of lubricating fluid from the bulbourethral glands.
3. Enlargement of the testes.

Female

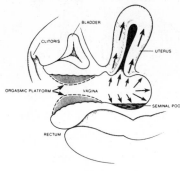

Orgasmic Platform, Seminal Pool

FIGURE 34

The responses in the female are:

1. Further enlargement of the breasts.
2. Elevation of the uterus away from the posterior wall of the vagina.
3. Congestion of blood in the outer lengths of the vaginal barrel produces a platform within the vagina. This platform is called the orgasmic platform because it contracts during orgasm (Fig. 34).
4. Withdrawal of the clitoris into its hood.
5. Secretions from Bartholin's glands.

The orgasmic phase

The orgasmic phase in both male and female consists of rapid muscular contractions that release accumulating tensions.

In the male, contractions of the full length of the shaft of the penis occur, producing ejaculation.

In the female, contraction of the orgasmic platform occurs. Muscles in the uterus and other parts of the female reproductive system may also respond.

In both males and females, the muscular contractions are approximately 0.8 second in duration.

The resolution phase

During the resolution phase, biological structures return to their pre-excitement state.

Male

In the male, the changes observed are:

1. Loss of erection.
2. Decrease in size of the testes.
3. Descent of the testes.

Female

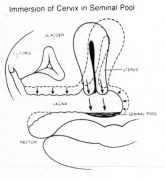

Immersion of Cervix in Seminal Pool

Changes in the female include:

1. Loss of nipple erection.
2. Loss of orgasmic platform (muscular contractions relieve congestion of blood).
3. Gaping of the entrance to the cervix.
4. Return of the clitoris from its protective hood.
5. Immersion of the cervix into the seminal pool (Fig. 35).

FIGURE 35

Special considerations

Because of their importance in the human sexual response, certain structures should be explained in more detail than that given up to this point.

Clitoris

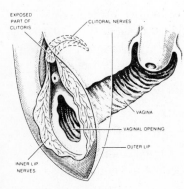

Nerve Endings Sensitive to Sexual Stimulation

The clitoris is a small organ partially hidden in a prepuce or hood (Fig. 36).

The prepuce resembles the foreskin of the penis, and the clitoris can retract inside the prepuce in much the same way that the penis retracts inside the foreskin.

The clitoris normally only retracts during sexual stimulation.

The clitoris exhibits an expanded portion or glans at its distal end much like the glans at the distal end of the penis.

The size of the glans of the clitoris increases during sexual stimulation secondary to congestion with blood.

It does not become erect as does the penis but simply enlarges.

The enlargement is rapid with direct manipulation of the clitoris but slower with breast manipulation, sexual intercourse, or fantasy.

FIGURE 36

Masters and Johnson[5] state:

1. "The clitoris and prepuce form the most consistently erotic area of the human body."

---

[5] Masters and Johnson, *op. cit.*, p. 45.

2. "The clitoris is . . . an organ system which is totally limited in physiologic function to initiating or elevating levels of sexual tension."

Many marriage manuals suggest that the male should locate the clitoris and remain in direct contact with it to heighten sexual tensions.

Masters and Johnson level the following criticisms at this recommendation:

1. The clitoris retracts during sexual stimulation and it is impossible for the penis to stay in direct contact with it.

2. Direct manual contact with the clitoris may produce irritation and this technique is usually rejected during female masturbation.

Traction or pressure on the hood that protects the clitoris appears to be more desired by the female.

Masters and Johnson conclude that female orgasm occurs in the same physiological way whether it is effected through clitoral stimulation, vaginal stimulation, or other means.

Anatomical and physiological variations in the clitoris appear to play little if any role in human sexual response.

Vagina

Masters and Johnson make the following observations relative to the vagina:

1. In the unstimulated state it is a potential rather than an actual space; i.e., the anterior and posterior walls are essentially in direct contact.

2. During the excitement phase the vagina enlarges to accommodate any size penis. Owing to this facility of the vagina, sexual inadequacy is seldom a matter of anatomical misfits.

3. Within 10 to 30 seconds after sexual stimulation, lubrication of the vaginal walls occurs. The lubricating fluid comes from the walls of the vagina.

4. During the plateau phase the outer third (lengthwise) of the vagina becomes congested with blood to form an orgasmic platform.

5. The platform contracts rapidly during female orgasm.

6. Following orgasm, the platform disappears.

Drugs that change the human sexual response

Aphrodisiac is the name given to any substance thought to increase the sexual drive or ability.

Throughout history man has carried on a never-ending search for aphrodisiac drugs.

This search has resulted in the use of extracts of trees, roots, flowers, insects, and animals, to list a few.

According to Dr. Kenneth Walker,[6] an eminent British physician, aphrodisiacs are thought to exert their physiological effects in the following ways:

1. By irritating the genital organs.

2. By stimulating the central nervous system.

3. By altering the mental state.

Spanish fly

Spanish fly (technically known as cantharides) is an example of an irritating drug. It is obtained from a beetle found in southern Europe.

When taken by mouth, this substance irritates the bladder and urethra during urination.

The irritation may invoke sexual tension.

Spanish fly, however, is a very dangerous drug.

Dr. Walker states:

> "[Spanish fly] . . . causes intense discomfort to the unfortunate patient and has been known to have fatal results.

> "It inflames the stomach and the bowels, evokes vomiting and diarrhea and produces congestion of the kidneys.

> "No one but a madman would take an aphrodisiac of this kind and only a criminal would prescribe it for anybody else."

Strychnine

Strychnine is an example of a drug that has been used to increase sexual drive by stimulating the central nervous system.

There is little proof that strychnine has any real aphrodisiac power, and it is a dangerous drug that should never be used by anyone other than a physician.

Its danger is suggested by the fact that it was first used to poison animals.

Substances that change the mental state

Alcohol, cocaine, hashish, and LSD have been touted as drugs that enhance sexual drive by changing the mental state.

It is possible that some of these drugs relieve inhibitions about sexual behavior, but there is no evidence that they are physiologically stimulating, with the exception of cocaine.

Although little evidence is available, some suggest that cocaine produces vascular engorgement of the genital organs.

Cocaine, however, is a highly dangerous drug.

LSD

There are a few claims that, under medical supervision, LSD has proved useful in the treatment of frigidity.

However, there are no carefully controlled studies available.

---

[6] Kenneth Walker, "Using Drugs to Heighten Sex Desire," *Sexology*, July, 1967, pp. 842-845.

Alcohol

As to the effects of alcohol, Dr. Nathaniel Shafer,[7] a New York City specialist in internal medicine, writes:

> Most people regard alcohol as a sexual stimulant in particular; hence the great popularity of alcoholic drinks at most parties and social gatherings.
>
> In one sense it may be considered thus, in that an individual under the influence of alcohol may lose his fears, inhibitions and tensions as they pertain to the sex act.
>
> His feelings of insecurity or inadequacy may be suppressed, allowing him to perform in a satisfactory manner.
>
> However, this is not due in any way to the sexual stimulating action of the alcohol, but is an effect of its tranquilizing or calming actions.
>
> Indeed any other sedative or tranquilizer would exert a similar effect.
>
> This is especially true since so many sexual problems are of emotional origin.

But whereas small amounts of alcohol may relieve inhibitions, increasing amounts may render the male impotent.

In summary, Dr. Walker has accurately described the current dilemma that attends the use of drugs to heighten sex drive:

> Throughout history, man has diligently sought far and wide for miraculous remedies, but in the end his search has always been thwarted. Either the action of the drug he has found proves erratic and uncertain or else the taking of it leads to his physical and mental degradation.
>
> In other words, man's search for an aphrodisiac has been attended with as limited success as has his search for the Philosopher's Stone and the Fountain of Youth. There is no such thing as a short-cut to Paradise.

---

[7] Nathaniel Shafer, "Alcohol and Sex," *Sexology*, December, 1966, pp. 351-354.

CHAPTER FIVE

Pregnancy, Childbirth and Lactation

Nine months after an East Coast electrical blackout, after a Midwest snow-storm, and after a flood in Italy, baby booms occurred. Such observations indicate not only that the human confined to quarters is a cuddly primate with a one-track mind, but also that pregnancy is a frequent consequence of something that occurs in such quarters.

Today many of the mysteries and old wives' tales that attend pregnancy have been elucidated, and the well-informed expectant mother avails herself of the most recent scientific knowledge by arranging for medical supervision during pregnancy (prenatal care). In addition to prenatal care, both the wife and husband can profit from a personal study of pregnancy and childbirth. This chapter attempts to highlight the most important details.

Preliminary to this section, however, we have included a very short and simplified discussion of the cellular basis of reproduction. The reader with a background in biology may wish to skip this introductory section and pick up the discussion on page 65.

CELLULAR BASIS OF HUMAN REPRODUCTION

100 trillion cells

The human body is made up of more than 100 trillion cells, each with a specific function.

For example, one type of cell permits movement, another thought; yet another makes reproduction possible.

Examination of a cell

When cells are viewed under a microscope, they somewhat resemble a slice of fruit: i.e., they have an outside membrane, an object in the center similar to the pit, and a pulpy mass filling the spaces between.

The outer covering is termed the cell membrane; the pulpy mass is called the cytoplasm; and the center pit (actually separated from the cytoplasm by a second membrane) is known as the nucleus.

Genes

The nucleus of a human cell contains over one million genes.

These genes, in turn, control the day-by-day activities of the cell.

The genes also provide the hereditary blueprint for reproduction.

Following the advent of the electron microscope, genes were chemically identified as giant molecules of a nucleic acid known as DNA (deoxyribonucleic acid).

Hence, it is DNA, operating from its protected position in the nucleus, that directs the activity of the cell and determines heredity.

Chromosomes

Each human cell (excluding sperm and ova) contains 46 chromosomes.

These chromosomes are composed of DNA and proteins, with proteins serving as a kind of "backbone" to support the genes.

Among the 46 chromosomes found in each normal body cell, 23 are duplicate descendants of the mother (maternal chromosomes) and the remaining 23 are duplicate descendants of the father (paternal chromosomes).

Consequently, human chromosomes are more accurately described as 23 pairs of homologous chromosomes.

Each chromosome pair carries genes that influence a specific trait, one member of the pair providing the maternal trait and the other the paternal trait.

Mitosis

Mitosis is the process by which a cell splits to form new cells.

The first step in mitosis is replication of the chromosomes to provide the new cell with a proper control system.

This first step is followed by several others leading to complete replication of cells every 10 to 30 hours.

Not all human cells exhibit mitosis, e.g., cells of the central nervous system.

Meiosis

Meiosis is the cellular division by which sperm and ova (gametes) are formed.

More commonly the process is referred to as spermatogenesis in the male and oögenesis in the female.

Sperm and ova, formed by meiosis, each contain 23 chromosomes and are capable of initiating formation of a new individual by fusion with each other.

It should be emphasized that sperm and ova contain only one-half the number of chromosomes that other body cells (somatic cells) contain.

For example, consider the following distribution:

Animal	Body Cells	Gametes
Dog	56 chromosomes	28 chromosomes
Horse	60 chromosomes	30 chromosomes
Human	46 chromosomes	23 chromosomes

The human life cycle

The human life cycle, therefore, consists of meiosis, fertilization, and mitosis.

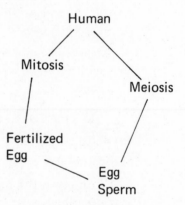

The sex chromosomes

Among the 23 pairs of chromosomes found in human cells is one pair of sex chromosomes.

These sex chromosomes contain the genes for development of maleness and femaleness.

Depending on their shape and size, sex chromosomes are termed X chromosomes or Y chromosomes.

Males exhibit an XY pair of sex chromosomes, females an XX pair.

This arrangement holds true for all cells in the body except germ cells (sperm or ova).

Sex determination

During oögenesis eggs containing 23 chromosomes are produced.

X

Each of these eggs contains an X sex chromosome, never a Y.

X or Y

During spermatogenesis sperm containing 23 chromosomes are produced.

Each of these sperm contains one sex chromosome—an X or a Y.

Male and female sperm

Therefore, sperm may be classified as male (having a Y chromosome) or female (having an X chromosome).

When the sperm fertilizes the egg, a full complement of 46 chromosomes (23 maternal and 23 paternal) is provided, including two sex chromosomes.

X and Y = Male

If a male sperm (Y chromosome) fertilizes the egg (always contains an X chromosome), the offspring will be a male (XY).

X and X = Female

If a female sperm (X chromosome) fertilizes the egg, the offspring will be a female (XX).

Acid-alkaline environments and sex determination

Based on the observation that acid environments are more destructive to male sperm and alkaline environments to female sperm, some physicians have recommended baking soda or vinegar douches to help determine the sex of a planned offspring.

To increase the probability of having a male offspring, the female is advised to douche with a solution of two tablespoons of baking soda to a quart of water.

If a female child is desired, a douche with two tablespoons of white vinegar to a quart of water is recommended.

Dominant and recessive characteristics

As we have seen, hereditary characteristics are determined by genes carried on the chromosomes.

When an egg is fertilized by a sperm, the maternal and paternal genes line up so that the genes for various traits, such as hair color, are next to each other.

If the maternal and paternal genes for a trait are different, then one set of genes overrides the other.

For example, following fertilization of the ovum, paternal genes for brown eyes might line up with maternal genes for blue eyes.

In this case, the genes for brown eyes are more influential, and the offspring would exhibit brown eyes.

The more influential genes are called dominant genes, and the ones they override are called recessive.

Thus, brown eyes are dominant over blue, dark hair over blond, and curly hair over straight, to list a few.

If the offspring inherits recessive genes (e.g., blue eyes) from both the mother and the father, then the recessive trait will manifest itself.

Sex-linked characteristics

Previously we have noted that each body cell contains 23 pairs of chromosomes, including a pair of sex chromosomes.

This latter pair of sex chromosomes, like other chromosomes, is known to carry genes.

And those hereditary characteristics transmitted on the sex chromosomes are said to be sex-linked.

The X chromosome carries genes for a variety of human characteristics.

On the other hand, the Y chromosome, with the exception of its ability to direct maleness, appears to be practically "empty" from a genetic standpoint.

Therefore, when some recessive hereditary defect is carried on the maternal X chromosome, such as red-green color blindness or hemophilia, the defect will manifest itself in the male offspring (XY).

This is true because the paternal Y chromosome carries no genes that could dominate the recessive defect carried on the maternal X chromosome.

However, recessive defects carried on the maternal X chromosome are far less likely to manifest themselves in female offspring (XX).

In the latter case, genes carried on the paternal X chromosome may dominate the recessive defect carried on the maternal X chromosome, producing a normal offspring.

If, however, both maternal and paternal X chromosomes carry recessive genes for a defect, it is sure to appear in the offspring.

Consequently, genetic defects transmitted by genes located on X chromosomes are far more likely to appear in male offspring than in females.

Biological basis of twins

Occasionally, ovulation may occur more than once during a cycle; if so, and if two eggs are fertilized by two different sperm, fraternal twins result.

Since fraternal twins result from two sperm and two eggs, they are no more alike than any other two children by the same parents.

Identical twins

Identical twins stem from one egg and one sperm; in this case, the fertilized ovum immediately divides into two individuals.

Since they have inherited the same chromosomes, identical twins are always of the same sex and very much alike.

Occurrence of multiple births

The approximate rate of occurrence of multiple births:

Twins 1 in 90 births
Triplets 1 in 8000 births
Quadruplets 1 in 500,000 births

PREGNANCY

Conception

The moment of fertilization is termed conception.

It normally takes place in the upper portion of the Fallopian tube.

The trip to the uterus

After fertilization, the ovum makes a three to four day trip through the lower portion of the Fallopian tube to the uterus.

En route, the ovum derives nutrition from secretions of the Fallopian tube.

With this nutritive support, the ovum exhibits cell division long before it reaches the uterus.

Preparation for implantation

The ovum spends four or five days in the uterus before it becomes implanted.

During this time it is nourished by secretions of the specially prepared uterine lining.

These secretions are sometimes called "uterine milk."

During this time the ovum is developing the physiological maturity required for implantation.

Implantation

Implantation usually occurs seven to eight days after conception.

This includes approximately three days of travel through the Fallopian tube and four to five days of development in the uterus.

When it is ready to implant, the developing ovum secretes enzymes that eat into the endometrium.

Then the cells of the ovum attach to the cavity formed in the endometrium.

Once the ovum is implanted, the cells multiply rapidly to enlarge the connection between mother and baby.

Placenta

As the ovum grows and develops it requires a means of obtaining nutrition and removing waste products.

This function is served by the placenta.

A physiological depot

The placenta is a physiological depot in which the transport systems of the mother and baby meet.

The mother's transport system brings nutrition and oxygen to the placental depot; the baby's transport system brings waste products.

These are exchanged through small pores in the walls of the placental depot.

No mixing of blood

No mixing of the blood occurs.

All substances are passed through the pores that separate these two transport systems.

Storage service

In addition to providing a meeting place for the circulatory systems of mother and baby, the placental depot offers a storage service.

Specially constructed compartments store various products until they are needed: calcium, iron, protein, glycogen, and other biological materials.

As we have already observed, the placental depot produces hormonal substances to support pregnancy.

In summary, the placenta serves as lung, kidney, liver, endocrine gland, and digestion system for the developing baby.

To accomplish this, the placenta starts to enlarge immediately after implantation, reaches approximately 3 inches in length by the fourth month and 8 inches by the eighth month.

By time of birth it has attained a weight of about 1 pound.

3/4 quart per minute

To insure effective service, the mother's circulatory system sends approximately 3/4 of a quart of blood through the placenta each minute.

Finally, a large number of substances may traverse the placenta and enter the fetal circulation. The following list includes a few of the well-known ones:

Some infectious organisms: e.g., viruses	Morphine
Antibodies	Cortisone
Nicotine	Penicillin
Ethyl alcohol	Streptomycin
Barbiturates	Tetracyclines
	Tetrahydrocannabinol (active ingredient in marihuana)

These substances can thus be transferred from mother to baby.

Hormonal secretions of the placenta

One of the most important tasks of the placenta is to prevent spontaneous expulsion of the growing embryo. In this connection, it is very important that the corpus luteum be maintained.

It will be remembered that:

1. The corpus luteum is formed in the ovary from follicular cells that discharged the ovum.

2. Formation of the corpus luteum is stimulated by LH from the pituitary gland.

3. The lining and muscles of the uterus are maintained in a state suitable for pregnancy by hormonal secretions of the corpus luteum.

Thus, the corpus luteum is important to normal pregnancy.

Indeed, if the corpus luteum disintegrates at any time prior to the eleventh week of pregnancy, expulsion of the embryo is likely.

Fortunately, the corpus luteum is maintained by hormonal secretions from the placenta.

Chorionic gonadotropin

The hormone secreted by the placenta has essentially the same effect as LH, but it is called chorionic gonadotropin.

Chorionic is an adjective coming from Greek and meaning the membrane that encloses the fetus. A portion of this membrane forms the fetal part of the placenta.

Gonad is the Greek word for seed; *tropin* is Greek for turning.

Thus, gonadotropic hormones turn the gonads or seeds toward maturity.

Turns gonads toward maturity

Gonadotropin, then, is a general name given to any hormonal substance that "turns the gonads" toward maturity.

These would include:

1. FSH and LH from the pituitary gland.

2. Chorionic gonadotropin from the placenta.

Chorionic gonadotropin not only prevents regression of the corpus luteum but also causes it to double in size by the end of the first month of pregnancy.

It also stimulates the production and release of greater amounts of estrogen and progesterone.

These hormones, in turn, maintain the uterus in a state suitable for pregnancy, thus preventing spontaneous abortion.

Chorionic gonadotropin and the testes

True to its name, chorionic gonadotropin turns the gonads of the male toward maturity.

And this takes place very early in intrauterine life.

Chorionic gonadotropin stimulates the testes to produce testosterone.

Testosterone, in turn, creates masculine sex organs and causes the testes to descend.

Estrogen and progesterone secretion during pregnancy

In the early stages of pregnancy, estrogen and progesterone are supplied by the corpus luteum.

Estrogen

During pregnancy, estrogen is secreted in large amounts to:

1. Enlarge the uterus, breasts, and external genitalia.

Progesterone

Progesterone is secreted in large amounts to:

1. Prevent contraction of the muscles of the uterus.

2. Prepare the breasts for lactation.

Physiological changes in the mother during pregnancy

Amniotic Sac

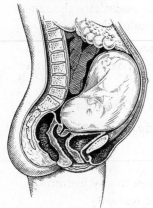

FIGURE 37

According to Dr. Arthur Guyton's *Textbook of Medical Physiology*,[1] the average weight gain during pregnancy is 24 pounds. This added weight is distributed in the following manner:

1. Seven pounds is fetus.

2. Four pounds is amniotic fluid surrounding the fetus (Fig. 37).

3. Two pounds represents the increased weight of the uterus.

4. Three pounds are due to enlargement of the breasts.

5. Three pounds are due to increased body fluids.
   A. The mother's blood volume increases as much as a quart.

6. Three pounds are due to increased lean body mass.

7. Three pounds are due to increased fat.

Appetite

During pregnancy some food substances in the mother's blood are extracted by the placenta.

This may increase the mother's appetite.

However, psychological factors that attend pregnancy may cause the woman to eat more than the body needs.

In women who overeat during pregnancy the body weight may increase by as much as 50 pounds.

Metabolism

During pregnancy the mother's metabolic rate increases to support the many physiological changes that take place in her body.

This may result in sensations of unusual warmness during pregnancy.

---

[1] Arthur C. Guyton, *Textbook of Medical Physiology,* W. B. Saunders Company, Philadelphia, 1971, Ed. 4.

The extra weight carried during pregnancy also contributes to extra heat production.

Nutrition

Since the pregnant woman has different nutritional needs during pregnancy, she should obtain the services of a physician early in pregnancy.

Thus, she will be assured of obtaining the extra minerals, vitamins, and proteins required.

Morning sickness

In the early stages of pregnancy, the mother may exhibit frequent vomiting—a condition termed "morning sickness."

The physiological cause of this condition is unknown, but there are two therories:

1. The placental secretions of chorionic gonadotropin in the early stages of pregnancy may, in some as yet unexplained way, be responsible for morning sickness.

According to this theory, the body develops a tolerance to chorionic gonadotropin during the later stages of pregnancy.

2. The second theory suggests that morning sickness is caused by chemicals released from cells that are destroyed as the ovum implants itself in the lining of the uterus.

This theory holds that chemicals released by cells (in the lining of the uterus) destroyed at time of implantation are the cause of morning sickness.

In support of this theory, it has been observed that degeneration of other tissues produces nausea.

Parturition

The technical name for the process of birth is parturition.

This process is initiated by a combination of hormonal and mechanical factors.

Hormonal factors

Hormonal factors prevent contraction of the uterus during pregnancy but initiate contraction at time of childbirth.

As it happens, progesterone inhibits uterine contraction, whereas estrogen increases uterine contractility.

The ratio of estrogen to progesterone therefore has an important effect on uterine contractility. After the seventh month of pregnancy, this ratio changes, for estrogen is secreted in proportionally greater amounts.

Oxytocin

Currently available evidence suggests that a hormonal substance called oxytocin is increased at time of labor.

Oxytocin is secreted by the pituitary gland, and its specific effect is to cause uterine contractions.

It is thought that irritation or stretching of the cervix is the stimulus for release of oxytocin.

Mechanical factors

The following mechanical factors are thought to increase uterine contractility:

1. Stretching of the smooth muscles of the uterus as pregnancy continues.

2. Intermittent stretching by movements of the fetus.

The following observations suggest that stretching or irritation increases uterine contractility:

1. Dilation of the cervix by the obstetrician frequently induces labor.

2. Rupturing of the membranes that enclose the fetus causes the head to irritate or stretch the cervix and may thus induce uterine contractions.

Labor

During the last months of pregnancy, weak rhythmic contractions begin in the uterus.

These contractions become stronger as the end of pregnancy approaches.

Finally, the contractions become strong enough to stretch the cervix and force the baby through the birth canal.

These final and more powerful contractions are called the contractions of labor.

Childbirth

During labor the muscles in the top of the uterus usually contract first, followed by contractions in lower portions.

The net effect is to force the baby downward toward the cervix.

The muscular contractions of labor may be 30 minutes apart during the early stages.

Then, as labor continues, the contractions may occur every one to three minutes.

And as the contractions become more frequent, they also become more forceful.

In the final stages of labor the muscles exert a pressure of approximately 25 pounds.

As might be expected, these strong contractions impede or even stop the flow of blood to the placenta.

Thus, it is fortunate that the contractions are intermittent.

First stage of parturition

Prolonged contractions (e.g., overdose of oxytocin) can cause death of the fetus.

Childbirth Sequence I

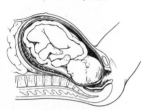

FIGURE 38

Childbirth Sequence II

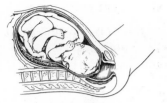

FIGURE 39

Stage two

Childbirth Sequence III

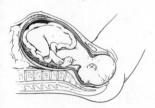

FIGURE 40

Childbirth Sequence IV

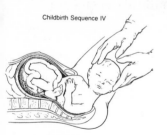

FIGURE 41

Childbirth Sequence V

FIGURE 42

The first barrier to parturition is the uterine cervix. However, the cervix has become soft during the last weeks of pregnancy, so that it stretches during labor. This stretching or dilation of the cervix is the first stage of parturition and lasts until the cervix is sufficiently dilated to allow the head of the fetus to enter (Figs. 38 and 39).

In terms of time, this may mean eight to 24 hours for the first child or only a few minutes for subsequent pregnancies.

Shortly after the cervix is dilated the baby moves into the birth canal (Fig. 40).

At time of entry into the canal the baby may be in a longitudinal (99 per cent of the cases) or a transverse position (1 per cent of the cases).

In the longitudinal presentation, the posterior part of the top of the head usually (95 per cent of the cases) enters first; occasionally, the brow (0.5 per cent) or the face (0.5 per cent) presents first.

In a longitudinal presentation, the buttocks, a knee, or a foot may enter first.

The latter are referred to as breech births; they constitute about 3 per cent of all longitudinal presentations.

In the transverse presentation, the shoulder or scapula (shoulder blade) enters the birth canal first.

Following entry of the baby into the birth canal, subsequent contractions of the uterus accomplish delivery (Fig. 41).

Childbirth Sequence VI

FIGURE 43

In terms of time, this stage may last up to half an hour in the first labor or be as short as 1 minute in subsequent pregnancies.

After the baby is expelled from the uterus, his only remaining connection with the mother is by way of the umbilical cord, which contains the arteries and veins to the placenta (Figs. 42, 43, and 44).

To accomplish final separation, the attending physician ties off the umbilical cord and cuts it.

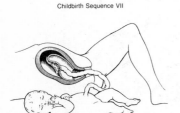

Childbirth Sequence VII

FIGURE 44

Stage three

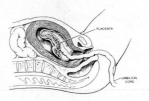

Childbirth Sequence VIII

FIGURE 45

Shortly after delivery (10 to 45 minutes) the uterus contracts to a very small size.

Since the placenta is unable to contract, it breaks or is sheared away from the walls of the uterus (Fig. 45).

The separated placenta is now expelled, together with a small amount of blood (average, 350 ml.).

Delivery of the placenta is sometimes referred to as delivery of the "afterbirth" (Fig. 46).

To prevent further blood loss, the uterus contracts tightly and closes off the blood vessels that went to the placenta.

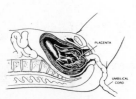

Childbirth Sequence IX

FIGURE 46

Cesarean birth

In approximately one in 50 births it becomes necessary to deliver the baby by making an incision through the abdominal wall and through the uterus.

This delivery is called a cesarean birth and is rendered necessary when the pelvic area is too small, when there is abnormal positioning of the baby, and in other circumstances.

A woman may successfully have as many as three to four cesarean deliveries. (One mother is reported to have jokingly requested that the doctor install a zipper after her sixth cesarean.)

Return to normal

Within a week following delivery, the uterus reduces its weight by one-half.

And within four to six weeks it returns to its approximate normal size.

Lactation

Production of milk by the breasts is termed lactation.

As we might expect, lactation is hormonally initiated.

The responsible hormone is LH, produced by the pituitary gland.

It happens this way:

1. During pregnancy, large secretions of estrogen and progesterone prepare the breasts for lactation: The ductile system grows and branches, and large amounts of fat are deposited.

2. At the same time, estrogen and progesterone prohibit release of LH by the pituitary.

3. Then when the placenta is delivered, the levels of estrogen and progesterone are suddenly decreased.

4. When the inhibiting force of these two hormones is removed, the pituitary gland releases LH.

5. LH, in turn, causes the breasts to produce milk.

The ejection of milk

Milk produced in the breasts is stored until the time of nursing.

The mechanism for release of milk is as follows:

1. As the baby suckles the breasts, a sensation is transmitted to the brain.

2. The brain, in turn, signals the pituitary gland to release oxytocin—a hormone.

3. Oxytocin enters the blood and within 30 seconds causes secretion of milk.

Continued production and secretion of milk

Continued milking of the breasts causes continued release of LH and thus continued production of milk. (The dairy industry is dependent upon this physiological mechanism.)

This production could be continued for several years if the breasts were continuously suckled. However, if milk is not removed from the breasts, they lose their ability to produce milk after about two weeks.

Other effects of lactation

After childbirth, the uterus returns to its normal size more rapidly in lactating women than in those who have not nursed their babies.

This is thought to occur because of a diminution in the amount of estrogen secreted during lactation.

Physiological factors associated with lactation may also prevent the normal menstrual cycle for the first few months following childbirth.

However, the lactating woman may have normal cycles, and she is capable of becoming pregnant.

Therefore, lactation is not a highly effective means of contraception.

Rh factor

Rh is the symbol for rhesus and stems from the discovery of an inherited protein substance first observed on the red blood cells of the Rhesus monkey.

People born with this protein substance on their red blood cells are said to be Rh positive.

Individuals without this protein are termed Rh negative.

Presence in population

The Rh factor is present in 85 per cent of the white population and 93 per cent of the black population.

The Rh factor occasionally becomes a medical problem because people who are Rh negative (i.e., who do not have the protein on their red blood cells) have the capacity to develop antibodies against the Rh protein.

Antibodies

This happens because the body has the capacity to develop antibodies against any protein that is not a part of that body.

Since most infectious agents are protein in nature, this mechanism of antibody production allows the body to protect itself.

The body has no choice but to treat the Rh factor in the same way it would bacteria, i.e., to build antibodies against it.

Attack red blood cells

Thus, if Rh protein enters the body of an Rh negative person, that person starts to produce antibodies that will destroy the Rh factor.

If these antibodies were to enter the body of a person with Rh positive blood, they might destroy the red blood cells and cause anemia.

There is a slight chance that such a condition could occur during pregnancy. It could happen:

1. If the mother were Rh negative and the father Rh positive.
2. If the baby inherited his father's Rh positive blood.
3. If the mother developed antibodies against the Rh factor.
4. If these antibodies passed through the placenta and attacked the baby's blood cells.

Then there is the possibility that the baby could become anemic.

But let's see what the chances are that this would actually happen.

First, the mother would have to be Rh negative; otherwise there would be no problem.

The father would have to be Rh positive and pass this factor on to his son or daughter. The chances are about 50 per cent that the baby would be Rh negative like the mother.

Even if the baby were to be Rh positive, there would be no problem until the mother's body had been stimulated to produce antibodies.

Sensitization

This ordinarily does not happen during the first pregnancy because the mother has not previously been sensitized by Rh protein.

However, there is a slight chance that the second pregnancy could present a problem if the baby were again Rh positive. This is true because the first pregnancy could sensitize the mother to Rh factor.

A new discovery

Fortunately, a very recent discovery makes it possible to prevent sensitization of the mother during her first pregnancy and thus avoid the Rh problem altogether.

A new treatment to prevent Rh sensitization

Antibodies produced in the body of one individual may be removed and injected into a second person to provide temporary protection against a specific invading agent.

Passive immunization

This process is called passive immunization.

Currently this method is being used to prevent maternal sensitization to the Rh factor.

Since sensitization apparently does not occur until after delivery of the fetus and its placenta, a special immunoglobulin (plasma extract) obtained from highly sensitized donors can be used as a source of antibodies for the recently delivered mother.

This immunoglobulin contains enough antibodies to destroy any Rh antigen that the mother might receive from her Rh positive baby.

Therefore, the mother, having enough antibodies from another source, produces none of her own.

In this way the Rh negative woman escapes sensitization that otherwise might have attended birth of an Rh positive baby.

It is hoped that this new discovery will render obsolete all Rh complications.

Even when the mother does become sensitized, blood transfusion both before and after childbirth is now available to prevent the baby from becoming anemic.

So there is really not much to worry about with the Rh factor if one consults a physician early in pregnancy.

Practical considerations

The preceding discussion has presented some of the more physiological details of pregnancy, childbirth, and lactation. The following topics are also of great practical interest:

1. Pregnancy tests.
2. Estimation of delivery date.
3. Changes that the expectant mother may observe in herself.
4. Growth of the baby.
5. Signs and symptoms of the onset of labor.
6. Danger signals during pregnancy.
7. Miscarriage.

Pregnancy tests

Pregnancy tests are based on the observation that the urine of pregnant women contains certain hormonal substances in greater concentration than would be expected in the nonpregnant patient.

These hormonal substances can be measured directly, but indirect tests are about 98 per cent accurate.

Traditionally these indirect tests have consisted of injecting the hormonal substances into other animals (mouse, rabbit, and frog) and observing the effects.

More recently slide tests have been developed that make it possible to perform a two-minute urine test to detect pregnancy as early as 12 days after a missed menstrual period.

Estimating the due date

On the average, babies are born about 280 days after the last menstrual period.

This, however, is only a mathematical average and few babies arrive exactly according to schedule. A baby may be born one to four weeks before or after this date.

Nevertheless, calculations based on a pregnancy of 280 days represent the best estimate.

This date is calculated by counting back three months from the first day of the last menstrual period and adding seven days.

For example, if the last period began on September 3, one would count back three months to June 3 and add seven days. The baby's due date would be June 10.

**Changes that the expectant
mother may observe in herself**

The breasts

The breasts become fuller and slightly tender to touch.

The nipple and dark surrounding area become darker and slightly puffy.

A tingling, prickling sensation may be felt around the nipples in early pregnancy.

Nausea

Some women experience morning nausea during the first three months of pregnancy.

This usually disappears by the fourth month.

For morning sickness, some physicians recommend a few dry crackers and half a glass of milk before getting out of bed.

Frequent urination

During pregnancy the uterus expands and exerts pressure on the bladder.

Since such pressure is the normal stimulus to urinate, the expectant mother frequently feels that she shouldn't get too far from the bathroom.

This is a perfectly normal occurrence during pregnancy. The increased urge to urinate is more frequent in early and late pregnancy.

One should not attempt to reduce water intake as a means of dealing with the problem because at least a quart of fluid should be ingested each day.

If frequent urination becomes a major concern for the expectant mother, she should not hesitate to discuss the problem with her physician.

A growing waistline

By the end of the third month of pregnancy the fetus may be 3 inches in length and weigh 1 ounce.

As the fetus continues to grow within the uterus, the abdomen must distend, causing the skin to stretch.

As the skin expands, pink horizontal stretch marks may appear.

These marks are normal and are more pronounced in some women than others; in general nothing can be done about them (i.e., rubbing, cold cream, or oil will not eliminate them).

Movement of the fetus

Beginning at conception, the embryo exhibits considerable movement within the uterus.

These movements become perceptible about midway through pregnancy.

At first they are detected as a gentle fluttering in the abdomen.

The movements grow stronger with each day, and later in pregnancy the baby's movements may be observed when the mother is standing before a mirror.

After periods of activity the baby may remain inactive for several days.

The mother should not be alarmed or worried if movements stop for a few days; this is normal.

Moodiness

Because of hormonal changes, moodiness is not unusual during pregnancy.

Hormonal changes may affect the emotions, and psychological ups and downs are likely.

Although each woman has her unique responses to pregnancy, most women find it a happy and interesting time.

Growth of the baby

Pregnancy is usually not suspected until three or four weeks after conception.

By this time the embryo is a quarter of an inch long, has a heart beat, a two-lobed brain, and a spinal cord.

Two months

After two months the embryo has started to form fingers, toes, and ears, and the beginnings of eyes and facial features are present.

It weighs about 1/30 of an ounce and is about 7/8 of an inch long.

After eight weeks, or the beginning of the third month, the embryo is called a fetus and is about 3 inches long.

Fourth month

By the end of the fourth month ears, toenails, and teeth have developed.

If it were possible to see inside the uterus, the sex of the child could be determined.

At the end of the fourth month the fetus is about 6 1/2 inches long and weighs about 4 ounces.

Fifth month

By the fifth month movement may be detected by the expectant mother.

The physician may be able to detect a heart beat at this time, but an infant born at this time would not live.

Six to eight months

At the end of eight months the fetus weighs about 5 pounds and is about 18 inches long.

If the baby is born during the seventh or eighth month, there is a 50 to 90 per cent chance that it will survive.

Full term

Full term (approximately nine months) girls weigh about 7 pounds whereas full term boys average about 7 1/2 pounds.

The range is between 5 and 9 pounds.

Full term babies are usually 19 to 21 inches in length.

How to know when real labor starts

Real labor is usually signaled by one of the following signs:

1. A discharge or gush of water from the vagina indicates that the sac of amniotic fluid that has cushioned the baby during pregnancy has ruptured.

This may occur before or during labor.

If it happens at home, it should be reported to the physician, as it usually means that labor is about to begin.

2. During pregnancy the cervix is sealed by a mucous plug.

This plug is discharged and travels down through the vagina as labor is about to begin.

This blood-tinged discharge is termed the "show."

3. The sign most frequently observed by the expectant mother is regular contractions of the muscles of the uterus.

Initially these contractions are 15 to 20 minutes apart and last about 45 seconds.

The physician usually asks to be notified when the contractions are about eight minutes apart (sooner if the mother is a long distance from the hospital).

Danger signals during pregnancy

William Birch and Dona Meilach,[2] in their well-written book, *A Doctor Discusses Pregnancy,* suggest that the following should be reported to the expectant mother's physician:

1. Any sign of bloody discharge from the vagina.

2. Persistent severe headaches.

3. Severe nausea and vomiting. Severe means several times within an hour.

4. Swelling of the ankles, feet, hands, and face, particularly if any of these puff up suddenly and your finger rings feel tight. (Slight swelling during the last months in hot weather is customary.)

5. Chills and fever of over 100° not accompanied by a common cold.

6. Continual abdominal pains that are not relieved by a bowel movement.

---

[2] William Birch and Dona Meilach, *A Doctor Discusses Pregnancy,* Budlong Press Company, Chicago, 1963, pp. 27-28.

7. A sudden gush of water from the vagina.

8. Very frequent, burning urination.

9. An increased, unusual thirst, with reduced amounts of urine. If you don't urinate for an entire day even though you have had normal intake of fluids, report the condition.

Miscarriage

When the baby is born before it is capable of surviving outside the mother's body, the event is called a miscarriage.

Most miscarriages occur during the second or third month of pregnancy.

More than 50 per cent of miscarried embryos exhibit deformity or biological malfunction.

Miscarriage is usually nature's way of insuring that full term babies are healthy.

Pregnancy and smoking

The Surgeon General's report (*The Health Consequences of Smoking*, 1971) states:

> Maternal smoking during pregnancy exerts a retarding influence on fetal growth as manifested by decreased infant birthweight and an increased incidence of prematurity, defined by weight alone. There is strong evidence to support the view that smoking mothers have a significantly greater number of unsuccessful pregnancies due to stillbirth and neonatal death as compared to nonsmoking mothers. There is insufficient evidence to support a comparable statement for abortions.

CHAPTER SIX

Contraception

Conception is the fertilization of an ovum by a spermatozoon. The frequency with which it occurs among women participating in normal sexual intercourse is termed the pregnancy rate. When no preventive measures are taken, the pregnancy rate is approximately 80 (i.e., if 100 women were to engage in sexual intercourse for one year, approximately 80 would become pregnant).

Contraception is the prevention of pregnancy and may be accomplished by a variety of chemical, physical or surgical means. Interception is the prevention of implantation of a fertilized egg, usually by postcoital (morning after) pills. Abortion is the early termination of pregnancy following implantation. Contraception predates interception, whereas interception predates abortion. Contraception and interception are the subject of this chapter, and abortion is discussed in the chapter to follow.

THE EFFECTIVENESS OF CONTRACEPTIVE METHODS

Theoretical vs. use-effectiveness
The effectiveness of any contraceptive is dependent upon several factors—theoretical effectiveness, motivation, knowledge of method, sociological stress, availability and acceptability—to mention a few.

The theoretical effectiveness of a contraceptive method refers to the pregnancy rate when instructions for use are followed in careful detail.

For example, the theoretical effectiveness of the oral contraceptive would be reflected by the pregnancy rate when, and only when, pills were taken exactly as prescribed.

In actual practice, the theoretical effectiveness of a contraceptive method is seldom achieved because of the high frequency of mistakes or inattention by the user.

81

In view of this, it is often more important for those evaluating contraceptives to know the use-effectiveness-pregnancy rate.

The discrepancy between theoretical effectiveness and use-effectiveness is clearly seen with the oral contraceptive; the former is attended by a pregnancy rate of less than one, whereas the pregnancy rate of the latter may be nearer to 16.

Conflicting reports of use-effectiveness

The student of sex education is often confused by widely conflicting reports of use-effectiveness-pregnancy rates. For example, rates of 3, 11, 12, 17, 28 have been reported for the condom. Which one is accurate?

Unfortunately, there is no simple way to resolve the differences between various reports. But Table 1 may be useful as a general guide.

This table attempts to contrast "constant and careful users" with "averages for all types of users."

A review of Table 1 reveals that the pregnancy rate is generally higher for coital related contraceptives (contraceptives that must be used with each coitus and which require advanced planning) such as the condom, diaphragm, spermicidal agents, and coitus interruptus.

Methods less subject to patient error appear to be more effective (i.e., IUD, tubal ligation, and vasectomy).

Choice of contraceptive method

It is the role of the sex educator to present information regarding the theoretical effectiveness, use-effectiveness, and safety of various contraceptives. Religious and esthetic aspects of individual choice are not within the purview of sex education.

TABLE 1. PREGNANCY RATES OF VARIOUS CONTRACEPTIVE METHODS

Type of Contraceptive	Constant and Careful Users	Average for All Types of Users
Tubal ligation	.04	.04
Vasectomy	.15	.15
Oral contraceptive	Less than 1	16.0
IUD	1.5–3.0	6.0
Condom + spermicidal agent	1.0	5.0
Condom	5.0	15.0
Diaphragm	8.0	12.0
Spermicidal agents	3.0–5.0	30.0
Coitus interruptus	16.0	25.0
Rhythm	15.0	40.0

This chapter discusses contraceptives in a sequence that accords with the frequency with which they are selected in the United States; i.e., (1) oral contraceptives, (2) surgical sterilization, (3) condom, (4) IUD, (5) diaphragm, (6) spermicidal agents, (7) rhythm, (8) douche, and (9) withdrawal.

ORAL CONTRACEPTIVES FOR WOMEN

Suppressed ovulation

In 1937, progesterone, a hormonal substance, was demonstrated to prevent ovulation in rabbits. This discovery prompted two questions in the minds of medical scientists:

1. Could progesterone be utilized as a human contraceptive?
2. If so, could a readily available source of progesterone be found?

In the early years progesterone was derived from animal tissues at a cost of $200 per gram.

The answers to both these questions were affirmative:

1. A synthetic substance having the physiological effect of progesterone was derived from the wild Mexican yam (progestin or progestogen).
2. In 1956 progestogen and another hormonal substance were combined as an oral contraceptive (trade name, Enovid) and found highly effective in tests conducted in San Juan, Puerto Rico.

Enovid

Thus the discovery that progesterone blocked ovulation led to the production of the first oral contraceptive pill.

But in addition to progesterone, Enovid included estrogen, added to control endometrial shedding and bleeding, thus assuring a normal menstrual-like flow each cycle.

Later it was found that synthetic estrogens alone prevented ovulation (natural estrogen had failed to produce consistent inhibition of ovulation).

Three types of oral contraceptives

Today, oral contraceptives are of three major types:

1. Sequentials
2. Combined
3. Progestational

The sequential and combined oral contraceptives contain both estrogen and progesterone.

Generally, the sequential types contain estrogen for the first 14 pills and both estrogen and progesterone for the remaining six or seven pills.

The combined orals contain both estrogen and progesterone throughout the cycle.

The progestational orals contain only low dose progestin (norethindrone). These are also known as the minipill.

Sequentials

The sequential oral contraceptives were designed to more nearly duplicate normal female physiology, i.e., increased levels of estrogen during the early part of the cycle and both estrogen and progesterone during the latter part.

But a higher pregnancy rate relative to the combined orals and an ever increasing list of side effects associated with estrogen have tended to render the sequentials unpopular in recent years.

The sequentials, however, appear to be especially suitable for persons with acne or hirsutism (excessive growth of hair).

Combined orals

The combined oral contraceptives derive their popularity from their theoretical pregnancy rate of only 0.1 per 100 woman-years.

By contrast, the theoretical pregnancy rates for sequentials and progestational pills are estimated to be 0.5 and 2.54, respectively.

It is estimated that approximately 18 million women in the United States now use combined orals.

How sequentials and combined orals work

The contraceptive effect of sequentials and combined orals was initially believed to be the simple blocking of ovulation.

But the observation that contraception can be achieved by hormonal dosages that do not achieve the suppression of ovulation has made it necessary to revise the initial hypothesis.

Five mechanisms

It would now appear that at least five mechanisms may be operative:

1. In sufficient dosage estrogen inhibits FSH, a pituitary hormone required for ovulation.

2. In sufficient dosage progestogen inhibits luteinizing hormone (LH), a pituitary hormone required for ovulation.

3. In the user of the oral contraceptive, a thick mucus is produced in the cervix that may act as a barrier to passage of sperm.

4. Also in the user, an endometrium not suitable for implantation may be present for a greater than normal portion of the cycle.

5. Progestins may inhibit motility of sperm or decrease the viability of the fertilized egg.

Dependent on dosage

The number of mechanisms involved in a given female user is dependent upon the amount of estrogen and progesterone taken.

This is important because the best contraceptive is the one that least affects normal physiology.

Thus, a pill that could be highly effective as a contraceptive and yet not block ovulation would be desirable.

Currently, however, it is important to note that the greater the hormonal dosage, the greater the effectiveness of the pill.

And pills that block ovulation are nearly 100 per cent effective when taken as directed.

In the meantime, research moves toward the discovery of a pill that will not suppress ovulation or disturb the endometrium but will be 100 per cent effective.

The minipill

Recently the Food and Drug Administration[1] approved for use in the United States an oral contraceptive containing only the progestational agent norethindrone (0.35 mg.).

This progestin-only oral contraceptive represents an attempt to avoid many of the side effects associated with the more traditional estrogen-progestin pill.

The FDA noted, however, that approximately eight per cent of the degradation products of norethindrone become biologically active estrogens.

The minipill is taken on a continuous basis as long as contraception is desired.

Although the minipill may be less productive of side effects, it has a higher drop-out rate for medical reasons than the combination oral contraceptive.

Two major drawbacks are:

1. A significant incidence of unpredictable bleeding.

2. A pregnancy rate of approximately three per 100 women-years.

On the other hand, side effects such as headache, nausea or vomiting, breast tenderness, and back and abdominal pain appear to be less with the minipill.

Research with the minipill has further confirmed the antifertility mechanism of progestogen:

1. Synthetic progestin suppresses luteinizing hormone release and prevents ovulation and corpus luteum formation in approximately 1/3 of cycles.

---

[1] *FDA Drug Bulletin,* December 1972.

2. Alteration of the endometrium to make it unsuitable to receive a fertilized egg may occur.

3. A thick mucus which may adversely affect sperm viability or motility may be produced in the cervix.

In releasing the minipill (marketed by Syntex under the name of Nor-20 and by Ortho as Micronor)[2] the FDA pointed out:

> . . . experience to date indicates that the effectiveness of progestin-only oral contraceptives is lower than that of sequential or combination oral contraceptives containing both estrogen and progestin. The overall pregnancy rate with the conventional oral contraceptives is generally less than one pregnancy over 100 women-years, while with the progestin-only products approximately three pregnancies might occur per 100 women-years.

Personal decision about oral contraceptives

The Boston Women's Health Collective, in advising women about contraceptive decisions, asserts:[3]

> Birth control pills are dangerous for some women, and in other women can cause side effects that range from nuisances to major pains and changes. But many women have taken the pill with no apparent side effects at all. Also 100% protection against pregnancy is a very important tool for many of us as we start to take control of our lives.

Prior to a personal decision regarding oral contraceptives it is important to discuss one's medical history with a physician. The following review of side effects may also be useful.

Side effects of oral contraceptives

The side effects of the pill are advantageous in some cases, disadvantageous in others, and serious or even lethal for a small number of women.

The following symptoms are potentially serious and should be reported to a physician at once:

1. Severe leg cramps

2. Chest pain

3. Severe headaches

4. Blurring or loss of vision

5. Sensations of flashing lights

Unwanted side effects

Blood clots

Studies completed in a number of countries have demonstrated a higher incidence of thromboembolic diseases (internal clotting disorders) among women who use oral contraceptives.

---

[2] *Family Planning Digest,* May 1973, Department of Health, Education and Welfare.
[3] Boston Women's Health Collective, *Our Bodies Our Selves,* Simon and Schuster, New York, 1973, p. 115.

Mortality

In Great Britain[4,5] the number of deaths resulting from blood clots of the lungs or brain was found to be several times higher for oral contraceptive users:

Deaths Per 100,000

	Age 20 to 34	Age 35 to 44
Oral contraceptive users	1.5	3.9
Nonusers	0.2	0.5

These figures should be interpreted against a death rate during pregnancy or delivery of approximately 25 per 100,000.

The thromboembolic mortality rate for oral contraceptive users is much less than the rate for pregnancy.

Morbidity

Women aged 20 to 44 years are hospitalized for venous thromboembolism (clots in veins) at a rate of approximately 6 per 100,000. Use of oral contraceptives increases this incidence to 66 per 100,000.

Effects of blood type

Among women taking oral contraceptives, the risk of thromboembolic disease is three times higher for those with blood types A, B, or AB than for those with type O.[6] It is unclear as to why this increased risk exists.

Estrogen factor

Studies[7] in the United Kingdom, Sweden, and Denmark have indicated that the incidence of thromboembolic disease is directly associated with the estrogen content of oral contraceptives.

Coronary thrombosis

The same study revealed a significant association of coronary thrombosis and oral contraceptive use.

Stroke

A study of 598 women in 12 university medical centers (with support from the National Institutes of Health) indicates an increased incidence of stroke among female pill users.

The risk for thrombotic stroke (caused by clot) was approximately nine times greater among women using the pill.

Stroke caused by hemorrhage was twice as high for pill users.

[4] W. H. W. Inman, "Role of Drug Reaction Monitoring in the Investigation of Thrombosis and the 'Pill.'" *Brit. Med. Bull.*, 26:248-256, 1970.

[5] W. H. W. Inman, and M. P. Vessey, "Investigation of Deaths from Pulmonary, Coronary, and Cerebral Thrombosis and Embolism in Women of Childbearing Age," *Brit. Med. J.*, 2:193-199, 1968.

[6] H. Jick, et al., "Venous Thromboembolic Disease and ABO Blood Type: A Cooperative Study," *Lancet*, 1:539-542, 1969.

[7] W. H. W. Inman, et al., "Thromboembolic Disease and the Steroidal Content of Oral Contraceptives: A Report to the Committee on Safety of Drugs," *Brit. Med. J.*, 2:203-209, 1970.

The study also indicates a much higher risk of stroke for women smokers. The latter findings suggest the need for additional studies of the interaction of smoking and pill use.

The risk of stroke, however, was greater among nonsmokers using the pill than among nonsmokers not using the pill.

Blood pressure

Research has established the fact that use of oral contraceptives results in a slight increase in blood pressure.

Severe hypertension, however, is an unusual occurrence. And it is uncertain as to whether a minimal increase in blood pressure is detrimental to these women.

The increase in blood pressure appears to be reversible; it returns to its previous level when pill use is discontinued.

Blood sugar

Use of oral contraceptives appears to cause an increase in blood sugar.

This effect also appears to be reversible.

The effects of the pill on glucose tolerance appear to be additive to the effects of age, obesity, and family history of diabetes.

The pill is contraindicated in diabetes.

The oral contraceptive does not appear to be diabetogenic (a cause of diabetes), but it does seem to exacerbate the condition.

Depression

In a study[8] of 5151 Kaiser Health Plan subscribers, it was found that 33.5 per cent had never used the pill, 27.9 per cent were former users, and 38.6 per cent were current users.

In this study, the current users exhibited less premenstrual moodiness and irritability than the other two groups.

There appeared to be no effect on users who had a previous history of depression.

The investigators further noted that the dosage of progestin taken appeared to effect premenstrual moodiness and irritability. Within a range of 0.5 to 10.0 mg, it was found that higher doses were associated with fewer symptoms.

In another study,[9] Dr. Joseph Goldzieher and his associates came to the following conclusion after a comparison of pill and non-pill users:

> It would seem that the majority of nervousness, depression, and weight gain noted in oral contraceptive users is either coincidental or associated with the psychological impact of taking these agents, rather than with any pharmacologic effect.

---

[8] *Family Planning Digest,* September 1973, Department of Health, Education and Welfare.

[9] Joseph W. Goldzieher, et al., "Nervousness and Depression Attributed to Oral Contraceptives: A Double-Blind, Placebo-Controlled Study," *Am. J. Obstet. Gynec.,* 111:1013, 1971.

Cancer

Studies[10-12] in both the United States and Great Britain indicate no relationship between use of oral contraceptives and breast cancer, benign breast lesions, cancer of the cervix, or precancerous cervical lesions.

Milk nutrients

Oral contraceptives reduce the amount of protein, fat, and calcium in the milk of the nursing mother.

Gallbladder functions

There is some evidence that use of oral contraceptives may increase the risk of gallbladder disease.

The pill and adolescent growth

As to the effects of the pill on growth, Dr. Louis Hellman states[13]:

> Fears that oral contraceptives might limit growth, if prescribed for young girls, have proved baseless. These fears were based on observations that large doses of estrogen hasten epiphyseal closure. These observations, however, were based on very large doses of estrogen administered prior to the growth spurt, which occurs somewhere between the tenth and twelfth year in the United States. It is unlikely that oral contraceptives would be used this early.

Other side effects

Other side effects reported to attend oral contraceptive use by some women include:

1. Increased susceptibility to Candida albicans vaginitis (a fungal infection of the vagina).

2. Fluid retention.

3. Nausea.

4. Loss of hair.

5. Acne may be worsened.

6. Altered thyroid function.

7. Women using contact lenses may observe irritation secondary to corneal edema.

8. Increased body hair (hirsutism).

Some beneficial side effects

The following side effects of oral contraceptives have been viewed as beneficial by some women:

1. Menstrual cramps are usually minimized.

2. The menstrual flow is generally reduced in both amount and duration.

3. Occasionally, acne is improved.

---

[10] J. G. Boyce, et al. "Cervical Carcinoma and Oral Contraception," *Obstet. Gynec.,* 40:139, 1972.
[11] "Tests on the Pill for Carcinogenicity," *Brit. Med. J.* 4:190, 1972.
[12] M. P. Vessey, et al., "Oral Contraceptives and Breast Neoplasia: A Retrospective Study," *Brit. Med. J.,* 3:719, 1972.
[13] Louis M. Hellman, "The Oral Contraceptives in Clinical Practice," *Family Planning Perspectives,* October 1969.

4.   Breast enlargement sometimes occurs.

5.   Menstruation is more likely to be regular.

**Prescription or
nonprescription
oral contraceptives**

In an attempt to minimize serious side effects, oral contraceptives are legally available only by prescription. However there is some controversy over this legal position. An examination of conflicting opinions on this question may help to provide a better perspective on oral contraception.

Some physicians have suggested that the advantages of the oral contraceptives so far outweigh the risks that it would be advisable to remove them from the list of prescription drugs—especially in the developing world.

In advancing this position, Dr. R. T. Ravenholt, Director of the Office of Population of the State Department's Agency for International Development (AID) states:[14]

> . . . now we have almost 13 years of experience, some 50 million women using oral contraceptives in the world, 10 million of whom are in the United States. We've had the opportunity to look at the impact of such use upon many indices, such as age-specific mortality rates related to certain diseases, infant mortality rates, congenital malformation rates—and we have a greatly improved basis for judging the effects of the pill.

Noting the "great hullabaloo" of the 1960's relating to an increased incidence of thromboembolism he stated: "All we could ascribe to the pill for young women in their teens and early twenties is something of the order of one death per 100,000 users per annum."

In advocating nonprescription use of oral contraceptives, Dr. Ravenholt noted:[15]

> We do not have any evidence to indicate that there's any marked difference in the effects of pills among 10,000 women who have been screened by physicians as opposed to 10,000 women who have not been screened by physicians. As far as we can see, it is very difficult to identify the woman—the occasional woman—who should not use the pill.

Other physicians do not agree with Dr. Ravenholt's views.

For example, Dr. Louis M. Hellman, Department of Health, Education and Welfare's Deputy Assistant Secretary for Population Affairs, states:

> There are numerous conditions for which the pill is definitely contraindicated, such as a history of thromboembolism, hypertension, migraine headaches, diabetes. We know that the incidence of serious complications associated with the pill is rare but we believe that a thorough medical history and examination of women who

---

[14] *Family Planning Digest*, July 1973, Department of Health, Education and Welfare.
[15] *Ibid.*

desire the pill obviously is desirable and may be lifesaving. Because of the metabolic changes associated with continued and prolonged use of these drugs, it is important that a woman's condition be monitored while she is taking the oral contraceptive to see that she is not developing conditions which may contraindicate its continued use. Such monitoring is especially important since we know little about what, if any, association there may be between pill use and disease entities which take very long periods to develop.

Maximizing your protection

It is probably advisable to use the pill for one cycle before becoming sexually active or to use another form of birth control during this time. This precaution is to protect against the possibility that an egg may have started to form before initiation of pill usage.

If a pill is missed, most physicians recommend that it should be taken as soon as remembered and the normal sequence of pill taking continue for the remainder of the cycle.

If two or more pills are missed, some additional form of contraception should be insititued for the remainder of the cycle.

There is no agreement as to how long a woman should remain on the pill, but if you decide to be cautious and come off the pill after a few years, be sure to select another acceptable and effective method of contraception.

The pill and fertility

It has been commonly believed that after using the pill the female becomes more fertile when she stops using them.

According to Dr. James Whitelaw, this belief was not arrived at by the scientific method but by poorly controlled observations.

In a paper entitled "The Myth of Oral Contraceptives in the Treatment of Infertility," published in *Fertility and Sterility,* Dr. Whitelaw concludes that not only are oral contraceptives of no value in the treatment of infertility but that they are contraindicated.

Indeed, infertility following oral contraceptive use has become a problem for many women.

Hormonal contraceptives by nonoral routes

The FDA has recently approved a low-dose long-acting injectable progesterone (medroxyprogesterone acetate, or Depo Provera).

For this contraceptive regimen, injections are required every three months.

Medroxyprogesterone acetate (DMPA) inhibits LH, thereby preventing ovulation. Its theoretical effectiveness is 0.3 to 0.5 pregnancies per 100 woman-years.

Women taking DMPA must sign a consent form instructing them about side effects. Side effects include excessive bleeding, cessation of menses, potential sterility, decreased libido, headaches, dizziness, and weight gain.

Vaginal ring

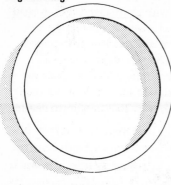

FIGURE 47

An experimental approach to the use of nonoral progestin involves a vaginal ring.

This rubber ring, about the size of a diaphragm, releases small amounts of progestin that are absorbed by the body.

The female user inserts the ring herself at the end of her regular cycle.

It is left in place for three weeks and then removed and thrown away.

Menstruation follows removal of the device.

Progestin implants

Progestin enclosed in a Silastic capsule may also be implanted under the skin for long-term contraceptive use.

Limited tests of progestin implants have yielded good results.

Postcoital contraception or interception

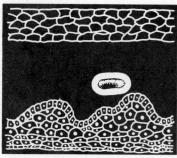

FIGURE 48

Recent research indicates that diethylstilbestrol (DES) is an effective postcoital contraceptive.

DES is a synthetic estrogen.

In a report[16] entitled "Interception: The Use of Postovulatory Estrogens to Prevent Implantation," Dr. John Morris and Gertrude van Wagenen noted in the *American Journal of Obstetrics and Gynecology* that in over 9,000 midcycle exposures treated with estrogens, only 29 pregnancies occurred.

The FDA, however, has urged that DES "be considered as an emergency treatment only and that it . . . not be considered as a method of birth control with continuous and frequently repeated therapy.[17]

The FDA has further proposed that warning labels be issued to persons who might use DES.

The labels would warn the patient of the association of estrogen with blood clots and other side effects.

DES has been associated with cancer of the vagina in young women whose mothers took it for other reasons during pregnancy.

How postcoital contraceptives work

At the present time, the mechanism whereby postcoital estrogen prevents pregnancy is unknown.

---

[16] J. M. Morris, and G. van Wagenen, "Interception: The Use of Postovulatory Estrogens to Prevent Implantation," *Am. J. Obst. Gynec.,* 115:101, 1973.
[17] *Family Planning Digest,* May 1973, Department of Health, Education and Welfare.

Dr. Richard P. Blye,[18] however, has suggested six possibilities:

1. Alteration of tubal transport
2. Prevention of embryonic viability
3. Prevention of sperm transport
4. Loss of sperm viability
5. Luteolysis (chemical breakdown of corpus luteum)
6. Asynchronism of uterine endometrium

Alteration of tubal transport

Among these theories, alteration of tubal transport appears to be one of the most popular.

Normally a newly fertilized egg spends three or four days in the Fallopian tube and another three or four in the uterus before it begins the process of implantation.

This is a carefully planned sequence and if the fertilized egg arrives too early, the endometrium is inadequately developed and the egg will degenerate.

Estrogens are known to increase the rate of secretion of tubal fluid, stimulate ciliary activity of the upper portion of the tube and increase peristaltic activity of the tubal muscles. In view of these effects, many researchers think that postcoital estrogens prevent pregnancy by altering the time sequence between fertilization and implantation.

Effectiveness of postcoital estrogens

Regarding the effectiveness of postcoital estrogens, Dr. Blye notes:

> Sufficient evidence has accrued to indicate that daily administration of 50 mg of diethylstilbestrol, 30 mg of conjugated equine estrogen, or 5 mg of ethinyl estradiol for 5 consecutive days is probably effective in preventing pregnancy if instituted within 72 hours of unprotected midcycle coital exposure.

SURGICAL STERILIZATION

Vasectomy

Vasectomy is a simple surgical procedure in which the vasa deferentes are cut to prevent the passage of sperm (Fig. 21).

Vasectomy does not interfere with ejaculation, since the sperm constitute only a very small portion of semen.

Sperm counts following vasectomy

Following vasectomy the male is generally considered sterile when two consecutive semen examinations are found to be negative, and when three weeks have passed.

However, recent studies indicate that approximately 34 per cent of postvasectomized males exhibit positive sperm counts

---

[18] Richard P. Blye, "The Use of Estrogens as Postcoital Contraceptive Agents," *Am. J. Obstet. Gynec.*, 116:1044, 1973.

12 weeks later. Irrigation of the distal end of the vas deferens with sterile water immediately after vasectomy reduces the problem somewhat but not entirely.

Table 2 summarizes the results of studies of 125 males having a vasectomy without irrigation and 111 having a vasectomy followed by irrigation with 20 ml. of sterile water.

Restoring fertility

Although the chances of restoring fertility following a vasectomy have improved in recent years, this cannot be counted on. Hence, the decision to undergo vasectomy should be considered definitive.

Vasovasostomy

A vasovasostomy is an operation to reverse a vasectomy.

According to a study[19] by Dr. Fletcher C. Derrick, Jr. of George Washington University School of Medicine (reported to the American Urological Association), the chances of successfully reversing a vasectomy are approximately 1 out of 5.

To improve the success rate of vasovasostomies, it is recommended that the vasectomy be done higher up, away from the convoluted portion of the vas deferens.

Autoantibodies to sperm following vasectomy

Blocked-up sperm may provide an antigenic stimulus in some men causing them to develop autoantibodies to their sperm.

In these cases, reversible vasectomy may not restore fertility.

Other side effects

Very little research exists relative to the side effects of vasectomy. This stems from the fact that changes are difficult to measure in the living male.

The evidence that is available, however, suggests that side effects are very minimal.

The *Family Planning Digest*[20] has recently summarized research into the effects of vasectomy in experimental animals:

[19] "Vasovasostomy Productive in Only 1 Out of 5," *Med. Tribune,* July 11, 1973, p. 25.
[20] *Family Planning Digest,* May 1973, Department of Health, Education and Welfare.

TABLE 2.   PERCENTAGE OF MALES EXHIBITING POSITIVE SPERM COUNTS FOLLOWING VASECTOMY*

	12 Weeks	15 Weeks	30 Weeks
Nonirrigated	33.6	25.5	5.6
Irrigated	16.2	6.3	0.0

* Adapted from Ian Craft, and John McQueen, "Effect of Irrigation of the Vas on Postvasectomy Semen-Counts," *Lancet,* 1:515, 1972.

In all species studied—rats, rabbits, hamsters and rhesus monkeys— swelling and, later, cyst-like lesions have been noticed in the different regions of the ducts leading from the testes, due to the accumulation of sperm, which continue to be produced.

These phenomena are most pronounced in lower animals and least evident in the highest, the monkey.

In the rats, there was a suggestion of a reduction in the output of testosterone.

In one experiment which used immature rats (the other studies used mature animals) researchers found exceptionally large cysts and a shrinkage in the size of testes.

Despite the presence of lesions and swelling, a study of vasectomized rhesus monkeys showed no difference between their postoperative sexual behavior and that of monkeys who had undergone only sham operation.

The degree of change observed varied from species to species. It is not certain whether any of these phenomena also occur in human males.

Drs. Robert Hackett and Keith Waterhouse have summarized the effects on humans.[21]

Bilateral vasectomy does not alter sexual potency or ejaculation or have any noticeable effect on seminal volume. Evidence that the endocrine status remains the same after vasectomy is supported by the fact that the plasma testosterone and seminal fructose levels are unaltered and there are no microscopic changes in the interstitial cells of the testis. Postvasectomy testicular biopsy shows normal spermatogenesis. . . .

Decision about vasectomy

The male requesting a vasectomy is usually informed about the procedure, advised as to the low probability of reversibility and provided a period of time to consider the matter.

Some physicians use specific criteria in determining eligibility for vasectomy, e.g., 30 years of age and at least two children. Others believe that vasectomy should be available to any adult upon request.

Surveys of men having vasectomies indicate that:

1. Approximately 60 per cent report the same frequency of sex relations.

2. An increase was reported by 38 per cent.

3. Only 2 per cent reported a decrease.

The few studies available indicate that vasectomy does not lead to greater promiscuity among men.

Currently there are approximately 750,000 vasectomies performed in the United States each year.

---

[21] Robert E. Hackett and Keith Waterhouse, "Vasectomy—reviewed," *Am. J. Obstet. Gynec.*, 116:438, 1973.

Female sterilization

Female sterilization involves abdominal surgery to tie off the Fallopian tubes and is thus more complicated as a surgical procedure than is vasectomy. But it is as safe as other surgical procedures (Fig. 49).

Tying off the tubes prevents the egg from passing to the uterus. Instead it harmlessly disintegrates in the tube.

Female sterilization does not in any way affect appearance or sexual desire.

Recent advances in female sterilization

Like a vasectomy, it is likely to be permanent, since the restoration rate is low.

Laparoscopic sterilization

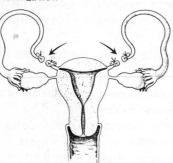

FIGURE 49

Sterilization by laparoscopy is a new surgical technique in which a laparoscope (instrument to visualize the abdominal area through a small incision) is inserted through the abdominal wall and the Fallopian tubes are cauterized with an electric current.

The procedure may be performed on an outpatient basis using only local anesthesia.

The woman is told to expect "three seconds of sharp pain" as each tube is cauterized.

Only about one per cent of such patients experience complications requiring additional abdominal surgery.

The procedure appears to be effective, convenient, and has a relatively low cost.

Following the procedure only a Band-Aid is needed to cover the incision. Some procedures require two incisions but a more advanced laparoscope makes it possible to complete the entire procedure through a single small incision.

Hysteroscopic sterilization

In hysteroscopic sterilization a device is inserted through the cervix into the uterus to visualize the openings of the Fallopian tubes. A cautery device is then inserted into the tubes (one at a time) and the tubes are burned. Subsequently, scar tissue forms over the injury, blocking the tubes.

Colpotomy

Colpotomy is a technique of female sterilization in which an incision is made in the vagina rather than in the abdomen.

The technique dates back to the early nineteenth century but has recently begun to attract new interest after extensive use in India.

In this procedure, the Fallopian tubes are tied through an incision in the vagina.

According to proponents of this procedure, it offers the following advantages: [22]

> Colpotomy can be performed either on an outpatient basis or with a minimal hospital stay.
>
> Only five to fifteen minutes are normally required for the operation.
>
> Local or spinal anesthesia, rather than general, is sufficient.
>
> There is less postoperative pain than with other techniques.
>
> There is no abdominal incision.
>
> There is no visible scar.
>
> Instruments are simple, cheap, and usually available wherever gynecological services are offered.
>
> Electrocautery is not required.
>
> Major complication and morbidity rates (in developing countries) are low.
>
> The failure rate is only about one per cent.
>
> It is possible to combine the procedure with early pregnancy termination or other gynecological procedures.

THE CONDOM

FIGURE 50

The condom is a mechanical barrier worn over the male penis to prevent sperm from entering the vagina (Fig. 50).

These are usually made of latex rubber and shaped like the finger of a glove.

Currently, condoms are being marketed in a variety of bright colors that may be more aesthetically pleasing to some users than the noncolored ones.

"Skins"

In their early history condoms were often referred to as "skins" because they were made from sheep intestines.

Today "skins" have been largely replaced with thin strong latex condoms.

Condoms may have a plain end or a small reservoir to contain the ejaculated semen.

Condoms do not require fitting by a physician, are harmless, and very easy to use.

Most widely used

The condom is the third most widely used contraceptive method in the United States.

Since 1938 condoms sold or shipped in interstate commerce have been subject to control by the Food and Drug Administration.

---

[22] "Sterilization," Population Report, Series C, Number 3, June 1973. (Department of Medical and Public Affairs, The George Washington University Medical Center, Washington, D. C.)

This has greatly improved their quality.

Rupture is the most frequent cause of failure with the condom.

In case of rupture, the female should immediately apply a contraceptive jelly.

The condom is also useful in preventing the spread of venereal disease.

Maximizing protection

The condom should be worn throughout sexual intercourse; an unexpected ejaculation might otherwise cause pregnancy.

When unrolling the condom, care should be taken to prevent formation of an air pocket in the tip. This could cause rupture.

A lubricant helps to prevent tearing and may be applied after the condom is in place. Prelubricated condoms are also available. Vaseline should not be used because it can decompose the rubber.

In withdrawing the male penis, the rim of the condom should be held to prevent spillage of semen.

The penis should be withdrawn soon after ejaculation.

Condoms carried in wallets may deteriorate because of heat.

Special use of condoms

Some women produce antibodies against sperm, resulting in infertility. In such cases, condoms may be used for 6 to 12 months to reduce the woman's antibody titre. Subsequent conception may become possible when the condom is not used.

Sex therapists often recommend condoms for premature ejaculation. Condoms tend to dull sensation and may delay ejaculation.

INTRAUTERINE DEVICES (IUD)

An old method

Although intrauterine devices have only recently come into the limelight in the United States, the basic concept of inserting something in the uterus to prevent pregnancy has been employed for more than 2000 years.

Uterine displacement

In the nineteenth century, intrauterine devices (stem pessaries) were used for the correction of uterine displacement as well as for contraception.

An early pioneer

In the early 1900's Grafenberg, a German scientist, developed a silver ring for insertion into the uterus.

After study of the effectiveness of the ring, he reported in 1930 that the pregnancy rate was only 1.6.

Despite this report of its effectiveness, Grafenberg's ring was poorly received. Placing something in the uterus just didn't seem like a good idea to medical scientists.

Thus, Grafenberg joined the list of scientists who will be remembered as being "ahead of the times."

Plastic IUD

Resurgence of interest in the IUD was prompted by the report of Japanese workers regarding the use of plastic material for intrauterine contraceptive devices (Fig. 51).

INTRAUTERINE DEVICES

Dalcon Shield

Saf-T-Coil

Copper-"T"

FIGURE 51

Through the cervical canal

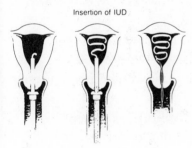

Insertion of IUD

FIGURE 52

Use of plastic IUD's made it possible to insert them through the cervical canal without dilating the cervix (Fig. 52).

This is accomplished by compressing the IUD into a small tube, inserting the tube through the cervical canal, and then discharging the IUD from the tube, allowing it to expand to its normal shape and size.

Some of the more popular devices include:

1. Margulies spiral (1959)
2. Lippes loop
3. The bow
4. Double spiral
5. Saf-T-Coil
6. Copper T (TCu)
7. Dalkon shield
8. Copper 7

Use of the IUD

Accurate figures as to the number of people using the IUD in the United States are not available, but it is estimated that approximately 10 per cent of the married women under 30 years of age use IUD's.

The relatively low price of the IUD makes it highly suitable for countries with nationwide family planning programs.

And since the effectiveness of the IUD is dependent upon the knowledge of the inserter and not of the wearer, it is well suited for use by uneducated populations.

As a part of their family planning programs, the following countries have extensively used the IUD:

1. India

2. Pakistan

3. South Korea

4. Taiwan

Biologic effect

The mechanism whereby the IUD has its antifertility effect is poorly understood because human experimentation is difficult, and the IUD has different effects with different species of animals.

In chicken and sheep, the IUD inhibits transport of spermatozoa.

In the rabbit, sow, cow, and ewe the function of the corpus luteum is impaired.

In the woman, the IUD does not prevent ovulation or menstruation.

Three theories

Currently there are three popular theories as to how IUD's prevent pregnancy:

1. *Altered tubal transport* prevents pregnancy by speeding movement of the egg through the Fallopian tubes.

2. *Mechanical interference* with implantation occurs as a result of abrasive action by the IUD.

3. *Changes in the internal milieu* of the uterus prevent pregnancy by rendering the walls of the uterus chemically unsuitable or gametotoxic.

Early work with the IUD appeared to support the theory of altered tubal transport and mechanical interference.

Presently, however, the evidence favors the theory that IUD's produce local inflammatory responses in which the internal milieu becomes toxic to either sperm or fertilized eggs.

The Advisory Committee on Obstetrics and Gynecology of the Food and Drug Adminstration states:

> Early histological studies disclosed no significant tissue alterations with the use of IUD's in humans. It was postulated on the basis of such observations that the devices acted mechanically: that they prevented implantation by an abrasive effect. Although endometritis was noted, it was thought to be a sterile reaction to a foreign body and of no significance. Several more recent studies have shown rather uniformly that there are alterations in the endometrium. These studies, based on the examination of endometrial biopsies and hysterectomy specimens, show grossly a thickening of the

endometrium with edema and pressure effects. Indeed, in many instances, an impression of the device may be seen on the endometrium with edema and pressure effects. Microscopic examination shows that the endometrium directly adjacent to the device is thin and ulcerated. . . .

Size of IUD's and pregnancy rates

Although the mechanism whereby IUD's prevent pregnancy is unknown, there is considerable evidence that the greater the surface area of the device the lower the pregnancy rate.

Table 3 indicates this inverse relationship.

Effectiveness of IUD

Regarding the effectiveness of the IUD, the Advisory Committee on Obstetrics and Gynecology to the Food and Drug Administration reports:

1. In the United States the most successful IUD's are associated with a pregnancy rate of from 1.5 to 3.0 per 100 women during the first year.
2. These rates tend to decline during successive years.
3. In general, the rates [pregnancy rates] vary inversely with the size of the device and with the age of the patient.
4. In terms of theoretical effectiveness, IUD's are less reliable than oral contraceptives. . . .
5. The IUD's are probably not more effective than the diaphragm or condom if these conventional forms of contraception are used correctly. In terms of use-effectiveness in clinic patients, however, the IUD's have proved far more reliable than the traditional methods and only slightly less reliable than the oral compounds.
6. About 80 percent of women will continue to use the device for the first year, 70 percent for the second, and, from the limited data available, about 50 percent at the end of the fifth year.

TABLE 3. PREGNANCY RATES AT TWO YEARS AND SURFACE AREA OF VARIOUS IUD'S*

Type of Device	Surface Area (mm.^{2})	Pregnancy Rate (%)
Small bow	390	16.1
Small loop	527	9.3
Large bow	730	7.1
Small coil	960	4.5
Large loop	960	4.1
Large coil	1200	2.2

* H. J. Davis and J. Lesinski, "Mechanism of Action of intrauterine contraceptives in women," *Obstet. Gynec.*, 36:350, 1970.

Safety of IUD

Insertion of IUD's is attended by a small risk of infection and uterine perforation.

The Advisory Committee on Obstetrics and Gynecology reports:

> There is no apparent carcinogenic [cancer causing] effect of the devices in the human being.
>
> Plastics of the type used for IUD's have been used extensively as prostheses in various parts of the human body and have in no instances resulted in cancer.

Abortion with IUD

The Committee further states:

> The incidence of abortion may be as high as 40 per cent if pregnancy occurs with the IUD in place. The proportion of these reported abortions that are induced, however, cannot be ascertained.

Ectopic pregnancy

The Committee also says:

> There is no evidence that IUD's cause ectopic pregnancies.

Fertility after IUD use

Research to date indicates that fertility is unimpaired among women who discontinue IUD's to plan pregnancy.

Recent studies of copper IUD's

In 1966, Dr. Howard J. Tatum designed a T-shaped device which had lower than usual medical removal rates but a pregnancy rate of 18 per 100 women-years.

Recent research has demonstrated, however, that winding a fine copper wire around the shaft of the Tatum T reduces the pregnancy rate to 0.5 to 1.5.

With the addition of copper, the device is now labeled a TCu.

Copper is gradually absorbed from the TCu and the device must be replaced periodically.

The amount of copper added to an IUD is generally measured in square millimeters. Hence a TCu-200 has a surface area of 200 mm.^{2} of copper.

The antifertility effect of copper appears to be proportional to its total surface area with an optimal effect obtained at 300 mm^2 of copper.

The mechanism whereby copper acts as an antifertility agent in humans is unknown. On the other hand, since copper does not affect the egg or impair the fetus in any way, it is hypothesized that its antifertility action is to prevent implantation.

One theory suggests that copper increases the number of white cells in the uterus and that these cells prevent implantation.

Cu_7

In addition to the TCu, copper has also been added to other types of IUD's. One of these is shaped like the number 7 (Cu_7).

Copper IUD's and gonorrhea

Dr. John Swanson,[23] University of Utah School of Medicine, has discovered that extremely small amounts of metallic copper can destroy colonies of gonococci in about 30 minutes.

It was further noted that the amount of copper released from current type IUD's should be sufficient to prevent gonorrhea.

Whether this theory is true in the human body or not awaits further investigation.

IUD's and salpingitis

On the other hand, current evidence suggests that use of regular IUD's by women who have contracted gonorrhea may predispose them to acute salpingitis.

Some newer type IUD's

Dalkon shield

The Dalkon Shield (Fig. 51) was developed by Dr. Hugh J. Davis, a gynecologist, and Irwin S. Lerner, a bioengineer at the Johns Hopkins University School of Medicine.

The Dalkon shield has a low expulsion rate thought to be due to its shape and composition.

A major advantage of the Dalkon shield is the fact that it may be used effectively with women who have not previously experienced childbirth.

Research in the United States indicates that a pregnancy rate of 1.2 per 100 women-years may be expected with the shield.

Progesterone T

Among the current IUD's is a T-shaped polymer device which continuously releases small amounts of progesterone into the uterus.

Preliminary research with this device suggests a very low pregnancy rate, and additional studies are underway.

Fluid-filled IUD

Medical scientists are currently experimenting with a nonrigid IUD filled with saline.

The device consists of a Silastic polymer reinforced with Dacron mesh. It is shaped like an inverted isosceles triangle.

In practice, this device is inserted into the uterus, and saline is injected through a tube.

Maximizing effectiveness of the IUD

In an attempt to further improve the effectiveness of the IUD, many physicians recommend the use of condoms or foam on days 10 to 18 of the cycle.

The diaphragm

The diaphragm is a shallow rubber cup with a reinforced perim-

---

[23] *Family Planning Digest,* May 1973. Department of Health, Education and Welfare.

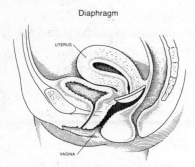

Diaphragm

UTERUS

VAGINA

FIGURE 53

eter consisting of a circular metal spring. Its diameter ranges in size from 55 mm. to 100 mm.

The diaphragm was developed about 90 years ago by a German physician, Wilhelm P. J. Mensinga.

For contraceptive use the diaphragm fits between the walls of the vagina and covers the cervix. (Fig. 53). Prior to insertion, however, spermicidal agents are applied to the inside of the diaphragm and around the rim.

It has been shown that the diaphragm is moved about during coitus; hence it is only partly effective as a mechanical barrier to sperm.

Its main contraceptive function is to hold the spermicidal agent near the cervical os.

Maximizing effectiveness

The diaphragm must be fitted by a physician, and the female user must be trained to insert it properly.

Since the vagina expands in the sexually responding female, the largest size diaphragm that can be worn without discomfort should be selected.

The diaphragm should be inserted not more than six to eight hours before intercourse, and should be removed eight to sixteen hours after coitus.

After use, the diaphragm should be washed with soap and water, dried, and coated with talcum powder.

Since the vagina may be stretched, the diaphragm should be rechecked after childbirth.

Cervical cap

The same points attend use of the cervical cap, which differs from the diaphragm in that it fits onto the cervix rather than lying diagonally across the vaginal tube.

Spermicidal agents

A variety of spermicidal preparations are available without prescription. These include:

1. Contraceptive cream
2. Contraceptive jelly
3. Vaginal foam
4. Foaming tablets
5. Suppositories

Spermicidal contraceptives consist of an inert base to hold the preparation in the vagina and against the cervix. Additionally, they include spermicidal chemicals, usually nonylphenoxypoly-ethoxy ethanol, which kills the sperm.

Use of spermicidal agents increases the effectiveness of both the condom and the diaphragm.

Maximizing effectiveness

Foams are generally more effective than creams or jellies.

Spermicidal preparations should not be applied more than 30 minutes before sexual relations, and they should not be removed for six to eight hours.

Spermicidal preparations should be reapplied if intercourse occurs again within eight hours of the original application.

But despite all precautions, spermicidal agents used alone do not represent an effective method of contraception.

THE RHYTHM METHOD

Normally a woman releases only one egg during each menstrual cycle and this egg must be fertilized within approximately 12 to 24 hours or not at all.

The objective of the rhythm method is to schedule sexual intercourse in such a way as to avoid the presence of sperm during the life span of the egg.

This is not an easy objective to accomplish. It is complicated by two problems:

1. There is no readily available sign to indicate that ovulation is about to occur.

2. It is now known that sperm can survive for at least seven days in the female reproductive tract.

Thus, the effective practice of rhythm requires some basic knowledge of physiology.

The calendar method

One way of practicing rhythm is termed the calendar method because it involves keeping records on a calendar.

The method is very ineffective and is described only as a matter of general information.

A more reliable method of rhythm will be described later.

How the calendar method works

It is commonly observed that women tend to ovulate about midway through their menstrual cycles.

Thus, if the length of the cycle were known, it would be possible to predict with some degree of accuracy the approximate time of ovulation.

However, the length of the menstrual cycle is no more predictable than the time of ovulation.

But the length of the menstrual cycle has one advantage—it can be objectively measured (i.e., the menstrual flow is an outward sign that the cycle has ended, whereas the time of ovulation is not attended by any outward sign).

The calendar method is based on the concept that the length of past cycles is a key to the future.

To use this method, the woman keeps a record of the length of each menstrual cycle for a year.

This provides her with some indication of the variability that can be expected in the length of her cycles.

The longest and shortest cycles represent the greatest variability.

In practice, 18 is subtracted from the number of days in the shortest cycle. This determines the first day on which intercourse is likely to result in pregnancy.

For example, if the shortest cycle were 24 days, then 24 minus 18 equals 6. Thus day 6 would be the first fertile day, and abstinence from sexual intercourse should begin on this day.

To determine the last fertile day, 11 is subtracted from the number of days in the longest cycle.

For example, if the longest cycle were 28 days, one would subtract 11 days from 28 to determine that the last fertile day would be day 17.

Thus in this example, days 6 through 17 would be unsafe for sexual intercourse.

Because the length of last year's cycles may not be an accurate index of the length of this year's cycles, this method is not recommended.

Basal body temperature method

Only one method of rhythm will be recommended here because it is currently the only one that is effective (Fig. 54).

Rhythm Method by Basal Body Temperature

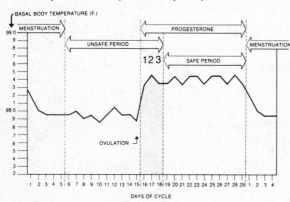

DAYS OF CYCLE

FIGURE 54

The method is based on a physiological clue that ovulation has occurred.

It happens this way:

1. After ovulation the follicle from which the egg was discharged develops into a corpus luteum.

2. This newly formed structure secretes progesterone into the blood.

3. Progesterone increases metabolism and thus increases body temperature.

The slight increase in body temperature that attends the secretion of progesterone is an outward clue that ovulation has occurred.

Although the increase in body temperature is a very small one (about 0.5° F.), it is a reliable clue if the temperature is properly taken and if no infection is present.

However, careful attention must be given to the details of this method.

It is immediately obvious that an infection or any factor that might produce a fever could constitute a false clue that ovulation had occurred.

Fortunately most fevers are attended by other signs or symptoms that are apparent to the woman.

Another source of concern is the fact that the body's metabolism increases with such factors as eating food, excitement, and physical exercise.

To avoid the influence of these factors, only the basal body temperature is used.

Basal temperature refers to the temperature when the body is at complete rest.

It is best determined before getting out of bed in the morning.

It may be taken orally or rectally, but rectal temperatures tend to be more accurate.

Temperature is best determined through use of a basal body thermometer, which may be obtained at any drugstore.

This thermometer ranges only a few degrees, from 96° F. to 100° F. with tenth-of-a-degree graduations.

The basal body thermometer makes it easier to determine small changes in temperature.

Period of increased temperature

Following ovulation, the newly formed progesterone effects a rise of about 0.5 of a degree in basal body temperature.

The observed rise continues until a day or two before menstruation.

As progesterone disappears the temperature returns to its former low level during the first day or two of menstruation.

If pregnancy occurs, the temperature remains high because progesterone is formed during pregnancy.

Pregnancy is the likely cause if the basal body temperature remains high for more than 18 days.

The safe period

Sexual relations may safely commence after the temperature rise has been observed for three consecutive mornings.

If the rise in temperature is due to progesterone (not infection), conception is highly unlikely during the remainder of the cycle.

In fact, if sexual relations are limited to this part of the cycle the rhythm method is as effective as the IUD, condom, or diaphragm.

But this means that there is no safe period prior to ovulation.

THE DOUCHE

The douche is a contraceptive technique in which the vagina is washed out with water or other substances.

The objective, when used as a contraceptive technique, is to remove semen before sperm can enter the uterus.

Of the contraceptive techniques discussed, douching is the least effective.

Sperm can be found in the opening of the cervix within 90 seconds after intercourse. This means that the douche usually would not be performed in time to be of any value.

Even when performed quickly the douche is very unreliable as a contraceptive technique.

WITHDRAWAL (COITUS INTERRUPTUS)

In the withdrawal technique the male withdraws the penis from the vagina just prior to ejaculation.

This method has been found unsatisfactory for the following reasons:

1. It is generally not satisfying from either a physiological or psychological standpoint.

2. The possibility of pregnancy is great because depositing even a few drops of semen in the vagina may cause pregnancy.

Contraceptive behavior among married couples

A recent national fertility survey[24] has served to describe contraceptive practices in the United States.

According to this survey, the oral contraceptive is by far the most popular method of contraception among married couples. It

---

[24] Charles F. Westoff, "The Modernization of U.S. Contraceptive Practice," *Family Planning Perspectives*, July 1972, pp. 9-12.

accounts for approximately 34 per cent of all current contraceptive practice,[1] exhibiting a 10 per cent increase since 1965.

The closest competitor to the pill is voluntary sterilization, accounting for approximately 16 per cent of the contraceptive population. Among couples electing sterilization, the ratio of male to female sterilization is approximately one to one (i.e., eight per cent for both males and females). This method of contraception is decidedly more popular among older married couples (aged 30 to 44). In the latter population, surgical sterilization accounts for approximately 25 per cent of current contraceptive practice.

The condom appears to be the third most popular choice and currently accounts for approximately 14 per cent of total contraceptive practice. This, however, is a significant decrease from 22 per cent in 1965.

Although the IUD is not as popular as the pill, condom, or surgical sterilization, its popularity appears to be rapidly increasing. A new surge of interest has attended improvement of the device, increased effectiveness for never-pregnant women, and concern over the side effects that attend the oral contraceptive. It is currently estimated that one out of every 20 couples of reproductive age now use the IUD—approximately 1.25 million married women.

The diaphragm, foam, and rhythm account for equal proportions of the contraceptive population—approximately six per cent in each case. The douche is the method of choice for approximately three per cent of current contraceptors, and withdrawal accounts for two per cent.

Contraceptive behavior among unmarried couples

A national survey[25] of never-married young women aged 15 to 19 reveals:

Less than half of the sexually experienced used any form of contraception at last intercourse.

And only 20 per cent used contraception on a regular basis.

When sex occurred six or more times per month, contraceptive use was more likely. Infrequent sex was associated with a higher degree of risk.

Socioeconomic status and educational level have a positive effect on contraceptive use.

Plans to marry had no significant effect on contraceptive use.

Oral contraceptives, condoms, and withdrawal were the most frequently used methods of contraception.

---

[25] John F. Kantner and Melvin Zelnik, "Contraception and Pregnancy: Experience of Young Unmarried Women in the United States," *Family Planning Perspectives,* Winter 1973, pp. 21-35.

**Contraceptive
failure**

Despite recent advances in contraception, only 66 per cent of those attempting to prevent a pregnancy altogether are able to do so for at least five years.[26]

Professor Norman B. Ryder of the Princeton Office of Population Research states:

> . . . contraceptive success is more likely, whatever the particular method, when the intent is to prevent rather than to delay, and when the woman is somewhat older rather than somewhat younger at the beginning of exposure to risk of an unintended conception. Standardized for intention and relative age, the failure proportions associated with each method are: pill, six per cent; IUD, 12 per cent; condom, 18 per cent; diaphragm, 23 per cent; foam, 31 percent; rhythm 33 percent; and douche, 39 per cent. These proportions reflect the characteristics of those who use each method, as well as of the method itself.

[26] Norman B. Ryder, "Contraceptive Failure in the United States," *Family Planning Perspectives*, Summer, 1973, pp. 133-142.

CHAPTER SEVEN

Abortion

Abortion

Laws permitting abortion should be fully implemented in order to assure that every woman who desires to terminate an unwanted pregnancy has prompt, dignified, and humane access to a medically safe abortion.

American Public Health Association

In January of 1973 the United States Supreme Court ruled (Doe v. Bolton and Roe v. Wade) that a state does not have the right to interfere with the decision of a woman and her physician to effect an abortion during the first trimester of pregnancy. The court further ruled that during the second trimester the state could impose only those regulations relating to the pregnant woman's health and safety, and that abortion could be prohibited during the third trimester only if such prohibition posed no threat to the woman's life or health. In striking down the abortion laws of Texas and Georgia, the Court in effect rejected the "right to life" theory that the fetus is a person with legal rights. This decision, coupled with the advances in medicine which render early abortion several times safer than childbirth, means that a woman and her physician have the right to decide this intensely personal matter—the legal blocks have been removed. It is now a social, psychological, philosophical or theological question for the individual woman and her physician. For these reasons, it now seems appropriate to discuss abortion in as much detail as pregnancy was heretofore described.

DEFINITIONS OF TERMS

To facilitate our discussion of abortion, let's begin with some definitions of terms.

Spontaneous abortion

Abortion occurring without outside intervention.

Induced abortion

Abortion brought on intentionally by use of drugs, instruments, radiation, or other means.

Threatened abortion

The appearance of the signs and symptoms of a possible abortion. Indicators include vaginal bleeding with or without intermittent pain. If the attachment to the uterus is not interrupted, pregnancy may continue.

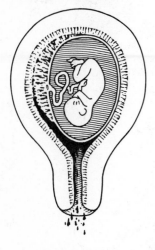

Threatened abortion

FIGURE 55

Imminent abortion

A condition characterized by bleeding and progressively increasing pain. If hemorrhage is slight, the condition may be reversed, but only in a hospital. If hemorrhage is severe, the uterus must be medically emptied.

Inevitable abortion

A condition in which bleeding and severe abdominal cramps progressively increase. Evidence of excessive blood loss may be present. The condition demands immediate curettage (scraping of the uterus) and blood transfusions where indicated.

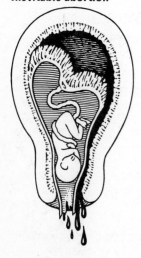

Inevitable abortion

FIGURE 56

Incomplete abortion

An abortion attended by continuous uterine bleeding because of retention of the products of conception. Surgical emptying of the uterus is indicated.

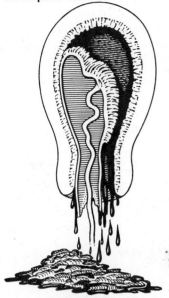

FIGURE 57

Incomplete abortion

Complete abortion

An abortion in which all the products of conception are expelled.

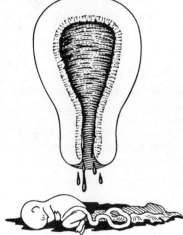

FIGURE 58

Complete abortion

Missed abortion

A condition in which a dead, nonviable fetus is retained in the uterus. Usually one waits for spontaneous expulsion to occur, but abdominal surgery may be necessary in rare cases.

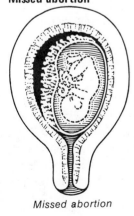

FIGURE 59

Missed abortion

Septic abortion

A condition in which there is an infection of the products of conception, usually resulting from an attempted interference during early pregnancy. Antibiotic treatment and curettage are necessary.

Habitual abortion

A condition in which the woman has spontaneously aborted three or more consecutive times, without apparent cause.

Therapeutic abortion

An abortion in which pregnancy is terminated in the interest of the woman's health.

Criminal abortion

Previously defined as an abortion deliberately produced for nonmedical reasons. Currently defined as an abortion that does not accord with public law.

Embryonic abortion

An abortion that occurs before the fifth week of pregnancy.

Fetal abortion

An abortion that occurs after the fifth week of pregnancy.

SPONTANEOUS ABORTION (MISCARRIAGE)

Although most of the contemporary interest appears to be directed toward induced abortion, it seems appropriate to begin our discussion with spontaneous abortion.

During the first eight weeks of pregnancy, the ovum is relatively poorly protected and nourished. It is not surprising, therefore, that between 10 and 15 per cent of all pregnancies end in spontaneous abortion. About 75 per cent occur before the sixteenth week, and the great majority occur before the eighth week.

Improved fetal attachment

Between the eighth and twelfth weeks, the incidence rate of spontaneous abortion decreases because of improved fetal attachment. However, there is a tendency to retain some of the products of conception should an abortion occur at this time.

After the first trimester of pregnancy, the placenta is firmly established and spontaneous abortion is far less likely.

Nature's way

Spontaneous abortion very often represents Nature's way of preventing a deformed fetus from going to full-term pregnancy; i.e., more than half of the aborted fetuses are clearly defective. In other cases miscarriage may be caused by maternal abnormalities; e.g., infectious diseases, hormonal abnormalities, or malnutrition. But in a large number of cases the cause of spontaneous abortion remains unknown.

**Vaginal bleeding
and cramps**

Miscarriage is usually signaled by vaginal bleeding (spotting) and subsequent cramps. At the first sign of a possible miscarriage, the woman should go to bed and notify her physician at once.

Following abortion, it is sometimes necessary to scrape the uterus to remove any remaining materials. To assist the physician in deciding upon the necessity for this procedure, any products of conception that are expelled should be retained for his examination.

Subsequent pregnancy

One spontaneous abortion does not mean that difficulty should be expected in subsequent pregnancies. Three or more spontaneous abortions without apparent cause indicates the need for special tests and sometimes bed rest during pregnancy. But even then, normal pregnancy is often possible.

The tendency to experience spontaneous abortion during the second trimester appears to be exacerbated by a previously induced abortion in which the cervix was dilated.

In a study[1] by a team of British physicians, a tenfold increase in the incidence of miscarriage among women who had had a prior abortion was observed.

For this study, postabortive women were compared with women who had undergone childbirth or a spontaneous abortion without cervical dilation.

INDUCED ABORTION

The authors subscribe to the view[2] that abortion is ". . . at best, a failure of contraception or, at worst, a failure of the healing and teaching professions to educate Americans effectively about contraception, and of society to make birth control services readily available to all who want them." We do not view abortion as human failure. On the other hand, we clearly recognize that an abortion always represents a crisis in a woman's life. Hence, the discussion that follows is an attempted answer to the question: what does a woman need to know in order to make an intelligent decision about whether or not to have an abortion?

**Frequency of different
types of abortions**

In a study[3] of 72,988 abortions, the Joint Program for the Study of Abortion has compiled the incidence rate of different types of abortions. The results are presented in Table 4.

---

[1] C. S. W. Wright, S. Campbell, and J. Beazley, "Second-Trimester Abortion After Vaginal Termination of Pregnancy," *Lancet,* 1:1278, 1972.

[2] Bonnie Douber, et al., "Abortion Counseling and Behavioral Change," *Family Planning Perspectives,* April 1972, pp. 23-27.

[3] Christopher Tietze and Sarah Lewit, "Joint Program for the Study of Abortion (JPSA): Early Medical Complications of Legal Abortion," *Studies In Family Planning,* 3(6):97-122, 1972.

TABLE 4.   PATIENTS WITH INDUCED ABORTIONS, BY PERIOD OF GESTATION AND TYPE OF PRIMARY PROCEDURE

Gestation (weeks)	Suction	D&C	Saline	Hysterotomy	Hysterectomy	All other	All procedures
			Number of Patients				
8 or less	16,117	1,267	0	30	79	11	17,504
9-10	20,989	1,230	0	64	121	18	22,422
11-12	12,915	671	0	150	199	19	13,954
13-14	2,480	106	1,092	186	141	39	4,044
15-16	461	37	2,926	173	118	59	3,774
17-20	0	0	9,066	285	124	98	9,573
21 or more	0	0	1,606	54	31	26	1,717
All gestations	52,962	3,311	14,690	942	813	270	72,988

Uterine aspiration (suction)

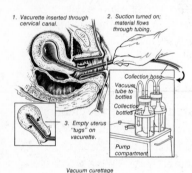

1. Vacurette inserted through cervical canal.
2. Suction turned on; material flows through tubing.
3. Empty uterus "tugs" on vacurette.

Collection hose
Vacuum tube to bottles
Collection bottles
Pump compartment

Vacuum curettage

FIGURE 60

The mechanical aspects of uterine aspiration are relatively simple medical procedures. A hollow tube is inserted into the uterus until it contacts the amniotic sac, whereupon vacuum pressure is turned on and the physician observes as the products of conception pass through a transparent tube and into a collecting bottle.

Preparation for uterine aspiration and follow-up care are, however, considerably more involved.

Cervical dilation

The cervix guards the entrance and outlet to the uterus and must be dilated to accommodate the size of an object that would pass through. Hence, dilation precedes uterine aspiration.

Mechanical dilation of the cervix is painful and the procedure necessitates use of an anesthetic.

For uterine aspiration, hospitals tend to use general anesthesia, whereas clinics, almost exclusively, use local anesthesia for paracervical blocking.

In paracervical blocking, Xylocaine, Carbocaine, or similar agents are injected in the posterior vagina behind the cervix.

When the cervix is dilated about the width of a finger, the physician inserts a vacurette (hollow tube) into the uterus until it contacts the amniotic sac.

The vacurette, in turn, is connected to a collection bottle via transparent plastic tubing.

At the appropriate time, vacuum pressure is turned on, and in less than a minute the physician observes the products of conception as they pass into the collecting bottle.

When the uterus has been emptied, a slight tug on the vacurette is observed. As an added precaution, the physician will scrape away any material that adheres to the lining of the uterus.

Recuperation

Following uterine aspiration, recuperation is almost immediate, and in a matter of a few hours the woman may resume her normal life style.

Menstrual-like bleeding usually persists for one to several days, and pads or tampons may be used.

Any fever, pain, or unusual bleeding following an abortion should be reported to one's physician immediately.

As may be seen in Table 4, most induced abortions (approximately 70 per cent) are by uterine aspiration. This procedure continues to increase in popularity, and it is estimated that by the late 1970's more than 90 per cent of all abortions will be by uterine aspiration.

The simplistic nature of the procedure renders it highly suitable during the early stages of pregnancy.

Physicians only

Although uterine aspiration is a relatively safe and simple procedure in the hands of a physician, it can be extremely dangerous when attempted by the layman. For example, a vacuum cleaner connected to the uterus may extract the uterus from the pelvic cavity and be immediately fatal.

Dilation and curettage

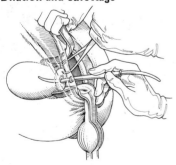

Dilatation of cervix
FIGURE 61

Dilation and curettage is the name given to the medical procedure in which the cervix is stretched open (dilated) and the lining of the uterus scraped (curettage). In a D&C, an object (shaped like a small spoon with a long handle) known as a curette is inserted into the uterus for purposes of scraping (Fig. 61).

The loosened products of conception are then removed from the uterus with forceps. The procedure requires approximately 15 minutes.

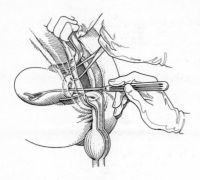

Curettage
FIGURE 62

Although a D&C may be used to terminate pregnancy, its most frequent use is to cope with abnormal bleeding, e.g., during the menstrual period, between periods, or after menopause.

Uterine aspiration has largely replaced the D&C as the most popular method for abortion.

Saline procedure

Uterine aspiration and D&C's are not generally recommended after the fourteenth week of pregnancy. And as may be seen in Table 4, none were performed after the sixteenth week.

Between the fourteenth and twenty-fifth weeks, the saline procedure was the method most often employed.

The saline procedure is based upon two physiological principles: (1) a strong saline solution kills the fetus, and (2) death of the fetus diminishes the secretion of placental hormones that sustain pregnancy.

In the saline procedure, a needle is inserted through the abdominal and uterine walls, and part of the amniotic fluid is removed. This fluid, in turn, is replaced with a strong saline solution.

During the subsequent 24 to 48 hours, the woman goes into labor and delivers the products of conception.

Hysterotomy

A hysterotomy is a surgical technique in which an incision is made through the abdominal and uterine walls, and the fetus and placenta are removed.

In recent years, the saline procedure has tended to replace the hysterotomy.

Menstrual extraction

In many locations it is possible to have a menstrual extraction following a missed period.

The procedure is similar to uterine aspiration and requires only a few minutes. The woman feels nothing more than a mild cramp.

Technically, menstrual extraction is not an abortion since pregnancy can be determined at this time. However, if a fertilized egg is present in the uterus, it is removed by the procedure, and pregnancy can be determined after the fact. Hence the procedure has been labeled "the perfect pregnancy test for women who didn't want to be pregnant."

Prostaglandins and abortion

In 1935 a class of biologically active substances was discovered in human seminal fluid. This class of long-chain fatty acids was labeled prostaglandins.

Today it is known that the prostaglandins are found in nearly all human tissues, and that they have a wide range of physiological effects.

These effects include uterine contractions and increased muscular activity in the Fallopian tubes.

Working from these observations, medical scientist have successfully used the prostaglandins to:

1. Induce labor

2. Induce menses

3. Induce abortion

Additional research suggests that the prostaglandins may have contraceptive value when used postcoitally to interrupt ovum transport or to inhibit progesterone formation by the corpus luteum.

Several problems remain, however, before the pharmacological application of the prostaglandins can be realized.

First, there is the matter of a high incidence of side effects.

Secondly, the prostaglandins are not potent by the oral route of administration, and the intravenous route can only be utilized in a hospital or clinical situation.

More recently, however, intravaginal administration has been demonstrated to be effective.

Thirdly, it appears that the success rate for inducing labor, menses, or abortion is considerably less than 100 per cent. This is also the case for postcoital interruption of ovum transport or inhibition of progesterone formation.

Postabortal complications

The complications that attend induced abortions are related to the time during pregnancy when the abortion occurs. During the first trimester of pregnancy, abortion is a very safe procedure.

The Joint Program for the Study of Abortion[4] reported no deaths among more than 30,000 women undergoing abortion during the first trimester.

Mortality

The overall mortality ratio for abortions performed in New York City was 5 per 100,000 (7.7 for residents and 3.5 for nonresidents). The mortality was nine times higher for abortions at 13 or more weeks than for those done at 12 or fewer weeks.

---

[4] Bonnie Douber, et al., "Abortion Counseling and Behavioral Change," *Family Planning Perspectives,* April 1972, pp. 23-27.

Mortality ratios by method of abortion are summarized in the following table.[5]

Method	Mortality per 100,000
Suction	1.1
D&C	2.4
Saline	18.8
Hysterotomy	208.3

Approximately one per cent of postabortal women exhibit serious complications. Some common complications include perforation of the uterus, hemorrhage, pelvic infection, damage to the cervix, and fever.

Ovulation following induced abortion

Following an induced abortion, contraception should be resumed or initiated at once.

Ovulation may occur as early as ten days following abortion.[6]

The average time for resumption is approximately 22 days.

The national scene

According to a Harris Survey taken in April 1973, 52 per cent of Americans favor the Supreme Court decision to legalize abortion during the first trimester. Forty-one per cent opposed this decision.

The following statistics, compiled for a recent year, present a global view of the abortion scene in this country (Abortion Surveillance Report, Health Services and Mental Health Administration).

— 480,259 legal abortions were reported.

— This means 136 legal abortions per 100,000 live births.

— Women less than 20 years of age accounted for 29 per cent of the abortions.

— Single, widowed, separated, or divorced women accounted for approximately two-thirds of all reported abortions.

— Approximately 80 per cent of the reported abortions were performed in the first trimester of pregnancy.

— 84 per cent were performed by either suction or D&C.

Repeat abortions

In a study of repeat abortions in New York City, Dr. Edwin F. Daily and his coworkers[7] found that only 2.5 per cent of induced abortions were by repeaters.

---

[5] *Family Planning Digest,* May 1973. Department of Health, Education and Welfare.

[6] E. F. Boyd, and E. G. Holmstrom, "Ovulation Following Therapeutic Abortion," *Am. J. Obstet. Gynec.,* 113:469, 1972.

[7] Edwin F. Daily, et al., "Repeat Abortions in New York: 1970-72," *Family Planning Perspectives,* Spring 1973.

Abortion—A personal decision

In addition to the factual information that attends induced abortion, there are a number of psychosociological considerations that enter into decision making. These, of course, are different for each individual—depending upon the principles and presuppositions operative in her personal life. Hence it is a difficult matter to advise another person about induced abortion, and the authors proceed with this discussion only on the basis of "what I would tell my own daughter about abortion."

The discussion presupposes (1) an open relationship with one's daughters and (2) previous discussions of premarital sexual behavior. It is not meant to stand alone.

Six psychosociological aspects of abortion are discussed.

What I would tell my daughter about abortion

Parental support

It is my hope that responsible contraceptive behavior will render an abortion unnecessary during your reproductive years. On the other hand, if you should ever be faced with a personal decision about abortion, I want you to know that I will support you in your decision—whatever it might be and whenever that decision might be necessary.

I want you to know that I agree completely with the ruling of the Supreme Court of the United States that the right to abort an unwanted fetus during the first three months of pregnancy resides with a woman and her physician. But if you should decide to have an abortion, I hope that you would also feel free to discuss it with me. Among the more obvious difficulties I might be able to assist you with are the selection of a physician and financial problems. At least know that I would be willing to try.

Punishment for illicit sex

I sincerely hope that you do not participate in coitus or become pregnant until after marriage, but if you should, I hope that you will not view your pregnancy as "punishment for illicit sex." It is possible that you did not exhibit responsible contraceptive behavior, but your pregnancy is certainly not a punishment. There are many unplanned and unwanted pregnancies both in and out of wedlock; none of these, however, is "sent as punishment."

Unhappy offspring

I further hope that you will not view abortion as "the person my baby is going to be should never exist because he or she will be unhappy." Your baby would probably develop into a very happy person. The point is this, you don't have to prove or feel guilty about what your child might have been. It is your personal right to participate in sex and not bear children if you so choose. This right of privacy emanates from the Fourteenth Amendment to the United States Constitution.

Exclusive category on Judgment Day

In my opinion, there is no good reason to think that those who have an abortion will occupy an exclusive category on Judgment Day. At best, abortion is necessitated by contraceptive failure, and at worst it is only one of the long list of human mistakes. One of the nice things about a country with a Fourteenth Amendment is that generally you have an opportunity to start your private life again—or have it remain the same. It is your choice.

The whole world knows

You should also know that it is a mistaken notion to think "the entire world can look at me and know that I have had an abortion." This is not the case although many postabortive women are troubled by the thought. Abortion, especially during the first trimester of pregnancy, is a very private matter. Only those people whom you choose to tell will know. If you ever decided to have an abortion, I would like to be among those that know. But if I were excluded, I would respect your right to privacy. On the other hand it is also your right to tell as many people as you like. It is your life and what other people know about it is primarily up to you. If you married a physician, he wouldn't know that you had had an abortion unless you choose to tell him.

Right to have your child

Even if you are unmarried at the time of pregnancy, I would want you to know that you also have the right to have your child if you wish. Do not allow a male who might be responsible for your pregnancy or anyone else to convince you that any of your personal attitudes toward abortion are merely brainwashing. You are a person with feelings that count, not a blank. It is your decision. In fact, it is unrealistic to view abortion as you would a "tooth extraction." It is a confusing and emotional experience, and there is nothing to be gained by denying this aspect of abortion; face it squarely. Some women have gained a greater command of their lives as a consequence of an honest decision to have or not to have an abortion. But it is a confusing experience. Don't go it alone. I sincerely hope that you will want to discuss it with me.

CHAPTER EIGHT

Venereal Diseases

Many authorities in sex education are of the opinion that venereal diseases should be considered only in connection with infectious diseases and not as a part of the sex education curriculum. They feel that a discussion of venereal diseases detracts from the "beauty" of sexuality. Inadvertently, this attitude promulgates the notion that nice people don't get and should not talk about venereal diseases. But an examination of health statistics indicates that thousands of nice people are contracting venereal diseases—not from doorknobs but in the same way that the more "common man" contracts these diseases. Indeed, venereal diseases are almost as dependent upon the sex act as pregnancy; the fact that disease is an undesirable consequence is not a justification for separating it from other aspects of sex education. To do so would be analogous to discussing the beneficial effects of a drug and delaying a discussion of any dangerous side effect until another time. In fact, the major reason that venereal diseases continue to exist is that they are so "undiscussable." Medical science has identified the causative agents, knows how these are transmitted, and has developed effective cures.

And venereal diseases are not out of place in a discussion of love. A major component of love is responsibility, which includes not transmitting a venereal disease to another person. Responsibility thus requires a knowledge of venereal diseases and how they are transmitted, which is the subject of this chapter.

CATEGORIES OF DISEASES

For convenience of study, diseases have been grouped into several broad categories. Three of these categories provide a perspective for the present chapter:

1. Hereditary diseases
2. Congenital diseases
3. Infectious diseases

Hereditary diseases are acquired at conception, whereas congenital diseases are acquired between conception and birth.

Infectious agents invade the body to produce the category known as infectious diseases.

Some venereal diseases are congenital, all are infectious, but none are hereditary.

VENEREAL DISEASES AND THEIR CAUSES

There are more than 20 human diseases that can be transmitted in a sexual way.

The most common venereal diseases are discussed in this chapter. These diseases and their causative agents are listed in Table 5 in the order in which they are discussed.

TABLE 5. VENEREAL DISEASES AND THEIR CAUSES

Disease	Organism	Agent
Gonorrhea	*Neisseria gonorrhoeae*	Bacteria
Syphilis	*Treponema pallidum*	Spirochetes
Chancroid	*Hemophilus ducreyi*	Bacteria
Lymphogranuloma venereum		Viruses
Granuloma inguinale	*Donovania*	Bacteria
Nongonococcal urethritis	*Chlamydia* (?)	Viruses
	Mycoplasma (?)	Bacteria
	Candida albicans (?)	Fungi
Herpes genitalis	Herpesvirus (type 2)	Viruses
Trichomoniasis	*Trichomonas vaginalis*	Protozoa
Monila	*Candida albicans*	Fungi
Pediculosis	*Phthirus pubis*	Parasites

GONORRHEA

Gonorrhea is an old disease—some medical historians believe that it was known to the Jews in Old Testament times, and it is described in the Book of Leviticus.

The word "gonorrhea" means "flow of seed" and was used by Galen in 130 A.D. to describe the signs of the disease that occur in males.

In the early history of the disease, it was thought that gonorrhea was a symptom of syphilis. This mistaken notion probably resulted from observations of patients with both diseases.

Indeed, the early medical scientist John Hunter inoculated himself with the pus formed in a patient with gonorrhea and contracted both gonorrhea and syphilis.

Not realizing that the patient had both diseases, Hunter concluded and taught that gonorrhea was the first stage of syphilis—a misconception that is still prevalent today.

In 1879, A. Neisser identified the bacterium that causes gonorrhea and named it the *gonococcus*.

Gonorrhea today

Among the infectious diseases reportable to public health authorities in the United States, gonorrhea currently ranks number one (Table 6).

TABLE 6.   INCIDENCE OF REPORTABLE INFECTIOUS DISEASES

1. Gonorrhea
2. Scarlet fever and streptococcal sore throat
3. Mumps
4. Syphilis
5. Hepatitis
6. Rubella
7. Measles
8. Tuberculosis
9. Salmonellosis
10. Shigellosis

Approximately 650,000 new cases of gonorrhea are reported yearly, but the actual number of treated cases probably exceeds 2,500,000.

Geographical factors

Gonorrhea is chiefly found in large metropolitan areas (Table 7).

TABLE 7.   GEOGRAPHICAL DISTRIBUTION OF GONORRHEA

Size	Incidence per 100,000
Small towns and rural areas	84
50,000 to 200,000	290
200,000 and over	610

The incidence is three times higher among males, primarily because the majority of infected females are asymptomatic.

The age range 20 to 24 years exhibits the highest rate, followed by teenagers (15 to 19 years).

World picture

The gonorrhea epidemic appears to be worldwide. Some comparative figures for the 1970's are found in Table 8.

TABLE 8. WORLD-WIDE INCIDENCE OF GONORRHEA

Country	Incidence per 100,000
Sweden	514
Denmark	319
United States	308
Britain	118
France	30

Numerous interwoven factors appear to be responsible for the increased incidence of gonorrhea. Some of these include the following.

1. Asymptomatic infections appear to have increased among males. This means that a smaller number of males are being effectively treated, a factor that contributes to the spread of gonorrhea.

2. Certain strains of the gonococcus are definitely less sensitive to antibiotics, and the recommended dosage of penicillin has now reached the full capacity that the buttocks can tolerate.

3. Increased population mobility has rendered contact tracing almost impossible.

4. Indiscriminate heterosexual and homosexual intercourse appears to have increased.

5. A number of medical scientists are of the opinion that oral contraceptives increase female susceptibility to gonorrhea.

   It appears that the pill increases pH in the area of the cervix and alters mucous secretions. Both conditions are thought to favor contraction of gonorrhea.

6. The condom appears to have decreased in popularity in recent years. This undoubtedly favors spread of gonorrhea.

7. Although no statistical data are available, many are of the opinion that oral and anal sexual practices have increased.

   At any rate, more cases of rectal and pharyngeal gonorrhea are currently being reported. This, however, may have resulted from an increased awareness among physicians.

The gonococcus

The bacteria that cause gonorrhea are bean- or kidney-shaped and are found in pairs.

In smears containing pus, the gonococci are seen inside white cells.

To survive, the bacteria require:

1. A pH of 7.2 to 7.6 and are killed by even weak acids.

2. A temperature of 35° to 36° C. and cannot survive a 3° change.

3. A moist environment and die immediately on drying.

4. Columnar or transitional epithelium and cannot attack the labia or vagina (stratified epithelium).

When the gonococcus dies, it releases an irritant (endotoxin).

Blood tests for gonorrhea

It is now clear that detectable antibodies are produced in gonorrhea.

Based upon this observation, a number of blood tests for gonorrhea have been developed. To date, however, none of them is reliable enough for general use.

No immunity

Despite the production of a small number of antibodies, an attack of gonorrhea confers no lasting immunity.

Transmission

Among adults, gonorrhea is spread almost exclusively by sexual intercourse. In children, infection by contaminated materials or pus is possible but not frequent.

The gonorrhea bacteria are ingested but not killed by white blood cells; thus, pus is infectious.

The organism dies quickly with drying but repeated use of bath water could be a means of transmission in young children.

Gonococcal conjunctivitis (infection of the eyes) may occur from passage through the birth canal of an infected mother.

If infected, the baby's eyes may be destroyed within a few days. This condition was at one time the most frequent cause of blindness in infancy.

Today most states require that the eyes of all newborn children be treated with silver nitrate or some other substance to kill the gonococcus (Fig. 63).

Also, most states require reporting of any inflammation of the eyes of a newborn to the health depeartment.

Application of Silver Nitrate at Birth

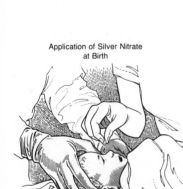

FIGURE 63

Transmission rate

Not all persons exposed to gonorrhea contract the disease. Although the true transmission rate is unknown, it is thought to be less than 50 per cent.

The reason for this seeming immunity is unknown. Recent evidence, however, suggests that the answer may be that other bacteria are known to prevent the spread of gonorrhea.

In studies of men, researchers have isolated 60 different bacteria that inhibit gonorrhea.

This finding could lead to medical application whereby physicians may attempt to modify the genital flora to decrease susceptibility to gonorrhea.

The course of gonorrhea

Having entered the human body, the gonococcus undergoes a short incubation period (three to seven days).

This short incubation period makes it possible for gonorrhea to be spread more rapidly than contacts can be traced.

Gonorrhea in the male

In the male the gonococcus attacks the mucous membrane lining the urethra (Fig. 64).

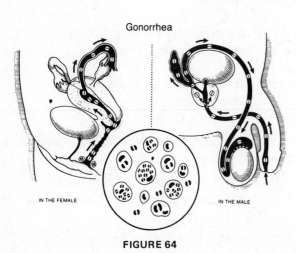

Gonorrhea

... IN THE FEMALE   ... IN THE MALE

FIGURE 64

The results of this attack are:

1. Swelling and irritation of the urethral tissue.

2. A painful, burning sensation with urination.

3. A yellowish discharge from the penis.

The pain is usually distressing enough to induce the male to see his physician. In other cases, however, there may be no pain.

Among infected males, approximately 10 per cent are asymptomatic.

To detect gonorrhea, the physician obtains a urethral culture (Fig. 65).

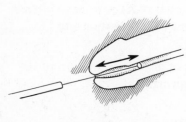

Urethral culture

FIGURE 65

If gonorrhea is diagnosed, treatment with penicillin can have dramatic results.

The urethral discharges may stop within 24 hours, and the disease may be completely abated in a short time.

However, some gonococcal bacteria are resistant to penicillin; and although other antibiotics are effective against gonorrhea, their effects are not so dramatic as those of penicillin.

Single-dose treatment for gonorrhea

Recently the FDA has approved a single-dose oral medication for gonorrhea.

The new drug tastes like lemon custard and is prepared by simply adding water to a bottle to dissolve a powder. The suspension is then ingested.

The oral suspension is a combination of ampicillin and probenecid and is reported to cure gonorrhea within 48 hours.

Bristol Laboratories market the drug under the name Polycillin TRB.

Biocraft Laboratories have also conducted tests on the drug and have requested permission from the FDA to market it under the name Clapicillin.

Probenecid is a drug that slows down the elimination of ampicillin from the body, affording it a better chance to kill the gonococci.

Untreated male gonorrhea

Untreated gonorrhea, like other infections, spreads to adjacent parts of the body.

In the male, it may spread to the posterior portion of the urethra, the prostate, the seminal vesicles, or the bulbourethral glands.

In advanced stages it may cause sterility or break through the walls that separate the reproductive system from other parts of the body, causing arthritis or heart disease.

Resistance

Great individual variation in resistance to gonorrhea has been observed.

If large numbers of gonococci are placed directly into the urethral canal, less than half the inoculated males will contract gonorrhea.

Prevention

The condom prevents contamination of the urethra and is undoubtedly the most effective measure for prevention of the spread of gonorrhea by sexual intercourse.

Gonorrhea and the female

In the female, gonorrhea passes through three stages (Fig. 64):

1. Infection of the urethra or cervix, which is often so mild as to go unnoticed.

2. Pelvic invasion by the disease.

3. A stage of residual and often chronic infection.

Hidden disease

During initial infection in women, the disease may cause no signs or symptoms. Thus the female becomes a chronic reservoir for the disease.

Approximately 90 per cent of infected women are asymptomatic.

Even the most advanced technique of smear and culture examinations yields a 20 per cent incidence of false negative results.

This difficulty in diagnosis of female gonorrhea is a major problem in controlling the disease.

Later complications

Complications of gonorrhea are more serious in the female because the disease may affect any of the pelvic organs or may even break through to attack other parts of the body.

The adult vagina is not susceptible to the bacteria, but the urethra, cervix, uterus, and Fallopian tubes may be attacked.

As the disease advances, the female may experience fever, nausea, vomiting, and lower abdominal pain.

Lower abdominal pain usually occurs when the infection has spread to the Fallopian tubes.

Treatment

Treatment is essentially the same as for males.

Follow-up

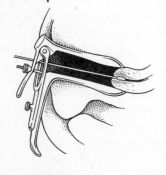

Endocervical culture
FIGURE 66

All patients treated for gonorrhea should have follow-up tests to be sure that the disease has been arrested. These tests consist of repeated cultures that are free of the bacteria.

The male is considered cured if a month passes without urethral discharge and if pus cells and bacteria are absent in the urine.

In the female, cure is considered to be accomplished when multiple successive examinations of the urethra and cervical canal indicate an absence of gonococcal bacteria.

In addition to follow-up care, all gonorrhea patients should have a blood test for syphilis.

Additional sites of infection

In addition to urethral and cervical infections, pharyngeal, rectal, and ophthalmic gonorrhea are of increasing concern.

Pharyngeal gonorrhea

At one time it was thought that the mucosa of the pharynx was unable to support growth of gonococci.

More recently, however, it has become clear that this was a misconception.

Indeed, pharyngeal gonorrhea has been reported[1] in 22 per cent of patients who were named as gonorrhea contacts and who also practiced fellatio. And in 13 per cent of this group, the pharynx was the only site of positive culture.

It has also been demonstrated that pharyngeal gonorrhea can spread to other parts of the body.

In general it is asymptomatic.

Rectal gonorrhea

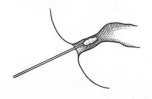

Anal culture

FIGURE 67

In a recent study[2] routine swabs of both the cervix and rectum were taken for 307 women in the Norfolk Venereal Disease Clinic.

Forty per cent of female patients diagnosed as infected also exhibited positive rectal cultures. And 20 per cent of the patients showed positive rectal tests but negative cervical tests.

Rectal gonorrhea is generally asymptomatic.

Ophthalmic gonorrhea

The gonococcus may be transmitted by fingers or moist towels to the eyes.

Failure to recognize and treat this type of infection may result in impaired vision.

Resistance of gonococci to antibiotics

In recent years a number of strains of gonococci have exhibited resistance to antibiotics.

This resistance may constitute a major problem in the control of gonorrhea in the future.

Dr. Frederick Sparling has summarized the problem to date:[3]

> Antibiotic resistance among gonococci has gradually increased in many areas of the world, including the United States, for over a decade. Resistance is often multiple in that strains relatively resistant to penicillin usually exhibit decreased sensitivity to tetracycline, erythromycin, chloramphenicol, and many other drugs, including streptomycin. Preliminary evidence suggests that there may be a common basis for resistance to several of these drugs. If this is substantiated, it is unlikely that use of combinations of these drugs would forestall development of resistance, nor would switch to generalized use of any one (tetracycline) lead to disappearance of resistance to the others (penicillin). Exceptions to this are sulfa drugs

---

[1] Henry Pariser, "Asymptomatic Gonorrhea," *Med. Clin. North Am.*, 56:1127-32, September 1972.

[2] Henry Pariser and A. F. Marino, "Gonorrhea—Frequently Unrecognized Reservoirs," *South. Med. J.*, 63:198, 1970.

[3] P. Frederick Sparling, "Antibiotic Resistance in *Neisseria Gonorrhoeae*," *Med. Clin. North Am.*, 56:1133-44, 1972.

(sensitivity has increased at the same time it has decreased to the others) and spectinomycin. The latter holds promise as an injectable drug for patients infected with gonococci which do not respond to penicillin or tetracycline. Resistance to all drugs except streptomycin is relative; presently available schedules of penicillin or tetracycline are still effective. Limited epidemiological data suggest that very intensive and perhaps more prolonged therapy may help prevent selection of still more resistant strains.

SYPHILIS

A spirochete infection

Syphilis is caused by spirochetes.

These organisms can only be seen against a dark background (in the same way that the moon and stars are only seen at night).

A pale, turning thread

But when it is seen in a microscope against a dark field, the spirochete appears as a pale, turning thread.

Because of this appearance, its discoverers called the agent that causes syphilis *Treponema pallidum* (trepein [Greek] — turn, nema [Greek] —thread, pallidum [Latin] —pale).

For those interested in biological classification, the causative agent in the case of syphilis is a member of the order of *Spirochaetales* and of the family *Treponemataceae*.

Since the causative organism of syphilis belongs to the order of spirochetes, the disease is sometimes referred to as a "spirochetal infection."

Characteristics of Treponema pallidum

Treponema pallidum is a living cell that requires special environmental conditions.

It is very susceptible to drying and dies in about 30 seconds on a doorknob or toilet seat.

It is very susceptible to high temperatures—above body temperature.

Elevating the body temperature to 106° F. for only a few hours causes destruction of a large percentage of active syphilitic organisms; this method was once used in treatment.

T. pallidum is killed by mild antiseptics, even soap and water.

Transmission

Syphilis is transmitted to another person in the following way: *T. pallidum* from the lesion of an infectious person passes through the intact mucous membranes or abraded skin of a second person.

Moisture is essential to transmission, a condition met by sexual intercourse and intimate kissing in the presence of infectious lesions.

Syphilis is thus not transmitted by doorknobs, dishes, or toilet seats.

Having entered the body, spirochetes are carried by the blood to every organ of the body.

If the infected person happens to be a pregnant woman, spirochetes may be passed into the fetal circulation, causing serious consequences or death of the fetus.

Congenital syphilis will be discussed in more detail in a later part of this chapter.

Spirochetes may also be found in menstrual blood, but they do not survive in the vaginal tract in the absence of a lesion.

If injected into a rabbit, *T. pallidum* will live, but humans are the only natural reservoir.

An asexual organism

Oddly, the spirochete so dependent on the human sex act for transmission does not itself mate but divides asexually approximately every 30 hours.

Stages of syphilis

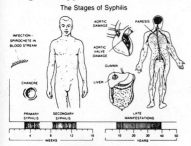

The Stages of Syphilis

FIGURE 68

Untreated syphilis passes through the following stages (Fig. 68):

1. Incubation period.

2. Primary stage.

3. Secondary stage.

4. Latent stage.

5. Late stage.

These stages will be discussed individually.

Incubation period

The incubation period consists of the time interval between the entrance of an infectious agent and the beginning of the signs and symptoms of the disease.

In the case of syphilis, the incubation period ranges from 10 to 60 days with an average of three weeks.

Assume that 1,000 bacteria entered the body by moist transfer. (Syphilis has been produced by as few as ten spirochetes.)

These spirochetes start to spread through the body and to multiply every 30 to 33 hours.

Spread of bacteria through the body

By the end of three weeks ten billion spirochetes have accumulated, and they have passed through the circulatory system and have been deposited around the blood vessels of tissues throughout the body.

It is doubtful that the spirochetes multiply in the blood, but when they are deposited in the tissues they resume multiplication.

Spirochetes cannot be detected in the blood during the incubation period. This is because blood tests for syphilis detect antibodies against syphilis rather than the presence of *Treponema pallidum.*

Thus, blood tests remain negative until antibodies have developed (approximately four to six weeks after infection).

Spirochetes multiply and spread through the body during the incubation period and later cause lesions of the skin or mucous membranes during subsequent stages of syphilis.

Primary syphilis

The primary stage of syphilis is signaled by the appearance of a lesion at the site of entry of the spirochete.

This stage may last one to five weeks.

The lesion that appears at this time is called a chancre (Fig. 68).

Chancre

It is usually 1/4 to 1/2 inch in diameter and is formed by white cells' packing themselves into the invasion area. The chancre usually begins as a red elevated area that breaks down to form a painless, ulcer.

The chancre is usually hard, but it can be soft.

It doesn't hurt.

It doesn't itch.

It usually does not fill with pus.

It is ordinarily not tender to touch.

It generally feels hard and button-like.

Multiple chancres may develop.

In approximately 95 per cent of the cases the chancre appears on or in the genital organs.

In women it commonly appears on the cervix, where it is often missed on examination.

In unusual cases the chancre may appear anywhere:

1. Homosexuals may develop lesions in the mouth or around the anus.

2. In a very unusual case syphilis was transferred by dual use of lipstick (this required that both women have a break in the skin of the lips).

3. One man is reported to have developed a chancre on his arm where his wife bit him.

4. Dentists and throat surgeons have accidentally contracted syphilis from treating infected patients.

Disappearance of chancre

The chancre usually disappears in about two weeks. (In unusual cases it may last as long as three months.)

Thus the individual who recognizes a new lesion and says, "I will wait awhile and see if it goes away before I see my doctor," makes a dangerous mistake.

Since the chancre is the only outward sign of primary syphilis, the individual who fails to report this to his physician passes untreated into the stage of secondary syphilis.

Dr. Lewis M. Drusin[4] has made the following important observation regarding the chancre:

Antibiotics given for another illness during this period may be sufficient to obscure the chancre without adequately treating syphilis.

Lymph node enlargement

In addition to the chancre, swollen lymph glands are usually exhibited during primary syphilis. These enlarged nodes (known as satellite bubo) are found in the site of the regional lymph drainage approximately three to four days after the appearance of the chancre. The nodes are round and rubbery without redness of the overlying skin. They are usually firm, freely movable, and nontender.

Diagnosis of primary syphilis

Since the chancre that attends primary syphilis resembles lesions caused by other factors, it is impossible to make an absolute diagnosis from the appearance of the lesion.

Absolute diagnosis can only be established by demonstration of *T. pallidum* in the local lesion.

A blood test for syphilis is likely to be negative at the time the chancre appears.

Remember that the incubation period averages approximately three weeks and that the primary stage of syphilis lasts approximately one to five weeks.

Since blood tests do not become positive until the fourth to sixth week, it is possible for the patient to pass through the primary stage of syphilis with a negative blood test.

Treatment

The preferred treatment for primary syphilis is penicillin.

When penicillin sensitivity prevents use of this drug, other antibiotics, such as erythromycin and tetracycline, may be used.

Primary syphilis is completely curable if properly treated.

Secondary syphilis

The secondary stage of syphilis begins about nine weeks (range, six weeks to six months) after initial infection.

---

[4] Lewis M. Drusin, "The Diagnosis and Treatment of Infections and Latent Syphilis," *Med. Clin. North Am.,* 56:116-74, September 1972.

During this stage, the spirochetes that have been spreading through the body produce lesions, especially in mucous membranes and in the skin (Fig. 68).

The skin lesions appear as a flattened, slightly raised red rash.

White patches may occur in the mouth and anus. Lymph nodes may enlarge.

These lesions contain many spirochetes, and if their outer covering is eroded spirochetes may escape and pass to another person.

Lesions covered with skin are not infectious.

Moist lesions frequently occur in the anogenital region and in the mouth.

The outer covering of these moist lesions is easily eroded, making them highly infectious.

Thus, the disease is spread by sexual contact for a purely biological reason—the moist lesion—not from any malevolent design to punish those who engage in sex.

Chancre vs. secondary lesions

Usually the first lesion that appears during syphilis is the chancre. And it usually appears in the anogenital region.

The chancre is easily eroded and highly infectious.

When *T. pallidum* enters the body, it passes via the blood to all parts of the body. Later these spirochetes will produce lesions.

The first lesion to appear is usually at the site of entry (chancre).

The chancre appears first for reasons of "seniority"; i.e., the spirochetes at this site have had more time to produce a lesion.

Secondary lesions appear at a later date after they have had time to develop.

But secondary syphilis is far more infectious than primary syphilis, because the secondary lesions are numerous, whereas there may be only one lesion during primary syphilis.

The secondary stage of syphilis represents the time span during which lesions are present and the disease is infectious.

This time span may range from three months to several years, with an average of two years.

During secondary syphilis the body develops antibodies against syphilis.

Thus, blood tests for syphilis are positive during this time.

When developed, these antibodies hold the spirochetes in check and bring an end to the lesions.

When this occurs the individual passes out of the secondary stage of infection.

The treatment of secondary syphilis is the same as that for primary syphilis. It is also readily curable.

Latent syphilis

"Latent" by definition means *hidden.*

Accordingly, there are no observable manifestations of the latent stage.

And since surface lesions are not present, the person with latent syphilis cannot transmit the infection.

There is one danger, however: the antibodies holding the spirochetes in check may lose control and allow the individual to revert to secondary syphilis. This is most likely to occur during the first year of latent syphilis.

Diagnosis and treatment

Latent syphilis can only be diagnosed by blood tests.

It is curable at this stage by antibiotic therapy.

Late syphilis

Late syphilis is the most serious stage for the infected individual.

This stage is often referred to as "symptomatic syphilis" because of the serious symptoms that occur.

Late syphilis may cause grave damage to any organs of the body, but the most frequently involved structures are (Fig. 68):

1.   Heart and blood vessels.

2.   Brain, spinal cord, and their coverings.

3.   Eyes.

Although the signs and symptoms of late syphilis may not occur until several years after the initial infection, the damaging spirochetes circulate to these structures early in the disease. These spirochetes are not eradicated at the time that other secondary lesions disappeared.

Late syphilis is treatable in that antibiotics will kill the spirochetes that cause the symptoms, but the damage itself is not reversible.

Late syphilis cripples, blinds, and kills many people every year, thus producing the most serious consequences of the disease.

Unfortunately, the primary and secondary stages of syphilis may go undetected. Thus, the first sign may occur in late syphilis, taking the form of a very serious consequence.

The natural course of syphilis

If a large group of people with syphilis go untreated, what would happen to them, and how often would these effects occur?

The answer to this question comes from a study completed in Oslo, Norway.

Being firmly convinced that the recommended treatment for syphilis was inadequate, Professor Boeck[5] withheld treatment from 1,978 patients between 1891 and 1910.

To protect the community, these patients were hospitalized until they had passed through the secondary stage.

When they were no longer infectious, they were released.

A follow-up study of 1,404 of these patients was completed in August 1951.

The results of this study represent the best information available about the natural course of untreated syphilis.

The findings

1. If syphilis is not treated, the patient may relapse from the latent stage to the infectious secondary stage.

The study revealed that 23.6 per cent of the patients exhibited relapse.

Among those who relapsed, 85 per cent exhibited lesions in the mouth, throat, or anogenital region where the lesions could be easily eroded and thus become infectious.

2. About one-third of untreated patients with syphilis will develop late destructive lesions of syphilis.

3. Approximately 23 per cent can be expected to die as a result of syphilis.

4. Two-thirds of total untreated patients can be expected to go through life with minimal or no physical inconvenience.

Tests for syphilis

Serous material taken from a moist lesion of primary or secondary syphilis may be examined under a darkfield microscope to confirm or deny syphilis.

It is estimated, however, that 70 per cent of syphilis is diagnosed on the basis of blood tests.

Blood tests for syphilis

There are two types of blood tests for syphilis—reagin and treponemal.

Both types are based upon antibody response to infection.

When spirochetes invade the human body, two types of antibodies develop—nonspecific antibodies (reagins) and treponemal antibodies.

Reagin tests

Reagins develop in response to tissue-treponemal reactions. With proper treatment and disappearance of treponema, the reagin titer returns to a low level.

Hence, reagin tests are useful both in diagnosis and as treatment criteria.

[5] E. Gurney Clark and Niels Denbolt, "The Oslo Study of the Natural Course of Untreated Syphilis," *Med. Clin. North Am.*, 48:3, May 1964.

The most widely used reagin test is the VDRL (Venereal Disease Research Laboratory test).

The VDRL test is relatively simple and widely used for screening.

But its value is limited to screening, since reagins are non-specific and may increase in such conditions as infectious mononucleosis, heroin addiction, leprosy and malaria, to mention a few.

The VDRL test is based on the observation that animal tissue extracts (heart and liver) cause reagins to aggregate.

These extracts are easily obtained and the VDRL test can be conveniently used in any laboratory situation.

Treponemal tests

If the VDRL test is positive, a treponemal test is usually required to guard against the possibility that the increased numbers of reagins may have been due to factors unrelated to syphilis.

Currently the FTA-ABS test (Fluorescent Treponemal Antibody Absorption test) is the most widely used treponemal test.

The FTA-ABS test is more difficult and expensive to perform, and it is usually recommended to follow positive VDRL tests.

In the FTA-ABS test, treponemal antigens are added to test-blood samples. If the sample contains specific antibodies, the treponemal antigens absorb them, and the process can be observed under a microscope.

Current status of blood test for syphilis

Regarding the current status of knowledge about tests for syphilis, Dr. Sidney Olansky states:[6]

> For many years syphilologists have strived to produce a single reproducible serologic test for syphilis which would serve as a standard test and a reliable specific test to eliminate biologic false-positive reactions. We have essentially accomplished both aims in the VDRL slide test for the former and the FTA-ABS test for the latter. With these two procedures essentially all problems in serodiagnosis can be resolved.

Blood tests following treatment of syphilis

Following adequate treatment of syphilis, serological (blood) tests exhibit the following pattern:

1. If treatment was given before the chancre develops, this first lesion will probably not appear and serological tests will remain negative.

2. When treatment occurs during the primary stage but before blood tests become positive, serological tests usually remain negative, and the chancre rapidly disappears.

[6] Sidney Olansky, "Serodiagnosis of Syphilis," *Med. Clin. North Am.,* 56:1145-50, September 1972.

3. If treatment is received during the primary stage but after blood tests are positive, serological tests require about 12 months to become negative again.

4. If treatment is delayed until the secondary stage, blood tests require about 18 months to become negative again. But 90 to 95 per cent of the patients do exhibit a negative reaction for syphilis following this 18-month period.

5. Individuals infected for two years or more before treatment may remain serologically positive for the remainder of their lives. This is true even though they are cured of the disease.

Congenital syphilis

A congenital condition is one acquired during development in the uterus and not through heredity.

Congenital syphilis is transmitted to the fetus through the placenta.

This seldom occurs before the fourth month of pregnancy.

It is hypothesized that the placenta contains a barrier to the bacteria (Langhans layer of the chorion) up until the sixteenth week.

Thus, treatment of the mother prior to the fourth month of pregnancy will prevent prenatal syphilis.

After this date bacteria pass through the placenta to infect the fetus.

Approximately 25 per cent of infected fetuses die before birth. Another 25 to 30 per cent die shortly after birth.

Of untreated children who survive, 40 per cent develop symptomatic syphilis.

CHANCROID—A LOCALIZED DISEASE

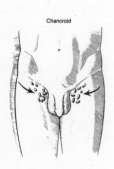

Chancroid

FIGURE 69

Chancroid is a localized venereal disease characterized by ulcerations at the site of inoculation (Fig. 69).

It does not spread to other systems of the body.

Chancroid is caused by a bacterium that is spread primarily by sexual contact.

The incubation period is three to five days.

Following the incubation period, the disease begins with a lesion that rapidly breaks down to form a tender, usually painful ulcer. These ulcers may spread and cause damage to adjacent structures.

Treatment

Effective treatment of chancroid may be accomplished with sulfonamides or tetracycline.

LYMPHOGRANULOMA VENEREUM

Lymphogranuloma venereum is a venereal disease caused by a virus.

The disease is found throughout the world but is more frequent in tropical areas. In the United States it occurs more often in the southern regions.

In the male, primary lesions appear on the genitals five to 21 days following sexual exposure. Frequently the primary lesion does not appear, and the first sign comes 10 to 30 days after exposure in the form of enlarged lymph nodes.

In the female, primary lesions are unlikely, but later there may be lesions of the urethra, labia, or vagina.

The enlarged lymph nodes commonly found in the male groin are uncommon in the female. But since lymphatic drainage from the vagina is toward the rectum, lymphogranuloma venereum is far more likely to cause serious inflammation of the rectum in the female than in the male.

The lesions of this disease are highly contagious.

Immunity does not follow an attack of the disease.

Treatment of lymphogranuloma venereum with tetracycline and streptomycin is somewhat effective.

It is not known whether these drugs attack the virus or only prevent secondary bacterial infections.

The disease is not fatal and is generally self-limiting. However, it may cause such serious complications as:

1. Loss of rectal control of defecation.

2. Loss of control of urination.

3. Damage to reproductive structures.

GRANULOMA INGUINALE—SKIN AND MUCOUS MEMBRANES

Granuloma inguinale is primarily a disease of the skin and mucous membranes. Occasionally the lymphatic system becomes involved.

It is a nonfatal disease, but the ulcerated lesions affect other parts and the disease spreads.

The disease is caused by a bacterium.

Lesions

The lesions that appear in granuloma inguinale are small, slightly raised, flat topped, and circumscribed.

The lesions become ulcerated with time and are infectious.

The lesions are usually localized to the genitals and anus.

Treatment

Granuloma inguinale can be effectively treated with tetracycline.

NONGONOCOCCAL URETHRITIS

Urethritis is an inflammation of the urethra. It may be caused by several factors, only one of which is gonorrhea.

When urethritis is not caused by gonorrhea, it is usually referred to as "nongonococcal" or "nonspecific" urethritis.

Two categories of nongonococcal urethritis are recognized:

1. Those spread in a venereal way.

2. Those spread in a nonvenereal way.

The cause or causes of nongonococcal urethritis are unclear. Some inflammations appear to be caused by viruses. Others are thought to be associated with mycoplasmas (a class of bacteria). For others there is no detectable cause.

HERPES GENITALIS

Herpes genitalis is probably the most common venereal disease after gonorrhea.

Genital herpes is an acute inflammatory dermatosis caused by a virus.

External lesions or groups of lesions measuring one or more millimeters in diameter appear in the genital area.

The infection may be accompanied by fever, headache, loss of appetite, and general malaise.

Regional swelling of lymph nodes is common, the nodes being very tender.

Compresses are mainstays in treatment. Silver nitrate, potassium permanganate, benzalkonium, and boric acid are frequent remedies. More recently the new antiviral drug, isoprinosine, shows great promise in treatment.

Pregnancy and the newborn

Infection of the newborn may be fatal. Such infections are thought to be transmitted within the birth canal. However, it is suspected that the virus can also pass through the placenta, and spontaneous abortion from the infection has been reported.

The child is thought to be safe if the disease has run its course 3 or 4 weeks before delivery.

Cervical cancer

There is substantial evidence that the herpes virus is related to cancer of the cervix. Although this is not unequivocally established, the evidence is highly suggestive.

TRICHOMONAL INFECTIONS (TRICHOMONIASIS)

The parasite Trichomonas vaginalis was described by Donné in 1836.

The parasite is a flagellate protozoon.

Trichomonas vaginalis is estimated to be present in 10 to 20 per cent of women of reproductive age and can be found in 12 to 15 per cent of those men exhibiting urethritis.

The parasite is usually transmitted sexually, producing vaginitis in the female and urethritis in the male.

The incubation period for this disease is thought to be four to 28 days.

Women

In women, the disease ranges from symptomless to very painful.

Frequently there is a greenish-yellow vaginal discharge attended by soreness and itching of the vulva and the skin on the inside of the thighs.

Dyspareunia (painful intercourse) may occur.

In some cases the woman is very miserable, and even walking is painful.

Men

Men are often symptomless carriers.

Sometimes there is a urethral discharge akin to that of gonorrhea.

Discomfort on urination is common.

Sometimes erections are painful and intercourse impossible.

Complications

Complications in women include urethritis, cystitis, bartholinitis (inflammation of Bartholin's gland), and infection of Skene's ducts.

Complications in men include prostatitis, cystitis, epididymitis, and urethral stricture.

Treatment

Treatment of trichomoniasis with oral doses of metronidazole is effective.

MONILIASIS (MONILA)

A yeast-like organism known as *Candida albicans* is part of the normal vaginal flora.

Occasionally it increases to cause a condition known as

moniliasis. Such increases are often secondary to diabetes, pregnancy, long-term antibiotic therapy and oral contraceptive use.

Candida albicans thrives on menstrual blood and often becomes troublesome just before and after menstruation.

The infection produces inflammation of the vaginal wall and causes white patches, resembling thrush, of the vagina and cervix.

The patient complains of severe itching and creamy-white discharges containing lumps.

In rare cases, the organism has entered the blood stream.

Candida albicans may be detected in a small percentage of males having nongonococcal urethritis. The extent to which fungi are causative in this condition is unclear.

Mycostatin vaginal tablets are used for treatment.

PEDICULOSIS PUBIS

Phthirus pubis is the technical name for a crab-type louse which infests the hairs of the anogenital region.

The ova of this organism attach to the skin at the base of pubic hairs.

Phthirus pubis causes an itching type of dermatosis.

Cure is usually rapid with parasiticides in the form of powder or lotion.

SECTION
3

PHILOSOPHICAL,
PSYCHOLOGICAL,
AND SOCIAL ASPECTS
OF HUMAN SEXUALITY

CHAPTER NINE

Intelligent Choice of a Sexual Life Style

Carefully consider the types of behavior listed in Table 9, and then decide which types are right or wrong according to your personal set of values.

TABLE 9. VALUES AND HUMAN SEXUALITY

Type of Behavior	Value Choice	
	Right	*Wrong*
Premarital sex	____	____
Abortion	____	____
Homosexuality	____	____
Masturbation	____	____
Oral-genital sex	____	____
Sodomy	____	____
Rape	____	____
Extramarital sex	____	____

Now consider your right-wrong responses and try to identify the criteria or criterion that you utilized in the decision making process.

A moral principle

In the experience of the authors, the most widespread contemporary principle for deciding right-wrong issues is this: an individual should be free to act, provided his actions adversely affect no one else.

This is not a new moral principle for the governance of human conduct, and those who subscribe to it find an old friend in the writings of John Stuart Mill.

Few persons have been able to describe the principle as clearly and succinctly as he did in his essay *On Liberty*.

> ... the sole end for which mankind are warranted, individually or collectively, in interfering with the liberty of action of any of their number is self-protection. That the only purpose for which power can be rightfully exercised over any member of a civilized community, against his will, is to prevent harm to others. His own good, either physical or moral, is not a sufficient warrant. He cannot rightfully be compelled to do or forbear because it will be better for him to do so, because it will make him happier, because, in the opinion of others, to do so would be wise or even right. These are good reasons for remonstrating with him, or reasoning with him, or persuading him, or entreating him, but not for compelling him or visiting him with any evil in case he do otherwise. To justify that, the conduct from which it is desired to deter him must be calculated to produce evil to someone else. The only part of the conduct of anyone for which he is amenable to society is that which concerns others. In the part which merely concerns himself, his independence is, of right, absolute. Over himself, over his own body and mind, the individual is sovereign.

Although Mill's principle is widely accepted today, it contains at least one major weakness in its application—a weakness that is nowhere as apparent as in matters of sexual behavior.

The weakness is this: the principle provides no guidelines to determine which actions adversely affect others, and, in case of disagreement, it does not specify who shall make the binding decision. The individual? Or society?

As a consequence, the 1970s are permeated by value conflicts over sexual behavior. For example, a few states have returned the right of homosexual behavior to the individual, but most states, in the words of Mill, "visit evil" on the homosexual. Likewise, the states do not agree in their laws regarding premarital sex, oral-genital sex, and sodomy. And although the United States Supreme Court has ruled that a state does not have the right to interfere with the decision of a woman and her physician to effect an abortion during the first trimester of pregnancy, most states have not changed their laws prohibiting abortion. Indeed, Congress is under great pressure at the present time to reverse this decision.

How do we determine which actions adversely affect others? In case of disagreement, who is to make the binding decision? Application of Mill's principle is no less difficult today than it was when he first asserted it in 1859.

CHOOSING A SEXUAL LIFE STYLE

A time of rapid change

Within a relatively short time span, ethical positions in the United States have changed from prescribed morality to acceptance of Mill's principle, "what you do is your own business as long as it doesn't adversely affect others."

In turn, accepted sexual life styles have been vigorously and persistently assailed.

Cultural expectations for woman have changed from "nonorgasmic responders" to "multi-orgasmic responders" and back to "nongoal-oriented sexual behavior," all within one decade.

Trends away from " premarital chastity" toward "sex with affection," "communal sex," "wife-swapping," and then back to "sex with love" have been observed.

Future trends

Currently, it appears that, with the exception of rape, most of the legal sanctions against differing modes of sexual behavior are headed for repeal.

Hence, the intelligent selection of one's own sexual life style constitutes the major contemporary concern.

Self-actualized sexual behavior

With a view toward self-actualized sexual behavior, the authors have discussed the following questions with thousands of people of all ages during the last decade:

How does one intelligently decide among such alternatives as:

- permissiveness vs. committedness

- masturbation vs. restraint in auto-eroticism

- premarital chastity vs. premarital sex

- heterosexuality vs. homosexuality

- oral sex vs. forbearance of oral sex

- marriage vs. singleness

- children vs. childlessness

- marital fidelity vs. extramarital sex ·

Discussion and research into these varieties of behavior have led us to the conclusion that no single alternative or set of alternatives holds a monopoly on happiness.

Hence, alternatives must be decided on an individual basis: there are no absolutes.

But the fact that societal prescriptions have been lifted and alternatives are now primarily a matter of choice does not mean that sexual happiness is more easily obtained.

In fact, coping with sexual freedom is a more difficult task for most people than being told what to do.

In this regard, Ayn Rand asserts:[1]

> Neither life nor happiness can be achieved by the pursuit of irrational whims. Just as a man is free to attempt to survive by any random means, as a parasite, a moocher or a looter, but not free to succeed at it beyond the range of the moment—so he is free to seek happiness in any irrational fraud, any whim, any delusion, any mindless escape from reality, but not free to succeed at it beyond the range of the moment nor to escape the consequences.

Self-actualizing people select their sexual life styles on the basis of careful thinking, not by the pursuit of irrational whims or the persuasions of others.

Rational selection of a sexual life style

Given several alternatives, intelligent decision making presupposes a basis for deciding—a criterion or set of criteria.

At present, the most popular criterion appears to be: if it makes you happy, then it's right, as long as it doesn't hurt anyone else.

In general this appears to be an excellent criterion, with one exception: it is a retrospective ethic that legitimizes any type of behavior with the excuse, "I thought it would make me happy, and I didn't have any idea it would hurt anyone."

A modified criterion

Because of this important exception, the authors recommend the following modified criterion: a selected life style component should be tested when, and only when, the probability of hurting one's self or others is small (i.e., one has the duty to be self-regarding and others-regarding).

This criterion rests on the presupposition that an individual does not have the right to be either self-destructive or others-destructive.

It also implies a moral obligation to study carefully the possibility that an action may be self-destructive or others-destructive.

Your sexual life style as a noncontradictory joy

The ultimate goal is to promote sexual behavior to the level of a noncontradictory joy.

In her book, *Atlas Shrugged,* Ayn Rand noted:

> Happiness is a state of noncontradictory joy—a joy without penalty of guilt, a joy that does not clash with any of your values and does not work for your own destruction.

Accordingly, the major question that attends the selection of a sexual life style becomes:

What are the conditions necessary to render one's sexual life style a noncontradictory joy?

In the opinion of the authors, the most enlightened answer to this question appears to be:

---

[1] Ayn Rand, *The Virtues of Selfishness,* New American Library, New York, 1961.

One's heterosexual or homosexual life style has the highest probability of contributing to a state of noncontradictory joy when it occurs within the framework of an interpersonal relationship that is permeated by love, attended by open communication, and guided by a knowledge of human sexuality.

Previous chapters have discussed love (Chapter one) and the biological knowledge that attends sexuality (Chapters two through eight), but before proceeding, let's discuss open communication.

Open communication

There appears to be a categorical imperative in the realm of human sexual behavior: thou shalt not discuss your likes and dislikes with others. This attitude appears to be widespread among people of all socioeconomic backgrounds, educational levels, and religious affiliations, and exists throughout the entire liberal-conservative continuum. And it is this same attitude that is at the root of many cases of sexual inadequacy.

The type of thinking that blocks open communication about sexuality is of at least two kinds:

1. Sexual behavior is intended primarily for procreation and only secondarily for pleasure. Open discussion of the pleasure aspects perverts one's total approach to sexuality.

2. Sexual behavior should be a natural joy. If it is not, there is something wrong—with one's biological or psychological self or perhaps one's partner. In either case it is too sensitive to discuss because it reflects inherent weaknesses or insincere interpersonal relationships.

But love demands that these sensitive communication blocks be removed. Love demands open discussion regarding penalties of guilt, clashes of values, and general likes and dislikes. Love demands that each partner work to promote sexual behavior to the level of a noncontradictory joy.

Permissiveness and committedness

The remainder of this chapter is a discussion of permissiveness versus committedness in heterosexual relationships.

The discussion includes marriage, nonmarriage contracts, opportunity and insincerity, trial marriage, and the playboy philosophy.

Other alternatives in sexual life style (e.g., homosexuality, masturbation, number of children) will be discussed in subsequent chapters.

In attempting to render participation in the sex act a noncontradictory joy, how does one decide between the alternatives of permissiveness and committedness?

Which has the higher probability of producing noncontradictory joy?

By now you are acquainted with the opinion of the authors: one's heterosexual or homosexual life style has the highest probability of contributing to a state of noncontradictory joy when it occurs within the framework of an interpersonal relationship permeated by love.

Note the probability sense of this opinion.

It does not contend that permissiveness is wrong or that it ought to be punished; it contends that committedness has a greater capacity for achieving a state of noncontradictory joy than does permissiveness.

Marriage as the commitment

Whereas there is general agreement on the need for committedness, the more troubling question appears to be:

How much commitment should attend the different types of sexual behavior.

For example, contemporary youth have vigorously and persistently claimed that a marriage certificate does not render sexuality a noncontradictory joy. And many would go a step further and suggest that marriage doesn't even increase the probability of promoting sex to the level of a noncontradictory joy.

A high divorce rate, widespread sexual inadequacy among the married, extramarital sex, and poor mental health among many married women add validity to this claim.

But clearly some degree of commitment should be reached before participating in the sex act. If not marriage, then what?

Nonmarriage agreements

In some countries, it is possible to negotiate a two or three day contract in which the two parties agree upon how to deal with any troublesome consequences of their sexual behavior.

Whatever else the contracts might represent, they at least include an element of responsible behavior. Such contracts clearly attempt to render sex more of a noncontradictory joy. But in the opinion of the authors, these contracts omit some important factors.

For this reason, the authors suggest that agreement to the following criteria should be obtained prior to participation in heterosexual intercourse. These criteria are designed to assist in promoting heterosexuality to the level of a noncontradictory joy.

Criterion 1

Both partners in sexual intercourse must be certain that they are not infected with one of the venereal diseases. The best way to achieve this certainty is through regular medical examinations, including blood tests.

In view of the fact that venereal diseases are widespread but easily curable, it is in the best interest of both parties involved and any offspring that might result to have precautionary tests for venereal diseases.

Anyone refusing to have such a test exhibits little concern for others.

The degree of risk that one is willing to take with a second person is directly proportional to his concern about that person.

Open agreement to tests for venereal diseases also represents a test of the maturity of the interpersonal relationship that exists between the two persons involved.

Criterion 2

Prior to participation in sexual intercourse, both partners must recognize their responsibility to love and care for any offspring that may result, or carefully evaluate the effect of an abortion.

An unloved, unwanted child begins life without the human dignity that should be everyone's birthright.

He is, in a sense, degraded from birth.

To disregard this responsibility violates an elementary principle of human conduct: One must accept the consequences of one's actions as they affect both one's self and others.

Consider the three statements that follow. Which represents the most desirable interpersonal relationship?

1. The pill is 100 per cent effective so we are not concerned about pregnancy.

2. The pill involves a slight chance of pregnancy if not properly taken so we agree to love any offspring that occurs, or to be supportive of each other before and after abortion.

3. We are not ready or desirous of having children, but if pregnancy occurs we are prepared mentally and financially to love and take care of any offspring or to undergo abortion.

You should know that unwanted pregnancies are not infrequent even among persons well-informed about contraception. And one large Midwestern university health service estimates 40 unwanted pregnancies per week among unmarried college girls.

Agreement to this criterion is not at all unreasonable.

As with the first criterion, open agreement to love any offspring or to be supportive before and after abortion, is a test of the maturity of the interpersonal relationship that exists between the two persons involved.

Criterion 3

Prior to participation in sexual intercourse the two people involved should have some notion of direction and goals in life and be able to answer the question: How does participation in sexual intercourse fit into the goals that I have set for myself and the goals of my partner?

Put another way, sexual intercourse is an activity for mature persons—for persons who are mature emotionally and psychologically, as well as physically.

A sexual relationship may be novel but it is not the way to find one's self.

The results of a study of unwed mothers by the Community Council of Greater New York will help to explain:

The majority of unwed mothers in this study:

1. Did not belong to clubs or other groups.
2. Did not enjoy visiting with other people.
3. Did not like sports and games.
4. Were attempting to find themselves through intimate sexual experience.

Criterion 4

One person must not exploit another. To counter exploitation it must be agreed that sexual intercourse is for the mutual improvement of both people involved.

Here are some motivations for sexual intercourse that tend to exploit the other person:

1. For self-gratification.
2. A way of gaining independence from parents.
3. A way of getting back at someone.
4. A way of trapping a husband.
5. A way of holding on to a boy or girl friend.
6. A way to become "popular."
7. A way to demonstrate manhood.
8. A way of relieving personal anxiety.

Criterion 5

Prior to participation in sexual intercourse, both partners should agree upon the desirability or undesirability of having children. If children are not wanted, a mutually acceptable and effective form of contraception should be planned.

Reasonable criteria

In the experience of the authors, most young people agree that these are reasonable criteria. Many, however, do not feel that their private agreement to these criteria necessitates marriage.

But the notion that today's young person is less moral than those of previous generations is a myth.

For example, they are far less likely to visit a prostitute than the youth of previous generations.

And they do not tolerate exploitation when they are able to discern it.

In a survey of over 500 students per year for each of the last five years, the authors have found that contemporary youth consistently locate themselves between steps six and seven on the Puritan-Permissiveness Continuum listed in Table 10.

It is interesting to note that most college women start at steps six or seven or somewhere in between.

TABLE 10. PURITAN—PERMISSIVENESS CONTINUUM

1. Premarital conversation with other "nice people."

2. Premarital nonsexual contact with special persons.

3. Premarital sexual contact above the waist with a person you love.

4. Premarital sexual contact below the waist with a person you love.

5. Sexual intercourse with a person to whom you are married.

6. Nonmarital intercourse with a person you love.

7. Nonmarital intercourse with a person for whom you have deep affection.

8. Nonmarital intercourse with a person who "turns you on."

9. Nonmarital intercourse for profit.

If or when they move up or down, it is usually a consequence of "how they were treated in the interpersonal relationship."

Students locating themselves between steps six and seven were asked: What would it take to move you up or down on the scale?

The most consistent answer for females was: for moving up or down on the scale—insincerity on the part of the male.

As a consequence of being hurt, college girls tended to become either more puritanical or more permissive.

The most consistent answers for males were: for moving down on the scale—opportunity; for moving up on the scale—falling in love with a girl that I really care for.

These findings suggest that the major problem in promoting heterosexual behavior to the level of a noncontradictory joy is not what ethic one subscribes to but what factors cause one to deviate from that ethical position.

Opportunity and insincerity

Opportunity and insincerity have constituted and probably always will constitute major problems in the sexual encounter.

In highly emotional situations humans often agree to things that they ordinarily would not agree upon; i.e., they compromise themselves.

It must be remembered that we humans have a highly developed capacity for sincere self-deception.

Further, the history of sexual relationships abounds with cases in which human beings have insincerely agreed to any or all proposals in order to gain the opportunity they wanted.

Regarding insincerity, Dr. Mervyn S. Sanders, associate clinical professor of obstetrics and gynecology at the University of Utah College of Medicine, has made an interesting observation regarding contemporary advocates of premarital sex.

> The verbal revolution about sexual freedom has some aspects of a national fraud.
>
> In an attempt to throw off all that resembles restraint, control, or delay of gratification, or to reject morality founded in any culture as primitive as the last generation, young people are spreading the 'new gospel of modern sexual freedom' as a startling new philosophical discovery.
>
> Most of the social and psychological ills of the race and of individuals supposedly will be corrected if people can jump into bed together without waiting for marriage.
>
> This advocation of license has been with mankind since the beginning of history.
>
> The only new facet is the endless public dialogue about what used to be attempts at private and largely individual persuasion.

Unfortunately, there is no satisfactory way to be sure that individuals will follow through on what they say they will do—i.e., that they are sincere in their statements. Marriage offers some advantages but no guarantee.

Marriage

Whereas the first edition of *Education for Sexuality* emphasized the disadvantages of premarital sex, the present discussion will focus more on the power of marriage to elevate human sexuality to the level of a noncontradictory joy.

Contrary to the opinions of some, the institution of marriage is not in jeopardy in the United States. More people than ever are getting married, and those who have been divorced exhibit little reluctance to remarry. Further, many of those who have experimented with heterosexual alternatives to marriage have returned to the list of the married.

Marriage appears to offer the following advantages for those interested in sexuality as a joy without penalty of guilt.

1. Public agreement to meet the five criteria previously described constitutes marriage and prevents a considerable amount of misunderstanding or insincerity. However, marriage often is reduced to legal exploitation. But the probability of exploitation in marriage is far less than for any other type of heterosexual relationship.

Nena and George O'Neill make an interesting observation on this point in their book *Open Marriage:*

> Theoretically, marriage should not be necessary to have a full one-to-one relationship. You should not even need marriage to legitimize a child, for that matter. In a world of true human understanding, a child should be legitimate just because he is born. All the requirements for succoring the young—maternal care, assuring interdependency and cooperation with others, as well as psychological intimacy—can

theoretically be met without legal marriage. The love and companionship existing between a couple does not need a piece of paper, a marriage document, to make it work, to assure its existence or its perpetuation. Or does it?

Commitment to another cannot be legislated. True commitment comes from within, not from outside a relationship. The signing of a contract cannot guarantee you another's commitment in the emotional sense; why should the absence of such a contract mean a lack of commitment? It shouldn't, of course. But unfortunately, it often does, often enough to make even those who are sure of their partner's commitment think twice. We would not need the marriage contract in actuality if all of us had reached a stage of human development that assured mutual responsibility and trust between all people. Unfortunately, this utopian brotherhood is far short of achievement. In our all too real world, the ultimate step in the establishment of trust between man and woman is still the marriage contract. *With this final step each says to the other: here's my deck of cards, the full deck, all of them open on the table, nothing held back.*

2. Marriage offers a major psychological advantage for both parties. It helps to prevent the feeling: "I am just on trial." It also provides the self-confidence that attends the feeling "I am accepted and loved as a total person—not just as a sexual partner."

3. Marriage offers the security needed to openly communicate one's problems, hang-ups, likes, and dislikes. This includes sexual inadequacies—especially male inadequacy.

In recent years, increasing aggressiveness on the part of the female appears to have created some problems for males—many of whom are in desperate need of understanding.

A college class taught by one of the authors has suggested an experiment designed to destroy any male self-image: Three girls report to the same male that he is a very nice person, that they enjoy being with him, but that his sexual performance is totally inadequate.

4. Marriage affords a stable framework within which one can more easily cope with value clashes related to contraception, pregnancy, and abortion.

The trial marriage

The main argument for a trial marriage goes like this:

To get to know someone, you must live with him. You have to see how the other person reacts to the minor upsets and major crises of daily living.

This argument implies that if you don't like the trial marriage partner when you "really" get to know him, you can at that point terminate the relationship and avoid further unhappiness.

And at first glance, trial marriages appear to include an element of value.

But when we dissect away the "outer coat," one frequently exposes other motivations for the trial marriage, especially as they are propounded in the United States.

For example, omit sex from the trial marriage situation and very few Americans retain their initial interest in the idea.

It is undoubtedly true that there are nonsexual aspects of human relationships that might be tested by living together that cannot be tested during courtship.

These nonsexual aspects, however, are usually not the object of concern in a trial marriage.

For most, being able to spend all of the waking hours together if they desire is a satisfactory condition under which a couple can "run checks" on nonsexual aspects of compatibility.

The major motivation for trial marriages stems from the popular misconception that most divorces result from sexual incompatibility rather than from poor interpersonal relationships in general.

Although the converse of this is true, most American trial marriages are prompted by the desire for a sexual tryout under conditions that are "more relaxed or more respectable than just premarital sex."

So let's be honest and discuss the value of a sexual tryout from the standpoint of human sexual response.

From a biological standpoint the female vagina is adjustable to any size penis.

From the male side, the size of the penis has little effect upon female satisfaction.

Thus one doesn't have to be concerned about "anatomical misfits."

A human being is not something that you have to try on for size like you do a hat or a pair of shoes.

Also, it is impossible to predict from initial experiences whether future experiences will be better, worse, or the same.

The two best indicators of sexual adequacy in the future are:

1. Attitude toward sexuality.

2. Feelings toward the partner.

And the one best predictor is one's feelings toward the partner.

It is true that sexual response is very much determined by one's attitude toward sexuality.

It is also obvious that attitudes toward sex can be poor even when two people love each other very much.

Such attitudes may reflect early training and value development and have little to do with feelings for the husband, wife, or partner.

But even the most irrational attitudes are learned, and thus with patience, understanding, and love there is a good chance that they can be unlearned.

The best criteria by which one can predict future sexual satisfaction are the same criteria that forecast good interpersonal relationships.

The Playboy philosophy

Although the Playboy philosophy is generally recognized for the exploitative philosophy that it really turns out to be, it does deserve discussion.

Harvey Cox, in his book *The Secular City*, makes these thought-provoking statements about the Playboy philosophy and *Playboy* magazine.

1. Playboy and its less successful imitators are not "sex magazines" at all. They are basically antisexual.

They dilute and dissipate authentic sexuality by reducing it to an accessory, by keeping it at a safe distance.

2. . . . Sex becomes one of the items of leisure activity that the knowledgeable consumer of leisure handles with his characteristic skill and detachment. . . .

The girl becomes a desirable—indeed an indispensable—"Playboy accessory."

3. . . . The infallible answer from the oracle never varies: sex must be contained, at all cost, within the entertainment-recreation area.

Don't let her get "serious."

4. . . . For the insecure young man with newly acquired free time and money who still feels uncertain about his consumer skills, Playboy supplies a comprehensive and authoritative guidebook to the forbidding new world to which he now has access. . . .

It tells him not only who to be; it tells him how to be it, and even provides consolation outlets for those who secretly feel they have not quite made it.

5. . . . Playboy really feeds on the existence of a repressed fear of involvement with women, which for various reasons is still present in many otherwise adult Americans.

So Playboy's version of sexuality grows increasingly irrelevant as authentic sexual maturity is achieved.

Despite its exploitative philosophy, *Playboy* has contributed toward bringing sex out into the open in the United States.

Dr. William Masters, coauthor of *Human Sexual Response,* says this of his interview with *Playboy:*

> We hope that something like this interview—appearing in the magazine I regard as the best available medium of sex education in America today—will help do it [it referring to the need for healthy objectivity about sexuality].

But Virginia Johnson, the other coauthor of *Human Sexual Response,* says in the same interview:

> What I'm about to say may not go over well with some Playboy readers, but the fact is that for the first time in many decades, the girl is running the sexual show.
>
> She is not a victim; she doesn't have to put up or shut up.
>
> Although this issue is still in limbo, we're on the right road toward placing value on sexual activity within a human relationship as opposed to simple emphasis on natural drives. . . .

Approaches to the permissiveness-committedness continuum

Although teachers and parents have taken countless approaches to the permissiveness-committedness continuum, most can be assigned to one of these four categories:

1. The "mute" approach in which no attempt is made to address the problem.

2. The "comfortable pew" approach in which adult society refuses to buck what it views as a widespread trend toward sexual freedom, choosing instead to limit its advice to methods of preventing pregnancy and venereal diseases.

3. The "indoctrination" approach in which the "goodness" of some specific code of behavior is expounded and reinforced.

4. The "interpersonal relationship" approach suggested by Kirkendall[2] and other contemporary writers, which recommends a sexual ethic based on satisfying interpersonal relationships.

Each of these approaches deserves comment prior to a summary of a fifth approach offered by the authors.

THE MUTE APPROACH

Finding themselves unable to select and adhere to a code of sexual behavior, many parents and teachers elect not to discuss the question at all with younger persons. If this approach were made explicit, it could be stated this way: "We as adults refuse to give you the results of our experiences with sexual behavior or our interpretations of the accumulated experiences of the generations before us. You must decide your code of sexual behavior on the basis of trial and error or any bits of information that you can find." Stated this way, most will agree, this is not a reasonable or effective approach.

---

[2] Lester Kirkendall, *Premarital Intercourse and Interpersonal Relationships,* Julian Press, New York, 1961.

THE COMFORTABLE PEW APPROACH

Pierre Berton in his critical analysis of the Anglican Church of Canada contends that the church in its attempts to remain popular has refused to speak out on issues of great importance and in so doing has turned its back on its first principles. He says it this way in his book, *The Comfortable Pew:*

> In the great issues of our time, the voice of the Church, when it has been heard at all, has been weak, tardy, equivocal, and irrelevant. In those basic conflicts that ought to be tormenting every Christian conscience—questions of war and peace, of racial brotherhood, of justice versus revenge, to name three—the Church has trailed far behind the atheists, the agnostics, the free thinkers, the journalists, the scientists, the social workers, and even, on occasion, the politicians. It has, for instance, virtually ignored the whole contemporary question of business morals, the tensions within industry and labour, the sexual revolution that has changed the attitudes of the Western world.

The comfortable pew approach as applied to sex education is one in which popular trends go unopposed. The attitude is one of: "Well, I guess it is all right if that's what everyone wants."

THE INDOCTRINATION APPROACH

If adult society could agree on a specific code of sexual conduct, and if young people were bits of clay that could be shaped, reinforced, and maintained in whatever way society had decided, then sexual ethics would be a matter of little concern. But even a superficial examination of adult sexual codes, in theory or practice, yields little agreement as to a single code of conduct. Attempts to shape or indoctrinate others to fit an arbitrary mold not only are doomed to failure in an enlightened society but are themselves immoral. Abraham H. Maslow,[3] writing on the topic, states:

> I believe this is the model of education which we all have tucked away in the back of our heads and which we don't often make explicit. In this model the teacher is the active one who teaches a passive person who gets shaped and taught and who is given something which he then accumulates and which he may then lose or retain, depending upon the efficiency of the initial indoctrination process and of his own accumulation-of-fact process. I would maintain that a good 90% of "learning theory" deals with learnings that have nothing to do with the intrinsic self that I've been talking about, nothing to do with its specieshood and biological idiosyncrasy. This kind of learning too easily reflects the goals of the teacher and ignores the values and ends of the learner himself. It is also fair, therefore, to call such learning amoral.

THE INTERPERSONAL RELATIONSHIP APPROACH

Lester Kirkendall and Roger Libby[4] state: "A sexual relationship is an interpersonal relationship, and as such is subject to the same principles of interaction

---

[3] Abraham H. Maslow, "Some Educational Implications of the Humanistic Psychologies," *Harvard Educational Review,* Fall 1968.
[4] Lester A. Kirkendall and Roger W. Libby, "Interpersonal Relationships—Crux of the Sexual Renaissance," *The Journal of Social Issues,* April 1966.

as are other relationships." This concept is so basic that its full meaning is frequently missed. Clearly translated, it means that sexual behavior must be evaluated in terms of its effects upon human relationships. Thus one can ask about a certain type of sexual behavior—does it improve or degrade the relationship (i.e., does it help or hurt yourself and the other person)? When viewed in this context, there is a criterion whereby sexual behavior can be evaluated. One can say more than "Oh, that's definitely wrong" or "That kind of behavior is all right." Rather, one can state, "That type of behavior degrades or improves human relationships." This latter approach facilitates communication since it replaces such essentially meaningless terms as "right" and "wrong" with more exacting terms that explain why certain behavior is considered right or wrong.

As an example, nearly everyone would agree that rape represents a kind of sexual behavior that makes it difficult for people to get along well together—it renders interpersonal relationships unpleasant, undignified, stressful, unhealthy, and unsafe. On the other hand, most people would agree that the ideal kind of interpersonal relationships are those that are mutually advantageous. Such relationships produce a climate in which each person can flourish, a climate that is far superior to what either can achieve alone.

A fifth approach	The present chapter has suggested a fifth approach to the problem of locating one's sexual life style on the permissiveness-committedness continuum. This approach started with Mill's moral principle that an individual should be free to act, provided his actions adversely affect no one else. The authors then suggested a modification of this principle: a selected life style component should be tested when and only when the probability of hurting one's self or others is very small. This modification was recommended on the basis of presuppositions held by the authors that an individual does not have the right to be either self-destructive or others-destructive and that before acting an individual has the moral obligation to study carefully the probability of both self-destructive actions and others-destructive action: i.e., one has the duty to be self-regarding and others-regarding. Finally, based upon study of the sexual encounter among heterosexuals, the authors recommended five criteria designed to promote sexual behavior to the level of a noncontradictory joy (i.e., joy that is neither self-destructive nor others-destructive).

CHAPTER TEN

Masturbation

In view of the extremely widespread occurrence of autogenital stimulation throughout the class Mammalia it seems illogical to classify human masturbation as abnormal or perverted.

This form of sexual expression appears to have its evolutionary roots in the perfectly normal and adaptive biological tendency to examine, to manipulate, to clean, and incidentally to stimulate the external sexual organs.

The human capacity for symbolic behavior has permitted marked increase in the sexual significance of masturbation by linking it with fantasy and imagination.

But the basic potentialities are a part of the biological inheritance of the species.

We believe that the relative infequency of self stimulation among mature people in most societies is a consequence of social conditioning.

Clellan S. Ford and Frank A. Beach, *Patterns of Sexual Behavior.*

What is masturbation?

For purposes of this chapter, masturbation will be defined as the deliberate manipulation of some part of the reproductive system in anticipation of an erotic reward.

Methods of masturbation

Different individuals masturbate in a variety of ways, and one individual may utilize several methods.

Some of the more common methods will be described.

Female masturbation

Probably the most frequent method of female masturbation is manipulation of the clitoral area.

Masters and Johnson report that very few women masturbate by applying direct pressure to the sensitive glans of the clitoris.

Rather, they manipulate the shaft of the clitoris or the mons area surrounding it.

Manipulation of the mons area appears to be just as effective after the clitoris is removed (clitoridectomy).

Another method of female masturbation involves thigh rubbing. Squeezing the thighs applies pressure to the labia and indirectly to the clitoris.

Other methods include:

1. Fingering or inserting something in the vagina.
2. Inserting something in the urethra.
3. Pulling clothing between the legs.
4. Stimulating the breasts.
5. Fingering the rectum.

Male methods

The male usually masturbates by manipulation of the penis with the hand.

Other methods involve coital movements against a variety of objects.

Fingering of the rectum is a seldom used method.

Dual masturbation

Dual masturbation is masturbation in the presence of another person who is also masturbating.

This type is most frequently observed among young boys.

Mutual masturbation

Mutual masturbation refers to two individuals who practice manual masturbation on each other.

Incidence of masturbation

Studies of the incidence of masturbation are not in complete agreement, but the following conclusions seem justified:

1. Almost all males masturbate at some time in their life.
2. The percentage of women who have masturbated ranges between 40 and 70.

Excessive masturbation

Whereas frequent masturbation may modify one's self-concept, it appears to have no long term biological effect. For example, Dr. Jan Raboch of the Sexological Institute of Charles University in Prague writes:[1]

> One of the most interesting patients that I have ever had was a 27-year-old Jew who came to our clinic shortly after World War II. He had spent a number of years in Nazi concentration camps. He stated that, in 1943 and 1944, the Nazis had grouped in a camp in Poland about twenty young and healthy men and fed them comparatively well.
>
> During twenty-one months they were forced, under inspection, to masturbate regularly every three hours, night and day. . . .

---

[1] Jan Raboch, "Men's Most Common Sex Problems," *Sexology*, November 1969, pp. 60-63.

Despite this ordeal, Dr. Raboch reported:

> We were unable, however, in spite of a most careful examination, to
> discover in him signs of any disturbance of the function of his genital
> organs. His fertility was found normal. When he married later, his
> potency was good.

**Philosophical
positions**

The Sex Information and Education Council of the United
States has defined four philosophical positions on masturbation:

A. The traditional view, which regards masturbation as always
   gravely sinful and as harmful to health—with some modification of its severity and rigidity in light of new scientific
   knowledge;

B. The view of many religionists, which sees masturbation often as
   an imperfect egocentric eroticism that deflects the individual
   from the Christian concept of sexuality as being ideally an essential relation with another;

C. An attitude of neutrality, which accepts masturbation, recognizes
   that further study of its various patterns is required, but is not
   prepared to encourage it as something positively good;

D. And a more radical position, which views masturbation as not
   only harmless, but positively good and healthy, and therefore
   encourages it among young people as an aid to more mature
   psychosexual growth.

**Developing your own
philosophical position**

In many respects, development of a personal philosophy toward
masturbation seems unimportant.

Since it is a harmless act, what difference does it make?

One student has likened it to "picking your nose"—as long as you
do it in private it really doesn't make any difference.

But many people experience considerable guilt about masturbation, and philosophical clarification is important.

A careful study of the four positions described above may assist
you with personal value clarification.

In addition to the conduct of your own sexual life style, it is
especially important that you consider how you might deal
with the masturbatory habits and attitudes of your children.

**Masturbation among
children**

In preparation for the guidance of children, it might be useful to
study the opinions of several medical experts.

After reviewing their work, try to formulate your own philosophy
toward masturbation.

Dr. Harrison S. Evans, a California psychiatrist, states[2]:

---

[2] Harrison S. Evans, "What Do You Tell Parents Who Are Concerned About
Their Children's Masturbation?" *Medical Aspects of Human Sexuality*,
1:3, November 1967.

A normal phenomenon

Masturbation in children is accepted by medical and psychiatric authorities as an essentially normal phenomenon, and it constitutes a phase in most children's development when they are exploring and becoming acquainted with their body.

Not a source of damage

Masturbation is not believed to be a source of damage to the child, either physically or mentally. It does not have a weakening effect on the body or mind. It does not draw out any of the child's vital energy, as old wives' tales would tend to suggest.

What it means to the child

There are two basic things for you to understand as you come to deal with your child's masturbatory activity.

Is he socially healthy?

First, as a parent, you should try to clarify what this activity means to the child. If the child is socially healthy, interested in his playmates and in his surroundings, and engages in masturbation as part of his curiosity and passing pleasure, then masturbation will probably subside as further maturation and social development take place

You can be quite sure that other things will come to absorb the child's attention and provide pleasurable outlets, and as a consequence there will be fewer occasions when the child will need to turn to autoeroticism (masturbation for pleasure and satisfaction).

A beneficial effect

Masturbation as a phase of experience can actually have a beneficial effect on the child's emotional development because it helps to establish the genitals securely within the body scheme so that at a later appropriate time they can become readily activated and used in a normal heterosexual manner as a part of a normal marriage.

Not always healthy

However, not all masturbatory activity is normal and healthy. If your child is shy, sensitive, and withdrawn, and if it appears that he has become too dependent on masturbation as a source of satisfaction and relief of tension, then in this instance masturbation might be considered a pathological reaction.

Not a normal phase of development

In a situation such as this masturbation is probably not a phase in normal development, but rather a symptom of psychological disturbances that need attention by a specialist, usually a child psychiatrist.

Your own feelings

The second thing of importance for you to understand is that as a parent you should clarify your own feelings about masturbation and your child's interest in sex and in his genitals.

In many instances it is the parents' feelings that constitute the real problem rather than the child's transitory sexual curiosity and exploration.

Dirty and wicked

Some parents, for various reasons, may see masturbation as something that is shameful, dirty, wicked, and an early sign of depravity rather than what it actually is, namely, a developmental phase.

If parents have these feelings, then they may very well overreact to the child's essentially normal behavior.

The parent may inappropriately threaten or punish the child, thus arousing guilts and repressions which later on in life may impair the child's adjustment.

How to react

It is my opinion that for you as a parent the appropriate reaction is to accept this behavior as essentially normal, handle it casually, guide and lead the child to interests outside of himself, provide a happy relationship of affection and security, and give answers that are simple and to the point when sexual questions arise in connection with masturbation and the dawning awareness of sexuality in general.

If there is evidence that masturbation is excessive or compulsive, and if the child has a poor social and psychological adjustment, do not threaten or punish but seek out help to understand the child's basic problem and work toward correcting this rather than focusing primarily on the masturbation itself, which in this instance is a symptom of underlying personality difficulty whose solution will also solve the masturbation problem.

Dr. Saul Harrison, professor of psychiatry at the University of Michigan, writes:[3]

Some children invest most of their attention and energy in compulsive masturbation. This may cause justifiable parental concern, not because of the myth about masturbation sapping one's reserve of energy, but because compulsive masturbation is a symptom of an emotional problem which also renders the child afraid or unable to engage in other age-appropriate activities. Such excessive masturbation serves as a means of consolation or as a substitute for relationships with other people.

Dr. Herbert A. Holden, president of the California Academy of General Practice, states:[4]

Masturbation occurs most frequently when the child is unhappy and bored. In older children, similar organization of the life pattern to fill the day with activity and interest is important.

Dr. Harry Bakwin, professor of clinical pediatrics at New York University School of Medicine, suggests:[5]

. . . A child who is unhappy or bored is more likely to resort to masturbation than one whose life is satisfying. However, the parents should not be made to feel that they are responsible for the child's practice. The intensity of the erotic urge varies widely, and masturbation is often practiced to excess even under the best of home surroundings.

Discussion with the adolescent consists first of all of a clarification of the nature of the habit. False ideas about the dire effects of masturbation are corrected. The universality of the practice is pointed out. In this way feelings of guilt, unworthiness, isolation, and shame are relieved.

[3] Saul Harrison, "Viewpoints," *Medical Aspects of Human Sexuality*, 1:21, 1967.
[4] Herbert A. Holden, "Viewpoints," *Medical Aspects of Human Sexuality*, 1:13, 1967.
[5] Harry Bakwin, "Viewpoints," *Medical Aspects of Human Sexuality*, 1:16-17, 1967.

This is not to say that the habit is to be condoned, much less encouraged. Its uselessness and misdirection of energy are pointed out. . . .

The home and school situation is reviewed and sources of unhappiness probed. It is helpful to be aware of the common reasons for concern in the adolescent—unpopularity, failure to live up to scholastic aspirations, failure in athletics, concern about the home situation, physical illness, short stature in the boy, tallness in the girl, and so on.

In addition to the foregoing discussion, the opinions of several medical experts regarding the general topic of masturbation are presented.

Dr. Lawrence Kolb[6] comments about parental attitude:

Masturbation, commonly practiced by children, requires treatment only if the parental or adult attitudes toward the act have instilled in the child anxieties and fears that affect his personality development adversely. More frequently the problems of masturbation in a child involve clarifying misconceptions of ill-effects of the procedure in the minds of the parents and preventing radical efforts to prevent the act.

The other varieties of body manipulation . . . are relatively of little importance.

Nelson's *Textbook of Pediatrics*[7] describes methods of masturbation, notes that although it is a normal activity it is inadvisable to encourage masturbation, and suggests that the most helpful treatment is to remedy the environmental situation:

Masturbation may be performed by manipulation of the genitals, by movement of the thighs or contraction of the perineal musculature, by copulatory movements sometimes with an object such as a pillow between the legs; or an equivalent sensation may be derived from tight clothing or activities such as horseback riding, straddling rails and climbing trees. In the younger child who is not aware of the cultural taboo against masturbation, the parents may observe the activity or the associated signs of intense concentration and excitement. Most children sense parental disapproval, however, and the activity is carried out in privacy. Rarely, the child may masturbate openly, an act which suggests poor awareness of social reality by the child or lack of censorship by the parents. Some well-meaning parents who know that masturbation is a normal activity may inadvisedly encourage it.

Within certain limits masturbation is normal. In the young child it represents a self-gratification analogous to thumb-sucking. In the older child, particularly the adolescent, it serves the purpose of exploring and experimenting with newly developing sexual capacities and feelings and may aid in gaining control over the sexual urges and becoming less afraid of them.

---

[6] Lawrence C. Kolb, *Noyes' Clinical Psychiatry*, W. B. Saunders Company, Philadelphia, 1968, Ed. 7.
[7] Calvin F. Settlage. In *Textbook of Pediatrics*, edited by Waldo E. Nelson, W. B. Saunders Company, Philadelphia, 1969, Ed. 8.

Masturbation occurs most commonly at bedtime when anxiety is increased owing to separation or fear of loss of control over sexual and aggressive impulses. For the same reasons the child is most likely to masturbate when he is alone and lonely. This fact leads to the logical, but usually mistaken, assumption that the urge to masturbate is the motive for rather than the consequence of being alone. Masturbation may also be performed, sometimes repetitiously and compulsively, as a reassurance against fear of injury to the private parts. Excessive masturbation suggests some problem or deficiency in object relationships. In some instances it is a symptom of a neurotic or more severe disorder.

It is appropriate for the parent to censor open masturbation and to be concerned about excessive masturbation, but to forbid it absolutely, to shame the child, to threaten punishment or to suggest injury to the genitals not only is ineffective, but also tends to create guilt and additional anxiety which may even increase the activity. The most helpful treatment is to remedy any environmental situation which is interfering with gratification of the child's needs or is causing tension and anxiety. It is important that the child be reassured that masturbation does not cause physical or mental deterioration. The adolescent should be given an explanation of ejaculation, orgasm and menstruation, so that he or she can understand them as normal body functions.

Ian Gregory[8] traces the evolution of attitudes toward masturbation:

Masturbation is sexual pleasure obtained by manipulation of the genitals or other erogenous parts of the body. Individual masturbation is widely practiced by the higher animals and by all races of mankind, particularly by immature males who have not yet established an adult heterosexual relationship, and by adults of both sexes who have been deprived of a normal heterosexual outlet. The use of artificial genitalia resembling those of the opposite sex has been reported in literature since the time of Aristophanes . . . and mutual masturbation may be practiced by males or females with members of the same or opposite sex. During the middle ages, the Church condemned all forms of sexual indulgence other than genital intercourse between husband and wife with the express purpose of having children. Masturbation became regarded as evil and perverse, and was frequently referred to as 'self-abuse.' Even in the present century it was thought by many physicians and other educated people to lead to insanity or other tragic consequences, and masturbation in girls sometimes led to surgical removal of the clitoris. More recently it has become regarded as a normal part of sexual activity and the accumulative experience reported in the Kinsey studies amounted to 93 per cent in males (decreasing from adolescence onwards) and 62 per cent in females (increasing to middle age). It is therefore regarded as abnormal only if practiced in public, or at the exclusion by choice of heterosexual genital union, as frequently occurs following certain of the deviant acts. . . .

---

[8] Ian Gregory, *Fundamentals of Psychiatry*, W. B. Saunders Company, Philadelphia, 1968, Ed. 2.

CHAPTER ELEVEN

Homosexuality

On December 15, 1973, I was instantly cured of mental illness together with millions of my gay brothers and sisters.

Gay statement to the press occasioned by the American Psychiatric Association's decision to remove homosexuality from its list of mental disorders.

Homosexual behavior refers to sexual relations, either overt or psychic, between individuals of the same sex. The word homosexual is derived from the Greek root *homo,* which means sameness. Homosexual behavior among females is often termed "lesbianism" after the female homosexual relations that were immortalized in the poetry of Sapho of the Greek isle of Lesbos. Depite use of this special term for the female homosexual it should be noted that such behavior is equivalent to sexual relations between males. Other synonyms for homosexuality include homogenic love, contrasexuality, homoeroticism, similisexualism, uranism, and sapphism (lesbianism).

History tells us that homosexual behavior is not of recent origin. For example, Dr. Frank S. Caprio[1] in his book *Variations in Sexual Behavior,* states:

Sodomy (usually refers to anal intercourse) is derived from the name of the town, Sodom, where the inhabitants, during Biblical times, incurred the wrath of God by wishing to consort sexually with the angels who had descended from Heaven. The town was therefore destroyed.

Pederasty (anal intercourse often with young boys) . . . was widely practiced in ancient times in Asia, the Orient and more specifically, in Greece . . . It is interesting to note also that pederasty in Rome was known as "Greek love."

---

[1] Frank S. Caprio, *Variations in Sexual Behavior,* Grove Press, Inc., New York, 1955, p. 85.

Dr. Panos Bardis[2] reports in a study of "Sex Life in Ancient Greece":

> . . . many of Greece's gods and heroes were often described as homosexuals: Poseidon, the god of the sea; Apollo, the god of the sun; Heracles (Hercules), the greatest hero in Greek mythology; Ganymede, the cup-bearer of Zeus; and numerous others.
>
> Among Greece's mortals, some of the most famous men were also homosexuals. Solon, the great Athenian lawgiver and elegiac poet, one of the Seven Sages of ancient times, was homosexual.
>
> The intrepid conqueror, Alexander, when he marched against Asia, was accompanied by his young male lover, Hephaestion. Later, during a magnificent and spectacular festival at Ecbatana, Hephaestion fell ill and, after 7 days, died.
>
> Alexander was so heartbroken and inconsolable that he fasted for 3 days; crucified Hephaestion's physicians; ordered the entire empire to go into mourning; had chapels erected to his beloved friend in many cities; and, in May 323 B. C., buried him in Babylon. The funeral, with a 200-foot-high pyre and other extravagances, was one of the most ostentatious, theatrical, and sumptuous ceremonies of all times.

Regarding other famous persons who were homosexual, Dr. Caprio[3] states:

> According to Moll, Octavius was supposed to have had sexual intercourse with Caesar, Tiberius was notorious for his cruelty and subjected boys to immoral sexual practices . . . Nero was another who indulged in sexual activity with young boys. . . .
>
> Michaelangelo, Shakespeare, Oscar Wilde, Byron, Walt Whitman, Tchaikowsky and numerous other famous men are said to have had homosexual tendencies. Wilde, in fact, was tried, sentenced and found guilty of homosexuality.

As for early female homosexuals, Agrippina and Levia were well-known Roman lesbians. It is generally held that homosexuality flourished in the Roman bath houses.

Thus, homosexuality has a long history and many of the current problems that relate to homosexual behavior are not really new ones. With this in view, the chapter that follows describes homosexual behavior, discusses its causes, and attempts to present some of the human problems that attend it.

VARIETIES OF SEXUAL BEHAVIOR

Autosexual behavior

Human sexual behavior may be divided into four major categories:

The first is autosexual behavior in which the individual focuses upon himself.

Masturbation is the usual form of autosexual behavior.

A variety of techniques and inanimate objects may be utilized in masturbatory behavior.

Heterosexual behavior

The second is heterosexual behavior in which the individual prefers a sexual partner of the opposite sex.

---

[2] Panos Bardis, "Sex Life in Ancient Greece," *Sexology*, pp. 156-159, October 1965.
[3] Caprio, *op. cit.*

Heterosexual behavior includes:

1. Sexual intercourse, in which the male penis is inserted in the female vagina.

2. Mutual masturbation, in which one or both partners masturbate the other.

3. Anal intercourse, in which the male penis is inserted in the anal canal of the female.

4. Cunnilingus, in which oral stimulation of the female genitals is provided.

5. Fellatio, in which the penis is inserted into the mouth of the female partner.

6. Soixante-neuf (French for 69) in which fellatio and cunnilingus are performed at the same time.

It should be noted that none of these six kinds of sexual behavior is considered homosexual when it takes place between partners of opposite sexes.

Homosexuality refers to the kind of sexual partner rather than to the type of sexual behavior.

Katasexual behavior

A third type of sexual behavior is termed katasexual.

In katasexual behavior the individual selects a nonhuman partner.

Bestiality is another name given to human-animal relationships.

HOMOSEXUAL BEHAVIOR

A fourth type of sexual behavior, the subject of this discussion, is homosexual behavior.

In homosexual behavior the individual has sexual relations with or emotional attachments to a partner of the same sex.

Overt homosexual behavior includes:

1. Mutual masturbation by two individuals of the same sex.

2. Sodomy—refers to any illegal sex act but most often is used to describe anal intercourse between two males. Pederasty is another term for anal intercourse, usually with minors.

3. Cunnilingus—oral stimulation of the female genitals by another female.

4. Fellatio—oral stimulation of the penis by another male.

5. Mutual cunnilingus (two females).

6. Mutual fellatio (two males).

**Realizing
homosexuality**

What is it like to realize that you are homosexual? In their book *Lesbian Woman*,[4] Del Martin and Phyllis Lyon answer:

It doesn't just happen to you. It isn't as if you wake up suddenly one morning and say to yourself, "I am a Lesbian." Or that you make a conscious decision—"that is what I'm going to be from now on"—as if it were an acceptable goal in life.

Though many Lesbians believe they were born that way, we tend to feel that persons are born sexual: not heterosexual or homosexual, just sexual. And the direction a girl's sexuality may take depends upon her individual circumstances and life experiences, and how she reacts to them. It's rather like a slowly emerging awareness of herself as someone who is different, who is responding in ways that are apparently not usual to others, and yet seem very natural to her.

Sometimes this awareness begins very early in life. While a child of five doesn't know anything about the sex act and couldn't care less, she can experience a strange attraction to other little girls, or perhaps just one girl singled out of the group. She may play with boys and feel a certain camaraderie and affection for them, but the emotional attachment she feels for girls may be entirely different.

Realization of male homosexuality appears to be somewhat similar.

**Etiology of
homosexuality**

Currently, the etiology of homosexuality is unknown. Although a number of theories have been advanced, the evidence presently available fails to substantiate any of them.

Homosexuality is not simply a matter of:

1. What one's mother did or one's father did not do.
2. Genetic or hormonal factors.
3. Early seduction by other homosexuals.
4. Arrested psychosexual development.
5. Mental illness.

Like heterosexuality, the etiology remains unclear.

**A sensitive
question**

Although the cause or causes of homosexuality are unknown, most homosexuals are very sensitive about questions relating to the etiology of their sexual orientation.

This probably stems from the fact that most heterosexuals asked the question in a sense that means—"What went wrong to make you different from the rest of us?"

---

[4] Del Martin and Phyllis Lyon, *Lesbian Woman*, San Francisco, Glide Publications, 1972, p. 26.

In a discussion of homosexuality that occurred in one of the author's sex education classes, a visiting homosexual speaker was asked: What caused you to be a homosexual?

Addressing himself to his male counterparts in the class, he answered with a series of revealing questions:

— Did you ever search the depths of your soul attempting to discover what makes you like women?

— Did you ever wonder what your mother did or your father didn't do to make you a heterosexual?

— Have you ever considered consulting a psychiatrist with a view toward correcting your problem of liking women?

— Thinking back carefully, were you ever molested by a female when you were a child?

— Could it be that your problem relates to the fact that most of your elementary school teachers were women?

— Does your like for women stem from a hate for men?

— Did some series of events arrest your psychosexual growth?

— Is there a history of mental illness in your family?

Most of you have never thought about the cause of your heterosexuality, and you probably aren't very concerned about it now.

Similarly, I do not know the cause of my homosexuality, and I am concerned about it only because the homosexual life style has been historically, and is currently, attended by a pervasive type of negativism that we (homosexuals) are trying to change.

But we don't want to be "changed to heterosexuals" anymore than you want to be "changed to homosexuals."

An important perspective

These comments do not tell us very much about the cause or causes of homosexuality, but they do provide an important perspective. Researchers should investigate the etiology of hetero-sexuality and homosexuality with equal vigor and objectivity.

This is an important perspective because heretofore most of the work in this area has focused upon theories to explain "what went wrong to make homosexuals different from heterosexuals."

Perhaps it would have been wiser to start with the question: What causes heterosexuality?

At any rate, the etiology of both homosexuality and hetero-sexuality remains obscure, or as George Weinberg aptly states it:[5]

> The fact is that the combination of physiological readiness and social experience resulting in the development of any erotic

---

[5] George Weinberg, *Society and the Healthy Homosexual,* New York, St. Martin's Press, 1972.

preference—homosexual or heterosexual—is so intricate that science has not been able to fathom it as yet. No group of experts in any field can predict who will be homosexual. . . .

Attitudes toward homosexuality

Although very little is known about the cause or causes of homosexuality, five rather well-defined opinions have developed.

Each of these opinions deserves careful consideration, and although we appear to live in a time of freedom of thought and discussion, it might be suitable to preface these opinions with a thought from John Stuart Mill:

> . . . Were an opinion a personal possession of no value except to the owner, if to be obstructed in the enjoyment of it were simply a private injury, it would make some difference whether the injury was inflicted only on a few persons or on many. But the peculiar evil of silencing the expression of an opinion is that it is robbing the human race, posterity as well as the existing generation—those who dissent from the opinion, still more than those who hold it. If the opinion is right, they are deprived of the opportunity of exchanging error for truth; if wrong, they lose, what is almost as great a benefit, the clearer perception and livelier impression of truth produced by its collision with error.

The five opinions are:

"Dirty perverts"

1. The homosexual is a dirty pervert who belongs in jail.

That this is a common heterosexual opinion is evidenced by the fact that homosexual acts are against the law in most states.

In some states the homosexual act is punishable by life in prison, while in others the sentence exceeds that for second degree murder.

Heterosexual tolerance

2. A second opinion is one of tolerance by heterosexuals. It holds that homosexuals will be tolerated if they don't touch or try to indoctrinate minors.

On the other hand, people of this persuasion will not allow homosexuals to teach in their schools or to hold high level government positions.

An illness

3. A third position holds that homosexuality is an illness that requires treatment.

This view appears to be widespread and often supported by psychiatrists.

For example, Dr. Warren Walker[6] writes:

> Most psychiatrists consider this condition definitely pathological, and believe that we are all biologically programmed to be heterosexual.

---

[6] Warren H. Walker, "Homosexuality—Current Concepts and Attitudes," *Rocky Mountain Med. J.* 66:42-43, 1969.

It is also believed by most psychiatrists that this condition is neither hereditary nor congenital nor constitutional, rather that early life experiences and relationships may in some way present barriers to the realization of the native biological programming.

Also in support of this view, Dr. Daniel Cappon[7] writes:

There is no evidence whatsoever of a hereditary, constitutional, hormonal, somatic or organic basis for homosexuality.

It is an exclusively psychogenic condition.

Moreover, it is never basic or primary but the end result of a number of overdetermined, layered psychopathologic factors.

Dr. George Kriegman,[8] clinical professor of psychiatry at the Medical College of Virginia, writes:

... let me make one thing clear: homosexuality as an enduring sexual pattern is an illness, no different than other illness, and is a symptom of deep-seated emotional difficulty.

Despite propaganda to the contrary, there is no such thing as a well-adjusted, happy homosexual.

Homosexuality is a psychoneurotic disorder.

Dr. Frank S. Caprio,[9] a world-known psychiatrist, states in his book, *Variations in Sexual Behavior:*

Female homosexuality at best is a form of cooperative or mutual masturbation—a symptomatic expression of a neurotic personality; a disturbance in the infantile psychosexual development; a regression to narcissism. . . .

Because of their socially disapproved modus vivendi, female inverts suffer from a pervading sense of loneliness and as a consequence are unhappy.

I personally am convinced that lesbians would not be healthy persons even if they lived in a society where sexuality with one's own sex was socially acceptable. There is seldom any permanence to a lesbian alliance. Lesbians become dissatisfied, jealous and change partners frequently.

In the foreword to his book, *Homosexuality,* Dr. Edmond Bergler[10] writes:

1. The homosexual of either sex believes that his only trouble stems from the 'unreasonable attitude' of the environment.

2. If he were left to his own devices, he claims, and no longer needed to fear the law or to dread social ostracism, extortion, exposure (all leading to constant secrecy and concealment), he could be just as "happy" as his opposite number, the heterosexual.

3. This, of course, is a self-consoling illusion. Homosexuality is not the 'way of life' these sick people gratuitously assume it to be, but a neurotic distortion of the total personality.

[7] Daniel Cappon, "Understanding Homosexuality," *Postgrad. Med.,* 42:A131-136, 1967.

[8] George Kriegman, "Homosexuality and the Educator," *The Journal of School Health,* May 1969, pp. 305-311.

[9] Caprio, *op. cit.*

[10] Edmond Bergler, *Homosexuality,* P. F. Collier, Inc., New York, 1962.

4. It is granted that heterosexuality per se does not guarantee emotional health; there are innumerable neurotics among heterosexuals, too.

5. But there also exist healthy heterosexuals, and there are no healthy homosexuals.

6. The entire personality structure of the homosexual is pervaded by the unconscious wish to suffer; this wish is gratified by self-created trouble-making. This "injustice-collecting" (technically called psychic masochism) is conveniently deposited in the external difficulties confronting the homosexual.

7. If they [fears] were to be removed—and in some circles in large cities they have been virtually removed—the homosexual would still be an emotionally sick person.

Sexual orientation disturbance

4. Homosexuality is a sexual orientation disturbance.

This is the current position of the American Psychiatric Association. Although they removed homosexuality from their list of mental disorders, they did not pronounce it normal. Instead, they inserted a new psychiatric disorder called "sexual orientation disturbance."

The latter category is reserved for those homosexuals who either want to change their orientation, or need to adjust to the one they have.

A different sexual orientation

A fifth and final position holds that:

1. Homosexual relationships have as much power as antidotes for human aloneness as do heterosexual ones.

2. Homosexuals are healthy and as capable of happiness as heterosexuals.

3. It is arrogant to view persons as perverted or ill simply because their sexual orientation is different from your own.

4. One should be sensitive and loving toward homosexuals, treating any sexual advances as compliments rather than as causes for rejection.

5. Interpersonal relationships should not be influenced by a knowledge of another person's sexual orientation; i.e., homosexuals and heterosexuals should be viewed and treated as human beings rather than as products of different sexual orientations.

Gay is good.

In support of this view, Dr. Franklin E. Kameny writes:[11]

> ... to those of my fellow homosexuals who may read this, I say that it is time to open the closet door and let in the fresh air and the sunshine; it is time to doff and to discard the secrecy, the disguise, and the camouflage; it is time to hold up your heads and to look the

---

[11] Franklin E. Kameny, "Gay Is Good," *The Same Sex*, Philadelphia, Pilgrim Press, 1969, p. 145.

world squarely in the eye as the homosexuals that you are, confident of your equality, confident in the knowledge that as objects of prejudice and victims of discrimination you are right and they are wrong, and confident of the rightness of what you are and of the goodness of what you do; it is time to live your homosexuality fully, joyously, openly, and proudly, assured that morally, socially, physically, psychologically, emotionally, and in every other way: Gay is good. It is.

Life style management

Based on their sociological studies, Drs. William Simon and John Gagnon state:[12]

... most homosexuals manage fairly well when we consider the stigmatized and, in fact, criminal nature of their sexual interest. In a group of homosexuals with extensive histories of homosexuality, we found about 80 per cent reported no trouble with the police, and an additional 10 per cent had had minor contacts but were not arrested. Only 20 per cent reported problems of managing relations with their parental families, and about 10 per cent or less reported difficulties in school work. Of those who had had military experience, only one fifth reported difficulties.

Commenting on the American Psychiatric Association's decision to remove homosexuality from their list of mental disorders, Dr. Robert L. Spitzer stated:[13]

We decided a medical disorder either has to be associated with subjective distress, pain or general impairment in social functioning. Homosexuality is not regularly associated with either.

Religion

In his book *The Lord Is My Shepherd and He Knows I'm Gay*, Reverend Troy Perry, founder and pastor of the first church for homosexuals, describes his aspirations:[14]

... I dream of that time when all people who are gay, all who are hiding it, will step forth freely into the light of truth, total acceptance and understanding. I fervently dream and pray for that time when there is an end to hiding, an end to fear, an end to being victimized. I dream that we can all come out of hiding, that we can all stand tall and walk with our heads held high, because we are gay and we are proud. We will throw our arms around each other's shoulders without any shame. We will laugh together, weep together, share together, and march together. There will be an end to fear! We will stand together! We will unite! We will all know that we are God's own creatures, that he loves us, that He created us, that He blesses us, that He's proud of us, that He cares for us!

Homophobia

George Weinberg[15] has coined the term homophobia to

---

12 William Simon and John Gagnon, "Homosexuality: The Formulation of a Sociological Perspective," *The Same Sex*, Philadelphia, Pilgrim Press, 1969, p. 17.

13 *Washington Post*, December 16, 1973.

14 Troy Perry, *The Lord Is My Shepherd and He Knows I'm Gay*, Los Angeles, Nash Publishing, 1972, pp. 227-228.

15 George Weinberg, *Society and the Healthy Homosexual*, New York, St. Martin's Press, 1972.

describe an "unreasonable fear of homosexuals," and Kenneth Smith[16] has developed a "homophobic scale."

To determine your homophobic rating, answer the following nine questions yes or no.

1. Homosexuals should be locked up to protect society.

2. It would be upsetting for me to find out I was alone with a homosexual.

3. Homosexuals should be allowed to hold government positions.

4. I would not want to be a member of an organization which had any homosexuals in its membership.

5. I find the thought of homosexual acts disgusting.

6. If laws against homosexuality were eliminated, the proportion of homosexuals in the population would remain about the same.

7. A homosexual could be a good President of the United States.

8. I would be afraid for a child of mine to have a teacher who was homosexual.

9. If a homosexual sat next to me on a bus I would get nervous.

"No" to 3, 6 and 7 and yes to the others is indicative of homophobia.

Questions without answers

How does one differentiate knowledge from speculation as they relate to homosexuality? In the absence of quality research, how does one filter the list of opinions to arrive at a personal view of homosexuality?

A struggle with these questions appears to bring only more questions:

Can homosexuality contribute to a state of noncontradictory joy? If not, why not?

How are these two questions influenced by the social arrogance of heterosexuals?

Can the sexual orientation of the homosexual be changed? Should it be changed?

These are confusing questions without clear answers.

On the other hand, good questions are the first step toward enlightened answers, and if this chapter does nothing more than render clear the major questions regarding homosexuality, it will have served a major purpose.

Legal reform

Putting the homosexual in jail is not in his best interest or in the interest of society. Hence, several attempts at legal reform have been initiated in this and other countries.

---

[16] Kenneth Smith, "Homophobic Scale," cited by George Weinberg, *Society and the Healthy Homosexual*, New York, St. Martin's Press, 1972.

The Wolfenden Report[17] in England is now a classic example of successful reform.

In 1954, the House of Lords appointed a committee to study the problem of homosexual offenses and prostitution.

Under the leadership of Sir John Wolfenden, the committee submitted its report in 1957.

Legal reform came almost exactly ten years after publication of this report.

The conclusions of this committee and the thinking that led to these conclusions were reviewed for the American Psychiatric Association by Sir John Wolfenden[18] in 1968.

In part, he stated:

> We came to the view that the function of the criminal law in this area of behavior is to safeguard public order and decency and to protect those who for whatever reason are properly regarded as the weak and therefore deserving society's protection.
>
> We conclude that in this area the private behavior of an adult individual, male or female, is no concern of the criminal law.
>
> I stress "an adult individual" because we were as deeply concerned as any other collection of 15 citizens to protect children, the mentally weak, and the officially subordinate.
>
> But I suggest that if this guideline is followed a coherent and logical pattern emerges. Let me be more explicit.
>
> It is no concern of the criminal law if two adult consenting males indulge in homosexual behavior in private.
>
> It may be a form of behavior of which you and I disapprove; we may be disgusted by it; we may, on all sorts of moral grounds, find it repugnant.
>
> But none of those subjective reactions of ours have anything to do with criminality. Every day I come across forms of behavior to which all these descriptions apply; but that fact does not entitle me to demand that those who behave in this way should be sent to prison.
>
> I disapprove of adultery; and so do a good many other people. We do so because we think this sort of behavior is immoral, or wrong, or "not right."
>
> But I do not demand that adulterers and adulteresses should be subject to the criminal law.
>
> If men and women, or men and men, or women and women, indulge in sexual acts in public, I not only disapprove, I think the law ought to do something about it.
>
> And I think this because I think the law's business is to protect me and my wife and children from affronts against decency.

---

[17] *Report of the Committee on Homosexual Offences and Prostitution,* H. M. Stationery Office (Cmmd. 247), London, 1957.

[18] Sir John Wolfenden, "Evolution of British Attitudes Toward Homosexuality," *Am. J. Psychiat.,* 125:792-797, 1968.

> I do not think this because I think such behavior immoral. I do not think the law has a right to enter, as it were, anybody's bedroom.
>
> Sexual behavior is nobody's business except that of those immediately concerned, unless their behavior offends against public order and decency.
>
> This is the basis in logic for the two halves of our recommendations, that homosexual behavior between consenting males in private should be no concern of the criminal law and that solicitation by prostitutes in public places should render them liable to prosecution.

In the United States, the American Law Institute in its *Model Code* came to the same conclusion as the Wolfenden Committee.

Regarding this conclusion, Dr. Ralph Slovenko,[19] professor of law at the University of Kansas, writes:

> The Wolfenden Committee in England and the American Law Institute in its *Model Code* have recommended that sexual relations of a homosexual nature between consenting adults should no longer be subject to law, provided they take place in private.
>
> The reasons given are the lack of harm to the secular community, the unenforceability of the penal law, the unsuitability of imprisonment for offenders, the undue interference in personal affairs, the strain placed by the law on limited police resources, and the opportunities created for blackmail.

In view of these recommendations, New York, Illinois, Connecticut, Colorado, Oregon, Hawaii, Delaware, Ohio, and North Dakota have removed homosexual acts (between consenting adults and performed in private) from the status of crimes.

Dr. Slovenko has compiled the following list of maximum penalties for crimes against nature (sodomy) in the various states of the United States.

ALABAMA	2 to 10 years
ALASKA	1 to 10 years
ARIZONA	5 to 20 years
ARKANSAS	1 to 21 years
CALIFORNIA	1 year
COLORADO	1 to 14 years [Repealed]
CONNECTICUT	30 years [Repealed]
DELAWARE	$1000 and 3 years [Repealed]
DISTRICT OF COLUMBIA	$1000 or 10 years
FLORIDA	20 years
GEORGIA	1 to 10 years
HAWAII	$1000 and 20 years [Repealed]
IDAHO	5 years
ILLINOIS	[Repealed]
INDIANA	$100 to $1000 or 2 to 14 years or both
IOWA	10 years
KANSAS	10 years
KENTUCKY	2 to 5 years

---

[19] Ralph Slovenko, "Homosexuality and the Law," *Medical Aspects of Human Sexuality*, 1:35-38, 1967.

LOUISIANA	$2000 or 5 years or both
MAINE	1 to 10 years
MARYLAND	1 to 10 years
MASSACHUSETTS	20 years
MICHIGAN	15 years
MINNESOTA	20 years
MISSISSIPPI	10 years
MISSOURI	2 years
MONTANA	5 years
NEBRASKA	20 years
NEVADA	1 year to life
NEW HAMPSHIRE	$1000 or 5 years or both
NEW JERSEY	$5000 or 20 years or both
NEW MEXICO	$5000 or 2 to 10 years or both
NEW YORK	[Repealed]
NORTH CAROLINA	5 to 60 years
NORTH DAKOTA	10 years [Repealed]
OHIO	1 to 20 years [Repealed]
OKLAHOMA	10 years
OREGON	15 years [Repealed]
PENNSYLVANIA	$5000 or 10 years or both
RHODE ISLAND	7 to 20 years
SOUTH CAROLINA	$5000 or 5 years or both
SOUTH DAKOTA	10 years
TENNESSEE	5 to 15 years
TEXAS	2 to 15 years
UTAH	3 to 20 years
VERMONT	1 to 5 years
VIRGINIA	1 to 3 years
WASHINGTON	10 years
WEST VIRGINIA	1 to 10 years
WISCONSIN	$500 or 5 years or both
WYOMING	10 years

Dr. Don Harper Mills,[20] associate clinical professor of forensic medicine and pathology at the University of Southern California, appears to speak for an increasing number of people when he states:

> Though discreet, consensual homosexuality is not a threat to public safety and decency, I do not pass on the issue of its effect on morality.
>
> However, I question the propriety of using the vehicle of criminal law to enforce any particular pattern of moral behavior, so long as it does not directly affect fundamental societal interests.
>
> Finally, is it not reasonable to conclude that restricting one's freedom of choice in areas of private morality by means of criminal law is itself morally improper?
>
> If homosexual behavior per se is morally wrong, its deterrence should be the responsibility of religious, social, and medical health bodies, not of the state.

[20] Don H. Mills, "Viewpoints," *Medical Aspects of Human Sexuality*, 1:51-52, 1967.

CHAPTER TWELVE

Population Stabilization

The assimilation of the baby-boom generation has been called "population peristalsis," comparing it to the process in which a python digests a pig. As it moves along the digestive tract, the pig makes a big bulge in the python. While the imagery suggests the appearance of the baby-boom generation as it moves up the age scale and through the phases of the life cycle, there is reason to believe that the python has an easier time with the pig than our nation is having providing training, jobs, and opportunity for the generation of the baby-boom.

Report of the Commission on
Population Growth and the
American Future

In the early 1970's the news media coined the term "baby bust" to describe a phenomenon in which birth rates declined when everyone was expecting them to increase. Population experts had suggested that births would increase significantly in the United States as the baby-boom generation reached reproductive age; instead they declined. In attempting to explain this surprising decrease in the number of births, three theories have been advanced. The first theory suggests that plummeting births are related to the fact that the age at which couples have children is gradually rising. According to this theory, the expected increase in births has simply been delayed for a short time. A second theory contends that today's young people are having fewer children. A third explanation relates decreasing births to the increased incidence of abortion. But whatever the reasons, by the mid 1970's the United States had achieved a birth rate of 2.08 per couple—slightly below the 2.11 "replacement level." The replacement level is set at 2.11 rather than 2 in order to compensate for those women who do not have children or who die in childbearing years before having had two children.

Although birth rates are declining, our population continues to increase. Currently the population of the United States increases by approximately 1.5 million per year. This yearly gain results from approximately 3.2 million births, 2 million deaths, and a net immigration of 350,000. The net increase is of the magnitude of 0.7 per cent each year. This rate is less than one-half the growth exhibited between 1947 and 1961, when the annual rate of gain ranged between 1.6 and 1.8 per cent.

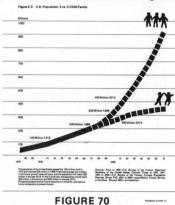

FIGURE 70

Figure 70[1] indicates that an average of two children per family will slow but not stop population growth. The fact that an increasing number of people are reaching the childbearing age means that birth rates will far exceed death rates for the remainder of the century, and it would indeed be unfortunate if we allowed the baby-bust psychology to lure us into unwarranted complacency regarding the future. Not only must we continue to work to stabilize our own population, but we must exhibit leadership in a world-wide effort to curb population growth. The world outlook is far more pessimistic.

POPULATION: A WORLD PROBLEM.

250 to 500 million

It is estimated that the world population at the time of Christ was approximately 250 million.

It required 1,650 years for this figure to double to 500 million.

500 million to one billion

Then by the year 1850, just two hundred years later, we had reached the one billion mark.

The population had doubled again by 1925, just 75 years later. At this date there were approximately two billion people in the world.

Estimates now present the following picture:

1969	3.5 billion
1980	4.0 billion
1990	5.0 billion
2000	6.5 billion

[1] Figure 70 from *Population and the American Future,* The Report of the Commission on Population Growth and the American Future, U. S. Government Printing Office, Washington, D.C., 1972.

United Nations population experts indicate that the population can be held to less than 6.5 billion in the year 2000 only if the current fertility rate in the underdeveloped countries can be cut in half in the next 30 years.

That this is a realistic expectation is suggested by birth control campaigns in a number of countries.

The food problem

To a family with inadequate food, a new baby is not a blessing. It is more comparable to a flood, a drought, or some other natural disaster that man is forced to live with.

In this connection it is currently estimated that of the world's children under six years of age, 70 per cent are malnourished.

To make matters worse, the world population is increasing at a rate of 2 per cent per year while the food supply is increasing at a rate of 1 per cent per year.

The average daily intake in the world today is 2,100 calories. By the year 2000 it is estimated that this will be reduced to 1,340-1,350 calories per day which is starvation level.

But a typical attitude held by young and old alike in the United States is that we don't have to worry about the population explosion because science will take care of it.

And it is indeed true that much can be done to increase the world food supply.

For example, it is estimated that one female green turtle could produce 7,200 pounds of meat per year if the mortality rate of her offspring were reduced.

But the plain truth is that currently planned programs of production provide no chance of keeping up with the population growth.

Even the most conservative estimates indicate that we will add a billion people to the world in the next 15 years. And even now there are very few countries in the world that are capable of producing the food they need.

A few years ago the United States and Canada had great surpluses of grains and other foods.

Today there are no surpluses anywhere in the world.

India, which has an annual population increase equal to the total population of Australia, already depends on the rest of the world for twenty million tons of food grain each year.

China, which has an annual population increase equal to the present population of Canada, is equally dependent.

Eastern Europe and the Soviet Union import millions of tons of food each year.

Since there is a very high correlation between the food supply an
the incidence of political violence both within and between coun
tries, we must attempt to find a solution.

The sex educator is an essential member of the team, because
experts in agriculture indicate that the problem cannot be solved
by focusing on food production alone.

Quality of life

Adequate food supply, if it were available, would insure physiolo
cal survival. But mankind deserves more out of life than mere
survival.

The population explosion also affects the quality of life, and
perhaps it is the quality of life that concerns us most in the
United States.

In this country our technology is very advanced and our rate of
population growth is relatively low—0.7 per cent per year.

This means that it is very likely that our food supply will more
than keep pace.

So it is undoubtedly the quality of life that will be of the greates
concern to us.

You yourself perhaps have encountered the problem in some of
the following ways:

1. Trying to find room to ski on the weekend.
2. Waiting your turn to play golf.
3. Trying to get a ticket for a hit Broadway show.
4. Looking for a clear spot to swim in a public swimming pool
    or beach.
5. Attempting to get a plane reservation during the holidays.
6. Trying to get a seat for an important athletic contest.
7. Attempting to find a place to hunt, fish, or camp.

These are but a few examples of problems that attend a population increase in an affluent society.

They are less important by comparison than the following:

1. Not enough doctors for medical care.
2. Fuel and power shortages.
3. Smog and air pollution alerts.
4. The feeling of being just a face in the crowd.

Individual liberty

It has been claimed for many years in the Western World that
an individual should be free to do what he pleases as long as it
doesn't interfere with others.

But with increasing numbers, almost everything you do starts
to interfere with others. This may even include the number of
children that you have.

Education

The population explosion has and will continue to have a drastic effect on the quality of education.

Dr. Charles J. Ping states:

> Mass education may well be a contradictory term. It is possible to train masses of people, but is it possible to educate . . . ? An infecting exposure to intellectual values demands close personal contact, but this is costly of time and persons, and cannot serve readily the needs of masses of people. The day is at hand when the slow and potentially dangerous process of problem solving by individuals represents a luxury numbers will not permit.

Solution

What do we do about the world population problem?

Minds that can develop atomic energy and send man to the moon might be equally successful with the population explosion.

Must we see people starving before our own eyes?

Must the air become too thick to breathe?

Must the water become too polluted to drink?

Must the nuclear warheads from a country too small to contain its population come at us before we decide to tackle the problem?

Voluntary childlessness

One approach to population control is voluntary childlessness for those who really don't want children.

Unfortunately, however, there is a tendency in most societies to label childless couples as abnormal, unnatural, immature, unhappy, and prone to divorce. And even in the United States, voluntary childlessness is relatively uncommon (approximately 5 per cent).

Regarding attitudes toward childlessness, Veevers notes:[2]

> Whether or not the negative stereotype is an accurate portrayal of the voluntary childless has not been established; in a sense its validity is unimportant if believed to be true, and hence is both a sanction in itself and a basis for further sanctions.

Despite the negative stereotype, the question of why one should have children is becoming increasingly popular as sex becomes more divorced from reproduction.

---

[2] J. E. Veevers, "The Violation of Fertility Mores: Voluntary Childlessness as Deviant Behavior," *Deviant Behavior and Societal Reaction.* Craig Boydell, et al. (ed.), Toronto, Holt, Rinehart and Winston, 1971, pp. 571-92.

SECTION
4

EDUCATIONAL ASPECTS
OF HUMAN SEXUALITY

In Chapter One we decided that sex education should be education for love, that it should attempt to render clear the constituents of love as they relate to sexual behavior. In view of this objective, the teaching units contained in this section are designed to aid the teacher with the task of developing a spiral of learning experiences to establish sexuality as an entity within healthy interpersonal relationships.

Units for the elementary grades

Many curriculum guides are available for the sex education of elementary school children. But the units contained in this section differ in one major respect—they are presented in detail, even including the dialogue between teachers and students. Since sex education is a relatively new addition to the total curriculum, the authors have included all of the details for the convenience of the teacher. These units are not recommended for use as a "cookbook" approach to sex education but are designed as examples for the many teachers who are just starting with sex education. The need for such units was expressed to the authors by those students enrolled in sex education workshops during the last several years. These sample units may be revised and enlarged to suit the needs of individual teachers.

Units for the junior and senior high school

In addition to teacher units for the elementary grades, this section also includes units for use in junior and senior high schools. These units are introduced and presented in Chapter Nineteen.

CHAPTER THIRTEEN

Sex Education of the First Grade Child

The development of certain basic concepts selected to serve as a foundation for sex education throughout the elementary years is an important and interesting objective for the first grade teacher. The units that follow are designed to help the first grade teacher develop a program specifically designed to meet this objective. The three units for the first grade are: (1) Our Body Parts, (2) Animal Families, and (3) Our Family.

OUR BODY PARTS

An Overview of Unit One

During the first grade, students are quite conscious of the differences between the male and female body parts, but many times they are uncomfortable in discussing them. The unit "Our Body Parts" is designed to help them overcome any self-conscious attitudes or hidden curiosity they have concerning the male and female body parts. As a part of this unit, first grade students are taken on a bathroom tour to casually but deliberately mention the difference between boys and girls—the penis and the vagina. After returning to the classroom, a review with the naming of all the body parts is scheduled. The genitals are reviewed with the other body parts to avoid drawing special attention to them.

ANIMAL FAMILIES

An Overview of Unit Two

Young children are especially interested in animals and their pets. The thoughtful teacher can channel this natural enthusiasm into a pupil-centered learning situation. The students begin the unit "Animal Families" by discussing their own pets and are gently led into a discussion of animal life in general. As the children play games with animal cutouts they learn the following concepts: (1) Life comes from life, (2) Life comes from the same kind of life, (3) All animal babies have a father and a mother in the beginning, (4) There are two kinds of life—male and female, and (5) All animal babies grow up to be adults. The first grade teacher will want to be careful to inculcate those concepts that will lay the foundation for future study of reproduction. However, the teacher can be somewhat flexible to allow the children to enjoy their exploration of animals in areas other than life structure. Flexibility will add to class enthusiasm and interest in the unit.

OUR FAMILY

An Overview of Unit Three

Important to the successful development of the child's future interpersonal relationships are the quality of his relationships within his family. The first grade teacher helps the child to explore his role in his family and his relationships with family members by guiding him into careful discussions and planning a family album with him. These activities develop within the child an understanding of: (1) the role of each family member in the family unit, (2) the role of each family member in the community, (3) the work the family shares as a unit, (4) the good times the family enjoys together, (5) the importance of good family relationships. The unit is designed to allow each child to explore his own family in depth, its chief feature being the encouragement of the child to share his carefully prepared family album with his own family.

UNIT ONE: OUR BODY PARTS

Building tour[1]

As children enter the first grade, the teacher should familiarize them with the school building. A building tour can be used to satisfy this need. The children should visit the principal's office, the nurse's office, the gymnasium, the school library, the auditorium, and the art room.

---

[1] This activity was taken from "Growth Patterns and Sex Education," *The Journal of School Health*, Vol. XXXVII, No. 52, May 1967, published by the American School Health Association.

Our Body Parts

Building Tour
Library, Gym, principals
nurse & office

Bathroom tour

During this tour a teacher can plan stops at both the girls' and boys' restrooms. At this time, the teacher can explain the differences between the boys' and girls' bathrooms—the urinal. She can point out the anatomical differences between boys and girls, explaining that little girls don't use urinals because they have a vagina instead of a penis.

Naming body parts

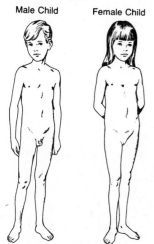

Male Child

FIGURE 71

Female Child

FIGURE 72

After returning to the classroom the teacher can show the class diagrams of male and female bodies. The children can name the body parts:

head	fingers	vagina
eye	thumbs	buttocks
nose	fingernails	thighs
ear	shoulders	legs
mouth	chest	knees
lips	abdomen	ankles
necks	pelvis	feet
arms	scrotum	toes
elbows	penis	toenails
hands	anus	navel

UNIT TWO: ANIMAL FAMILIES

LESSON 1

Demonstration guidelines

For presentation of this unit the teacher may use a large feltboard and felt cutouts of nine different animal families: dog, cat, duck, bear, horse, lion, rabbit, cow, and human. At the end of this unit are simple pictures of these animal families. The teacher may cut these out and use them as patterns.

An alternate way to present this unit might involve a bulletin board with thumb tacks to attach the animals.

As the unit is presented, the different animal families will be placed on the feltboard. Allow the children to place the animals on the animal family board. After each lesson the children will make cutouts for their own animal family board.

...mal friends and.
...es

Today I thought we might talk about our animal friends and their babies.

Some of our animal friends live right at home with us while others live in the zoo.

Our pets who live with us

Our animal friends who live at home with us are called pets; many of you have baby animals for pets.

How many of you have a pet at home? What kind of pet do you have? *Mary? Sue? John?* (Call on several children to talk about their pets to gain their attention.)

It's fun to talk about our pet animals, isn't it?

Today I brought some pictures of our zoo and some pet animal friends, and we are going to learn about them.

An animal family board

Our animal friends have families just as you and I do. We are going to make an animal family board together to learn about their animal families.

On our board we are going to put the animals in each of the different animal families together.

Feltboard in miniature

Before presenting the following unit on animal families have each of the children make a feltboard in miniature. For their feltboards each child will need an empty cigar box, a small amount of contact paper, rubber cement, a roll of colorful binding tape, and a piece of felt no larger than the size of the box cover.

Have each child cover the sides and cover of the box top with the contact paper. Next, have each cover the inner face of his box cover with felt. Rubber cement may be used to attach the felt to box cover. Colorful binding tape is used to edge each side and the top of the box. This binding provides extra reinforcement.[2]

The dog family

Let's begin by talking about a family we all know; in this family is a familiar animal many of us have for pets.

See if you can guess which animal this is.

This animal is known as "man's best friend"; it barks when a stranger comes near and wags its tail when it sees a friend.

Who knows what this animal is? (*A dog.*)

Dogs belong to a family

A dog belongs to a family just as you and I do; he belongs to the dog family.

---

[2] From Robert Olson, *Grade Teacher*, Vol. LXXIX, Number 2, "Feltboard in Miniature," October 1961, page 47.

(Show the picture of the puppy.) What do we call a dog when it is a baby? (*A baby dog is called a puppy.*)

How many of you have a puppy?

A story about puppies

Listen to this funny story one man wrote about puppies; it might remind you of a puppy you know.

I Had a Dog and a Cat
by
Karl Capek

All puppies are alike; they are all born with the same habits and grow according to the same rules of the game.

They crawl into places where they have no business; make seventy-seven puddles a day; tear people's socks; eat what they ought not to, for instance chairs, strings, soaps, carpets, and fingers; sleep in the basket on the clean washing; cry for help every five minutes; learn to bark; and are quiet only when they are causing some . . . damage.

All this is a . . . law of Nature, valid for all of the puppies in the world.

If you have a puppy, he probably chews your slipper and makes puddles on your rug just as the man in the story said.

Don't be too angry, though. Remember that all puppies are alike in these mischievous ways.

**All puppies have a
mother and a father**

Puppies are alike in another way too; every puppy has a mother and a father. (Place the mother and the father dog on the animal family board.)

All puppies have parents

The puppy's mother and father are called his parents; all puppies have parents.

The mother, the father, and the baby belong to each other. We call them a family.

Would someone like to put the baby puppy alongside his parents on our family board, since they all belong to each other?

**Unit activity: feltboard
in miniature**

Have the children make their own dog family for their animal feltboard in miniature. You can make several patterns for them to use from the picture provided at the end of this unit. While the children are working on their dog families you can ask them questions individually:

Does a dog belong to a family?
What is a dog called when it is a baby?
What mischievous things do dogs do?
How are all puppies alike?
What are a puppy's mother and father called?
What do we call a mother, father, and baby who belong to each other?

LESSON 2

All animals belong to a family with a mother and a father

All baby animals belong to a family with a mother and a father.

This probably doesn't seem strange to you, since you belong to a family with a mother and a father, too.

Let's learn about some other baby animals and their families.

The cat family

Who knows of a family that has a baby that purrs and plays with yarn? (*The cat family.*)

Come pick out the members of this family. (Allow one of the children to choose the mother, father, and baby animal belonging to the cat family.)

(Holding up the picture of the kitten.) What do we call the baby in this animal family? (*A kitten.*)

The baby kitten's mother is called a tabbycat. (Hold up the picture of the mother cat.)

The baby kitten's father is called a tomcat. (Hold up the picture of the tomcat.)

A mother and a father who have a baby are called parents

The mother tabbycat and father tomcat have a baby, so we call them parents.

All mothers and fathers who have a baby are called parents. We will put Mr. Tomcat, Mrs. Tabbycat, and baby kitten close to each other on our animal family board because they are a family and belong together.

Who would like to do this for me?

We will have to put them close together because there will be many families to place on our animal family board.

We already know about two families, and we still have all of these animals and their families left. (Refer to the animal cutouts still not on the animal board.)

There are many, many animal families in the world; let's learn about another animal family.

The duck family

I will tell you about the family, and let's see if you can guess the name of the family without seeing the picture of the animal.

This family lives in the water. The animals in this family go "quack, quack." They are the . . . (point to a child to guess) (*duck family*).

(Pick a child.) Come show us the mother, the father, and the baby who belong to the duck family. (Place the animals he has chosen on the animal family board.)

(Ask the class if he has picked the right animals for the duck family.)

But I wonder how we can be sure that we have picked the right mother and father and baby to belong to each other?

(Ask the child who volunteered to find the family.) Why did you pick this mother, this father, and this baby to belong together as the duck family?

Family members are alike

Yes, you are right. We know that they are a family because they are so much alike.

A mother and a father have a baby like them

Families are always alike. A mother and a father will always have a baby who is just like them.

The baby kitten was very much like her mother tabbycat and father tomcat. (Point to them on the animal family board.)

The baby duckling is very much like its parents too. (Refer to them on the animal family board.)

It's very much like its mother duck and very much like its father duck.

How do we know which animals belong to a family? (*Family members are alike.*)

Unit activity: feltboard in miniature

Have each child make his own cat and duck family for his animal feltboard in miniature. You can make several patterns for them to use from the pictures provided at the end of this unit. As the children are working on their cat and duck families you can ask them questions individually:

> What is a cat called when it is a baby?
> What do we call all mothers and fathers who have a baby?
> How can we be sure that we have picked the right mother and father and baby to belong to each other?

LESSON 3

Family members are all alike

Now that we know that family members are very much alike, it will be easy for us to identify many other families.

The bear family

Let's take the bear family next.

When a bear is a baby, it is called a cub.

Who can pick out the baby cub for me and show it to the class? (Allow a child to do this.)

Who can pick out the mother bear and the father bear? (Place them on the animal family board.)

How do we know that this one is the cub (point to the picture the child has chosen) and not this one? (Point to the father or mother bear.)

A baby animal is much smaller than its parents

(Allow the children to guess) You are right. Although the cub looks like its parents we can pick it out easily because it is so much smaller.

When a cub is born it is so small that it is only the size of its mother's paw; it weighs only one-half pound.

Imagine how tiny the cub looks next to his parents. Each of his parents weighs over 600 pounds!

But the cub will weigh 600 pounds when he grows up too.

All babies grow up

All babies grow up, and as they grow up they become bigger, just like their parents. (Point to the cub and then to his parents.)

When they grow bigger and have had many birthdays, they are n longer babies; they are grownups.

When babies grow up they are adults

Another word for "grownup" is adult; when babies grow up the are adults.

Your mother was once a baby girl, but she grew up and is an ad now.

Your father was once a baby boy, but he grew up and is an adul now.

This cute little baby cub will grow up too. What will we call the baby cub when he grows up? (*Adult.*)

If you have a pet you probably already know how fast baby animals grow up to be adults.

It seems that whenever we get a kitten or a puppy for a pet in a short time it is grown up.

All animals grow up to be adults. Who can come up to our anim family board and show us an adult animal?

(Allow several children to come and point to the adults. As the child points to an adult animal you will say:) Yes, the tomcat is an adult. He was a kitten when he was a baby, but he grew up.

Unit activity: feltboard in miniature

Have each child make his own bear family for his animal feltboard in miniature. You can make several patterns for them to use from the pictures provided at the end of this unit. As the children work on their bear family you can ask them questions individually:

> What is a bear called when it is a baby?
> How big is a cub when it is born?
> Will a cub ever be as big as his parents?
> What is another word for grownup?
> What is a baby cub called after he grows up?

LESSON 4

The horse family

We know that all baby animals grow up to be adults. Let's meet the horse family and see how their babies grow up to be adults.

A baby horse is called a foal.

The horse parents, the father stallion (show him) and the mother mare (show her) have two baby foals.

Have one of the children put the mare and the stallion on the family board.

One of their baby foals is a filly (girl) and the other baby is a colt (boy).

When a baby is born it is either a boy or a girl

When animal babies are born they are either girls or boys.

A boy baby is a male

If the animal baby is a boy we call him a male.

What is another name for a baby colt? (*Male.*)

What is another name for a baby boy cub? (*Male*)

What is another name for the baby boy kitten? (*Male.*)

Boys are always males

A boy is always a male—when he is born, when he is growing, and even when he grows up to be an adult.

Fathers are males too

Fathers were born as boy babies; fathers are males too.

Let's put the baby colt by his father; they are both males. (Pick a child to do this.)

A girl baby is a female

If a baby animal is a girl she is a female; the baby filly is a female.

What do we call the baby girl kitten? (*Female.*)

What do we call the baby girl cub? (*Female.*)

Girls are always females

A girl is always a female—when she is born, when she is growing, and even when she grows up to be an adult.

Mothers are females too

Mothers were born as girl babies; mothers are females too.

Let's put the baby filly by her mother; they are both females. (Pick a child to do this.)

In our class we have many boys and girls; this means that there are many males and many females in our class.

Ask different children whether they are males or females.

Unit activity: feltboard in miniature

Have each child make his own horse family for his animal feltboard in miniature. You can make several patterns for them to use from the pictures provided at the end of this unit.

As the children are working on their horse family you can ask them questions individually:

What is a horse called when it is a baby?
What is another name for an animal baby that is a boy?
What is another name for an animal baby that is a girl?
Is a mother a male or a female?
Is a father a male or a female?

LESSON 5

The remaining families

How lucky we are to have males and females, fathers and mothers, girl babies and boy babies, and families for them to belong to.

Speaking of families, we still have all of these families left. (Point to the animals not yet on the animal family board.)

We will want all of them to be together with their families on our animal family board.

Let's put the rest of the animals with their families.

The deer family

Who would like to put the deer family together on our animal family board?

The lion family

Who would like to put the lion family together on our animal family board?

The rabbit family

Who would like to put the rabbit family together on our animal family board?

The cow family

Who would like to put the cow family together on our animal family board?

The human animal family

Now that we have learned so much about families, you may have been wondering why it is that animal families are so much like your own.

After all, you have a mother and a father; they are your parents.

We are a lot like animals

You are very much like them; you belong to them and people call you . . . (point to different class members) *the Jones family, the Brown family, and the Smith family* instead of the dog family, the cat family, or the bear family.

We are animals too

The truth is that you are an animal too; your family is the human animal family.

Your father and mother are called human beings, and human beings have human babies who grow up to be just like you.

Who would like to put the human animal family on the animal family board?

Now we have all of our animal friends with their families; let's see how much we can remember about animal families.

ACTIVITIES FOR REVIEW

Animal family alphabet

To develop the concept that all animals have a family with a mother and a father have the children go through the alphabet naming an animal family for each letter, i.e., antelope family, bear family, cat family, dog family, elephant family.

Streetcar game[3]

One child is the conductor. He stands behind the chair of the first child in the group. Teacher shows a card. If the conductor says the word first he continues to be conductor and moves to the next child. If a child who is seated says the word first, he becomes the conductor.

The words to be printed on cards for use in this game are:

animal	parents	horse
friend	cat	colt
pet	kitten	girl
baby	duck	boy
family	bear	male
dog	cub	female
puppy	grownup	lion
mother	adult	rabbit
father	human	cow

A quiz with teams

Divide the class into two teams. Keep score on the blackboard. Ask them the review questions. You will find these questions at the end of this unit.

A color reviewing activity

You may use the two page coloring activity, "Animal Families," to review the concepts the child has learned in this unit. (This two page coloring activity is included at the end of this unit and may be duplicated for distribution.) Pass the sheets out to the class. You will then read the directions with the child. For example, begin by saying "Color the baby." Point to the three choices. Have the children color the baby. Then read the next set of directions, "Color the parents." You will want to read the directions with the children to make sure that you are testing family concepts and not reading ability. When the children are finished, collect the color drawings and check to see that the children have grasped the concepts. You will want to clear up any mistakes the child has made. After you have started them on the following activity the children will be busy working by

---

[3] The source for the framework of the streetcar game is Mary Jackson Ellis and Mayon Atherton's *The First Grade Log,* T. S. Denison and Company, Minneapolis, 1956, vol. I.

themselves. During this time you might pass back their drawings and help the children who have made mistakes individually.

Unit activity: feltboard in miniature

Have the children make cutouts of different animal families for their feltboards in miniature. Encourage them to make cutouts of animals other than those that have been used already in class. When they have finished, have them show the class their cutouts and tell about the animal family they have made.

A drawing activity

It was fun to talk about the cat family, the bear family, the dog family, and all of these other families; it is great fun to talk abo our own families too.

I'm going to give each of you a sheet of paper to draw your fam When you have finished, you can tell us about your family.

(After all the class members have drawn their families, they are ready to go on to the first grade lesson on family members.)

REVIEWING THE UNIT

Questions for review

1. What are our animal friends who live at home with us called?
2. What are our animal friends who belong to each other called?
3. In what ways are all puppies alike?
4. What are a baby animal's father and mother called?
5. What do we call all mothers and fathers who have a baby?
6. How can we be sure that we have picked the right mother, father, and baby to belong to each other?
7. What will a mother and father's baby look like?
8. What do we call a baby when he grows up?
9. How can we tell which animals belong to a family?
10. How can we tell which is the baby animal in a family?
11. When a mother and a father have a baby, what are they called?
12. What do we call a baby when it grows up?
13. When a baby is born it can be either a boy or a ——?
14. What can we call a baby animal if it is a boy?
15. Is a boy always a male, even when he grows up?
16. What is another name for a baby animal that is a girl?
17. Is a girl a female when she is growing up?
18. Is a mother bear a female?
19. Do you belong to an animal family?
20. What is the name of the family we all belong to?

Animal Families

COLOR THE BABY

COLOR THE PARENTS

COLOR THE MOTHERS

FIGURE 73

COLOR THE FEMALES

COLOR THE FAMILY

COLOR THE MALES

COLOR THE HUMANS

FIGURE 74

The Bear Family

Animals can be arranged
on feltboard like this

FIGURE 75

The Deer Family

Animals can be arranged
on feltboard like this

FIGURE 76

The Cat Family

FIGURE 77

The Dog Family

FIGURE 78

The Rabbit Family

FIGURE 79

The Duck Family

FIGURE 80

The Horse Family

Animals can be arranged
on feltboard like this

FIGURE 81

The Lion Family

Animals can be arranged
on feltboard like this

FIGURE 82

The Cow Family

Animals can be arranged
on feltboard like this

FIGURE 83

The Human Family

Figures can be arranged
on feltboard like this

FIGURE 84

UNIT THREE: OUR FAMILY

Introduction

Introduce this unit by having the children show to the class the pitcture they have drawn of their families. You will ask them the following questions about their families:

How many people are there in your family?

How many brothers do you have?

Are your brothers older or younger than you are?

How many sisters do you have?

Are your sisters older or younger than you are?

Unit activity: family album

The children will make a family album with this unit. The materials needed are leather for the cover, yarn to bind the cover, and minila filler paper. Have the children design the cover and title the album "Our Family." The first insert in the album will be the picture the child has drawn of his family.

Our home

Read the following poem to the class.[4]

Our House
by
Dorothy Brown Thompson

Our house is small—The lawn and all
Can scarcely hold the flowers;
Yet every bit, the whole of it,
Is precious for it's ours!

From door to door, From roof to floor,
From wall to wall we love it;
We wouldn't change for something strange
One shabby corner of it!

The space complete in cubic feet
From cellar floor to rafter
Just measures right, and not too tight
For us, and friends and laughter!

Have the children discuss their homes. Draw a picture of the home for the family album.

Our family makes our home happy

Each child will tell the class one way that his family makes his home happy. Then have the children draw a picture of their

---

[4] From Wilma McFarland, *For a Child,* Westminster Press, Philadelphia, 1947.

family making their home happy. Put the picture in the family album with the following poem:[5]

> "Aren't families nice?
> A mother and a daddy?
> A sister and a brother,
> All snugly living in a house,
> And loving one another."

Our fathers

Discuss the following questions with the class:

What do you like best about your father?

Why does your father work?

What kind of work does your father do?

How can you help your father?

Unit activity: family album

Draw a picture of father at work for the family album.

Our mothers

Have the children give examples of times that mother has scolded them for being bad. Bring out the concept that mothers forgive and love their children all the time. Read the following poem:[6]

A Boy's Mother
by
James Whitcomb Riley

> My mother she's so good to me,
> If I was good as I could be,
> I couldn't be as good—no sir!—
> Can't any boy be good as her!
>
> She loves me when I'm glad er sad;
> She loves me when I'm good er bad;
> An'; what's a funniest thing, she says
> She loves me when she punishes.
>
> I don't like her to punish me—
> That don't hurt—but it hurts to see
> Her cryin'!—'Nen I Cry; An' nen
> We both cry an' be good again.
>
> She loves me when she cuts an' sews
> My little cloak an' Sund'y clothes;
>
> An'; when my Pa comes home to tea,
> She loves him 'most as much as me.
>
> She laughs an' tells him all I said,
> An' grabs me up an' pats my head;
> An' I hug her, an' hug my Pa
> An' I love him purt' nigh as much as Ma.

---

[5] Mary Jackson Ellis, Pearl Esko, and Robert Kane, *The First Grade Log*, Minneapolis, T. S. Denison and Company, 1962, vol. II.

[6] James Whitcomb Riley, *Joyful Poems for Children*, Bobbs-Merrill Company, New York, 1946. Copyright © 1940, 1960 by the Bobbs-Merrill Company, Inc.

Discuss the following questions with the children:

What do you like best about your mother?

Does your mother work?

What kind of work does your mother do?

What kind of work does your mother do at home?

How can you help your mother?

Unit activity: family album   Draw a picture of mother at work for the family album.

My brother   Have the children discuss the following questions about their brothers:

Do you have a brother?

Is your brother bigger or smaller than you?

What kinds of things does your brother like to do?

What have you learned from your big brother?

Have you ever helped your little brother to learn to do new things?

What do you like best about your brother?

Unit activity: family album   Have the class draw a picture for the family album entitled "My Brother and I."

My sister   Have the children discuss the following questions about their sisters:

Do you have a sister?

Is your sister bigger or smaller than you?

What kinds of things does your sister like to do?

What have you learned from your big sister?

Have you ever helped your little sister to do new things?

What do you like best about your sister?

Unit activity: family album   Have the children draw a picture for the family album entitled "My Sister and I."

A new family member   For the discussion of a new family member, bring a baby doll to class. Other materials necessary: diapers, safety pins, powder, wash cloth, towel, small tub, soap, baby bottle. As you discuss helping mother with the baby, you can show the children how to bathe the baby, how to give the baby a bottle, and how to change the diapers. Emphasis should be placed on helping the new family member.

Discussion questions for "A New Family Member":

Do any of you have a baby in your family?

Is the baby a boy or a girl?

What "special" things do mothers and fathers have to do for babies?

Do mothers and fathers sometimes have to spend a lot of time with baby? Why?

What things do you like to do for the baby?

Why does a baby need older brothers and sisters?

Unit activity: family album

Have the class draw a picture for the family album entitled "Baby and I." Those children who do not have a baby in the family can draw a picture of what they think they were like when they were a baby.

Our family works together

Arrange to have two empty bulletin boards, one for the boys and one for the girls. Have the boys look through magazines, cutting out picture examples of the work that they, their brothers, and fathers do around the house. They can also bring things from home. Have the girls look through magazines, cutting out picture examples of the work that they, their sisters, and mothers do around the house. They can also bring things from home.

Allow each child to tell about one of his pictures. Discuss how children can help their fathers and mothers. Have the children plan ways that they can help at home.

Each day a child does something at home to help let him tell the class. Then he gets to put one of his pictures on the bulletin board. The boys will put their pictures on one bulletin board and the girls will use the other bulletin board.

Unit activity: family album

Have the children draw a picture for the family album of the family working together with the title "Being Helpful." Have them copy the following poem for their album.[7]

Being Helpful

I love to help my mother.
Mother loves to help me too.
So now we help each other
To get the work all thru.

I love to help my daddy.
He likes to help me, too.
So I found out that helping
Is the best thing to do.

Family relationships

Preceding the discussion of this topic, the children have discussed sharing work with the family. To introduce the topic of "Family

---

[7] Ellis, Esko, and Kane, *op. cit.*

Relationships" begin with the idea that there are many, many things to share with the family other than work. Ask the children what other things they can share with their families.

> I am going to give you some examples of things that could happen in any family. Then I would like to have you tell me what you would do to help.
>
> If you have trouble deciding, pretend that you are another member of the family and try to think what kind of help you would like.
>
> Baby brother has knocked over your favorite toy. It is lying on the floor, broken into many pieces. Baby brother starts to cry. What should you do?
>
> Last night father promised that he would take you to the movies tonight. Father comes home tonight looking very tired and weary. Father had a very hard day at work. What would you do?
>
> Younger sister and you have had a very bad fight. Both of you were wrong. Younger sister says, "I'm sorry." What should you do?
>
> Older sister has a chance to go to the lake, but she cannot go unless the dishes are done. She only has a few minutes to get ready and many, many dishes to dry. What should you do?
>
> Older brother has come home with very good grades in school. He tells you about his good grades. What should you do?
>
> Has something special, good or bad, ever happened to you that you wanted to share with your family? How did your family help you?

Unit activity: family album

Have the children draw a picture of their family sharing something special, good or bad, together.

Puppet show

To review the role of different family members have the children make paper bag puppets—mothers, fathers, sisters, brothers, babies. Divide the children into groups to give the following puppet shows:

> "The Way Sisters Are"
>
> "The Way Brothers Are"
>
> "The Way Mothers Are"
>
> "The Way Fathers Are"
>
> "The Way Babies Are"

Completing the family album

Ask the children whether there are any other pictures they want to color to include in their album. The children might have some good suggestions for the class. Allow time for them to complete the pictures, which were their own ideas.

SUGGESTED BIBLIOGRAPHY FOR THE FIRST GRADE

Boegehold, Betty, *Three to Get Ready*. New York: Harper & Row, Publishers, 1965. A clever story about a cat family, illustrating the fairness and sharing that are necessary for a happy family.

Buck, Pearl S., *Johnny Jack and His Beginnings.* New York: John Day Co., Inc., 1954. A beginning book written in story fashion for children who wonder where they came from. The story creates a sense of wonder about reproduction.

Burkhardt, Richard W., and McGuinness, Al G., *Our Family.* Chicago: Beckley-Cardy Company, 1954. A reader that shows how the behavior of a person in the family influences his happiness and the happiness of others.

Darby, Gene, *What Is a Cow?* Chicago: Benetic Press, 1957. A simple but informative book about the cow and her calf. It also explains the dairy and the milk we drink.

Ets, Marie, *The Story of a Baby.* New York: The Viking Press, 1969. A well illustrated book containing information on fertilization and gestation. Intended to be read aloud to the young child.

Gregor, Arthur, *Animal Babies.* New York: Harper Brothers, 1959. A picture book of animals with their babies. The captions accompanying the large illustrations try to show that mothers care for their young.

Guy, Anne, *A Baby for Betsy.* New York: Abingdon Press, 1957. Betsy longs for a baby sister and her mother cannot have one. The family goes through the process of adoption. Illustrates how adopted family members are loved as if they were true members of the family.

Hill, Elizabeth Starr, *Evan's Corner.* New York: Holt, Rinehart & Winston, Inc., 1967. Evan wants to have a place all his own, so his mother gives him a corner. Evan spends much time making his corner an interesting place to be. Somehow Evan realizes that all his work has been in vain. His mother tells him that he will be happier if he spends his time helping others.

Hoban, Russell, *A Baby Sister for Frances.* New York: Harper & Row, Publishers, 1964. The reactions of Frances to the arrival of a new sister. A good book to be used with children who are expecting a new member in the family.

Hoban, Russell, *The Solely Trying Day.* New York: Harper & Row, Publishers, 1964. A clever story of a day when father comes home to hear the bitter fighting of his family. When he asks what the difficulty is, each member blames another. Develops the idea that we must share the blame for wrongdoings.

Hobson, Laura Z., *I'm Going to Have a Baby.* New York: John Day Co., 1967. The preparation of Chris, an only child, for a new baby. Can be used with children expecting their first brother or sister.

Hoffman, Elaine, and Hefflefinger, Jane, *Family Helpers.* Chicago: Melmont Publishers, 1954. An excellent book to illustrate the role of the different family members. Shows how each family member has certain tasks for which he is responsible.

Horvath, Betty, *Jasper Makes Music.* New York: Franklin Watts, Inc., 1967. A story to read to the class about a boy who works very hard shoveling snow to earn money for a guitar. His parents cannot buy him one because there are too many other things the family needs.

Lenski, Lois, *The Little Family.* New York: Doubleday & Co., Inc., 1932. A story about the Little family and how they work together. Develops the role of the father and the mother and shows that a boy helps the father, and a girl helps her mother.

Matmueller, Felix, *We Want A Little Sister.* Minneapolis: Lerner Publications, 1965. A story about a family expecting a baby. The children in the family are encouraged to ask mother and father any questions they have about the coming of the baby. Answers typical questions posed by young children in this situation.

Meeks, Esther, and Bagwell, Elizabeth, *The World of Living Things.* Chicago: Follett, 1969. Discusses the different forms of reproduction with a build-up to human reproduction. Emphasizes the differences between maleness and femaleness and the importance of the family.

Meeks, Esther, and Bagwell, Elizabeth, *Families Live Together.* Chicago: Follett, 1969. A photographic explanation of the family situation and of warm, loving family relationships.

Meeks, Esther, and Bagwell, Elizabeth, *How New Life Begins.* Chicago: Follett, 1969. Explains

the different life cycles on earth and the life cycle and generation of humans. Emphasizes
the need of baby's for the protection and care of parents.

Miles, Betty, *A House for Everyone*. New York: Alfred A. Knopf, Inc., 1958. A picture book
for the small child with emphasis on the idea that a house is a place where we live with
and enjoy loved ones.

Radlaver, Ruth Shaw, *Fathers at Work*. Chicago: Melmont Publishers, 1958. A well illustrated
book of the occupations of different fathers. The teacher will need to read with the child,
for although the subject is appropriate for grade 1 concepts, the vocabulary is difficult.

Schlein, Miriam, *The Way Mothers Are*. Chicago: Albert Whitman & Co., 1963. A well illustrated
book dealing with the concept of love. A very good illustration showing that family members
must love each other all the time.

Zolotow, Charlotte, *Big Sister and Little Sister*. New York: Harper & Row, Publishers, 1966.
Clearly illustrates the care and sharing among family members. Also shows how younger
members of the family learn how to be good family members from their brothers and
sisters.

Zolotow, Charlotte, *When I Have A Little Girl*. New York: Harper & Row, Publishers, 1964.
A little girl explains how she will change the rules for little girls when she is a mother.
May be used to open discussion on the topic, "Do mothers and fathers know what's
best for their children?"

Zolotow, Charlotte, *When I Have A Son*. New York: Harper & Row, Publishers, 1967. A little
boy tells how he will change things so that when he has a son, the son will not have to do
all the things he doesn't like to do. A good book to open discussion on why parents ask us
to do certain things we don't want to do.

SUGGESTED FILMS FOR THE FIRST GRADE

A Day With Your Family. Society for Visual Education, 1345 Diversey Parkway, Chicago,
Illinois 60614. An eight minute filmstrip showing a day with a family. Emphasizes
having fun and sharing work.

Animal Babies Grow Up. Coronet Films, 65 E. South Water Street, Chicago, Illinois 60601.
This film clearly shows 1. that some baby animals look like their parents as soon as they
are born; 2. that some baby animals do not look like their parents when born and must
go through several stages before becoming adults but eventually do resemble their parents;
and 3. that animals care for their young in different ways and for different lengths of
time. Used to develop two concepts in the first grade—Life Comes from the Same Kind
of Life.

Birth of Puppies. Coronet Films, 65 E. South Water Street, Chicago, Illinois 60601. Children
look forward to the birth of puppies and assume different responsibilities.

City Pets: Fun and Responsibility. Coronet Films, 65 E. South Water Street, Chicago, Illinois
60601. This film stresses the special care of our animal pets—dogs, cats, hamsters, white
mice, parakeets, canaries, and goldfish. Helps the children to develop a sense of responsibility for their pets.

Helpers Who Come to Our House. Coronet Films, 65 E. South Water Street, Chicago, Illinois
60601. This film can be used with the unit "Our Family" to discuss the occupations of
the children's fathers. The children learn about the many helpers who come to their
home to provide services—the mailman, the milkman, the garbage man, and others.

Helpers in Our Community. Coronet Films, 65 E. South Water Street, Chicago, Illinois,
60601. This film can be used with the unit "Our Family" to discuss the occupations
of the children's fathers. The setting for the film is a classroom discussion about the
different kinds of helpers in the community; we meet many of these interesting people
(street repairman, doctor, bus driver) and learn about the important work that they do.

Our Family Works Together. Coronet Films, 65 E. South Water Street, Chicago, Illinois 60601. The home is a pleasant place in which to live when family members cooperate in work and play. Mike and Susan help plan a surprise to share with father. They also share in the family's work.

The Family Has a New Baby. Society for Visual Education, 1345 Diversey Parkway, Chicago, Illinois 60614. A filmstrip depicting a family prior to and after the arrival of a new baby. Illustrates family sharing and responsibility.

What Do Fathers Do? Churchill Films, 626 N. Robertson Blvd., Los Angeles, California 90069. A young boy spends a day with his father and learns what father does and how father balances a budget to take care of his family.

Zoo Babies. Coronet Films, 65 E. South Water Street, Chicago, Illinois 60601. This film explains the relationship of zoo babies to their animal parents. It answers such questions as, "Do all baby animals look like their parents? "How do they get their food?" and "How are they protected?"

CHAPTER FOURTEEN

Sex Education of the Second Grade Child

Second grade children are interested in the growth of all living things. They are curious about the origin of life, how new life grows and develops, and how new life is reproduced. Their interest focuses on life itself, not necessarily on reproduction in sexual terms. The second grade teacher's main objective is to give the children an overview of the origin and development of the living things in their surroundings. The two units that follow are designed to accomplish that end.

SEED EXPERIMENT

An Overview of Unit One

Second grade children are interested in exploring and manipulating the environment on their own. The second grade unit, "The Seed Experiment," allows the children to study the growth and development of different seeds through their own experiments. Art projects and nature walks are added to allow the children to express creativity in their learning. The basic concept to be developed in this unit is that life comes from the same kind of life. Children also learn that "the bringing about of the birth" of a new plant of the same kind is called reproduction. This unit is a deliberate effort to present the groundwork for the study of human and animal reproduction.

LIVING THINGS THAT COME FROM EGGS

An Overview of Unit Two

Upon completion of the seed experiment the children will have developed their first basic concepts of fertilization and will be ready to proceed to a more complex study of reproduction. The unit, "Living Things That Come from Eggs," provides a stepping stone from reproduction in animals to reproduction in humans. The teacher uses classroom demonstrations to explain animal reproduction. The following concepts are developed: (1) Different kinds of eggs grow into different kinds of animals. (2) Living things need only parents to make them. (3) All babies are made by joining a sperm and an egg. (4) Eggs must be fertilized before they can grow. (5) Mammal eggs grow in the mother's uterus. The unit capitalizes on the safety of the uterus as a nest for the growth of an egg. The children have a corner in the classroom with the nests of different animals to show the contrast. Thus, reproduction in higher animals is distinguished from reproduction in the lower animals.

UNIT ONE: THE SEED EXPERIMENT

What is a seed?

Here is a seed. (Show the children a seed.)

A seed is a little plant.

A seed is a little plant that has not yet started to grow.

A seed will grow, though.

We want to find some seeds and watch them grow.

Before we go looking for seeds let's look at some of the seeds we have here on our seed chart.

The seed story

Let's read the seed story on the seed chart together.

The following poem should be reprinted in large letters on a chart Beside each line should be a picture of a seed to show as an example. Also have each of the following seeds to pass around to the children for them to see.

Seeds are funny things.

Some have stickers; (cottonwood seeds)

Some have wings; (maple seed)

Some are big; (peach seed)

Some are small; (flower seed)

Some are round and flat; (lima bean)

Some are like a ball; (acorn seed)

Some are hidden inside of fruits; (orange seed)

Some are in pods; (sweetpeas)

Some are in roots under the ground; (radish)

Some seeds are food and good to eat; (pumpkin seed)

Corn and beans and fruit for a treat.[1]

Seeds are everywhere

Seeds are everywhere!

Have the following poem printed on a chart and read it with the children.[2]

Some little seeds have parachutes
To carry them around.
The winds blow them
Swish, swish, swish
Then gently lays them on the ground.

Finding seeds

Arrange for the class to go on a nature walk. If you cannot arrange for the walk, ask the children to take a walk with their mothers or fathers to look for seeds.

We are going on a walk to look for seeds that lie on the ground.

If we look carefully, we will find many, many seeds outdoors.

There are many seeds indoors too; ask your mother to help you find some seeds in her kitchen and bring them to school.

Tomorrow we will plant the seeds that we find.

What kinds of seeds do we have?

Allow the children to show the seeds they have brought. Ask them what kind of seed they have. If they don't know, tell them. If you don't know, tell the child that you will try to find out what kind of seed it is for him. Give the child one of your seeds so that he will know what kind of seed he has. Every child must know the name of the seed he plants.

We have many, many kinds of seeds.

Each one of our seeds will grow into the kind of plant it came from.

If we know the kind of plant the seed came from, we will always know what the seed will grow into.

Here is a bean seed; the bean seed will grow into a bean plant.

Here is a grapefruit seed; the grapefruit seed will grow into a grapefruit plant.

---

[1] From Mary Jackson Ellis and Mayon Atherton, *The First Grade Log*, T. S. Denison and Company, Minneapolis, 1962, vol. I.

[2] From Mary Jackson Ellis, Pearl Esko, and Robert Kane, *The First Grade Log*, T. S. Denison and Company, Minneapolis, 1962, vol. II.

Activities to develop the concept that life comes from the same kind of life

FIGURE 85

Play a game. Each child will stand and say "I have a _____ seed. What will grow from my _____ seed?" The class will guess.

Before we plant our seeds we are going to draw a picture of the kind of plant that it will grow into.

I have a grapefruit seed; I am going to draw a picture of a grapefruit. (See Figure 85.)

After we finish our pictures we are going to tape the picture to a stick and put the stick in the soil by our seed.

Then we will know for sure what kind of plant is growing.

Pass out paper to the class for their drawings. The paper should be about 4 by 4 inches. Use popsicle or pushup sticks or pencils to support the pictures.

Now we are ready to plant our seeds.[3]

Make a hole with your finger in the soil of your (eggshell, tin can, old cup, flowerpot).

Put your seed into the hole and cover it with soil.

Sprinkle the soil with water and put the seed in the sunlight.

The sun will shine down into the soil and the water will soak into the seeds; the seeds will grow.

Plan for a "caring" period each day. The children will water their seeds and watch for their growth. Wait until the plants have sprouted through the soil before going on.

Seeds grow into the kind of plant they came from

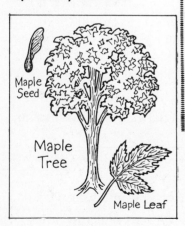

FIGURE 86

We planted many, many kinds of seeds.

Each of our seeds grew into the kind of plant it came from.

Let's make a bulletin board to show what we have learned about seeds.

On the top of our bulletin board we will print, "Every seed grows into the kind of plant it came from."

There are so many different kinds of seeds that each of us will have a job to do.

Decide how much room you will have on your bulletin board for posters. Divide the class into that number of groups. Each group mounts a seed in the upper left-hand corner of their poster. They print the name of the seed under the mounting. In the middle of the poster paper they draw the plant the seed comes from, e.g., grapefruit, lemon, maple tree. In the lower right-hand corner they mount one of the leaves from the plant. They will print the name of the plant under the leaf. (See Figure 86.)

[3] Adapted from Millicent Selsam, *Seeds and More Seeds*, Harper and Row, Publishers, New York, 1959.

Where do seeds come from?

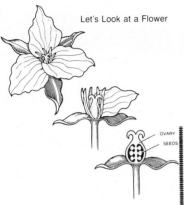

Let's Look at a Flower

FIGURE 87

We know that every seed grows into the kind of plant it came from, but where is the seed when it is inside the plant?

Let's see if we can find out where seeds come from.

You will need a flower and a magnifying glass for this teaching activity. (The teacher can use Figure 87 on the overhead projector also.)

Let's look at a flower.

In the flower, just above the point where the flowers join the stem, there is a special place called the *ovary*.

If you want to see the ovary you can pull the petals off the flower.

The ovary is the green thing in the center of the flower.

Inside the ovary are tiny little *eggs*.

If you want to see the eggs you can pull apart the ovary very carefully.

Eggs grow into seeds

The eggs grow until they become seeds.[4]

Then they stop growing; before they can start growing again they must be placed in the ground.

Sometimes we speak of the ground as mother earth.

The earth is the great mother in the body of which seeds begin to grow to be plants—flowers, vegetables, trees and grain.

Reproduction

This bringing about of the birth of a new plant of the same kind is called reproduction.

When a mother plant dies she leaves new seeds.

These seeds grow into more plants.

How lucky we are to have seeds!

Review activity

Have each child plant a flower seed in a flowerpot for his mother. The children can fingerpaint the flowerpots. Then have each one write a story to his mother about the flower. Have the class work together on the story. You can help them by printing the story on the blackboard. You will want the story to include these concepts:

1. The seed comes from the ovary of the plant.

2. The seed assures us that there will be more of the same kind of plants.

3. The seed will grow to be a plant in the ground.

Preparing for the next unit

The explanations the children have for the story will indicate to you whether they are ready for the next unit on eggs, where they come from, and where they grow.

---

4 From Karl DeSchweinitz, *Growing Up*, The Macmillan Company, New York, 1947.

UNIT TWO: LIVING THINGS THAT COME FROM EGGS

LESSON 1

Many, many eggs

As the teacher introduces the lesson she holds up pictures of a variety of eggs.

> Eggs, eggs, eggs! White eggs, speckled eggs, tremendous eggs, tiny eggs. Eggs with hard shells and with soft coverings.

Same kind of life

> How different they are from each other. And no wonder! Because different kinds of eggs grow into different kinds of animals.[5]

Life comes from life

You see, life begins in the same way for all these living things. (Show pictures of plant, fish, turtle, frog, bird, dog, cat, human baby).

All these living things began life as an egg—a very tiny egg at that!

Bulletin board suggestion

Have your class make different kinds of eggs from colored paper or clay. You might allow the children to color some hard-boiled eggs. Put your egg display beneath a bulletin board on a table. Title the bulletin board "Living Things That Come from Eggs." Have the children draw living creatures that come from eggs to put on the board.

An egg copies

Have you ever copied anything? A picture? A poem? Some words? (Allow for responses.)

Everywhere around us we see things that are copies.

Sometimes it takes many, many people to make a copy of something.

Many needed to copy nonliving things

Many people and machines are needed to copy nonliving things. (Show pictures of car, truck, house, school.)

Complicated nonliving things are sometimes made in factories. (Have a picture of an assembly line in a factory.)

Stop here for a discussion of the many things made in factories. You might want to have a picture of an automobile factory and a model of a toy car. You can discuss the many complicated parts of a car. Then discuss the number of men and machines that are needed to make cars.

---

[5] From Millicent Selsam, *All About Eggs*, William R. Scott, Inc., New York, 1952.

Many, many people are needed to copy a complicated nonliving thing.

A car is not living; many men and machines are needed to make a car.

A truck is not living; many men and machines are needed to make a truck.

A house is not living; many men and machines work together to make a house.

Turtles, cats, dogs, ponies, kittens are living; they have many complicated parts. Who makes them?

Parents needed to copy living things

Living things only need parents to make them; parents make everything that is necessary for new life to begin.

Father and mother bear make everything that is necessary to make baby bear.

Father and mother cat make everything that is necessary to make baby kitten.

Father and mother dog make everything that is necessary to make baby puppy.

Parent factories

Parents have factories in their bodies to make what is necessary to have a baby that is just like them.

(Using a felt board or a blackboard make two column headings "Mother" and "Father.")

The egg factory

The mother has a factory within her body that makes eggs. (Put the word "eggs" under the Mother heading.)

You might have already guessed the name of the egg factory; it is called . . . the ovary.

Put the word "ovary" under the Mother column.

The sperm factory

The father has a factory within his body that makes seeds. (Put the word "seeds" under the Father heading.)

The father's factory for making seeds is called the testes. (Put the word "testes" under the Father heading. Have the children repeat the word.)

The father's seeds are called sperms. (Put the word "sperms" under the Father heading in place of the word "seeds." Have the children repeat the word "sperm.")

Two important factories

Now we know the names of the two important factories in parents.

1. What is the mother's factory called? *The ovary* (point to the word on the board).

2. What is the father's factory called? *The testes* (point to the word on the board).

All necessary parts are made

We also know that these factories make two parts that are necessary to make a baby.

1. What does the mother's ovary make? (*Eggs.*)

2. What does the father's testes make? (*Sperms.*)

Factory parts must be put together

Now we can ask, how is a baby made?

First, let us see how other factories make things.

In a car factory there are many parts—windows, doors, seats. Can anyone think of any more parts?

A car is made

All these parts are put together and we have a car. (Allow children to help put a toy car model together.)

A book is made

Let us suppose we are in a book factory. What parts do you suppose we'd find there? Pages, cover, pictures. (Have these materials available plus tape and glue.)

Who can make a book from these parts? (Allow children to construct the book from the parts.)

We would put the pages and pictures together, and we'd have a book.

Now we know how a car and a book are made:

1. To make a car we put together all the necessary parts that are made in a car factory.

2. To make a book we put together all the necessary parts that are made in a book factory.

A baby is made

How do you suppose we make a baby?

A baby is made the same way that a book, a car, a doll, and a toy are made; all the necessary parts are put together.

Only two parts

One thing is different though: the only parts that are necessary to make a baby are the egg from the mother and the sperm from the father.

The egg and the sperm join

All babies are made by joining an egg and a sperm.

When an egg from a mother bear and a sperm from a father bear come together, a baby bear is made.

What is made when an egg from a mother cat joins a sperm from a father cat? (*Kitten.*)

What is made when an egg from a mother duck joins a sperm from a father duck? (*Duckling.*)

How is a puppy made? An egg from a mother dog joins with a sperm from a father dog.

Now we know how all living things are made: a sperm joins with an egg.

When you make the following statement, write the words "sperm" and "egg" on the board and then join them to show fertilization. It will look like this:

Fertilization

When a sperm joins an egg, we say that the egg has been fertilized.

This is just another way of saying that all the necessary parts are together and that the baby can now start to grow.

Review questions

Review: This is a good place to end the lesson to review the concepts before going on. Use the review questions and suggestions below.

1. Does life begin the same way for all living things?

2. How do all living things begin life?

3. What will a frog egg grow into?

4. What will a fish egg grow into?

5. Who makes a car?

6. Who makes a truck?

7. Who makes living things?

8. Who makes a puppy?

9. Who makes a kitty?

10. What kind of factory does a mother have in her body?

11. What is the name of the mother's egg factory?

12. What kind of factory does a father have in his body?

13. What do we call the father's sperm factory?

14. How is a car made?

15. How is a book made?

16. How are all babies made?

17. How is a baby bear made?

18. How is a baby fish made?

19. What do we call the egg when the sperm joins together with it?

20. What do we mean when we say the egg is fertilized?

Mailman game

Give each of the children a card with one of the words below written on it. Tell the children not to show anyone their cards. Have each of the words below printed on another set of cards. Place the cards in a line across the chalk tray. Choose a postman. Each child will come up to ask the postman if he has any mail for him. Instead of asking for mail with his name on it he will ask for the word printed on his own card. The postman must find the card the other child asks for. If he can find the right card he remains the postman. If not, the other child becomes the postman. Keep playing the game until every child has had a chance to ask for a word. Also, make sure that several children have a chance to be the postman. The words to use for the cards:

testes	living
sperm	father
seeds	mother
eggs	ovary
parents	fertilization

LESSON 2

Sperm joins egg

We learned yesterday that a sperm must be joined with an egg in order for a baby to begin.

All living things begin new life in this way.

Sperm and egg join in different ways

But for different living things the sperm from the father meets the egg from the mother in different ways.

The way the sperm and egg meet determines where the fertilized egg will grow into new life.

Fish eggs

Sometimes the sperm from the father and the eggs from the mother meet in the water; this is where the eggs of most fish have their homes or nests.

Let's see how the father's sperm and the mother's eggs meet.

Demonstration guidelines

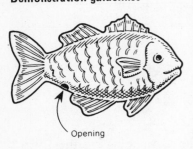

Opening

FIGURE 88

As you explain the lesson outlined below on fish fertilization to the children, you should demonstrate. For your demonstration you will need a fishbowl with sand and rocks in the bottom. You will also need two clay models of fish. When you are modeling the clay fish, make a small opening under the mother fish's body and a small opening under the father fish's tail. (See Figure 88.) Allow your models to harden so that they can be placed in water. Model some very tiny eggs and fill the hole of the mother fish with them. Mold some very tiny sperm and fill the father fish with them. Use different colors of clay for the egg and the sperm so the children can tell the difference between them. You will want to mold the eggs and sperm just prior to the demonstration so that they are soft and pliable. When you are finished cover the holes with invisible scotch tape to keep the eggs and sperm inside the fish. Now you are ready to demonstrate.

(As you present the lesson, begin by demonstrating how fish make nests for their eggs. For this you will need a fishbowl, water, sand, and rocks. To make the nest, place sand in the bottom of the fishbowl. Cover half of the sand with rocks. Fill the fishbowl with water.)

When the nest is complete, you can put the mother fish over the nest; pull the tape off the opening and the mother's eggs will fall in the nest. The mother fish swims away. Now put the father over the nest; pull off the tape and the sperms will fall over the eggs. With your fingers join the sperms and the eggs (illustrating fertilization).

Point out to the children that the fish have left their eggs. Now put models of other sea creatures into the fishbowl. Allow them to attack the eggs, allowing only a few to survive. This illustrates the idea that many fish eggs must be laid to insure the birth of a few new fish because of the low level of protection afforded them.

Mother fish has ovaries

The mother fish is like all other mothers; she has an egg factory in her body.

In fact, the mother fish has two egg factories.

You might have already guessed the name of the mother fish's egg factories. They are called ovaries.

A nest for the fish eggs

She has many eggs in each ovary waiting to be laid; before she lays them, a nest is made.

Sometimes the father fish digs a nest for these eggs on the bottom of the pond.

Scoop, scoop, scoop. He scoops up the sand with his tail.

Sometimes the mother fish cleans off a rock or a stone for the nest.

Brush, brush, brush. Mother fish clears a space on a rock or stone for her eggs.

Mother fish's task

Mother fish releases her eggs into the nest through an opening under her body.

Her job is complete; the eggs are in a nest ready to be met by the sperms.

The eggs must be met by the father's sperms so that they will be fertilized.

When eggs are fertilized they can grow.

Father fish's task

As soon as mother fish has laid her eggs, father fish gets ready for his half of the job.

Father fish swims over to the nest. He pours his sperms out through an opening under his body near his tail.

His sperms cover the eggs.

Fertilization

When one of the sperms joins one of the eggs, the egg is fertilized.

A fertilized egg can grow into a baby fish.

You might think that many, many new fish babies would begin to grow since there were so many sperms and eggs.

Actually, very few new fish babies develop.

An unsafe nest

You see, the eggs that are fertilized (met by sperm) are not in a very safe nest.

There is not much protection for the eggs while they are growing in the nest in the water.

The hungry enemies

Many fish and other animals who are very hungry are swimming around looking for something to eat.

They see the eggs. Gobble, gobble, gobble. They are a tasty meal.

Poor fish eggs—some of them never get to grow up to be fish.

The water is not a very safe nest for eggs to grow in.

Frog's eggs

The eggs of most frogs have their homes in the water too.

Let's see how the frog's sperms and eggs meet.

Mother frogs have ovaries

We remember that all mothers have ovaries. Mother frogs have ovaries too.

She has many, many eggs in her ovaries. Here is the way she releases the eggs.

An unusual meeting

Father frog sits on mother frog's back.

He presses his large thumbs against the mother frog's sides. (Figure 89.)

This causes several thousand—that is many, many eggs!—to come out of mother frog.

As the eggs come out of mother frog, father frog pours his sperms over them.

FIGURE 89

Fertilization

If one of father frog's sperms reaches and enters one of mother frog's eggs, the egg will be fertilized and begin to grow.

But where will the eggs begin to grow into a frog? Father and mother frog didn't make a nest for the eggs.

Eggs without a nest

The fertilized eggs have no nest to grow in. They just float around in the water. (See Figure 90.)

Some of them grab onto weeds or twigs in the water and grow there. Others begin to grow as they float in the water.

We know that many, many frog eggs begin to grow. Do you think many of the frog eggs grow into frogs?

You are right. Frog eggs aren't any luckier than fish eggs.

FIGURE 90

The hungry enemy

Many fish and other animals who are very hungry are swimming around looking for something to eat.

They see the frog eggs. Gobble, gobble, gobble. They are a tasty meal.

Poor frog eggs—some of them never get to grow up to be frogs.

The vicious sea

The water is not a very safe nest for many kinds of eggs to grow in.

ACTIVITIES FOR REVIEW

Bulletin board

Allow children to make a bulletin board with the caption, "The Sea Is a Dangerous Home for Eggs." Cover the bulletin board with blue paper. Select different children to make the following out of construction paper: mother fish, father fish, eggs, sperms, rock nests, sand nests, and hungry enemies. Place these on the bulletin board. Pin light blue plastic over the bulletin board.

Shoe box nest

The nest and its safety is the theme used in this lesson and in the lessons to come. You will want to have an ongoing activity in the classroom where the children can draw conclusions and make comparisons. Shoe box nests for each lesson will suffice to keep this ongoing project.

Have the children make a display of the sea and the nest for the fish eggs in a shoe box. Choose a corner in the room for the display. As the following lessons are presented, other shoe box displays are put in the corner.

LESSON 3

Demonstration guidelines

The following lesson is presented as the teacher demonstrates. You will need a bird's nest, a clay model of a mother bird, a clay model of a father bird, clay sperms and eggs, and a straw 1 inch long.

In this lesson it is difficult to show the clay birds actually mating, but you can show the children where the openings in the mother's and father's bodies are. You also will be able to show the tube in the mother bird that leads to the outside of the body. When you are modeling the mother bird, make her opening round enough and long enough so that you can slip the straw into the hole. Also make sure that you make the mother bird's eggs small enough to pass through the straw.

After you have told the children how the sperm meets the egg, you can pull the straw out of the mother bird and show it to the children. You can show them the fertilized egg passing down the tube.

A new nest

Birds and chickens grow from eggs like the fish and the plants but instead of growing in the water or in the ground, they grow in a nest.[6]

Mother hen makes a special nest

The mother hen makes a special nest for her eggs. She gathers straw from the farmyard.

The mother hen then goes looking for little chips of wood and twigs.

She gathers the straw, the wood chips, and the twigs and piles them in a safe place.

The mother hen goes about building a nest.

Twist, turn. Twist, turn. She uses her beak to weave all the pieces together.

The nest is done

At last the nest is done; the mother hen is ready to lay her eggs.

Father rooster is close at hand; he knows that the nest is finished.

He begins to make circles around the hen; it's a strange sight!

Squawk! Squawk! Squawk! Father rooster makes a lot of noise.

Finally father rooster jumps on mother hen's back.

He presses his tail feathers very close to the mother hen's tail feathers.

Two important openings

He presses very closely at one spot; this is the spot where the father rooster has a very small hole in his body.

The hen has a very small hole by her tail feathers too.

---

[6] DeSchweinitz, *op. cit.*

The father rooster tries to get his tiny hole right next to the tiny hole in the mother hen.

Father's sperms pour into the mother's body

When the father rooster gets the two holes next to each other, he sends his sperms from a place inside his body through his tiny hole into the hen's tiny hole and to a place inside her body.

The mother hen's tiny hole leads to a place where she keeps her eggs.

The sperms from the father rooster meet the eggs.

Joining of the sperm and the egg

When one of father rooster's sperms gets inside one of the mother hen's eggs, the egg is fertilized.

The beginning of a chick

The fertilized egg can begin to grow into a baby chick.

A shell for protection

A hard shell forms over the egg. Lucky egg! The shell will help to keep the egg safe.

After the hard shell covers the egg, the mother hen lays the egg.

The egg journey

The egg goes from the place where eggs are stored in the hen down a little tube which looks like a straw, and drops into the nest. (Use models to demonstrate.)

A safe nest

The nest is a safe place for the egg to grow; the baby chick grows inside the egg.

The mother hen helps the egg grow by sitting on it to keep it warm.

The baby chick keeps growing, growing, growing.

A chick is born

One day the baby chick is ready to be born. The baby chick breaks the shell with his beak.

The baby chick is born.

Lucky chick eggs—most of them get to grow up to be chickens.

They are much safer in their nest than the fish eggs or the frog eggs.

FIGURE 91

ACTIVITY FOR REVIEW

Rather than having a committee make a shoe box nest for the display, each child will make a bird's nest this time. You can have them bring twigs and straw and mud to work with. If you

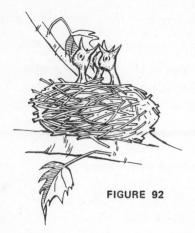

FIGURE 92

have clay available, you can have them model a bird and eggs. If not, the children can use construction paper to do this. As they are working on their nests you can mingle among the children, asking them questions individually to make sure that they have understood the lesson. When their shoe box displays are done, you can put the following poem on the board. The children can copy it. Then they can take their shoebox nests and poem home to their parents.

What Robin Told
by
George Cooper[7]

How do robins build their nests?
   Robin Redbreast told me—
First a wisp of yellow hay
In a pretty round they lay;
Then some shreds of downy floss,
Feathers too, and bits of moss.
Woven with a sweet, sweet song;
This way, that way, and across;
   That's what Robin told me.

Where do robins hide their nests?
   Robin Redbreast told me—
Up among the leaves so deep,
Where the sunbeams rarely creep.
Long before the winds are cold,
Long before the leaves are gold,
Bright eyed stars will peep and see
Baby robins—one, two, three;
   That's what Robin told me.

LESSON 4

Many kinds of eggs

So many different kinds of eggs. Eggs in water, eggs in the sand, rough eggs, smooth eggs, big eggs, and little.

Then outside of the mother's body they break open their shells or coverings; and out come . . . frogs . . . chickens . . . baby robins.

The case of the missing eggs

Other animals have babies too. But you never see their eggs at all. Where are they?[8]

The dog, the elephant, the mouse, and the four-legged animals grow from eggs but they do not grow in the ground or in the water.

They grow up in the nest but the nest is not in the trees or bushes or in the grass.[9]

Let's see if we can find the nest where dog eggs change into puppies.

---

[7] From Wilma McFarland, *For a Child,* Westminster Press, Philadelphia, 1947.
[8] Selsam, *op. cit.*
[9] DeSchweinitz, *op. cit.*

Demonstration guidelines

Male Dog   Female Dog

FIGURE 93   **FIGURE 94**

For the following lesson use pictures of male and female dogs for demonstration. As you present the lesson, point out the different anatomical features. The picture of the male dog should clearly show the penis. The picture of the female dog should clearly show the vaginal opening.

Eggs in the ovary	We know where the mother dog keeps her eggs, don't we? Who can tell us? . . . (*The mother dog keeps her eggs in the ovary.*)
A tube passageway	If we could see inside the mother dog, we would find a tiny tube leaving the ovary.
	The mother dog's eggs are waiting in the tiny tube for the father dog's sperms.
Mother dog's important openings	The mother dog has an opening outside her body that leads inside her body to where she stores her eggs.
	This opening is right by mother's tail. It is called the vagina. (Have the children repeat the word. Point to the vaginal opening of the female dog in the picture.)
Vagina leads to eggs	This opening called the vagina is where the father dog's sperms can get inside mother dog to meet with her eggs.
	Do you remember where the father dog's sperms are made? . . . (*The sperms are made in father dog's testes.*)
A long journey	The father dog's sperms have a long trip to make to meet the mother dog's eggs.
The fingerlike penis helps	The father dog has a special part of his body called the penis to help his sperms make this trip.
	You may have seen the penis of a father dog.
	The penis looks like a large finger. It is between the father dog's hind legs. (Point to the penis of the father dog on the drawing.)
	When father dog wants his sperms to enter the mother dog, he climbs upon her back.
Mating	He puts his penis into mother dog's opening (vagina) and sends many, many, many sperms into her body. This is called mating.
	The sperms have little tails; sperms beat their tails back and forth so they can swim.

The beginning of a puppy

The sperms swim to meet the mother dog's eggs. When one of father dog's sperms enters into one of mother dog's eggs, the egg is fertilized.

A nest inside the mother

FIGURE 95

But instead of the fertilized egg's dropping out of mother dog's body into a soft nest as a mother bird's eggs do, the egg begins growing in a nest inside the mother.

(Show the picture of the puppy growing in the uterus of the mother dog.)

The nest inside the mother dog is a warm, safe place for the egg to grow in. It looks something like a small sac.

It is called the uterus. (Have the children repeat.)

The uterus is the nest where the fertilized egg grows to be a puppy.

When the egg has grown into a puppy, the puppy leaves the mother through an opening by her tail. (*Vagina.*)

A puppy is born

The puppy is born. Puppies are lucky!

The safest nest of all

What better place could there be in which to grow? The eggs which fish lay in nests under the water can be washed away and hurt by storms, and sometimes bird's eggs are broken by being blown out of nests.[10]

But nothing like this can happen to an egg that grows up to be a baby inside its mother's uterus.

Here are some pictures of other babies growing inside the uterus of their mother. (Show the pictures of the other baby animals growing in the uterus. Use the animal flashcards at the end of this unit.)

Review

FIGURE 96

Show the children the picture of the baby calf growing in the cow's uterus. Use Figure 96 with the overhead projector. Have the children work as a class on a story to tell what has happened.

After the children have finished their story they can draw a baby calf beside its mother. The children can read the following poem together.

The New Baby Calf
by
Edith Newlin[11]

Buttercup, the cow, had a new baby calf,
   a fine baby calf,
      a strong baby calf,
Not strong like his mother
But strong for a calf
For this baby calf was so new!

---

10 DeSchweinitz, *op. cit.*
11 From May Hill Arbuthnot, *Time for Poetry*, Scott, Foresman and Company, Glenview, Illinois, 1959.

Buttercup licked him with her strong warm tongue,
Buttercup washed him with her strong warm
    tongue,
Buttercup brushed him with her strong warm
    tongue.
And the new baby calf liked that.

The new baby calf took a very little walk,
        a tiny little walk,
            a teeny little walk,
But his long legs wobbled
When he took a little walk,
And the new baby calf fell down.
Buttercup told him with a low soft 'Moo-oo!'
That he was doing very well for one so very new
And she talked very gently, as mother cows do
And the new baby calf liked that!

The new baby calf took another little walk
        a little longer walk,
            a little stronger walk,
He walked around his mother and he found the
    place to drink
And the new baby calf liked that!

Buttercup told him with another low moo
That drinking milk from mother was a fine
    thing to do.
That she had lots of milk for him and for
    the farmer too.
And the new baby calf liked that!

The new baby calf drank milk every day,
His legs grew so strong that he could run and
    play,
He learned to eat grass and then grain and hay,
And the big baby calf grew fat!

LESSON 5

Many nests

We have seen how the eggs of different animals are fertilized and grow into baby animals. (While you are reviewing, show pictures of the following eggs and their nests. You can also have the children refer to their shoe box displays.)

Fish nest

The eggs of the fish are fertilized in the water and grow into baby fish in nests of sand or rocks.

Frog nest

The eggs of frogs are fertilized in the water and grow into baby frogs while they hang on twigs in the water.

Bird nest

The eggs of birds are fertilized inside the mother bird and then laid into a nest of twigs and mud to grow into baby birds.

Dog nest

The eggs of dogs are fertilized inside the mother and grow into puppies in a little sac inside the mother called the uterus.

Horse nest

The eggs of horses are fertilized inside the mother and grow into foals in a little sac inside the mother called the uterus.

Cow nest

The eggs of cows are fertilized inside the mother and grow into calves in a little sac inside the mother called the uterus.

Human nest

Human eggs are fertilized and grow in the same way that dogs', horses', and cows' eggs do.

Demonstration guidelines

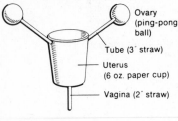

FIGURE 97

As you explain the lesson on human fertilization outlined below, demonstrate. (See Figure 97.) This will make the lesson more meaningful to the child. The following materials are needed: two ping-pong balls, one 6 ounce paper Dixie cup, one 3 inch straw, two 4 inch straws, and a pea. Assemble the demonstration kit as pictured in the left-hand margin. Attach the demonstration model to a manila outline of a woman. As you progress through the following lesson, use your demonstration model to explain fertilization to children.

Human egg factory

Human eggs are made in the egg factory where all mothers make their eggs; do you remember where eggs are made in the mother? (*Ovary.*)

Yes, the eggs are made in the ovary. The ovary looks like a ping-pong ball. (Show the children the demonstration model and use the model for the remainder of the lesson.)

There are two ovaries inside every mother. In one of these ovaries a very, very tiny egg forms. (Use the pea.)

This egg moves from the ovary (ping-pong ball) into a little tube (straw).

The egg moves slowly through the tube waiting for the father's sperm to meet it.

Human sperm factory

Do you remember where sperms are made in the father? (*In the testes.*)

Demonstration guidelines

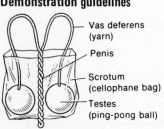

FIGURE 98

As you explain the parts of the male use a demonstration model to make the lesson more meaningful. You will need rope or knitted yarn, two ping-pong balls and a very small bag. Place a ping-pong ball on each side of the small bag. Attach the demonstration model to a manila outline of a man.

Yes, the sperms are made in the father's testes. The testes are in a sac between the father's legs. (Show the children the demonstration model.)

Human mating

When a mother and a father who love each other decide to have a baby, the father must send his sperm inside the mother to meet the egg.

The father has a penis (coiled yarn or rope) to help his sperms get inside the mother.

Father puts his penis (coiled yarn or rope) inside an opening between mother's legs called the vagina (straw). The father's sperms swim out of the penis into the vagina.

Fertilization

The sperm swims, swims, and swims to meet the egg; when a sperm meets an egg the egg is fertilized.

Now all the necessary parts are joined together for a human baby to grow.

Human nest

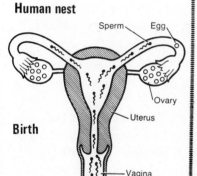

The fertilized egg moves all the way through the tube and drops into a nest inside the mother.

Do you know the name of the nest inside the human mother where the egg grows to be a baby? (*Uterus.*)

The fertilized egg grows and grows inside the uterus until the baby is ready to be born.

Birth

When the baby is ready to be born, it passes out of the uterus and through the vagina.

The baby is born. The nest inside a human mother is the safest nest of all.

FIGURE 99

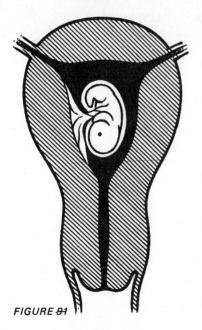

FIGURE 91

FIGURE 100

ACTIVITIES FOR REVIEW

Review of the lesson

The children need to review this lesson individually in order to grasp all concepts as well as the anatomy presented. Set up five stations. At each station have the following materials:

> two ping-pong balls
> one 6 ounce paper Dixie cup
> one 3 inch straw
> two 4 inch straws
> one pea
> an outline drawing of a woman
> one small bag
> yarn or rope
> two ping-pong balls
> an outline drawing of a man

Have the children work together to assemble the man and the woman. This activity will aid in reviewing the location of the important sex organs.

Then ask a child from each station to show the class the man and woman his group has assembled and to explain fertilization.

Animal nest game

To review "the living things that come from eggs" that the children have learned, play the animal nest flashcard game using the pictures of mother animals and of fertilized eggs growing into baby animals. (Figs. 101, 102, 103, 104). Cut out each of these animals separately and glue them to cardboard flashcards. Place all the flashcards with animal mothers on them together. Place all the flashcards with fertilized eggs growing into babies together. Have the children match them properly. As they match the mother with the fertilized egg, ask them which father animal fertilized the egg and where the egg will grow into a baby animal.

Example:

> Flashcard? *Mother cow.*
> Who fertilized the egg? *Father cow.*
> Where is the nest for the egg to grow? *Inside the mother.*

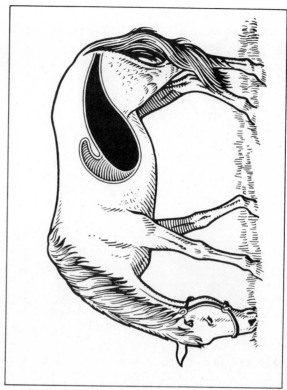

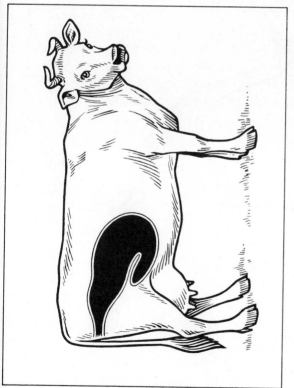

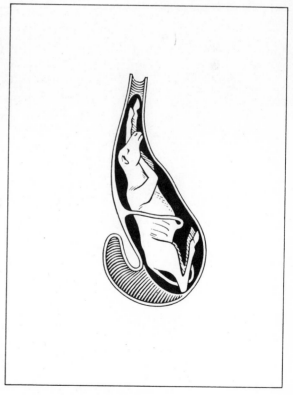

FIGURE 101

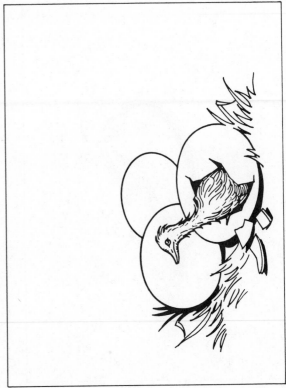

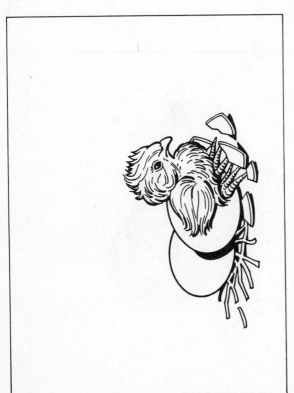

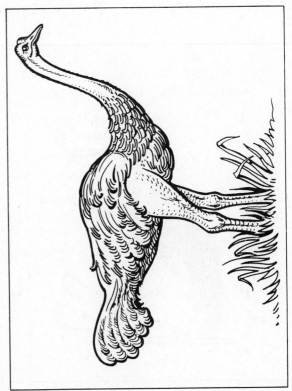

FIGURE 102

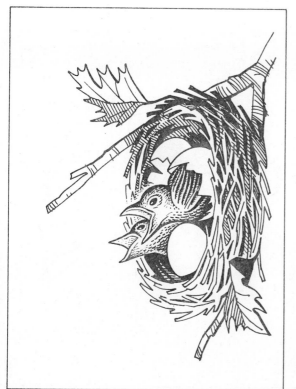

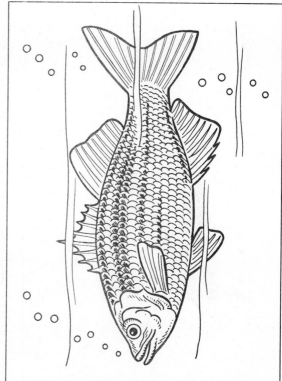

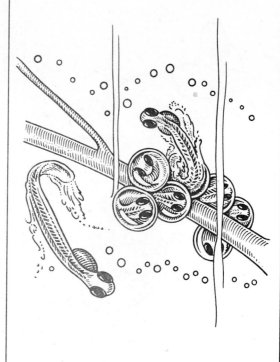

FIGURE 103

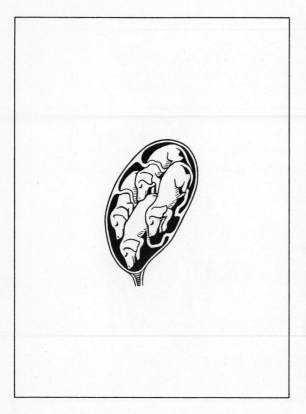

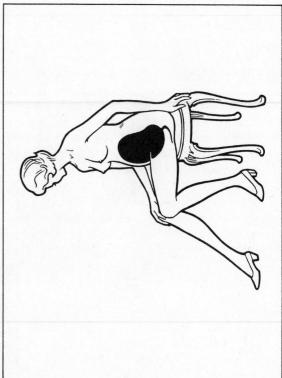

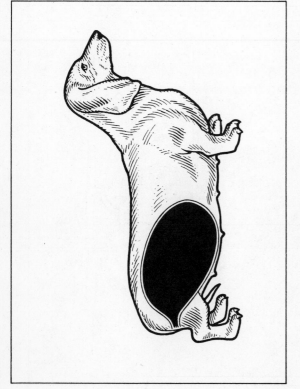

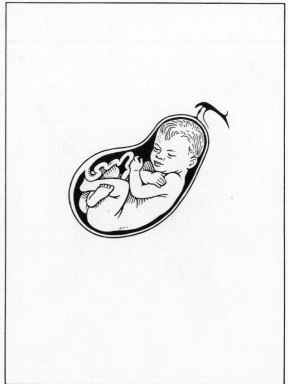

FIGURE 104

SUGGESTED BIBLIOGRAPHY FOR THE SECOND GRADE

Blough, Glenn O., *Who Lives in This House?* New York: McGraw-Hill Book Co., 1957.
    A story of animal families and how they build nests for their eggs. Can be used before explaining that the human egg grows inside the mother rather than inside a nest.
Darby, Gene, *What Is a Turtle?* Chicago: Benetic Press, 1960.
    Explains where baby turtles come from—eggs. Very clear explanation of the mother's laying eggs and leaving. May be used when the different ways animals have their families are discussed.
DeSchweinitz, Karl, *Growing Up*. New York: The Macmillan Co., 1967.
    Good analogies are drawn among fish, animals, and humans as to how they begin. The book is a good preface to human reproduction.
Gruenberg, Sidonie M., *The Wonderful Story of How You Were Born*. New York: Doubleday & Co., Inc., 1970.
    A well illustrated story told by a grandmother about the beginning of life. Begins with an animal and plant analogy and ends with human reproduction.
Jordan, Helen J., *How a Seed Grows*. New York: Thomas Y. Crowell Co., 1960.
    By explaining a simple experiment the book illustrates the growth of seeds. The children could do the experiment after hearing the story, and the class could discuss the results.
Mandel, Elias, and Meilach, Donna, *A Doctor Talks to 5 to 8 Year Olds*. Chicago: Budlong Press, 1967.
    A simple expectation of life for children. It is well illustrated and intended to be shared by parent and child.
May, Julian, *Living Things and Their Young*. Chicago: Follett, 1969.
    Describes different methods of reproduction and development of family life from the lower animals to human animals.
Podendorf, Illa, *The True Book of Plant Experiments*. Chicago: Children's Press, 1960.
    An interesting book of facts that David learns from doing plant experiments. The children can listen to the story and then repeat David's experiments. The experiments demonstrate the growth of a seed.
Schwartz, Elizabeth, and Schwartz, Charles, *When Animals Are Babies*. New York: Holiday House, Inc., 1964.
    This picture book develops the concept that all animals have mothers and fathers, but that not all of them live as family units.
Selsam, Millicent E., *All About Eggs*. New York: William R. Scott, Inc., 1952.
    A story about how eggs change into animals. The story tells about the growth of eggs of the lower animals in the water or nests. It contrasts this with the growth of higher animals and humans in the body.
Selsam, Millicent E., *Seeds and More Seeds*. New York: Harper & Row, Publishers, 1959.
    A story about a little boy who grows different kinds of seeds. Illustrates the concept that life comes from the same kind of life.
Showers, Paul, and Showers, Kay S., *Before You Were A Baby*. New York: Thomas Y. Crowell Co., 1968.
    Explains the story of reproduction in a family setting. Well illustrated.

SUGGESTED FILMS FOR THE SECOND GRADE

A Child is Born. Warren Schloat Productions, Inc., Pleasantville, New York 10570.
    A basic explanation of human reproduction.
All Kinds of Babies. Carousel Films, Inc., 1501 Broadway, Suite 1503, New York 10036.

Explains that all life comes from eggs. Contrasts the care needed by different babies, emphasizing the helplessness of human babies who must be cared for and loved.

Fertilization and Birth. E. C. Brown Trust, Henk Newenhouse, Inc., 1826 Willow Road, Northfield, Illinois 60093.

This film is an excellent summary for the unit, "Living Things That Come from Eggs." This film shows fertilization in fish, dogs, sheep, horses, and human beings. The meeting of the sperm and the egg is depicted as well as the growth of the egg. For each female animal, the egg and the embryo are located. Anatomical locations in the male are also presented. The child should have a clear idea of testicles, penis, and vagina after seeing the movie.

How Babies Are Made. Creative Scope, Inc., 1 E. 42nd Street, New York 10017.

Thirty four slides beginning with the story of reproduction in flowers and animals and developing into the basic story of human reproduction.

How Flowers Make Seeds. Coronet Films, 65 E. South Water Street, Chicago, Illinois 60601.

An excellent film to illustrate the parts of a flower that function in the production of seeds. This film can be used when the concept of "ovary" is introduced in the seed experiment unit.

Human and Animal Beginnings. E. C. Brown Trust, Henk Newenhouse, Inc., 1826 Willow Road, Northfield, Illinois 60093.

A film depicting how life begins for all kinds of babies (duck, fish, rabbit, human). Shows where the eggs come from and where they grow into baby animals. Relates the importance of planning for a human baby, since human beings need to stay with their babies for a long time as they grow up.

It Takes A Lot of Growing. Carousel Films, Inc., 1501 Broadway, Suite 1503, New York 10036.

The feelings and roles of a family unit and the changing responsibilities from childhood to adulthood.

Kitten: Birth and Growth. Bailey Films, Inc., 6509 DeLongpre Avenue, Hollywood, California 90028.

Two small children have a cat named Millie that is shown giving birth to four kittens. The kittens are nursed, crawl, play, and are weaned in the film. The film is an introduction to birth and growth designed to facilitate discussion of the birth process and motherhood.

Let's Watch Plants Grow. Coronet Films, 65 E. South Water Street, Chicago, Illinois 60601.

This film can be used with the unit on seed experiments. It shows a class planting seeds and watching for the growth of the seeds. The care that the seeds need to grow properly is illustrated. The film should be shown before the children plant their seeds so that they will know how to take care of them.

Living and Nonliving Things. Coronet Films, 65 E. South Water Street, Chicago, Illinois 60601.

After your class discusses the differences between living and nonliving things, you might show this movie in which Tony learns five basic differences. You can compare the differences Tony learns with the list of differences the class has made.

Seeds Grow Into Plants. Coronet Films, 65 E. South Water Street, Chicago, Illinois 60601.

Children will learn the conditions necessary for seed growth from this film. They will also learn how seeds travel, how the embryo plant develops inside a bean seed, and how the seed grows into a small plant.

CHAPTER FIFTEEN

Sex Education of the Third Grade Child

The third grade child is fascinated with his environment and may spend days, often weeks, in examining and exploring his interests in detail. These interests, coupled with his newly formed interest in his interactions with others, provide the third grade teacher with a favorable setting for the development of concepts of sex education. The objectives of the third grade teacher are to explore in depth the development of new life and to assist the third grade child in developing and evaluating his interpersonal relationships. In view of this, two units have been planned: (1) Growth of a Chick and (2) Friendship.

GROWTH OF A CHICK

An Overview of Unit One

The teacher who plans carefully can develop a unit that encompasses many areas of the curriculum. Reading, writing, art, and mathematics may be carefully woven into the daily curriculum to study the growth of a chick. The teacher can capitalize on this integrated approach, allowing ample time to spend on a 21 day classroom project. The classroom suspense and curiosity in the breeding of baby chicks will afford the third grade teacher numerous opportunities to explain fertilization and embryonic development—appropriate third grade concepts.

FRIENDSHIP

An Overview of Unit Two

A child develops successful interpersonal relationships from his experiences in a variety of situations, including those experiences with his family, with his friends, and within the classroom. The third grade unit on friendship recognizes the experiences that can be deliberately planned by the third grade teacher to enhance pupil interaction. Children learn that they must make a concentrated effort to develop qualities and activities that will enhance their interactions with others. They also explore their own abilities and evaluate their success in being a friend to themselves. This unit develops the following attitudes, values, and concepts: (1) an appreciation for the enjoyment one receives from a solitary activity, (2) a desire to choose activities he can perform to improve himself, (3) a respect for the solitary activities of one's friends, and (4) a desire to form stable, long-lasting friendships.

UNIT ONE: GROWTH OF A CHICK

TEACHER ORIENTATION

Introduction to the teacher

The following unit on the fertilization of a hen's egg and its growth to a chicken provides a valuable background for the child on growth and reproduction. The children will be better able to grasp the life concepts involved if their attention is kept by allowing them maximum involvement. For this purpose this unit is organized into several activities that cover a time-span of a short lesson each day for four weeks. A calendar accompanies this unit to allow the teacher to effectively plan the necessary activities.

Purchase of fertilized eggs

The teacher should arrange ahead of time to purchase fertilized eggs for the classroom experiment. Plan to have them delivered to your classroom on a Wednesday morning.

Constructing a homemade incubator

Construct a homemade incubator for the fertilized eggs. You will need a tub filled with straw, a thermometer, and an infrared light. Place the infrared light beside the fertilized egg or eggs to keep them warm. The thermometer should also be placed beside the eggs so that one can easily see whether the temperature in the tub is being maintained at 100° F.

Classroom activity: a diary of events

The lessons that follow are coordinated with the 21 day incubation period of the chick egg. The objective of the lesson is for the child to understand how the egg became fertilized and how the egg grew into a chick. In order to have the child grasp the scope of this project he should keep a diary for this 21 day period. The contents of the diary are outlined day by day for the teacher (weekends are not included); see the accompanying "Calendar of Events: Birth of a Chick."

A CALENDAR OF EVENTS: BIRTH OF A CHICK

MONDAY	TUESDAY	WEDNESDAY	THURSDAY	FRIDAY	SATURDAY	SUNDAY
		1 Day 1 diary, eggs in incubator	**2** Day 2 diary, review	**3** Day 3 diary	**4**	**5**
6 Day 6 diary, candling the eggs	**7** Day 7 diary	**8** Library reading, film study, bulletin board	**9** Library reading, film study, bulletin board	**10** Library reading, film study, bulletin board	**11**	**12**
13 Day 13 diary	**14** Homemade brooder, feed trough, chick waterer	**15** Homemade brooder, feed trough, chick waterer	**16** Day 16 diary	**17** Poems for diary	**18**	**19**
20 Day 20 diary	**21** Birth diary, naming and caring announcements	**22** Review				

DAY 1: INTRODUCTION TO GROWTH AND REPRODUCTION

Demonstration preparation

Place fertilized eggs in an incubator in the classroom. Make sure that you choose an area that is visible to as many of the children as possible.

Introduction to classroom project

Class, we are going to have a special project for the next 21 days. We are going to watch this egg grow into a chick.

You have probably seen eggs that look like this one before. You may have eaten them for breakfast or used them to bake a cake.

But those eggs are not the same as the eggs we have here.

Two kinds of eggs

Although both kinds of eggs were laid by a mother hen, there is still a very important difference.

Grocery store eggs

The eggs you buy at a grocery store have not been joined by the father's sperm cells.

No sperm—no chicks

That is why you cannot hatch a chick from an egg that you eat for breakfast or an egg you use to bake a cake.

New life—an egg, a sperm

We know that for new life to begin to grow, an egg cell from the mother must be joined with a sperm cell from the father.

The mother

The Chicken's Egg-laying System

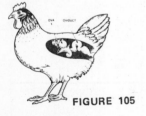

FIGURE 105

Here is a picture of the mother hen. (Show Figure 105 on an overhead projector.) Look at the opening under her tail feathers.

You will see a long tube inside the mother hen. This tube is called the oviduct.

The long oviduct

The oviduct is a long tube inside the mother hen that leads to the mother hen's ova or eggs.

An egg in the oviduct

Almost every day in a mother hen's life one of her eggs gathers a lot of food around it and enters the oviduct.

Gathering food for the trip

The food that an egg gathers around it is a yellow color. It is called yolk.

The yolk of an egg

Have you ever seen the yolk of an egg? (Crack an egg and show the children the yolk.)

---

[1] Figures 105 and 106 adapted from Louis Darling, *Chickens and How to Raise Them*, William Morrow & Co., Inc., New York, 1955.

Germspot—a cloudy spot

See the little white cloudy spot on the egg yolk? This is called the germspot.

A special place for sperm

The germspot is a special place on the yolk for a sperm cell.

If no sperm cell from the father rooster is in the germspot, no chick can grow.

The egg will be laid by the mother hen. You will use it to bake a cake or to eat for breakfast.

But we already know that! Let's find out how an egg grows into a chick.

Father rooster's sperm

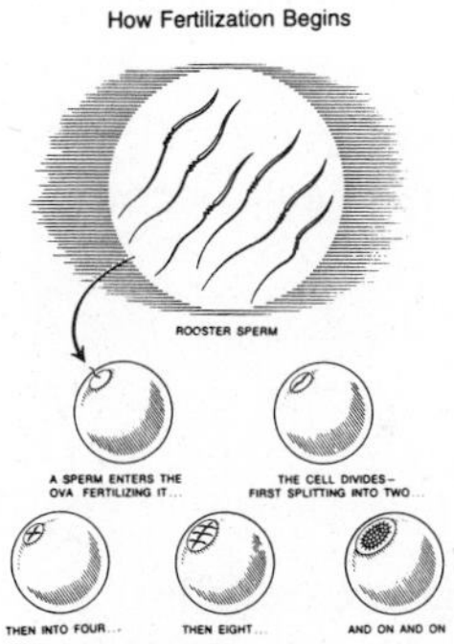

How Fertilization Begins

ROOSTER SPERM

A SPERM ENTERS THE OVA FERTILIZING IT ...   THE CELL DIVIDES— FIRST SPLITTING INTO TWO ...

THEN INTO FOUR ...   THEN EIGHT ...   AND ON AND ON

FIGURE 106

Here is a picture of some sperms from a father rooster. (Show Figure 106 on an overhead projector.) Sperms are made inside the father rooster.

The father rooster wants his sperms to get inside the mother hen so her egg will grow into a chick and will not be a breakfast egg.

Beneath the tail feathers

Father rooster has a hole beneath his tail feathers too.

He makes a lot of squawking noises and circles around mother hen to get her attention.

The two openings meet

The father rooster then presses the opening beneath his tail feathers against the opening beneath the mother hen's tail feathers.

Father rooster sends sperm into the hen

When the two openings are touching, the father rooster sends many, many sperms into the mother hen.

Sperms swim toward egg

The sperms are now in the oviduct. They will swim toward the egg.

One of the sperms will meet with the egg. Do you remember where the sperm will meet the egg? (*The germspot.*)

Germspot starts to grow

Now the germspot on the egg can start growing into a chick.

A nest for the egg

The hen makes a very comfortable nest for the egg to grow into a chick. The nest is made of straw and twigs.

When the nest is done, the mother hen will lay the egg. It will pass down the oviduct and come out of the hole beneath the hen's tail feathers.

Egg white surrounds the egg

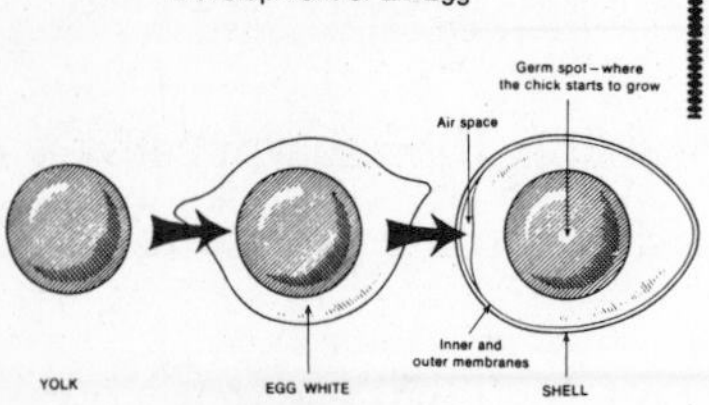

Development of an Egg

Germ spot — where the chick starts to grow

Air space

Inner and outer membranes

YOLK   EGG WHITE   SHELL

FIGURE 107

As the egg comes down the oviduct, it is surrounded by egg white. You have probably seen the white of an egg. (Use Figure 107 on an overhead projector.)

Two sacs and a shell

Then two sacs form a cover around the egg. At last a hard shell covers the egg.

A well protected egg

The egg is well protected when it comes out of the hole beneath the mother hen's tail feathers and is laid into the nest.

21 days of growing

The egg will have a lot of growing to do before it can become a chick. It will grow for 21 days.

Calendar activity

Have each of the children make a calendar. They can decorate their calendars by drawing a chick at the top.

Class activity: a diary of events

Explain to the children that the class is going to carefully observe the growth of the chick. Each student is going to keep a record of happenings in a diary called "Egg to Chick."

Give each child materials to make a diary: leather and yarn for a cover, construction paper for inserts. Have them design a cover carefully.

Diary of events: day 1 contents

For the first day in the diary have the children draw a picture of the mother hen showing her oviduct and some eggs. Then have the children draw a picture of the sperms, which come from the father rooster. Last, in the classroom, have the children draw a picture of the nest that has the egg in it.

Lesson for day 1

A magic change begins in the egg when it is kept warm. Most of the time an egg is kept warm by the mother hen.

The mother hen sits on the eggs to keep them warm. Our eggs are warm too.

A warm substitute

Classroom Incubator

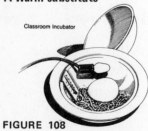

FIGURE 108

We are keeping our eggs in an incubator. An incubator is a warm nest that is a substitute for the mother hen.

We don't need the mother hen to keep our eggs warm because they are in the incubator.

The germspot grows

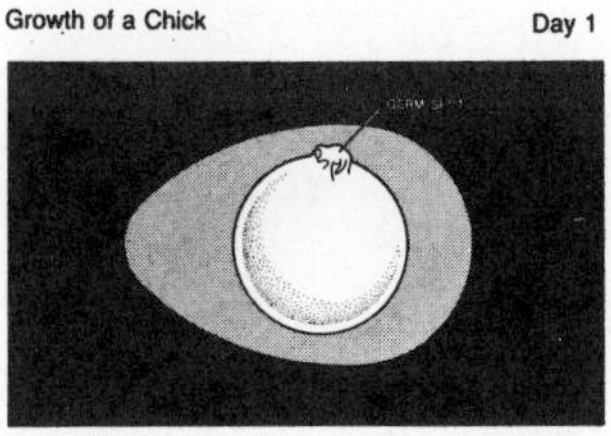

Growth of a Chick   Day 1

FIGURE 109

When the eggs are kept warm, the germspot starts to grow. It will take the form of a baby chick in a day or two. (Use Figure 109.)

Recording the events in the diary

Have the children make a page for their diary numbered "day 1." The diary recording should include:

1. An explanation of how an egg is fertilized.
2. An explanation of the protective coatings the egg gathers.
3. An explanation of how an egg is laid.
4. An explanation of the beginning of growth in the egg.

LESSON FOR DAY 2

Reviewing the lesson for day 1

List the following sentences on the board. Have the children put these sentences in the right order.

1. The rooster sends his sperm into the hen.
2. The egg is kept warm.
3. The egg begins to grow into a chick.
4. The hen makes an egg.
5. A yolk covers the egg.
6. A shell covers the egg.
7. The hen lays the egg.
8. White covers the yolk of the egg.

Lesson for day 2

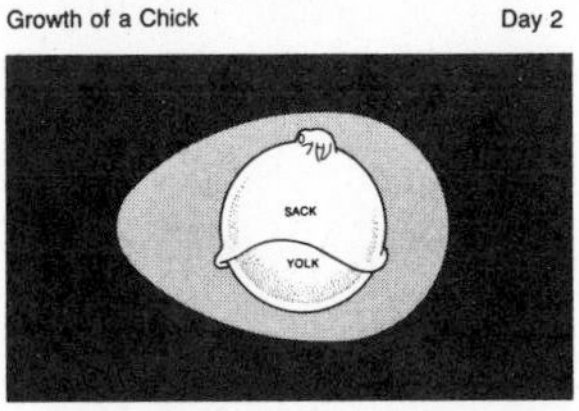

Growth of a Chick   Day 2

FIGURE 110

Let's learn what is happening in our egg today. (Put Figure 110 of the sac forming around the yolk on the overhead projector.)

When the egg has been growing for two days, a sac-like skin grows around the yolk.

This sac is attached to the stomach of the chick. This is how the chick gets its food.

Recording the events in the diary

Have the children make a page for their diary numbered "day 2." The diary recording should include:

1. An explanation of the formation of a sac-like structure.
2. An illustration of the diagram projected for the class.

LESSON FOR DAY 3

Calendar activity

Have the children subtract today's date from the date that the chickens will hatch to find out how many days remain.

Lesson for day 3

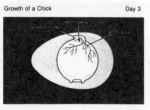

Growth of a Chick   Day 3

FIGURE 111

Who can tell the class how many days the chick has been growing in the egg? (*Three days.*)

Let's take a look to see how our chick is coming along. (Show overhead Figure 111 for day 3.)

Now that the egg has been growing for three days, we can notice many changes.

Sac surrounds the yolk

Look at the sac we talked about yesterday. The sac completely surrounds the yolk today.

Red tubes bring food

Look at all the red tubes that are going from the yolk to the chick. Do you know what these red tubes are? You have them in your body. (*Blood vessels.*)

Yes, they are blood vessels. The blood vessels carry blood with food from the yolk to the growing chick.

We said that the yolk and the white were going to help the egg grow into a chick. Do you know how?

The yolk and the white are the food the growing chick is using.

The chick needs a lot of food. It's beginning to take shape and look more like a chick.

Embryo—chick takes shape

We call the chick an embryo when it begins to take shape.

Look carefully at the chick embryo, and you will see that a head is starting to form.

The end of three days

At the end of three days the chick has a head, it has many blood vessels, and it has a heart.

Recording the events in the diary

Have the children make a page for their diary numbered "day 3." The diary recording should include:

1. A picture of the embryo after three days.

2. A description of the embryo after three days.

LESSON FOR DAY 6

Calendar activity

Have the children subtract today's date from the date that the chickens will hatch to find out how many days remain.

Lesson for day 6

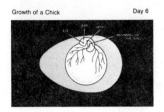

Growth of a Chick   Day 6

FIGURE 112

Now our egg has been growing for six days. It needs more and more food.

That is why there are so many more blood vessels. These extra blood vessels covering the yolk are bringing more food to the growing chick. (Show Figure 112 for day 6 on the overhead projector.)

The chick has grown a great deal. What can we see now?

1. A wing.

2. An ear.

3. The heart.

4. An eye.

Candling the egg[2]

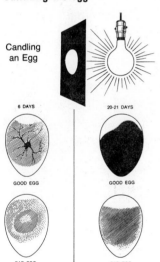

Candling an Egg

6 DAYS   20-21 DAYS

GOOD EGG   GOOD EGG

BAD EGG   BAD EGG

FIGURE 113

On the sixth day your class should examine the egg or eggs to see whether the chicks are developing. The process for examining the chick is called "candling." (Use Figure 113 in the overhead projector.)

> To see what is going on inside the egg, candle it. Cut an oval hole a little smaller than the egg in a piece of black paper or carboard. Hold the cardboard over a strong light. Place the egg in the hole. You will find that you can see the shape of the growing chick quite well.
>
> There will be a small dark spot in the center of the egg with a network of fine lines radiating from it. The dark spot is the beginning of a chick, and the lines in the network are blood vessels, which are bringing food from the yolk to it so that it can grow. If the egg is not good, there will be no definite lines or shapes in it, and it should be thrown away. When you are candling eggs, do not keep them away from the hen too long or let them become chilled.[2]

Recording the events in the diary

Have the children make a page for their diary numbered "day 6." The diary recording should include:

1. A picture of the embryo after six days.

2. A description of the embryo after six days.

3. An explanation of candling.

---

[2] From Louis Darling, *Chickens and How to Raise Them,* William Morrow & Co., Inc., New York, 1955.

LESSON FOR DAY 7

Lesson for day 7

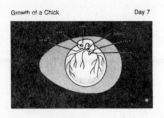

Growth of a Chick   Day 7

FIGURE 114

The embryo has been growing for one week now. At last it has begun to take the shape of a baby bird.

If we look closely at the chick embryo (show Figure 114 for day 7 on the overhead projector), we can see that it has all its body parts.

Name the parts of the chick that you see:

1. Tail	4. Ear
2. Beak	5. Eye
3. Wings	6. Feet

Recording the events in the diary

Have the children make a page for their diary numbered "day 7." The diary recording should include:

1. A picture of the embryo after seven days.

2. A description of the embryo after seven days.

Calendar activity

Have the children subtract today's date from the date that the chickens will hatch to find out how many days remain.

LESSONS FOR DAYS 8, 9, and 10

Teacher orientation

During the next three day period the children will be exposed to outside materials and activities related to their project. Below are some suggested activities. Perhaps your students will have some additional ideas of their own.

Library reading

Assemble a collection of library books for the children to read. There are many books available on eggs and chickens for this purpose. These books are listed in the Suggested Bibliography for the Third Grade. In addition to books on eggs and chickens, gather books on the development of eggs in other animals. Allow the children to read during class.

Film study

Perhaps you would like to show one of the many films listed under Suggested Films for the Third Grade. This serves as a useful review for the children.

Bulletin board

Have the children plan a bulletin board for the classroom. Allow the children to decide what they would like to have on this bulletin board. Have the class decide how they are going to divide the responsibilities so that each child will have a job to do.

Recording the events in the diary

Have the children make pages in their diary numbered "day 8," "day 9," and "day 10." The children will have participated in different learning experiences on these three days. They should record in their diary what they have learned from the outside material they consulted.

LESSON FOR DAY 13

Lesson for day 13

Growth of a Chick   Day 13

FIGURE 115

After 13 days have passed the unborn chick is quite well formed. (Show Figure 115, the 13 day old embryo, on the overhead projector.)

The chick has been growing and growing and using up its supply of food.

The growing chick embryo has used almost all the white of the egg.

Some of the white still remains. It is still enclosed in a sac connected to the stomach of the chick.

This yolk will be used by the chick in the final growing days. Let's find out how many growing days are left.

Calendar activity

Have the children subtract today's date from the date that the chickens will hatch to find out how many days remain.

Recording the events in the diary

Have the children make a page for their diary numbered "day 13." The diary recording should include:

1. An illustration of the embryo after 13 days.

2. A description of the food that remains after this 13 day growing period.

LESSONS FOR DAYS 14 AND 15: PREPARATION FOR THE BIRTH OF THE CHICKENS

Teacher orientation

Young chicks are hard to raise and require a great deal of care. Explain to the children that the class will need to prepare for the birth of the chickens. The class should prepare a comfortable home for the chicks to replace the nest. (See Figure 116.[3])

---

[3] Figures 117, 118, and 119 and accompanying text adapted from Darling, *op. cit.*

A Brooder for Chicks

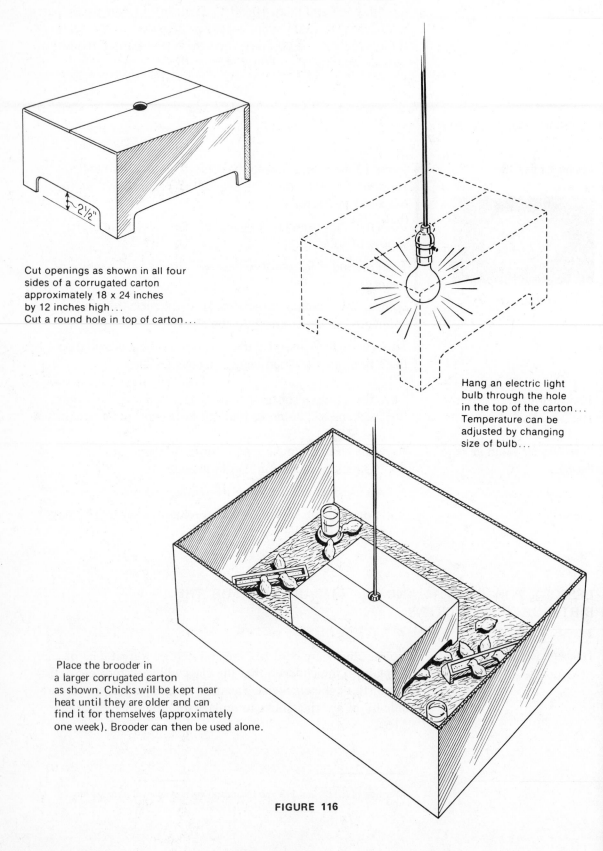

Cut openings as shown in all four
sides of a corrugated carton
approximately 18 x 24 inches
by 12 inches high...
Cut a round hole in top of carton...

Hang an electric light
bulb through the hole
in the top of the carton...
Temperature can be
adjusted by changing
size of bulb...

Place the brooder in
a larger corrugated carton
as shown. Chicks will be kept near
heat until they are older and can
find it for themselves (approximately
one week). Brooder can then be used alone.

FIGURE 116

Homemade brooder

The younger chicks are hard to raise and require a great deal of care. They must be kept warm with artifical heat from 4-6 weeks. A heater for this purpose, called a brooder, can be made from two big cardboard boxes and an electric light. Infrared bulbs, which are especially good for brooders, can be bought at most hardware stores and from mail order houses. The bulb should be big enough to keep the temperature at about 90° F.[3]

A home for the chicks

The homemade brooder should be placed in a large crate with litter covering the floor. The litter can be bought at a feed store. Litter can also be made from dried grass, clippings, dry leaves, chopped hay, shavings, or sawdust. You will also want to place a chick waterer and feed trough in the crate. Below are diagrams showing how to make them. Allow the children to make them.

Chick Waterer

Cut hole in metal jar lid...

Attach short lengths of wood to lid as shown...

Chick Feed Trough

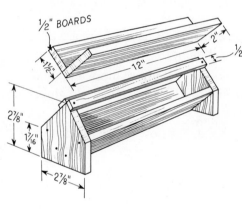

1/2" BOARDS

2"

1/2"

12"

1 1/2"

2 7/8"

1 7/16"

2 7/8"

FIGURE 117

Fill jar with water and screw on lid. Hold small pie pan or dish, upside down, against wood... Turn over quickly.

FIGURE 118

Purchasing feed for the chicks[4]

Many different kinds of feed are sold to persons planning to raise chickens. Feed is available at feed stores and at your local market. You will need two kinds of feed—scratch and mash.

Mash is a combination of cod liver oil; meat scraps; alfalfa; fish; and ground corn, wheat, and oats. Three types of mash

[4] Adapted from Louis Darling, *Chickens and How to Raise Them*, William Morrow & Co., Inc., New York, 1955.

can be purchased: starting, growing, and laying mash. Purchase starting mash for the chicks for the first five to six weeks; then switch to growing mash until they are four months old.

Scratch feed is a combination of corn, oats, and wheat. Intermediate size scratch is fed to the growing chicks.

In addition to mash and scratch feed, purchase some calcium and some grit. Calcium is used by the hen to make eggshells, and grit is used to help grind the food in their gizzards.

If you should need additional information on feeding the chicks, call a local feed store or veterinarian.

Recording the events in the diary

Have the children make pages for their diary numbered "day 14" and "day 15." The diary record should include a description of the preparations being made for the birth of the chicks.

LESSON FOR DAY 16

Calendar activity

Have the children subtract today's date from the date that the chickens will hatch to find out how many days remain.

Lesson for day 16

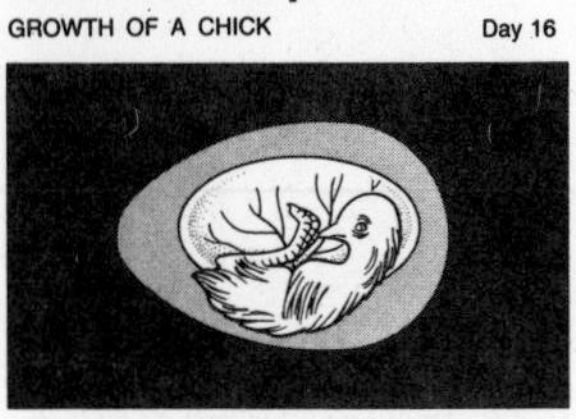

GROWTH OF A CHICK   Day 16

FIGURE 119

The chick embryo has been growing 16 days. There are only five more days before the egg hatches.

You can see that as the chick embryo grows, more and more of the yolk is used. (Show Figure 119, the 16 day old embryo, on the overhead projector.)

The chick has really taken shape. See how nicely his feathers are growing.

Recording the events in the diary

Have the children make a page in their diary numbered "day 16." The diary recording should include:

1. An illustration of the 16 day old embryo.

2. A description of the embryo after 16 days of growing.

LESSON FOR DAY 17

Poems for the diary

Have the children write stories and poems about chickens for their diaries. Some of these stories and poems can be placed on a bulletin board in the classroom.

LESSON FOR DAY 20

Calendar activity

Have the children subtract today's date from the date that the chickens will hatch to find out how many days remain.

Lesson for day 20

GROWTH OF A CHICK   Day 19

FIGURE 120

GROWTH OF A CHICK   Day 20

FIGURE 121

Only one day is left until our chicken will pop out of the egg to come out into the world.

The growing chick is making its last minute preparations. Do you remember when we said earlier that the special sac was so important for food?

Now the sac begins to pull the remaining yolk into the chick's stomach. (Show the illustration of the 20 day embryo; Figure 121)

This will fill up the chick's stomach so that the chick will have enough food in its stomach for two days after it is born.

The chick is starting to breathe now. Air comes through very small holes in the shell of the egg.

Recording the events in the diary

Have the children make a page in their diary numbered "day 20." The diary recording should include:

1. An illustration of the 20 day old embryo.
2. A description of the embryo after 20 days of growing.

LESSON FOR DAY 21: THE BIRTH OF THE CHICKS

Calendar activity

Have the children subtract today's date from the date that the chickens will hatch to find out how many days remain.

Lesson for day 21

The 21 days that the chick grows inside the shell are over. We have to keep a close watch on the nest now.

Birth of the chick

The first sign that the chick is ready to be hatched is a tapping sound coming from the egg.

The egg tooth

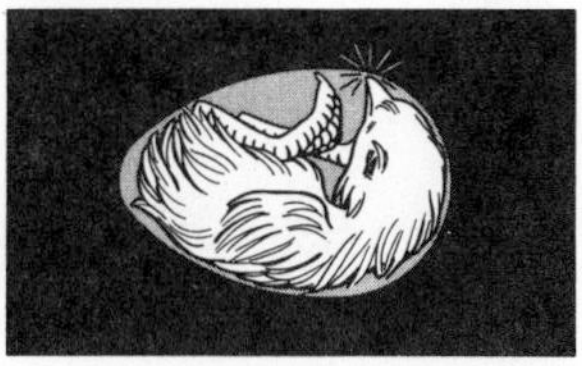

GROWTH OF A CHICK   Day 21

FIGURE 122

The little chicks have a tiny, hard point right on the end of the bill.

This tiny, hard point is called an egg tooth. The chick uses the egg tooth to tap against the shell.

Tap, tap, tap. The chicken pecks at the shell. (Show the illustration of the 21 day old chick breaking the shell; Figure 122.)

The chicken taps for a while and then rests a while. By tapping the inside of the eggshell the chick can break it.

Four hour birth

It takes about four hours for the chick to break the eggshell. Then at last the chick comes out of the egg slowly.

The chick is very weak from all its tapping. The chick is also very wet from being inside the egg.

After three hours the chick dries out and is a fluffy yellow chick, which needs a lot of care.

Keeping the chick warm

For the first week of its life a chick must be kept very warm. Usually the chicks stay under the mother hen just as you curl under your soft blanket on a cold night.

The warm brooder

We made a brooder for our chicks. The brooder is a warm place for the chicks to crawl into.

Mash is like cereal

The chicks will soon need food. Chicks eat mash. Mash looks like the cereal you eat for breakfast.

Chicks grow up

If we keep our chicks well fed and warm, they will grow up.

More roosters—more hens

Some of the chickens will grow up to be father roosters. Other chickens will grow up to be mother hens.

More chicks!

Then a father rooster and mother hen can get together and have more chicks.

Recording the events in the diary

Have the children make a page in their diaries called "The Chick's Birthday." The diary recording should include:

1. A description of the birth of the chick.
2. A drawing of the newborn chick.

Naming and caring for the chick

Have the class decide upon a name for the chick or chicks. Then have the class decide how they would like to divide the responsibility of caring for the chicks.

Announcing the chick's birth

Have the children make birth announcements, announcing the birth of the chicks and inviting the rest of the school to see the chicks. These can be sent to the principal, nurse, librarian, and other classrooms.

REVIEWING THE UNIT

Questions for review

1. How does all animal life begin?
2. Where does an egg come from?
3. What is the oviduct?
4. What is the name of the yellow food that gathers around the egg?
5. What is the germspot?

6. What is the difference between a breakfast egg and an egg that will grow into a chick?

7. How do the father rooster's sperms get into the mother hen?

8. What part of the egg starts to grow into a chick?

9. What protective coverings does the egg gather as it comes down the oviduct?

10. How long does it take for an egg to grow into a chick?

11. What are two ways of keeping the eggs warm?

12. When the egg has been growing for two days, what grows around the yolk?

13. Why does the chick have red tubes coming to him from the yolk?

14. What do we call a chick when he begins to take shape?

15. How do you candle an egg?

16. What happens to the yolk the day before a chicken is hatched?

17. How does the chicken get air to breathe before it is hatched?

18. What is the first sign that a chick is ready to hatch?

19. What part of the chick helps it to break the eggshell?

20. How long does it take the chick to break the eggshell?

21. What does the chick look like when it finally comes out of the eggshell?

22. How does a chick stay warm when it is first born?

23. What do baby chicks eat?

24. When the chicks grow up what will they be?

25. If there are more hens and more roosters there will be more _____.

UNIT TWO: FRIENDSHIP

Introduction

Let's pretend that all of you are coming to my house for dinner tonight. I don't know what to serve for dinner, so I'm going to make a list on the board of what you would like to eat.

My, we have a long list, don't we? If I serve all these different foods I can make each one of you happy.

Making others happy

When you make someone else happy, you are usually happy yourself. That is why it is so important to make others happy—both of you will benefit.

Let's make another list. This time we'll pretend that you are going to someone's house after school.

You may choose any play activity you want with your friend. What would you choose?

(List the activities on the board. Make a long list with many varieties of activities.)

Now let's review our list. We know that to make someone else happy we like to share play activities of his choosing.

I'll read down the list of activities, and you can mark down a point for yourself each time I name an activity you like to do and know how to do.

You can look at your number of marks and evaluate the number of interests you share with your classmates. How many of your classmates could you share something with?

One of the best ways to make new friends is to share common interests with them. Expressing a sincere interest in the activities of others lets them know that we would like to have them as our friends.

A "tasting" party

(Have each child bring to class the necessary equipment or toys he needs to demonstrate an activity he enjoys. Divide the class into groups, allowing each child to get a "taste" of some activities with which he is not already familiar.)

Solitary activities

We have learned many new activities to share with our friends. As we grow we will keep learning and improving ourselves until we have many interests and abilities.

Boys and girls who have many interests and abilities, numerous likes and few dislikes, will have many friends to choose from. They will certainly have many good times.

There are times, though, when friends aren't around. It's really important to know how to be a friend to yourself.

Stop and think of the last time you were alone. Did you find many interests to occupy your time?

Class discussion	(Discuss hobbies: What are they? What are different types of hobbies? Why are hobbies important? Have the children tell about their hobbies and plan new hobbies for the year.)
	We have been learning about the interests and activities of our friends. We learned that boys and girls who have many interests and abilities, numerous likes, and few dislikes will have many friends to choose from.
Personal friendship qualities	But interests and abilities are not the only characteristics of good friends. There are many personal characteristics that people have that make them better friends.
	I like a friend whom I can tell a secret to and my friend will never tell anyone else. What kind of a friend do you like?
Class discussion	(Have the children name as many personal characteristics involved in forming friendships as they can think of.)
	There is an old saying, "To have a friend you must be a friend."
	We have named many important qualities that good friends have. To be a good friend we must work very hard to have all the qualities we mentioned.
Class activity	Let's write a list of friendship qualities and keep it in our desk drawers. Each day before we go home from school we'll look at our list and ask ourselves how hard we are trying to be a friend to others.
	Of course you'll want to keep your list to yourself because it is very personal, but if you are working hard to be a good friend, others will certainly know it.

SUGGESTED BIBLIOGRAPHY FOR THE THIRD GRADE

Beim, Jerrold, and Beim, Lorraine, *Two Is a Team*. New York: Harcourt, Brace & Co., 1945.
Ted and Paul are the best of friends until they begin to build a coaster. Each wants his own way, so they part. Each builds his own coaster. After the coasters are finished, the boys have a race during which they have several expensive accidents. In order to pay for the damages, the boys decide to work together as a team.

Craig, M. Jean, *The New Boy on the Sidewalk*. New York: W. W. Norton & Co., Inc., 1967.
Joey meets a new boy on the sidewalk, and the two are highly jealous of each other. Instead of making friends, they are bitter enemies until two older boys begin to pick on them. Joey and the new boy jump to each other's defense and learn to share their possessions.

Darling, Louis, *Chickens and How To Raise Them*. New York: William Morrow & Co., Inc., 1955.

A good source book for the classroom that explains in detail how to raise chicks. Presents a good overview of the life cycle of the chick as well.

Estes, Eleanor, *The Hundred Dresses.* New York: Harcourt, Brace & Co., 1944.
Peggie and Maddie are best friends. Peggy continually teases Wanda, a poor girl in the class, about having only one dress. Wanda is so lonely and tired of ridicule that her family decides to move away. Maddie realizes that she should have encouraged Peggy to be a kinder person. Maddie decides that she is never going to stand by and say nothing again.

Hess, Lilo, *Easter in November.* New York: Thomas Y. Crowell Co., 1964.
On Gail's ninth birthday her father buys her a dozen chicks. The story tells how the mother hen, Brownie, cares for these chicks. The story also includes additional information on chickens that can be used to supplement the class project.

Kay, Helen, *A Summer to Share.* New York: Hastings House, Publishers, Inc., 1960.
Merry decides to stay home rather than go to a summer camp with her friend, Linda. Soon Merry begins to feel bored and lonely. Her parents arrange for a city girl to come to the country to spend the summer with Merry. Merry and her visitor, Susan, learn to appreciate each other's differences, dislikes and likes and become good friends.

Lexau, Joan, *Cathy is Company.* New York: The Dial Press, Inc., 1961.
Cathy is going to be away all night for the first time at her cousin Barbara's house. The two girls share a good time together. The book may be used by the third grade teacher to discuss being a guest and being a hostess to friends.

Lexau, Joan, *I Should Have Stayed in Bed.* New York: Harper & Row, Publishers, 1965.
Sam gets up on the wrong side of the bed, and everything goes wrong for him. He decides that he "should have stayed in bed." At the end of the day his best friend, Albert, stays after school with him. It doesn't look like such a bad day after all.

McCarthy, Agnes, *Room 10.* New York: Doubleday & Co., Inc., 1966.
Room 10 is a humorous novel about the classroom adventures of a third grade class. The story begins with the first day of school and ends as the children are promoted to the fourth grade. The children can discuss their own classroom and their interpersonal relationships in their classroom after reading this study.

O'Neil, Mary, *People I'd Like to Keep.* New York: Doubleday & Co., Inc., 1964.
A story about a child's thoughts and feelings about people in her everyday life—the teacher, the doctor, and the bakery man. Develops a sensitivity to, and awareness of, those we react with in our lives.

Randall, Blossom E., *Fun for Chris.* Chicago: Albert Whitman & Co., 1956.
Chris has learned to love and be kind to all persons, including his new friend, Toby, a Negro boy. Together they learn that sharing a friendship is more important than worrying about skin color. Another boy, Jimmy, doesn't want to play with Toby, but Chris and his mother help to show Jimmy how unimportant skin color is. The children also learn that skin color depends on the skin color of one's parents.

Schloat, Warren G., *The Wonderful Egg.* New York: Charles Scribner's Sons, 1952.
Warren and Andy visit an egg farm to learn about hens and the eggs they lay. The book includes the following subjects: "Eggs That Produce Chicks," "Eggs for You to Eat," "How to Cook Eggs."

Selsam, Millicent, *Egg to Chick.* International Publishers Co., Inc., 1964.
An excellent book for the children to read on the changes in the egg as it grows into a chicken. The book is well illustrated and a good supplement to the class project.

Watson, Nancy D., *Kathie's Chickens.* New York: Alfred A. Knopf, Inc., 1965.
Kathie has a fat brown mother hen and a big father rooster, which are expecting little chicks. The story explains how the hen cares for the eggs and how the eggs hatch into chicks.

SUGGESTED FILMS FOR THE THIRD GRADE

How Do You Know You Are Growing Up. Henk Newenhouse, Inc., 1826 Willow Road, Northfield, Illinois 60093.

Explains how children grow physically, emotionally, and mentally.

Developing Responsibility. Coronet Films, 65 E. South Water Street, Chicago, Illinois 60601.

This film stresses to children the idea that responsibility entails hard work, difficult decisions, and missing out on some fun, but that the rewards usually make up for these.

The Golden Rule, A Lesson for Beginners. Coronet Films, 65 E. South Water Street, Chicago, Illinois 60601.

The Golden Rule is taught to children as a basic standard for their behavior in daily living. Daily living situations are dramatized to show the children how the Golden Rule is applied.

Mother Hen's Family. Coronet Films, 65 E. South Water Street, Chicago, Illinois 60601.

Jerry and his father follow the process of the laying of eggs up to the hatching of chicks. To help children develop their understanding of the relationship between time and the growth of the chick, the incubation period of the eggs is followed on a calendar. An excellent movie to accompany study of the laying and hatching of eggs in the classroom.

People Are Different and Alike. Coronet Films, 65 E. South Water Street, Chicago, Illinois 60601.

People around us have many different visual traits—eyes, ears, height, and dress. At first, people appear to be very different, but beneath these differences people are alike in many ways—they all need friendship and love, food and a place to live, education, fun, and happiness.

CHAPTER SIXTEEN

Sex Education of the Fourth Grade Child

In the fourth grade the attention of the normally inquisitive and curious child is transferred from the living things around him to himself. Children in this age group are fascinated by the human body, its many parts, and their functions. The fourth grade teacher's main objective is to help the child learn more specific details about his body and about male and female roles in reproduction and heredity. Two units are suggested for fourth grade: (1) Where Babies Come From and (2) Heredity.

WHERE BABIES COME FROM

An Overview of Unit One

Fourth grade children vary immensely in their ability to grasp and retain new concepts. This often presents the fourth grade teacher with a problem in introducing a new unit. The authors have inserted the story, "Where Babies Come From," to alleviate the teacher's difficulty. The authors grant permission to the classroom teacher to reproduce this story and the pictures by mimeograph or Xerox for each student. The pictures accompanying the story are included in the atlas. Thus, an alternate method for having the class learn the material is for the teacher to read the story slowly, showing the illustrations at the appropriate time on the overhead projector. From the story the children learn at their own speed of mastery that: (1) the human body is made of many small parts called cells; (2) the cell is governed by DNA; (3) half of the DNA in each cell comes from the mother and half from the father; (4) all of the body's cells developed because of orders sent out by the DNA boss in the very first cell; (5) half of the first cell comes from the mother and half of the first cell comes from the father; (6) therefore, it takes both a mother and a father to have a baby; (7) to have a baby the father puts his penis inside the mother's vagina so that the sperm that carry his half of the DNA can get into the mother's body to look for the egg; and (8) unless a man and a woman really love each other they certainly will not be able to love and take care of children, and that is why you should get married before you try to have children of your own.

HEREDITY

An Overview of Unit Two

An effective teacher will organize learning in such a manner that new concepts will build upon concepts previously mastered. The unit, "Heredity," is developed as an expansion of the concepts mastered in "Where Babies Come From." The children are aided in their organized sequential learning situation by visible demonstration models of the hereditary process. Demonstration techniques are included for assistance in the mastery of the following subject matter: (1) the inheritance of chromosomes from the mother and the father; (2) the sex determination of a new baby; (3) the pairing of chromosomes and genes; and (4) the role of dominant and recessive genes in heredity. The teacher can use these visual aids for the lesson, for review, and for individual student interaction.

UNIT ONE: WHERE BABIES COME FROM

FOREWORD

Dear Boys and Girls:

We are writing this book to answer a question that you have frequently asked: Where do babies come from?

When you have finished reading the book, your parents or teacher will help you with any other questions that you might want to ask.

FIGURE 123

The human body is made up of many small parts called cells. The cells are like the bricks in a house: it takes many bricks to make a house and it takes many cells to make a boy or a girl.

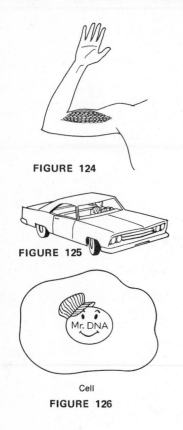

FIGURE 124

FIGURE 125

Cell
FIGURE 126

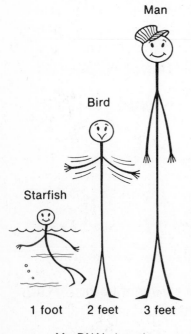

Man

Bird

Starfish

1 foot   2 feet   3 feet

Mr. DNA's length
FIGURE 127

Some of your cells make it possible for you to move; these are called muscle cells. Other cells produce tears to wash your eyes. Some cells help you to fight disease and to get well when you are sick. The cells that allow you to think are called brain cells. The food that you eat is taken to your muscles through tunnels that have walls made of cells. Thus, cells make up all parts of your body.

A car, like a person, is made of many parts. It has tires, an engine, windows, seats, and other parts. But a car needs a driver to make it go. The driver decides how fast it will go and in what direction it will move.

A train also has many parts but it needs an engineer to make it go. The engineer determines how fast and in what direction the train will move.

Each of the cells in your body has its own driver or engineer. His name is Mr. DNA. He is not a real man, just a long string of chemicals. But scientists refer to him as the boss of the cell, and we shall call him Mr. DNA.

Mr. DNA is a very bossy boss because he tells the rest of the cell just what to do and what not to do. But he is a good and wise boss that was passed on to you by your parents. Half of Mr. DNA in each of your cells came from your mother, and half came from your father. And the DNA in the cells of your mother and father came from your grandmothers and grand-fathers. So you see, Mr. DNA has been around for a long time and has a great deal of wisdom. His wisdom or knowledge fills up 46 books that are kept right inside the cell.

Most books are written by putting the letters of the alphabet together in different ways to make words. But Mr. DNA has a very short alphabet made up of only four letters. These letters are A, T, C, and G. Thus, Mr. DNA's books are hard to read. Some of the words look like this: Ta CG AT CG. Scientists haven't learned to read Mr. DNA's code yet, but they do know that the four letters in his alphabet stand for four chemicals. It is a very hard code to understand.

When scientists first saw Mr. DNA's books, they looked like tiny colored bodies. For lack of a better name, they were called colored bodies. But that was a long time ago, and the scientist of that day used the Greek language. So Mr. DNA's books were called chromosomes (kro'-mo-sohms), the Greek word for colored bodies. Today we know that they are like very tiny books that contain the knowledge that Mr. DNA needs to run his cell.

Mr. DNA is really a curled-up string of chemicals. If he were taken out of the cell and uncurled, he would be about 3 feet long. Mr. DNA in a cell of a starfish is about 1 foot long, and in the cell of a bird he is about 2 feet long.

There are many DNA bosses in your body: one in every single cell. They know when your body needs to grow, and when it should stop growing. They know when to make new cells, and when to replace old worn-out ones. And when new cells are made, the old Mr. DNA makes a new Mr. DNA for the new cell.

When you are born, your body is already made up of many cells, each with its own DNA boss. But all these cells developed because of orders sent out by the DNA boss in your very first cell.

Where do you think this first cell came from? Half of it came from your mother and half of it from your father. You see, it takes both a mother and a father to have a baby.

A mother has a place in her body where this first cell can grow and develop. This place is about the size of a pear and is called the uterus (yoo′ ter-rus). And as this first cell grows into many cells, the uterus gets bigger and bigger until it can hold a full size baby.

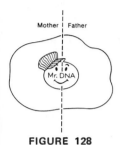

The mother's uterus is just below her navel (children sometimes call this the belly button). It is shaped like a bottle except that the bottle is turned upside down so that it opens like a tunnel between the mother's legs. When you were born, you came out through this tunnel, which is called the vagina (vuh-jy′-nuh).

The uterus, then, is the place where the first cell starts to grow and develop. And we know that half of the first cell comes from the mother and half from the father. But how do the two halves get together in the uterus?

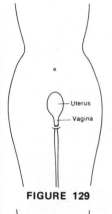

FIGURE 129

Fortunately, the uterus has three tunnels leading into it. The tunnel that goes down to open between the mother's legs we already know as the vagina. And at the top of the uterus there are two more tunnels that connect with two egg factories. These factories are called ovaries (o′-va-ries). Each month an egg leaves the factory and goes down one of the tunnels toward the uterus. But eggs are only one half of the DNA boss. They must combine with another half from the father before a new baby can start to grow.

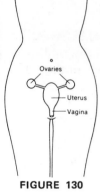

FIGURE 130

The father also has a factory to make his half of the first DNA boss. This factory is found in a small sack just behind his penis (pe′nis). When the mother and father decide to have a baby, the father puts his penis in the mother's vagina tunnel so that his half of Mr. DNA can get inside the mother's body. In just a few minutes, the father's DNA halves are swimming up the vagina to the uterus. These halves from the father are called sperms.

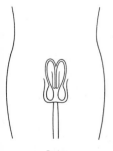

Penis
FIGURE 131

The sperms swim through the uterus and up to the tubes that lead to the egg factories. If an egg that has recently left the egg factory happens to meet one of the father's sperm, the two halves of the DNA boss zip themselves together, and you have the first complete DNA boss. He now takes control and makes all future decisions about growth and development. He decides how tall you will be, what color your eyes will be, and even what size shoes you will wear. All this information is contained in Mr. DNA's library books or chromosomes.

Perhaps you have wondered why some babies are born girls and some boys. As you might expect, the answer is in Mr. DNA's 46 books. First, we should point out that 23 books come from the father and 23 books come from the mother. Thus, when the two halves of Mr. DNA are zipped together, he has a full new library of 46 books or, as scientists would say, 46 chromosomes. But not all new libraries are the same: Some contain the knowledge needed to form a boy, and others contain the knowledge needed to form a girl.

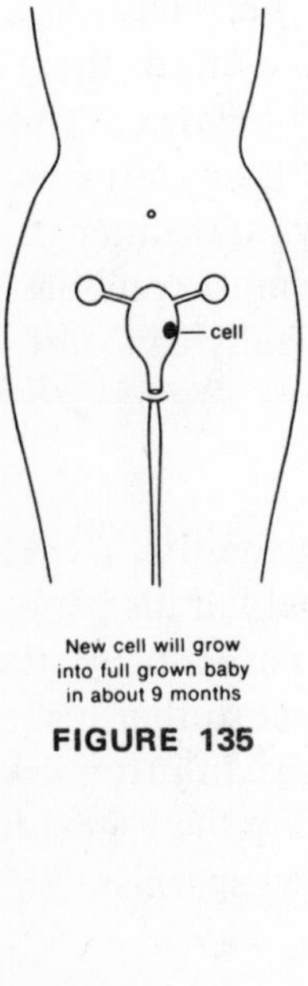

The 23 books or chromosomes that come from the mother never contain the information needed to form a boy. But some sperms carry a book of information about boys and some carry a book of information about girls. If a sperm with one of these books about boys is zipped together with the egg, a new baby boy will be born. If a sperm with a book of girl information combines with the egg, the baby will be a girl. Thus, it is the type of book carried by the sperm that determines whether the baby will be a boy or girl.

After the sperm and the egg combine in the tunnel between the uterus and the egg factory, the new cell starts to grow and to move down the tunnel to the uterus. It plants itself in the side of the uterus and starts to grow rapidly. After about nine months, it is a full-grown baby. When the baby is ready to be born, the mother feels a slight pain and goes to the hospital. There the doctor helps the baby to come out of the tunnel between the mother's legs.

One day you may want to become a mother or a father, so you should know when and how to have babies.

First, you should know that girls don't produce eggs and boys don't produce sperms until about the time that they become teenagers. So young children couldn't become mothers or fathers even if they wanted to.

When you grow up, you may find a boy or girl that you like very much. Then you decide to get married. When you get married, you promise to love and take care of each other. This is very important because unless a man and woman really love and take care of each other, they certainly will not be able to

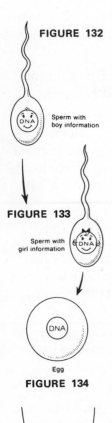

FIGURE 132

FIGURE 133

Sperm with boy information

Sperm with girl information

DNA

Egg

FIGURE 134

New cell will grow into full grown baby in about 9 months

cell

FIGURE 135

love and take care of children. That is why you should get married before you try to have children of your own.

P.S.

You may also be interested to know how fish have babies, since the mother and father fish never fall in love or get married. The mother just releases her eggs into the water and the father releases his sperms into the water. The two halves of the DNA boss zip themselves together and form the first cell of a fish. Unfortunately, there is no uterus to protect the first fish cell so many of them don't get to grow up. Humans are lucky that they develop in their mother's uterus where they are protected. Humans are also lucky that they have a mother and father who love each other and who love and care for their babies. If mothers and fathers didn't love each other enough to plan to take care of their children, babies wouldn't be much better off than fish. Poor fish.

QUESTIONS

1. The human body is made up of many tiny units. What are they called?
2. What do we call the cells that allow us to move?
3. How does a cell know how fast to grow or what job to do?
4. What is DNA?
5. What is the half of the DNA boss that comes from the mother called?
6. What is the half that comes from the father called?
7. Where do the sperm and egg come together to form the first DNA boss?
8. How does the father's sperm get inside the mother?
9. After the egg and sperm come together, how long is the time before a new baby is born?
10. Where in the mother's body does the baby develop?
11. Why are some babies born boys and some girls?
12. How does the new baby get out of the mother?
13. When should people have babies?
14. Why are human babies more fortunate than fish babies?

UNIT TWO: HEREDITY

Demonstration guidelines   The following lesson on heredity is presented as a demonstration. Read through the lesson and assemble the entire kit before beginning.

The cell model

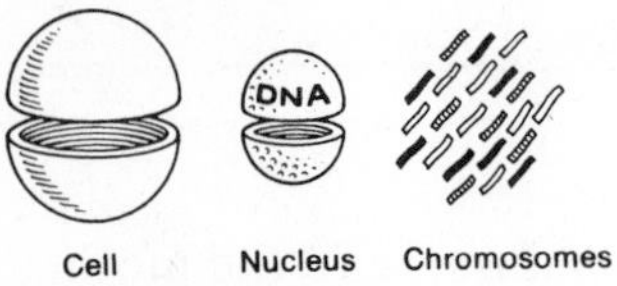

Cell   Nucleus   Chromosomes

FIGURE 136

Tennis ball

Golf ball

Paper strips

FIGURE 137

The cell lesson

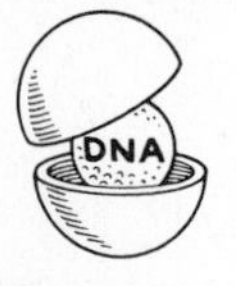

FIGURE 138

FIGURE 139

The first cell model

Soup bowls

Colored paper strips (inside bowls)

FIGURE 140

Put colored paper strips inside sperm

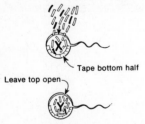

Tape bottom half

Leave top open

FIGURE 141

The first cell lesson

To clarify the cell, DNA, and chromosomes, make your own model. You will need a tennis ball cut in half, a plastic golf ball cut in half, and strips of different colored construction paper.

The tennis ball represents the cell. The golf ball represents the nucleus containing the DNA. Using fingernail polish, print DNA on the golfball. The strips of colored construction paper represent the chromosomes. Put the strips of colored paper inside the golf ball. Close the golf ball. Put the golf ball inside the tennis ball. You can use a rubber band to hold the tennis ball together.

You are ready to demonstrate. Use your model and explain the following:

There are many, many cells that make up your body.

One scientist estimates that there are twenty-six trillion five hundred billion.

There are many different kinds of cells.

Do you remember the many kinds of cells in the story?

Each cell in the body has a driver or an engineer. What is his name? *(Mr. DNA.)*

Here is where Mr. DNA lives inside the cell. (Open the tennis ball and show the children the golf ball with DNA painted on it.)

Mr. DNA is a very bossy boss. He tells us how fast to grow, what color eyes to have, and what size shoes to wear.

Where does Mr. DNA learn so much? *(Mr. DNA gets his wisdom from his 46 books or chromosomes.)*(Open the golf ball and pull out the strips of colored paper representing the chromosomes.)

To illustrate clearly where the first cell gets its DNA and chromosomes, assemble the following models. To construct your models you will need two soup dishes, manila paper, and construction paper.

The soup dishes can be placed together to represent the egg. Place the soup dishes together one on top of the other upside down so that they fit together. Now take 22 strips of colored paper and an x and place these inside the soup dishes.

Make four halves of sperms out of manila paper. Tape two halves together at the bottom, leaving the top open so that you can slide the 22 strips of colored paper plus an x inside the sperm. Thus, you have a female sperm.

Tape the other two sperm halves together at the bottom, leaving the top open so that you can slide the 22 strips plus a y inside the sperm. Thus, you have a male sperm.

How did Mr. DNA gather so much information? Mr. DNA

Colored strips and X

FIGURE 142

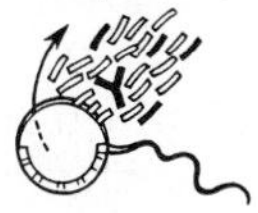

Pull out colored strips
from untaped area

FIGURE 143

Fertilization

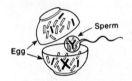

Sperm

Egg

FIGURE 144

Sex determination model

Sex determination lesson

FIGURE 145

learned half of his knowledge from his mother and half of his knowledge from his father.

The knowledge Mr. DNA got from the mother was contained in the egg. (Show the children the egg and pull out the chromosomes or colored bodies of construction paper.)

The mother's egg contains 23 books of knowledge called chromosomes.

The mother's books contain knowledge about the qualities of all her ancestors—her mother, her father, her grandmother, her grandfather, her great grandmother, her great grandfather.

The knowledge Mr. DNA got from the father was contained in the sperm. (Show the children the sperm and pull out the chromosomes or colored bodies of construction paper.)

The father's sperm contains 23 books of knowledge called chromosomes.

The father's books contain knowledge about the qualities of all of his ancestors—his mother and father, grandmother and grandfather, and great grandmother and great grandfather.

We know that when a mother and father decide to have a baby, the father puts his penis in the mother's vagina tunnel so that his half of Mr. DNA can get inside the mother's body.

Once his sperms are inside the mother they swim about, looking for the egg.

If the egg happens to meet one of father's sperm, the two halves of the DNA boss zip themselves together and you have the first complete DNA boss. (Take one of the sperms and put it inside the egg.)

This new cell has a DNA driver with all the knowledge it needs: 23 books of wisdom from mother and 23 books of wisdom from father. (Open the soup dishes and show the children the 46 chromosomes.)

For this demonstration use the soup dishes with 22 chromosomes and the x chromosome inside. Also use the two sperm models. In one model put 22 chromosomes (colored strips) plus an x. In the other model put 22 chromosomes (colored strips) plus a y.

One of mother's 23 books or chromosomes contains the information needed to make a girl.

Scientists call this book "x."

Let's look inside the egg and see if we can find this book or chromosome. (Open the soup dishes and pull out the 22 strips of colored paper. Pull out the x chromosome last.)

Father's 23 books or chromosomes sometimes have a book about girls and sometimes have a book about boys.

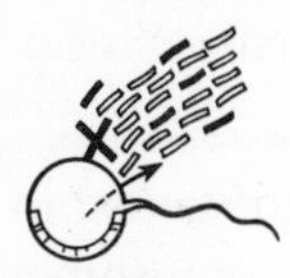

FIGURE 146

FIGURE 147

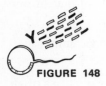

FIGURE 148

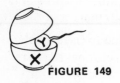

FIGURE 149

Here is one of father's sperms. Let's look inside it to see whether there is a book about boys or girls.

(Open up the sperm. Pull out the 22 strips of colored paper. Pull out the x chromosome last.)

Here is an x book. Who remembers what kind of knowledge is inside an x book? *(Girl knowledge.)*

If this sperm carrying an x book zips together with mother's egg, a new baby girl will be born.

(Take the sperm containing the x chromosome and put it inside the egg. Now show a picture of a baby girl.)

Here is another sperm from father. Let's look inside this sperm to see whether there is a book of information on boys or girls.

(Open up the sperm. Pull out the 22 strips of colored paper. Pull out the y chromosome last.)

Here is a y book. What kind of information do you suppose is inside the y book? *(Boy knowledge.)*

If this sperm carrying the y book zips together with mother's egg, a new baby boy will be born.

(Take the sperm containing the y chromosome and put it inside the egg. Now show a picture of a baby boy.)

The gene model

FIGURE 150   **FIGURE 151**

To illustrate clearly the relationship of the many genes to the chromosomes, construct the following book model. For your model you will need colored construction paper, tape, and cardboard.

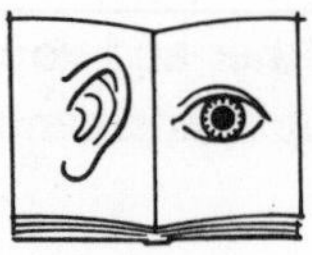

Cover the cardboard with colored construction paper to make a book cover. Fill the book with pages of different colors of construction paper. Paste pictures on the different pages to represent inherited traits—curly hair, eye color, shoe size, etc.

The book can be used to represent one of the chromosomes. The pages can be used to represent the genes on the chromosomes.

The gene lesson

FIGURE 152

FIGURE 153

Mr. DNA's books have many pages containing information on many, many things.

Let's look at one of Mr. DNA's books or chromosomes. (Take one of the chromosome books and open it to the different pages with the inherited traits pasted on them.)

This page contains the information needed to color the baby's eyes. (Show the picture on the page.)

This page contains the information needed to make the baby's hair curl. (Show the picture on the page.)

This page contains the information needed to make the hair red. (Show the picture on the page.)

FIGURE 154

You can see that every one of Mr. DNA's books or chromosomes contains pages of information on many topics.

These pages of information in Mr. DNA's books or chromosomes are called genes.

Each one of Mr. DNA's books or chromosomes contains thousands of pages or genes.

Every cell in the body contains Mr. DNA's books or chromosomes, and therefore, every cell contains thousands of pages or genes.

These genes decide what color skin you will have, how tall you will be, what color eyes you will have, and if your hair will be curly.

Demonstration guidelines

FIGURE 155

Using large sheets of manila construction paper, draw the head of a man and the head of a woman. These figures can be used later with the lesson as column headings to represent the genes inherited from the mother and the genes inherited from the father.

Do you remember how the cell got its library of 46 books or chromosomes? (Place the figure heads of the mother and the father on a board.)

Twenty-three books or chromosomes came from the mother's egg and 23 books or chromosomes from the father's sperm.

FIGURE 156

(Place the soup bowl model of the egg containing 23 chromosomes under the mother. Place the construction paper model of the sperm containing 23 chromosomes under the father.)

This means that half the books or chromosomes in a fertilized egg contain pages or genes from your mother, and the other half contain pages or genes from your father.

FIGURE 157

(Place a fertilized egg between and below the model of the egg and the sperm. Place 46 chromosomes in the model.)

Make a large egg out of construction paper. Inside the egg match up 23 pairs of chromosomes. Make divisions on the chromosomes and make them different colors to represent the genes. Match the colors on both the chromosomes in a pair and in the same place. This illustrates the idea that a gene for a particular trait from the mother and the same gene from the father are located at the same point on matching chromosomes.

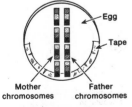

FIGURE 158

Now make a large model of a chromosome, pairing the traits from the father and the mother as illustrated in the left-hand margin. This illustrates the idea that one gene for each trait comes from the mother and one gene for each trait comes from the father.

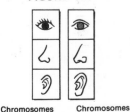

FIGURE 159

Let's look more closely at the 46 books or chromosomes in a fertilized egg; these chromosomes seem to do something very strange.

They seem to line up inside the egg in two's.

One of father's books or chromosomes is always right beside one of mother's books or chromosomes. (Use Figure 150.)

These books or chromosomes have a very special reason for being beside each other.

They contain the same kind of information.

Here is one of the books or chromosomes from the father, and here is one of the books or chromosomes from the mother. (Use Figure 150.)

Look closely at them, and you will see that they contain the same kind of information.

We already know that the information on the chromosome or book is called a gene.

A scientist would say that the chromosomes contain similar genes.

If we lined the chromosomes up next to each other, we could see that there is a pair of genes for each trait.

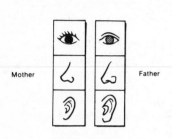

Mother   Father

Chromosome pair
FIGURE 160

(Point to the simple drawings on the chromosomes from the mother and father.)

Here is some information on mother's chromosome about eyes.

We call this the eye gene.

Here is some eye information on the chromosome that came from the father.

What do we call this information (*Eye gene.*)

Here is some nose information on the chromosome that came from the mother.

What do we call this information? *(Nose gene.)*

Here is some information on the chromosome that came from the father.

What do we call this information? *(Nose gene.)*

You see, a human being has two genes or pages of information on every topic telling him what to do.

There are two genes deciding how big your feet will be.

There are two genes deciding how tall you will be.

There are two genes deciding what color your eyes will be.

Dominant and recessive genes

To illustrate dominant and recessive genes for eye color make two sets of eyes out of construction paper. Make one set of eyes brown and the other set of eyes blue.

Now turn the pair of brown eyes over and tape blue eyes on the back of them. This can be used to demonstrate that al-

Mother—
Brown on front,
blue on back

Father—
Blue on front,
blue on back

Baby—
blue eyes

FIGURE 161

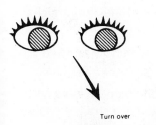

Turn over

FIGURE 162

though a person has brown eyes he can still be carrying a gene for blue eyes. Therefore, a brown- and a blue-eyed parent can have a blue-eyed child.

Many times the two genes will agree. This might happen if the eye color gene you get from mother is brown and the eye color gene you get from father is brown.

In this case the two genes agree and your eyes will be brown.

Sometimes the genes do not agree. This might happen if the eye color gene you get from mother is brown and the eye color gene you get from father is blue.

One of the genes wants your eyes to be blue and the other gene wants your eyes to be brown.

What happens? Fortunately some genes are much more bossy than others, and they always get their own way.

A gene for brown skin always wins an argument with a gene for white skin.

A gene for being tall always wins an argument with a gene for being short.

A gene for curly hair always wins an argument with a gene for straight hair.

A gene for brown eyes always wins an argument with a gene for blue eyes.

When the eye color gene from the mother is brown and the eye color gene from the father is blue, the baby will always have brown eyes.

This is not the same as saying that if your mother's eyes are brown and your father's eyes are blue your eyes will be brown.

Remember that everyone alive has two genes for everything.

If your mother has brown eyes, you know that one of her eye genes is brown but what about the other one? (Show the brown eyes that have blue on the back.)

This mother has brown eyes; she has one gene for brown eyes (turn over) and her other gene is for blue eyes.

You see, when her brown eye gene argued with her blue eye gene over what color eyes she should have, her brown eye gene won.

But she still has both the brown eye gene and the blue eye gene; this means that her baby could get a blue eye gene from her.

Here is a mother with brown eyes and a father with blue eyes. What color eyes will their baby have?

We know that the color of eyes the baby will have depends upon what genes the baby gets from its mother and father.

Let's suppose the baby gets a brown eye gene from the mother and a blue eye gene from the father. What color will the baby's eyes be? *(Brown eyes.)*

Let's suppose the baby gets a blue eye gene from mother and a blue eye gene from father. What color will the baby's eyes be? *(Blue eyes.)*

Demonstration guidelines

FIGURE 163

To illustrate the dominant and recessive genes for curly hair make the following model. Cut out a mother with straight hair on both sides of the construction paper. Cut out father with curly hair on both sides of the construction paper. By showing the children the front and back of both construction paper models you can illustrate that the mother carries two genes for straight hair and that the father carries two genes for curly hair. Curly hair is the dominant gene. Therefore, the child will have curly hair since the father does not carry the recessive gene for straight hair.

Here is a mother with straight hair and a father with curly hair.

(Turn the model of the mother over to show that she has two genes for straight hair.) The mother has two genes for straight hair.

(Turn the model of the father over to show that he has two genes for curly hair.) The father has two genes for curly hair.

The genes do not agree. One gene wants the baby to have curly hair, and the other gene wants the baby to have straight hair.

Do you know which gene will win the disagreement? *(The gene for curly hair.)*

A mother with two genes for straight hair and a father with two genes for curly hair can only have a baby with curly hair.

Demonstration guidelines

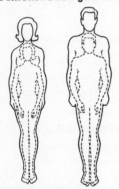

FIGURE 164

To illustrate how two tall parents can have a short child, construct two tall parents out of construction paper. Then construct two short parents out of construction paper.

Pin the short parents on the board. Pin the tall parents over the short parents so that the short parents cannot be seen. Now it appears that both parents are tall so all of their children will be tall. Lift up the tall parents and show the class that the parents are each carrying a gene for being short. Because of this the parents have a short child. Pin the short child on the board.

Here are two tall parents. (Lift up the tall parents to show that they each carry a gene for being short.)

Although the mother is very tall, she has a short gene too.

The father also has two genes. He has one gene for being tall and one gene for being short.

The baby will get one gene from each parent. Let's see whether the baby will be tall or short.

Suppose that the baby gets a gene for being tall from the mother and a gene for being tall from the father.

Will the baby be tall or short? *(The baby will be tall.)*

Now suppose that the baby gets a gene for being tall from the mother and a gene for being short from the father.

The two genes disagree. One gene wants the baby to be tall. The other gene wants the baby to be short.

Do you remember who wins the argument between a tall gene and a short gene? *(The tall gene. The baby will be tall.)*

Now let us suppose that the baby gets a gene for being short from the mother and a gene for being short from the father.

Will the baby be tall or short? *(The baby will be short.)*

Now we can see why it is possible for two tall parents to have a short child.

The parents' genes are more important than what the parents look like.

Demonstration guideline and review

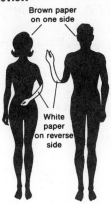

Brown paper on one side

White paper on reverse side

FIGURE 165

The foregoing lesson can be repeated using skin color. Cut out two brown construction paper figures. On the back side of these figures paste white paper. Although the mother and the father have brown skin, the white paper on the back indicates that they both are carrying a white gene. Have the children discuss the different possibilities for inheritance.

UNIT ACTIVITIES[1]

Inherited characteristics

Ask students to bring to class individual snapshots of themselves taken when they were 5 years of age in which their facial features are clearly visible. The teacher then could take small group pictures of students. Make a bulletin board display with the current pictures in the center and the childhood snapshots around the edge and

---

[1] These activities were taken from "Growth Patterns and Sex Education," *The Journal of School Health* Vol. XXXVII, No. 52, May 1967, published by the American School Health Association.

let the students see if they can identify childhood snapshots of each other by comparing facial characteristics in the snapshot with those in the current pictures.

Heredity and our ancestors

The study of heredity can be enhanced by having each student make a list of his inherited characteristics such as eye and hair color, whether hair is curly or straight, etc., and then trace his characteristics as far back through his family as he can. This activity will afford the teacher an opportunity to help students distinguish between the characteristics which are inherited and those which are acquired.

Class discussion

Have the students discuss the following statement, "What a person becomes is determined by his heredity, his environment, and to some extent what he wants to be.

SUGGESTED BIBLIOGRAPHY FOR THE FOURTH GRADE

Andry, Andrew, and Steven Schepp, *How Babies Are Made.* New York: Time-Life Books, 1968.
> The story of plants, animals, and humans in detail. Photographs help to make the explanations clear and simple.

Chicago Museum of Science and the University of Illinois, *The Miracle of Growth.* Urbana: University of Illinois Press, 1967.
> A detailed discussion of conception, birth, and development from infancy to adolescence, giving special consideration to heredity.

Cockefair, Edgar, and Cockefair, Ada, *The Story of You.* Wisconsin: Milam Publications, 1955.
> The story of where babies come from. The book was illustrated by children. It can be reviewed by the class, and then the class can make their own illustrations.

Cosgrove, Margaret, *Eggs—And What Happens Inside Them.* New York: Dodd, Mead & Co., 1966.
> An explanation of the embryology of new life—tadpoles, chicks, reptiles, elephants, and humans. Reviews concepts about the egg learned in the second grade and the chick material of the third grade, in addition to explaining human embryology, a fourth grade topic.

Evans, E. K., *The Beginning of Life.* New York: The MacMillan Co., 1962.
> A discussion of human reproduction with special focus on the special loving feelings involved in human mating, family relationships, and the excitement and joy at the arrival of a baby.

Health Education Services, *The Gift of Life.* Mental Health Materials Center, 1951.
> The physical process of reproduction, birth, and growth is clearly and simply explained in this small picture pamphlet. If possible, the teacher should purchase a pamphlet for each child.

Lerrigo, Marion, and Cassidy, Michael, *A Doctor Talks to 9 to 12 Year-olds.* Chicago: Budlong Press, 1964.
> A discussion of how life begins and how the family interacts as a social unit. Specially geared for this age group.

Levine, Milton, and Seligman, Jean, *A Baby Is Born.* New York: Golden Press, 1966.
> A careful story of how a baby is born with emphasis on family love. The book can be used to review the lessons in the fourth grade unit.

May, Julian, *How We Are Born.* Chicago: Follett, 1969.
> The story of human reproduction from conception to the birth of the baby. Discusses fetal development and care of the baby by the parents after birth.

Power, Jules, *How Life Begins*. New York: Simon & Schuster, Inc., 1965.
> Where babies come from and how they develop are creatively expressed in text, photographs, and drawings. An excellent supplement for use in the fourth grade classroom.

Scheinfeld, Amram, *Why You Are You*. New York: Abelard-Schuman, Ltd., 1958.
> An excellent book for the fourth grade unit on heredity, dealing with such topics as the wonders of genes and chromosomes and how they work in heredity; what makes boys and girls; the way children get their looks; how twins are produced; and how different races developed. An understanding of environment accompanies the heredity material.

Strain, Frances Bruce, *Being Born*. New York: Appleton-Century-Crofts, 1954.
> An excellent discussion of where babies come from with carefully drawn analogies. The book is also well illustrated and contains a good discussion of mating and marrying.

Zeichner, Irving, *How Life Goes On*. New Jersey: Prentice-Hall, Inc., 1961.
> An excellent book for reviewing units in elementary grades one to three and supplementing the unit for grade four. Plant and seed experiments are described, and the growth of a chick is outlined. Parental care in its highest form completes the cycle of life presented.

SUGGESTED FILM FOR THE FOURTH GRADE

There is a limited supply of films covering the topic of heredity at a level appropriate for fourth grade students. The fourth grade unit contains many ideas for class demonstrations to compensate for the lack of films on heredity.

Human Growth. E. C. Brown Trust, 220 Alder Street SW, Portland, Oregon 97204.
> Shows growth changes in boys and girls from ages 3 to 21. Deals especially with the changes at puberty in preparation for parenthood. The film may be used as a summary of the male and female reproductive systems and an introduction to pregnancy. The film depicts the different stages in pregnancy quite clearly as well as keeping the facts at an easy-to-digest level for the fourth grade child.

CHAPTER SEVENTEEN

Sex Education of the Fifth Grade Child

In the fifth grade, the student finds himself in a flux of change—accelerated growth accompanied by anxieties, fears, and tensions. The objective of the fifth grade teacher is to help the children overcome these worries by giving them adequate knowledge about the new changes in their bodies and the reasons for these changes. The teacher must create a reciprocal, comfortable, permissive environment to maximize pupil learning. The unit suggested for the fifth grade is "Discovering Yourself."

DISCOVERING YOURSELF

An Overview of Unit One

 One of the most rewarding objectives a fifth grade teacher can have is to help her students gain enough knowledge about their bodies and their body changes to become comfortable with themselves. The unit, "Discovering Yourself," has been included at the fifth grade level to provide specific teaching in areas of concern to the child. This unit includes (1) a lesson on reproductive cells, (2) a lesson on the anatomy and physiology of the male reproductive system, (3) a lesson on the anatomy and physiology of the female reproductive system, (4) a lesson on feminine hygiene for girls only, and (5) review activities. At the fifth grade level, students may be more comfortable if members of the opposite sex are not present. The decision whether or not to separate the sexes rests upon each individual teacher and depends entirely upon the structure and maturation of the class. The maturation of the boys in the class will also determine whether the section on menstrual protection can be included in the lesson on the female reproductive system. If the boys are mature enough to handle the discussion, it is a valuable addition to the fifth grade curriculum. It will satisfy the growing boy's curiosity about the sanitary vending machines in ladies' restrooms. However, the more detailed lesson on feminine hygiene is prepared for girls only. The girls are uncomfortable about their new changes in femininity and the hygiene unit covers their questions in depth. It is best handled by a qualified woman who can help the girls feel comfortable and identify with a feminine figure. It is especially important to adequately review the information in this unit. If any of the material in "Discovering Yourself" is not properly reviewed, misconceptions may result. The fifth grade teacher should make use of the review activities.

UNIT ONE: DISCOVERING YOURSELF

LESSON 1: REPRODUCTIVE CELLS

Class activity

Have the class model living things out of clay—bird, horse, dog, human—or make models of living things from construction paper. Discuss with them the topic, "Living Versus Nonliving Things."

Living vs. nonliving

We have been modeling and drawing examples of living things. Let us take one of our models (clay bird model) and compare it to a _____ (bird) that is alive.

Using the blackboard list the differences between the clay bird model (or other model) and a living _____(bird):

    1. Living bird breathes.

    2. Living bird flies.

    3. Living bird sings.

    4. Living bird grows.

    5. Living bird dies.

Difference in modeling

We want to add to our list another difference between living and nonliving things.

Remember when you began to model your living thing out of clay? You began with a hunk of clay and molded your (bird, cat, dog).

You knew that you were not really going to make something living at all—but a copy of something living.

Mother Nature copies living things	Mother Nature copies living things too—only her copies will be living. So Mother Nature has to begin her model in a different way.
The cell—a special modeling clay	She begins with a tiny piece of living modeling clay called the cell.
	The cell is a very different type of modeling clay. It is smaller than the tiniest grain of sand.
The cell is living	But because the cell is living it can model a living thing all by itself.
	You are probably wondering how such a tiny cell can model one of the elephants you see at the zoo.
	You may also wonder how the tiny cell forms a human being.
Cell can do special tasks	The cell is a very special kind of modeling clay—so special that it can do very special tasks.
	One of its special duties is to divide and divide itself until there are millions of cells.
	This is a very important task because each type of cell that models human beings has a special job to do.
Body cells keep us alive	These cells make up all parts of your body. They are called body cells. Body cells are concerned with keeping people alive.
The work of cells	Let's look at the work done by these very tiny body cells.
	Some of these cells make it possible for you to move; these are called muscle cells.
	Other cells produce tears to wash your eyes. Some cells help you to fight disease and to get well when you are sick.
	The cells that allow you to think are called brain cells. The food that you eat is taken to your muscles through tunnels that have walls made of cells.
	To sum up the work of the cell, we could say that everything that keeps you alive—running, jumping, eating, sleeping, thinking—is a special job performed by one of the body cells.
	Since the body cells can do everything that is necessary to keep us alive, we wouldn't think that a human being would need any other kind of cell.
Human beings have two kinds of cells	But all human beings have two kinds of cells. And although body cells are very important because they keep us alive, the other kind of cells is important too.
	These other cells are not concerned with us but with making more human beings.

Reproductive cells to make new human beings

These cells are called reproductive cells. All men and women have body cells to keep them alive and reproductive cells to make new human beings.

We all know that men and women are different. We also know that it takes both a mother and a father to have a baby.

Two kinds of reproductive cells

Therefore, it probably won't seem strange to you that it takes two reproductive cells, one from the father and one from the mother, to make a new human being.

The egg cell

The reproductive cell that comes from the mother is called the egg cell.

All mothers have body cells to keep them alive and egg cells to make new human beings.

The sperm cell

The reproductive cell that comes from the father is called the sperm cell.

All fathers have body cells to keep them alive and sperm cells to make new human beings.

LESSON 2:   MALE REPRODUCTIVE SYSTEM

Demonstration guidelines

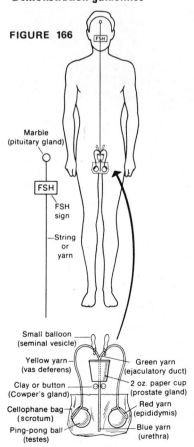

FIGURE 166

Marble
(pituitary gland)

FSH

FSH
sign

String
or
yarn

Small balloon
(seminal vesicle)

Yellow yarn
(vas deferens)

Clay or button
(Cowper's gland)

Cellophane bag
(scrotum)

Ping-pong ball
(testes)

Green yarn
(ejaculatory duct)

2 oz. paper cup
(prostate gland)

Red yarn
(epididymis)

Blue yarn
(urethra)

Before beginning the unit, assemble the following simple kit to demonstrate with. Materials you will need: one cellophane lunch bag, two ping pong balls, four different colors of yarn (red, yellow, blue, green), two small uninflated balloons, one very small dixie cup, a small chunk of clay, cardboard, and a marble.

These materials represent the anatomical parts of the male:

1. The small cellophane lunch bag is the scrotum.

2. The two ping pong balls are the testes.

3. The red coil of yarn on top of the testes (ping pong balls) represents the epididymis.

4. The yellow yarn leading up into the body is the vas deferens.

5. The two small uninflated balloons are the seminal vesicles.

6. The green yarn leading through the Dixie cup is the ejaculatory duct.

7. The small Dixie cup is the prostate gland.

8. The blue yarn leading out of the Dixie cup is the urethra.

9. The two small balls of clay attached to the blue yarn are the Cowper glands (you could use round bottons with a hole in them and sew them to the yarn).

10. The cardboard can be used to make the outline of a man. (Then attach the reproductive organs to the outline.)

11. Attach the marble to the brain of the cardboard outline to illustrate the location of the pituitary gland.

As the journey of the sperm is discussed, trace the route of the sperm for the class using the demonstration model.

Reviewing yesterday's lesson

1. Living vs. nonliving

Yesterday we learned the difference between living and nonliving things. Who remembers this basic difference? *(The cell.)*

2. Two kinds of cells

We also learned that human beings have two kinds of cells. Can someone tell us the names of these two cells? *(Body cells and reproductive cells.)*

3. Body cells

What are body cells concerned with? *(Body cells are concerned with keeping us alive.)*

4. Reproductive cells

What are reproductive cells concerned with? *(Reproductive cells are concerned with making new human beings.)*

We are interested in our body cells

We have all been very interested in our body cells as we have been growing up.

That is probably why we seem to know more about our body cells than about our reproductive cells. Let's see how much we know about our body cells.

Our muscle cells

Who knows what body cells make us able to swing a bat? *(Muscle cells.)*

Where are the muscle cells? *(They are in the muscle.)*

Our skin cells

Who knows what cells cover the body? *(Skin cells.)*

Show us some skin cells. Of course when we point to the skin we are pointing to many skin cells because we know that our eyes cannot see one cell.

Unit activity: "Growing Up" notebook

For this unit the students should make a notebook entitled "Growing Up." One section of the notebook will be a sex education dictionary of terms. As this lesson is presented, have the students copy the terms in their notebooks and define them. Have them define the terms in their own words. Make sure that all the words underlined in this lesson appear in the notebook. You will find these words defined at the end of this lesson.

Where reproductive cells are made

Now who can tell us where the reproductive cells are made?

1. Female reproductive cells or eggs are made in the ovaries, which cannot be seen because they are inside the body.

2. Male reproductive cells or sperms are made in the testes, which are located in a little sac between the boy's legs.

A boy's body has a lot of growing to do before he can produce sperm. This growth period toward sexual maturity is called puberty.

During puberty, several changes occur in the boy's body:

1. Deepening of the voice.

2. Growth of body hair.

3. More manly appearance.

4. Growth of testes, penis, and scrotum.

5. Muscle growth.

These changes, called the secondary sex characteristics, are necessary before a boy can produce sperm.

And of course a sperm must fertilize the egg for new life to start.

The sperm cell must meet the egg cell

In order for a sperm and an egg to meet so that a new baby can begin to grow, the sperm cell must travel from the testes out of the penis and into the mother's body.

A long journey for the sperm cell

You would think that this would be a short trip, since the testes and the penis are so close together.

But this isn't true. The sperm has to pass up into the body as it has many preparations to make before it can get where it's going.

Sperm's journey and growing up

The sperm also has to wait until a boy is grown up to make this trip. No sperm makes this trip until a boy is about 11 or 12 years old.

Alarm clock alerts testes

When a boy is about 11 or 12 years old, a tiny alarm clock in his brain sends out a signal that tells the testes that it is time to prepare for the sperm's journey.

This tiny alarm clock is called the pituitary gland, and the message it sends to the testes is called FSH. *(A hormone).*

FSH tells testes to make sperms

FSH tells the testes to begin working to make many sperms.

You probably have helped your mother make cake or cookies. If you have, you know how important it is to make them at just the right temperature.

Sperms produced at optimum temperature

Sperms have to be made at just the right temperature too. Do you remember the little sac between the boy's legs?

The scrotum regulates the temperature of the testes	The little sac that holds the boy's testes is called the scrotum. The scrotum helps the testes to make the sperms by keeping the testes at just the right temperature.
The journey begins	After the sperms are made they do not stay in the testes long, for they have a long journey to make.
First stop: epididymis	The very first stop on our trip is a little resting place right above the testes, called the epididymis.
The sperms grows up to look like a tadpole	While the sperm is resting up for its long journey, it is growing up. A grown-up sperm looks like a tadpole.
The sperm has a head and a tail	Have you ever seen a tadpole? A sperm has a head and a tail just like a tadpole.
A sperm can swim	Where does a tadpole live? *(In the water.)* A sperm moves like a tadpole too— it swims.
	Now that the sperm is grown up it must wait its turn to be used.
Vas deferens: the waiting station	It waits in a long tube that winds its way up into the body. This tube is called the vas deferens.
	At last it is time for the trip; the sperms pass up into the body through the long vas deferens.
Energy stop: seminal vesicle	Energy is needed for the long journey ahead, and so a very small filling station empties some sugar into the vas deferens. This little filling station is called the seminal vesicle.
Ejaculatory duct: a fork in the road	As the sperms leave their fuel stop they come to a fork in the road. The sperms are now going to travel along a very short path called the ejaculatory duct.
A long swim ahead	As the sperm empties into the ejaculatory duct it remembers the long swim ahead. Better get more water to swim in!
	Luckily the ejaculatory duct is right in the middle of a milk-water storage tank.
Prostate gland: milky water for the swimming sperm	This storage tank for water is called the prostate gland. The prostate gland empties some milky water into the ejaculatory duct.
Semen: the final mixture	Now the sperm is in a milky-sugary substance. This is called semen.
The ingredients in semen	Let's stop for a minute to see if we can remember all the ingredients that are in semen.

1. Sperms from testes

First, there was the sperm. Where did the sperm come from? *(Testes.)*

2. Sugar from seminal vesicles

Next, some sugar was added for the sperm to have energy for the trip. Where did the sugar come from? *(Seminal vesicle).*

3. Milky water from the prostate gland

Last, some milky water was added to help the sperms swim easily. Where did the milky water come from? *(Prostate gland.)*

So you see there are three ingredients in semen:

1. Sperms from the testes.
2. Sugar from the seminal vesicles.
3. Milky water from the prostate gland.

Dead end road

Now we are ready for the final state of the trip. The ejaculatory duct comes to a dead end where there is only one road to take.

Urethra: the last road

This is a long road leading out through the penis. This road is called the urethra.

Urethra and urine

We know that urine also leaves the body through this same road, the urethra. But they never travel together.

In fact, the semen with the sperm in it wants to make sure that there is no urine left on this road.

Right beside the urethra are two cleaning stations called the Cowper glands.

The Cowper glands squirt some cleansing fluid down the urethra to clean the road for the semen.

Now the road is clear for the semen, but wait: we must be sure that the semen gets inside the mother so it can look for the egg.

Remember that we said the urethra was a long tube inside the penis. The father can use his penis to place the semen inside the mother.

The penis is usually very soft and hangs down between the boy's legs. But when semen is going to come out of the penis, the penis becomes very hard.

This makes it easier for the father to put his penis into the mother's vagina.

When the penis is inside the vagina, the semen comes out and the sperms begin to swim about looking for the egg.

Reviewing the male reproductive system

It is very important that the teacher review the male reproductive system thoroughly before beginning the female reproductive system. Below are some review questions:

1. Where are the male reproductive cells made?

2. Where are the female reproductive cells made?

3. How old is a boy when he begins to grow up and make sperms?

4. What is the name of the tiny alarm clock in the brain?

5. Where does the FSH message come from?

6. What does FSH tell the testes to do?

7. How does the scrotum help the testes to make sperms?

8. Where do the sperms "grow up"?

9. How is a sperm like a tadpole?

10. Where does the sperm await its turn to be used?

11. What does the sperm use for energy?

12. What is the name of the short path between the vas deferens and the urethra?

13. Where does the sperm get the milky-water to help it swim?

14. What are the three ingredients in semen?

15. What is the name of the long tube inside the penis?

16. Do urine and semen ever travel down the urethra at the same time?

Sex education dictionary

Have the class go over the definitions they have written in their notebooks on the male reproductive system. You will find suitable fifth grade definitions at the end of this unit. As the students go over the definitions have them point out the anatomical structures on the model.

Male anatomical drawing

Pass out to the students a diagram of the male reproductive system. Have the class label the diagram together.

"Growing Up" notebook

Have each student write a summary of the journey of sperm and put it in his notebook on growing up. The sex education dictionary should be in this notebook also.

SEX EDUCATION DICTIONARY

Testes

The place where the male reproductive cells, the sperms, are made. The testes look like two small balls and are located in a small sac between the boy's legs.

Pituitary gland

A small gland about the size of a marble in the brain that sends a message to the testes telling them to make sperms.

FSH

A message from the pituitary gland that tells the testes to begin working to make many, many sperms.

Scrotum

A small sac between the boy's legs and under his penis. The sac holds the two testes. It helps the testes to make sperm by keeping the testes at the right temperature.

Epididymis

A small tube like a resting station on top of each testis. It is here that the sperms grow up to look like tadpoles.

Sperm

The male reproductive cell, made in the testes. The sperms look like tadpoles—each has a head and a tail. They move by swimming in milk-water. They use sugar for fuel.

Vas deferens

At first the vas deferens is a waiting station where the sperms wait their turn to be used. Then when it is time for the sperms to be used, they travel along the vas deferens, which becomes a long road that goes up into the body. The vas deferens ends when it comes to a path called the ejaculatory duct.

Seminal vesicle

A filling station that provides the sperms with sugar energy. There are two seminal vesicles.

Ejaculatory duct

A connecting road. The ejaculatory duct connects the vas deferens and the urethra.

Prostate gland

A storage container for milk-water. The prostate gland dumps milk-water into the ejaculatory duct to help the sperm swim more easily.

Semen

A milky, sugary liquid containing the sperms. The semen contains the sperms from the testes, sugar from the seminal vesicles, and milk-water from the prostate gland. The semen is a liquid, which finally leaves the male body through the urethra in the penis.

Urethra

A tube inside the penis. The semen empties into the urethra by way of the ejaculatory duct. The semen travels down the urethra and out of the penis.

Cowper's glands

Two small cleaning stations beside the urethra. Cowper's glands squirt out a cleansing fluid to clear the urethra.

Penis

Located between the boy's legs. It is soft and hangs down and looks like the thumb. When semen is going to come out the penis, it becomes very hard. Then the penis is put inside the mother more easily.

LESSON 3:   FEMALE REPRODUCTIVE SYSTEM

Demonstration guidelines

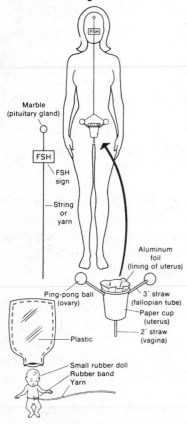

Marble
(pituitary gland)

FSH
sign

String
or
yarn

Aluminum
foil
(lining of uterus)

Ping-pong ball
(ovary)

3˝ straw
(fallopian tube)

Paper cup
(uterus)

Plastic

2˝ straw
(vagina)

Small rubber doll
Rubber band
Yarn

FIGURE 167

Before beginning the unit, assemble the following simple kit to use for demonstration. The following materials are needed for demonstration of the menstrual cycle: a small marble, an index card with FSH written on it, some string or yarn, two ping pong balls, two 4 inch straws, one 3 inch straw, a Dixie cup, a piece of aluminum foil, two pieces of clear plastic cut in the shape of an upside-down milk bottle stapled together except at the lower end, a small doll which has a mark for the navel, an 8 inch string of knitted yarn, a rubber band, and cardboard.

The model can be used to demonstrate the following anatomical locations:

1. The marble represents the pituitary gland.

2. The FSH sign with the string attached leads to the ovary and represents the hormone signal for growing up.

3. The two ping pong balls represent the ovaries.

4. The two 4 inch straws represent the Fallopian tubes.

5. The one 3 inch straw represents the vagina.

6. The Dixie cup represents the uterus.

7. The aluminum foil can be shaped to line the Dixie cup to represent the inner lining (endometrium) of the uterus.

8. The pieces of clear plastic stapled together with an opening left at the bottom can be used to place the rubber doll in to show pregnancy.

9. The yarn can be attached to the navel of the doll by attaching it to a rubber band at the doll's waist. The other end can be attached to the uterus to represent the umbilical cord.

10. Childbirth can be domonstrated by bringing the doll out of the opening between the two pieces of clear plastic and pulling off the yarn.

11. The cardboard can be used to make the outline of a woman. Then attach the reproductive organs to the outline.

Now that your demonstration kit is fully assembled you are ready to begin the fifth grade lesson on the female reproductive system and growing up.

Discovering yourself

If the primary secret of human happiness could be contained in two simple words they would be: Know Yourself. It is the basic principle of existence from which all good things flow. But knowing yourself is no easy assignment. It doesn't happen overnight.[1]

---

[1] From *Your Years of Self Discovery*, The Life Cycle Center, Kimberly Clark Corporation, Neenah, Wisconsin.

You are always changing

You are continually changing, always growing, always having new feelings.

This means that to really know yourself you'll have to work at it over the whole of a lifetime.

Know and understand others

Also, you'll have to work hard to know and understand others. This is an important part of knowing yourself.

Girls must understand boys

You can see why it is so important for a girl to know all about boys and how they grow to be men and fathers.

Boys must understand girls

You can also see why it is so important for boys to know all about girls and how they grow to be women and mothers.

**Unit activity:
"Growing Up" notebook**

For this lesson the students will continue their notebook on "Growing Up." One section of the notebook will be a sex education dictionary of terms describing the female reproductive system. As this lesson is presented, have the students copy the terms in their notebook and define them in their own words. Make sure that all the words that are underlined in this lesson appear in the notebook. You will find these words defined at the end of this unit.

The same alarm clock

Boys and girls are both signaled to grow up by a tiny alarm clock in the brain called the pituitary gland.

The age the alarm sounds

In boys we said that the alarm clock rings about the age of 11 or 12. In girls the pituitary gland or alarm clock may ring as early as 9 or 10.

Girls begin to grow up one or two years earlier than boys.

Do you remember where the egg cells or reproductive cells of a female are made? *(In the ovary.)*

Drowsy baby eggs

There are thousands of baby egg cells sleeping soundly in each ovary until the pituitary alarm clock sends out its FSH signal.

FSH stirs sleepy eggs

"Wake up, you sleepy eggs," says FSH. "This girl is grownup now and grownup girls' bodies prepare to have a baby each month."

Body changes in growing up

The body of a girl makes some immediate changes after getting this "grownup" message:

1. She begins to look more like her mother and other grownup girls she knows.

2. Her hips become wider.

3. Her breasts become larger.

4. Hair begins to grow under her arms and where her legs come together.

These changes will make it easier for a girl's body to prepare for a baby each month.

Rather exciting, isn't it? Boys want to know about the nest for babies inside the mother and girls want to know all about the changes happening in their own bodies.

Monthly nest preparation

This exciting event is known as the menstrual cycle. The menstrual cycle is just another way to say that the girl's body prepares a nest for a baby to grow in each month.

Let me tell you how this nest is formed.

The grownup egg

After the FSH wakes up the sleeping baby eggs in the ovary, some of the eggs begin to grow. One of these eggs becomes a grownup.

Be on the alert—nest needed

The girl's body is alerted that an egg is about to begin its journey looking for a sperm. A very comfortable nest must be prepared for the egg in case it meets the sperm.

Uterus—a comfortable nest

Does anyone know the name of the nest in the mother where the eggs grow? (*The uterus.*) (Show the class the Dixie cup on the demonstration model.)

So that the baby would have a comfortable nest to grow in, a very soft lining of blood and food lines the uterus. (Show the aluminum foil.)

This lining looks something like red velvet. It makes a very safe, comfortable nest.

Now the grownup egg will go looking for the sperm. The grownup egg won't find any sperm in the ovary so it decides to leave.

A long hallway

Right outside the ovary is a long hallway called the Fallopian tube. (Show the 4-inch straw.)

Persuasive little fingers

At the end of this hallway and very close to the ovary are a lot of little fingers pointing to the egg saying, "Come this way into the Fallopian tube."

So the egg travels into the Fallopian tube and begins to journey down the tube toward the uterus next.

If any sperms are in the Fallopian tube they will begin to swim toward the egg. (You can stop here to review how the father puts his penis into the mother's vagina and how the sperm swims toward the egg.)

Demonstration guidelines

To review the demonstration of fertilization used previously at a lower grade level, make a sperm from construction paper and have two soup dishes. Place the soup dishes together. To show fertilization, open the two dishes and put the construction paper sperm inside.

A lifetime partnership

When one sperm meets the egg and they make friends, they form a partnership. This partnership is called fertilization.

In a fertilization partnership each partner gives part of what it knows to form a new baby. (Use soup bowl and construction paper sperm.)

The living modeling clay

The sperm cell and the egg cell are now joined together as one cell. This one cell is the living modeling clay from which a new baby will grow.

The cell needs a very comfortable nest to do all this important modeling, so it journeys the rest of the way down the Fallopian tube until it reaches the uterus. (Show this using the model.)

Uterus—growing room

The uterus is a very comfortable room. Its walls have all the nourishment and comfort for a new baby to grow. The cell attaches to this wall.

A very small cell

This cell is smaller than the tiniest grain of sand. You can see that it has a lot of growing to do in the nest.

The cell and nest grow

The uterus has to keep getting bigger to keep the nest big enough for the cell to grow into a baby. (Show the clear plastic uterus model with the doll inside it.)

The pregnant mother

You have probably seen a mother with a baby growing inside her. The word we use to describe her is "pregnant."

Not the stomach!

A mother with a baby growing inside her is pregnant. Some people look at a pregnant mother and think that the baby is growing in her stomach.

But we know better. We know that it is her uterus that is getting bigger to hold the growing baby.

Extra food supply needed

While the baby is growing inside the mother, it needs extra food supplies.

A special attachment

A special cord connects the baby to the mother so that the baby can get all the supplies it needs.

(Show this attachment by placing the doll with the yarn attached to its navel inside the clear plastic uterus.)

A food and garbage exchanger	This cord is called the umbilical cord. At one end it attaches to the baby at his navel; the other end attaches to a special place in the uterus called the placenta. The placenta is a food and garbage exchange service station.
	It brings all the things that the baby needs from its mother and takes away everything that the baby cannot use.
Nine-month growing period	With all this comfort and care inside the mother, the baby will soon grow old enough to be born. This growth takes nine months.
The birth tunnel	When a baby is ready to be born, it usually comes head first down through the tunnel between the mother's legs.
	We already know that the name of this tunnel is the vagina. The baby is born when it comes through the vagina. (Using the demonstration model, pull the baby through the opening at the bottom of the clear plastic to show birth.)
A cord without a job	After a baby is born it no longer needs to be connected to its mother's nest. The long cord comes out with the baby.
	The doctor ties the cord off and cuts it. (Detach the knitted yarn from the doll by taking off the rubber band.) The mark that is left on the baby from this cord is the belly button or navel.
	A new life has begun. The mother and father will take care of this baby until it grows up.
	Now we know a little bit more about ourselves: We know why our bodies are changing. We know why we have to know about both boys and girls and how they grow up. . . .
Natural changes important to the future	. . . Because the changes that are happening to you are natural and will be very important to you when you want to marry and have your own family.
	You probably aren't much interested in marrying and having a family now. There are many things you want to do and things you want to learn first.
Mother Nature's advance preparations	You will be getting your ideas and education in tune before deciding to marry. Meanwhile Mother Nature is getting your body in tune.
	Mother Nature makes both boys' and girls' bodies ready to have babies long before they marry. You will soon be noticing these preparations.
Noticeable growing changes in boys	Boys may notice an occasional discharge of clear, sticky fluid from the penis.

This is the semen, which is beginning to form during the early period when the boy is growing up.

Semen overflows

Quite frequently the semen overflows at night, leaving a small spot on the sheets or pajamas.

Semen may be accompanied by a dream

Sometimes this overflowing of semen is accompanied by a dream about girls or a dream about growing up.

"Wet dream"—seminal emission

This is why some people call this secretion a "wet dream." Scientifically a wet dream is called a seminal emission.

A boy who does not understand this experience may be sleeping and awaken to find himself frightened and disturbed.

Wet dreams are a normal part of growing up

There is no reason for a boy to be upset. This is a normal part of growing up. It is a sign that semen is being made and that a boy is becoming nearer the age where he might marry and have children.

Girls' bodies prepare for motherhood

Girls' bodies are preparing for marriage and babies too. Remember when we talked about the menstrual cycle?

We said that the menstrual cycle was just another way of saying that a girl's body prepares each month to have a baby.

Let's review what we already know about the menstrual cycle. (Use the demonstration model.)

The baby egg grows up

Each month one of the baby eggs grows up. Where does this egg grow up? *(The ovary.)*

The long hallway

Then the egg leaves the ovary and enters the long hallway. What is this hallway called? *(The Fallopian tube.)*

A comfortable nest of blood

At the same time that the egg is traveling down the Fallopian tube a comforable nest of blood is being made. Where is this nest? *(Uterus.)*

Partnership results in new life

We know that if an egg forms a partnership with a sperm in the Fallopian tube a new life beings. This life will grow into a baby in the uterus.

But what happens if the egg does not join with a sperm?

Egg and lining not needed

Then the egg and the blood lining of the uterus are not needed. (Show the aluminum foil lining in the Dixie cup.)

Together they leave

The egg and the blood leave the uterus and come down the vaginal tunnel.

Demonstration guideline

To explain to the child exactly what the hymen is and how the menstrual flow leaves through an opening in the hymen, assemble a demonstration model. Use a large straw or other device to represent the vagina. Cover one end with clear plastic or cellophane; this will represent the hymen. Now puncture a small hole in the cellophane or clear plastic to represent the perforation in the hymen. It is through this perforation in the hymen that the menstrual flow leaves the body. It is through this same perforation that the tampon is inserted.

A thin covering

A very thin piece of skin called the hymen covers the opening of the vagina. (Show the model.)

In the middle of the hymen is an opening. (Point to the hole in the cellophane or plastic hymen.)

The egg and blood come through this opening to the outside of the body.

This is called the menstrual flow. It lasts about three to five days.

Collecting the unwanted blood

During the menstrual flow or menstruation a girl has to wear some protection to collect and absorb this blood.

Demonstration guideline

Both boys and girls should be familiar at this age with menstrual hygiene products. As you explain this simply and factually, show the class the napkin, sanitary belt, and tampon.

Sanitary napkins to absorb blood

A sanitary napkin is a soft disposable pad used to absorb the menstrual flow. (Show one.)

Sanitary belt to hold napkin

A narrow elastic belt called a sanitary belt is used to keep the napkin firmly in place. (Show the belt.)

The belt is worn around the waist next to the skin. The pad is attached to the belt. (Attach a pad to the belt.)

A tampon for internal absorption

The tampon is another easy way of absorbing the menstrual flow. (Show tampon.)

The tampon is worn inside the vagina. It is put into the same opening through which the menstrual fluid leaves the body.

Just like a blotter

A tampon works something like a blotter. It absorbs the blood as it flows from the uterus into the vagina.

A girl will only need to wear some type of sanitary protection for the three to five days in her menstrual cycle when the unneeded blood is trickling down the vagina.

When the menstrual flow is over, it is time to begin the monthly preparation of a nest all over again.

The cycle repeats itself

This preparation occurs over and over again, every month for years and years . . . and each month that this preparation is not needed it leaves the body.

So you see the changes that will be happening to you are very natural and also very important.

Why early changes?

Nature begins these changes long before you are ready to marry and have children, for a very good reason.

Many years to understand the body

We also know that it takes many years to adjust to these changes in our bodies and to understand them fully.

Many years to understand self and others

We also know that it takes many years to learn about ourselves

Marriage and family

These years of learning and growing changes are important in having a good marriage and in becoming good parents in the future.

Reviewing the female reproductive system

It is very important that the teacher review the female reproductive system thoroughly. The students should be familiar with the biology of sex at the end of the fifth grade. Below are some review questions:

1. Why is it important to know yourself?
2. Is it important for boys to know about the growth changes in girls? Why?
3. Is it important for girls to know about the growth changes in boys? Why?
4. Who is signaled to grow up first, boys or girls?
5. What message does the alarm clock pituitary gland send out in girls?
6. What is the menstrual cycle?
7. How many of the sleepy eggs in the ovary become grownup each month?
8. Where is the nest that is prepared each month in the mother and what does it look like?
9. How does the egg get from the ovary to the uterus?
10. Where does the egg usually meet a sperm?
11. Where does the living modeling clay from which a baby is made come from?
12. Why does the uterus get bigger and bigger?
13. What do we mean when we say a woman is "pregnant"?
14. How does a baby get extra food supplies when it is growing inside the mother?

15. How long does a baby grow inside its mother?

16. How does a baby get out of the mother?

17. What is the navel?

18. How do boys know when they are growing up and beginning to make semen?

19. What happens to the comfortable nest of blood in the uterus if it is not needed?

20. How long does the menstrual flow last?

21. What does a girl wear to collect the menstrual blood?

Class discussion

After the class has reviewed the biological phases of growing up, begin a class discussion on the sociology of growing up. Below are a few questions you might use to stimulate class discussion:

1. Why do the many body changes in growing up begin years before we are ready to marry?

2. What are some of the other ways we need to grow up before we will be ready to marry?

3. What are some of the other ways we need to grow up before we will be ready to have children?

You might want to list the students' ideas on the blackboard and then have them add these ideas to a separate section of their "Growing Up" notebook.

Sex education dictionary

Have the class go over the definitions they have written in their notebooks on the female reproductive system. (You will find suitable fifth grade definitions at the end of this unit.) After the students go over the definitions have them point out the anatomical structures on the model used for demonstration.

Female anatomical drawing

Pass out to the students a diagram of the female reproductive system. Have the class label the diagram together.

"Growing Up" notebook

Each student should write a summary of the menstrual cycle and put it in the notebook on growing up.

SEX EDUCATION DICTIONARY *(CONTINUED)*

Pituitary gland

An alarm clock about the size of a marble in the girl's brain. The alarm clock rings at about the age of 9 or 10 and sends out a message called FSH to tell the girl that it is time for her body to remodel for motherhood.

Ovary

There are two ovaries or storage rooms filled with thousands of sleeping eggs. Each month some of these eggs wake up and one of them becomes a grownup. The ovaries look like ping pong balls.

FSH

A message from the pituitary gland, which tells the baby eggs sleeping in the ovary to wake up and begin to grow.

Menstrual cycle

The preparation of a comfortable nest for a baby to grow in each month. This nest is in the uterus, and if it's not needed it leaves the body at the end of a month's time.

Uterus

A nest inside the girl about the size and shape of a pear. It has a rich red velvet lining and is comfortable for a baby to grow inside. The uterus can get bigger and bigger as the baby grows larger.

Fallopian tube

A long hallway with many fingers pointing near the end by the ovary. The fingers point to the grownup egg, telling it to come inside this hallway and meet a sperm. If the egg and sperm are to form a partnership their meeting place is within the Fallopian tube. The Fallopian tube or hallway ends at the uterus.

Fertilization

A partnership or joining of a sperm and an egg. In this partnership each partner gives part of what it knows to form a new baby.

Pregnant

A word used to describe a mother with a baby growing inside her uterus.

Placenta

A food and garbage exchange that connects a mother and her baby. It brings all the things that the baby needs from its mother and takes away everything that the baby cannot use.

Vagina

A tunnel between a girl's legs. This tunnel has three purposes:

1. A man puts his penis in this tunnel to release his sperms.
2. A baby can be born through this tunnel when it is ready to leave the uterus.
3. An unwanted nest of blood from the uterus can leave the body through this tunnel.

Navel

A mark that is left on the baby, showing where the baby was attached or connected to its mother. This mark is also called the "belly button."

"Wet dream," "seminal emission"

When a boy is growing up and beginning to make semen, occasionally this semen overflows at night. It may leave a small spot on his sheets or pajamas. Sometimes this overflowing of semen is accompanied by a dream about girls or a dream about growing up. This is why some people call this secretion a "wet dream." Scientifically a wet dream is called a seminal emission.

Hymen	A thin piece of membrane that covers the opening of the vagina to the outside of the body. In the middle of the hymen is a small opening. The menstrual flow comes down the vagina and leaves the body through this opening.
Menstruation	The unwanted egg, lining of the uterus, and blood, which leave the uterus each month no baby is made. This blood trickles down the vaginal tunnel for about three to five days. Some protection must be worn to absorb this blood.
Sanitary pad or napkin	A sanitary pad or napkin is a soft disposable pad used to absorb the menstrual flow.
Sanitary belt	A narrow elastic belt used to keep the napkin firmly in place. The belt is worn around the waist next to the skin. The pad is attached to the belt.
Tampon	A tampon is used to absorb the menstrual flow inside the vagina. It is put into the same opening through which menstrual fluid leaves the body. A tampon works something like a blotter. It absorbs the blood as it flows from the uterus into the vagina.

LESSON 4: FEMININE HYGIENE

Preparing for this lesson	Before presenting the following lesson, write a letter home to the girl's parents asking them to purchase a starter kit for their child to bring to school. This kit should include a tampon, a sanitary napkin, and a sanitary belt.
	If you prefer you could merely send home a letter indicating that you will be covering menstrual hygiene in class and would like to purchase a starter kit.
	A starter kit may be purchased separately at a drug store or can be obtained in a package from one of the following manufacturers of sanitary products whose addresses are listed in a subsequent paragraph: Personal Products Company, Tampax Incorporated, and Kimberly Clark Corporation.
About this lesson	The following lesson on feminine hygiene is a summary of five excellent pamphlets written for girls who are about to begin to menstruate. This summary will be most meaningful if the pamphlets are distributed to the girls for reading and for discussion with their mothers.

Growing Up and Liking It and *Strictly Feminine* (Director of Education, Personal Products Company, Box SS-6, Milltown, New Jersey 08850)

It's Time You Knew (Educational Director, Tampax Incorporated, 161 East 42nd Street, New York, New York, 10017)

World of a Girl (Scott Paper Company, International Airport, Philadelphia, Pennsylvania 19113)

Your Years of Self Discovery (The Life Cycle Center, Kimberly Clark Corporation, Box 551, Neenah, Wisconsin 54956)

Equipped for parenthood	We learned in our previous lesson about growing up and the many changes that are made to equip boys to become fathers and girls to become mothers.
All girls menstruate	One of the most important changes in your own body is the beginning of your menstrual cycle. This is something you have in common with all other girls.
	All girls menstruate. That is why all of the girls in our class are here together today, to talk about menstruation.
Knowing yourself completely	You probably already have many questions about menstruation. This is quite natural as it is one more part of knowing yourself completely.
Menstruation is natural	Menstruation is quite natural. It starts and stops each month.
Menstruation varies among girls	Although menstruation is natural and happens in all girls, it is not the same for all girls, just as not all girls are the same height and the same weight.
Menstrual warning signals	Many girls, but not all girls, have some warning signs, which tell them that their menstrual flow is approaching.
Tiredness and the blues	Some girls feel tired or "down in the dumps."
Back discomfort	Other may have some back discomfort midway between their waist and buttocks.
Blemishes and bulges	Frequently girls feel a little fatter and have a few blemishes when their period is approaching.
	These signs of menstruation are not serious, though, and they quickly disappear.
The menstrual flow varies	Just as the advance signs of menstruation are not the same for all girls, neither is the menstrual flow itself.

The menstrual flow usually changes in color and amount from the beginning to the end of menstruation.

Changes in menstrual blood color

At first the menstrual blood may be a pale rusty or brownish hue; then it turns red—the color you normally think of blood. Toward the end of the flow it is sometimes dark brown or black. Then it takes on a rusty color again at the very end of the flow.

Amount of menstrual flow

Only 6 to 8 tablespoons of blood come through the vagina during menstruation. It may look like much more, but it really isn't.

The amount of blood doesn't matter; neither does its color.

Be at ease

The important rule concerning menstruation is to be at ease.

Be prepared

Normally we are more at ease in life when we are prepared. Each of you is prepared with a sanitary protection kit to absorb your menstrual flow when you begin to menstruate.

Let's look at each product in this kit. Maybe you'll have some questions to ask me about these products.

Sanitary napkins to absorb flow

Here is a sanitary napkin. The napkin is a soft disposable pad worn outside the body to absorb the menstrual blood.

Sanitary belt to hold napkin in place

The sanitary napkin is attached to a sanitary belt to keep the napkin firmly in place. Let's attach one of the napkins in our kit to the belt.

Demonstration guidelines

The following tips for attaching the sanitary pad to the sanitary belt are found in the booklet "World of a Girl" (Scott Paper Company).[2]

How to use the sanitary belt

1. Place narrow end of the pad on the body at a position slightly beyond the rectum.
2. With the pad held firmly against the body, between the thighs fasten the wide tab to the front of the belt with pins or clasp.
3. Make certain the pad is snug against the body and fasten back tab firmly.
4. Now try walking, sitting, twisting. If your pad is correctly adjusted it will stay firmly in place.

If your pad is held firmly in place by a sanitary belt, it will be unnoticeable to you and to others.

---

[2] Scott Paper Company, International Airport, Philadelphia, Pennsylvania 19113.

Caring for the sanitary belt

You will want to take extra special care of your sanitary belt, since you will be wearing it next to your body just like underwear.

1. Keep two belts.

It is a good idea to have at least two belts so that you can put a freshly cleaned belt on each day of your period.

2. Wash carefully.

To wash your belt use mild suds and rise thoroughly.

3. Dry carefully.

Then lay the belt on a flat surface to dry. Smooth out any wrinkles so it will dry flat.

A belt will last through many washings if you care for it properly.

If washed and dried correctly, the belt will hold the pad firmly against your body without any telltale bulges.

Change napkin four times daily

You will want to change your pad often, though. Four times a day is a good rule—before breakfast, before lunch, before dinner, and before bedtime.

Have a spare

If you will be away from home for the day, perhaps at school, you will want to have extra pads with you.

Spare should be clean and fresh

It's a good idea to wrap the pads you take from home in a tissue or put them in a cosmetic kit to keep them clean and fresh.

A spare for your locker

You might want to keep a few extra sanitary pads or napkins in your locker at school.

A spare in the restroom

If you should be caught by surprise without a napkin or pad, there are machines that sell them in the girls' restroom.

A spare with safety pins

They usually come in a handy packet with two safety pins. You can use these pins to pin the pad to your underpants if you don't have your belt with you.

Tampons are available

The tampon or sanitary protection that is worn inside the vagina is also sold in machines in the ladies' restroom. (Show the tampon.)

Tampon inserts through hymen

The tampon is much smaller than the pad. It is put into the vagina through the small opening in the hymen.

Tampon smaller than hymen

Although the opening in the hymen is small, the tampon is much smaller. A tampon will not break or tear the hymen.

Let's learn how to insert the tampon.

Demonstration guidelines

For this demonstration use the tampon charts in the atlas (Figure 159). As you explain the tampon insertion, point to the diagram. You can show the girls how to hold the tampon applicator. If they would like to practice insertion, tell the girls to do it at home. If they need any additional help, tell them to ask their mothers.

The following explanation of tampon insertion is quoted from *Strictly Feminine,* published by the Personal Products Company.[3]

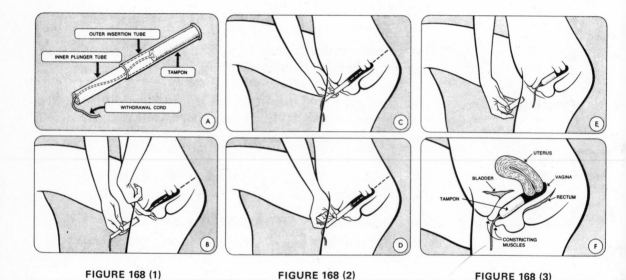

FIGURE 168 (1)   FIGURE 168 (2)   FIGURE 168 (3)

Holding the applicator correctly

Be certain that you know how to hold the applicator in the proper way. Hold the plastic applicator toward your body. Place your thumb and your middle finger (or your fourth finger) on the finger grip. Place your index finger (or your middle finger) on the end of the plunger.

Use whichever finger position is most comfortable for you. And don't worry if it takes a little practice to feel comfortable holding the applicator. Remember that these two recommended ways of holding the tampon are designed especially to help position it properly in your body.

Tampon rule

Remember that the most important rule for all tampon users, especially for first time users, is to relax.

How to use a tampon

Insert the tampon with a slight rotating motion. Remember that each girl and woman is a little different. Some girls slant the applicator toward the back of the waist, others toward the base of the spine and some even lower. Also you may have to slant the applicator differently depending on whether you are sitting, stand-

[3] Milltown, New Jersey 08850.

ing, or lying down. If you relax and insert the applicator gradually, you will soon find the method and direction of insertion which suits you best.

Insert the applicator until your fingers, on the finger grip, touch your body. When this is done, gently push the plunger with your fingers until the ends of the plunger and applicator tubes are even. Remove them from your body and dispose of them in the wastebasket.

Tampons are a very safe, comfortable way to absorb the menstrual blood.

No odor from tampon

Many girls like them better than pads because the blood is absorbed inside the body and there is no smell or odor.

Safe for swimming

Also, because no blood gets out of the body when using the tampon, the tampon is safe for swimming.

A tampon should be changed as often as a pad—four times a day.

Disposing of the tampon and napkin

Girls must be careful in disposing of pads and tampons that have been used.

Soiled pads and tampons should be placed in a paper bag and thrown into a wastebasket or a restroom container.

They should never be flushed down the toilet. This usually will cause clogging.

No matter what type of sanitary protection you use—the tampon or napkin—you will be well protected.

Accidents do happen

Occasionally, though, you may find a spot of blood on your underpants, nightgown, or bedsheets.

Accidents occasionally happen, but they are no problem if you know how to quickly take care of them.

Washing a blood stain

As soon as possible wash the blood stain with cold water and mild soap. Usually the stain will quickly disappear.

Occasional discomfort

Occasionally a girl may have cramps accompanying menstruation.

Cramps during menstruation

Cramps are the occasional pains a girl gets below her waist during menstruation.

Mistaken ideas about menstruation

Sometimes cramps are caused by mistaken ideas a girl has heard about menstruation:

1. That a rainy day causes menstrual cramps.

2. That eating a lemon will start your menstrual flow ahead of time.

3. That taking a bath during menstruation will cause TB.

4. That a girl who is menstruating is possessed by an evil spirit.

5. That flowers will wilt if you touch them while menstruating.

You can see how a girl who believes any of these silly things can be frightened and feel sick inside during menstruation.

Constipation—unnecessary menstrual cramps

Other girls have menstrual cramps because they are constipated. Constipated is a word that describes a condition in which bowel movements are difficult.

The water and fruit cure

Constipation may cause menstrual pains. The best way to avoid this is to drink plenty of water and to eat lots of fruit.

The poor posture villain

Other girls have cramps because they have poor posture, which pushes all the important body parts together and makes menstruation more difficult.

Sit tall—feel better

It's good to sit tall when you feel yourself slumping at your desk. Here is a good exercise that you can do:

A sit tall exercise

Sit in your chair with part of your back touching the back of your chair. Now put your arms straight down at your side.

Take the palm of your hand and place it on the chair with your fingers pointing away from the chair.

Now push down on the palms of your hands as much as possible and count to five.

You should feel yourself sitting taller. This exercise is fun to do whenever you feel yourself slumping.

Exercises—an aid to growing up

Incidentally, exercises are very good for a girl at the age at which she begins to menstruate.

They help a girl to feel better and get her body in top notch running order.

Rare menstrual discomfort

A girl who has a daily program of exercise rarely has menstrual cramps.

Demonstration guidelines

Familiarize your girls with exercises for painful menstruation. Have the girls dress in gym clothes and meet in the gym. Together the girls can learn the following exercises:

Abdominal pumping exercises[1]

Sit on the floor with your knees bent and your feet flat. Put one hand on the lower abdomen (below your waist) to feel muscle movement.

On count of "one" inhale deeply, pushing the abdomen out. On "two" pull the abdomen in holding your breath. On "three" exhale completely through the mouth. Repeat several times.

FIGURE 169

Twisting exercise[4]

FIGURE 170

Lie on your back with your legs straight and your arms spread out straight from your shoulders. Raise your left leg, keeping your knee straight, and swing your leg over to touch the palm of your right hand with your toes. Return your leg by first bringing it straight up in the air and then returning it to its starting position. Repeat the exercise, using your right leg. Do this exercise several times with each leg.

Cat exercise[4]

FIGURE 171

Assume a crawling position with your hands and knees on the floor. Lower your chest to the floor and arch your back by pulling in your abdominal muscles (the muscles below your waist). Return to a resting position. Repeat several times.

Other exercises

In addition to these exercises you will want to do at least one vigorous exercise each day.

You might want to play your favorite record and solo dance for 15 minutes when you come home from school each day.

It's also fun to take a brisk 15-minute walk before or after your homework.

On some days, but not very often, menstrual cramps may need some special attention.

Postures[4]

FIGURE 172

Sometimes lying in a special way seems to ease menstrual discomfort. Try these positions to find the one that makes you most comfortable.

Lie on your back on the floor with your knees bent and your feet resting on a low chair or stool.

Lie on your back on the floor or on a firm bed with your head on a small pillow and your knees pulled up to your chest.

Kneel on the floor with your knees about 12 inches apart and lower your chest until it touches the floor. Turn your head to one side with one hand on each side of the head.

Additional tips to relieve discomfort

All the exercises and postures we have learned should help, but in addition you may want some extra tips on how to relieve menstrual discomfort:

1. Place a hot water bottle or electric heating pad on your stomach.

2. Relax in a warm tub of water.

---

[4] Adapted from *Exercises for Dysmenorrhea*, Department of Health, Physical Education, and Recreation, University of Toledo, Toledo, Ohio.

Now you know many facts and many of the things all women know about their menstrual periods.

The menstrual period is quite normal and natural if you are always at ease and always prepared.

Perhaps you have some questions to ask . . . .

UNIT ACTIVITIES

My menstrual cycle

Have the girls make a booklet of calendars for the next 12 months. Title the booklet "My Menstrual Cycle."

On the first page of the booklet have the girls copy the following paragraph, which explains how to keep a calendar of the menstrual cycle:

Circle the day you start to menstruate. Then count off 28 days into the next month and draw a box around the date. That is approximately when your menstrual flow is due again. Be sure to make another circle around the day you actually do begin menstruating the next month, and make a note of how long overdue you were. This will give you a due date for the next time.

Explain to the girls that a record of their menstrual periods will be helpful in understanding themselves completely. It will help them to know:

1. The length of each menstrual cycle (28 to 35 days).

2. The number of days that they flow (3 to 5).

3. When their next menstrual flow will be.

4. If they have any menstrual irregularities.

Tampon or napkin carrying case

The girls will want to carry a tampon or napkin in their purse when their period is nearing. An additional activity might be to make a carrying case. The girls can use yarn and leather or plastic and boondaggle. If class time does not permit, you might pass the materials out in class and have the girls make the carrying case with their Girl Scout troop or with their mothers. An outside-class activity such as this might promote discussion between the girls and other competent adults.

"Growing Up" notebook

Have the children complete their "Growing Up" notebooks. Each notebook should include:

1. The journey of the sperm.

2. The menstrual cycle.

3. The sex education dictionary.

Collect the notebooks and check to see that the students have the correct information. Pass back the notebooks and allow the children to take them home to discuss with their parents.

First letter of information

At the close of the fifth grade the students should be familiar with the biological changes in growing up. As a review activity have each child write a letter to a fourth grade child explaining the process of growing up in detail. Tell your class that you plan to keep the letters and give them to the fourth grade children when they are in the fifth grade. Explain to your class the importance of being at ease with growing changes and the ease and assurance their letters will be to the other children if their explanations are clear. Put the letters in envelopes addressed to a fourth grader.

Second letter of information

After your sex education program has been instituted in your school system for more than one year you will have a set of letters to pass out to your fifth grade students. Pass out these letters to your class after you have covered and reviewed this unit. Have the children read the letters to themselves. Then have the children list on the blackboard some of the points made in the letter they read. After you are finished with this activity, erase the blackboard, collect the letters, and have the children begin writing their own letter to a fourth grader.

SUGGESTED BIBLIOGRAPHY FOR THE FIFTH GRADE

A Guide for Educators on Menstrual Hygiene. Education Department, Personal Products Company, Milltown, New Jersey 08850.
   A manual for teachers to help cover the topic of menstruation. Includes an outline for covering "The Facts of Menstruation," "Typical Questions about Menstruation," "Healthful Exercises," and "Good Grooming Suggestions." In addition there is a glossary and a list of suggested films.
Accent on You. Educational Director, Tampax Incorporated, 161 East 42nd Street, New York, New York 10017.
   A series of questions and answers from thousands of girls of this age group. Answers many of the questions girls have as well as reassuring them that other girls are puzzled also. Available in quantity for your students.
Beck, Lester, *Human Growth.* New York: Harcourt, Brace & Co., 1949.
   This book is recommended for the sixth grade child as a quick review of the material he has learned in grades one to five. At the fifth grade level the discussion of changes during puberty is important.
From Fiction to Fact. Educational Director, Tampax Incorporated, 161 East 42nd Street, New York, New York 10017.
   An educational guide for teachers who are helping young girls to understand the process of menstruation. An excellent coverage of the anatomy and physiology of menstruation.
Growing Up and Liking It. Educational Department, Personal Products Company, Milltown, New Jersey 08850.
   An educational pamphlet available in quantity for the teacher to use with her students in discussing the menstrual cycle. Discusses the menstrual cycle step by step and then carefully covers the hygiene of menstruation. One of the most complete booklets available.
How Shall I Tell My Daughter? Educational Department, Personal Products Company, Milltown, New Jersey 08850.

A booklet for mothers who are perplexed about discussing the topic of menstruation with their daughters. The teacher might order the booklet for the mother prior to covering this topic in class. This will assure preparation on the mother's part if the child should come home from school with additional questions.

It's Time You Knew. Educational Director, Tampax Incorporated, 161 East 42nd Street, New York, New York 10017.

A booklet for menstrual age girls explaining menstruation and how menstruation affects daily living. Available for classroom use.

Kind, R. W., and Leedham, J., *You Grow Up.* London: Longmans, Green & Co. Ltd., 1968.

A programmed booklet for teaching children about the biology of growing up. The booklet is very straightforward in discussing menstruation protection. Diagrams are clear and useful for this topic.

Lerrigo, Marion O., and Southard, Helen, *A Story About You.* Chicago: American Medical Association, 1961.

A review of the beginning of life. Most important, this book deals with the growth changes of the child and the emotional changes accompanying growth.

Limbacher, Walter, *I'm Not Alone.* Dayton: George A. Pflaum, 1969.

Explains "being human" and its implications for adults and little children. Can be included in a unit on self discovery.

Strain, Frances B., *Being Born.* New York: Hawthorn Books, 1972.

An excellent discussion of where babies come from with carefully drawn analogies. The book is also well illustrated and contains a good discussion of mating and marrying.

Strictly Feminine. Educational Department, Personal Products Company, Milltown, New Jersey 08850.

A booklet available for teachers to use with their girls in discussing the menstrual cycle. Very clear and detailed information in this booklet on the tampon—its safety and insertion.

The Miracle of You. Kimberly Clark Corporation, Box 551, Neenah, Wisconsin 54956.

A booklet written for the premenstrual age girl to help her understand and appreciate the many physical changes that occur in her life, particularly the process of menstruation. Available in quantity for classroom use.

World of a Girl. Scott Paper Company, International Airport, Philadelphia, Pennsylvania 19113.

A booklet available in quantity to teachers that deals with the changes in a girl's body as she grows up. Presents growth toward womanhood as a continuum.

You and Your Daughter. Kimberly Clark Corporation, Box 551, Neenah, Wisconsin 54956.

A booklet written for mothers (can be used by teachers), suggesting ways of answering a young girl's questions about growing up. The booklet is written in a question-answer form. It can be used to familiarize the adult with some of the questions of a young girl and some possible ways of answering these questions.

Your Years of Self Discovery. The Life Cycle Center, Kimberly Clark Corporation, Box 551, Neenah, Wisconsin 54956.

A booklet available in quantity that covers the topic of femininity and the sociology of femaleness as well as the biology of menstruation. Can be used after the child already understands menstruation thoroughly and is ready to understand the greater implications of growing up.

SUGGESTED FILMS FOR THE FIFTH GRADE

As Boys Grow. Medical Arts Productions, Inc., P.O. Box 4042, Stockton, California 94102.

A film for boys on the bodily and emotional changes accompanying growth.

Boy to Man. Henk Newenhouse, Inc., 1826 Willow Road, Northfield, Illinois 60093.
   Explains the many changes accompanying growth—skin, voice, body hair, glandular and
   sexual maturation.
Girl to Woman. Henk Newenhouse, Inc., 1826 Willow Road, Northfield, Illinois 60093.
   Explains the growth and development from girlhood to womanhood as well as describing
   the male reproductive system.
Growing Up (Preadolescence). Coronet Films, 65 E. South Water Street, Chicago, Illinois 60601.
   Nicky and Peggy show that growing up is an uneven process that differs between boys and
   girls, varying with individuals and age. The role of the endocrine glands in the growth
   process is illustrated.
Helen in Paris. Personal Products Company, Milltown, New Jersey 08850.
   A menstrual hygiene film made especially for use with black communities.
It's Wonderful Being a Girl. Personal Products Company, Milltown, New Jersey 08850.
   Two girls differ greatly in their rate of development and the time of the first menstrual
   flow. An excellent film to point out these differences. The film also covers sanitary
   protection and mother-daughter relationships and presents a fine philosophy of being
   a girl.
Milly Grows Up. Personal Products Company, Milltown, New Jersey 08850.
   A discussion of menstruation and menstrual hygiene.
Story of Menstruation. Kimberly Clark Corporation, Neenah, Wisconsin 54956.
   A general film introducing the facts about menstruation through the use of animated
   drawings and diagrams. Deals primarily with the physiology of menstruation and the
   misconceptions surrounding it.
The Miracle of Nature. Glenn Education Films, Inc., P.O. Box 371, Monsey, New York 10952.
   A menstrual film for the premenstrual age girl. The film presents menstruation in its
   proper perspective as a normal physiological function of the maturing body.

CHAPTER EIGHTEEN

Sex Education of the Sixth Grade Child

Throughout the elementary school years, sex education results in a spiral of learning. Each new unit reinforces and expands upon previous learning experience. In the earlier elementary years the children have learned specific content appropriately chosen for their degree of maturation. By the sixth grade, the maturation of the child and the vast learning experiences he retains have laid the foundation for the study of human sexuality in detail. The objective of the sixth grade teacher is to review and expand the child's understanding of the male and female sexual cycles, fertilization, pregnancy, and married and family love. A pretest to assess the knowledge of your class is followed by the fundamental sixth grade unit, "The Family as the Basic Unit of Society."

"PRETEST"

The administration of a pretest serves as a valuable educational tool for evaluating the current status of your students. The pretest is designed to help the sixth grade teacher identify the subject matter that needs to be reviewed prior to beginning the unit. In addition, it allows the student to identify his own needs and limitations within the spiral learning process. The location of the concept by grade level accompanies each question to enable the teacher to quickly obtain the material for review.

THE FAMILY AS THE BASIC UNIT OF SOCIETY

An Overview of the Unit

"We all belong to families that have experienced the joy of new life. In later years when we marry, we will belong to another family and we will be concerned with the raising of another generation. For this reason we will want to learn about life from its earliest existence and trace through its development step by step." So begins the unit that culminates the elementary sex education program. The program has built upon concepts and subject matter each year to arrive at a unit in the sixth grade in which each concept can be interwoven into a singular point of view—that sexual love and the upbringing of another generation are the basic functions and responsibilities of the family. The sixth grade program, "The Family as the Basic Unit of Society," includes a discussion of (1) the male and female reproductive systems, (2) ejaculation and the sex act, (3) intercourse and married love, (4) fertilization and heredity, (5) and pregnancy and childbirth.

PRETEST: THE BEGINNING OF NEW LIFE

Part I. Human and animal beginnings

Below are listed ten statements about the beginning of human and animal life. If the statement is false place a (0) in the blank. If the statement is true place a (+) in the blank.

+ 1. Human beings belong to the animal kingdom. (Grade 1)

+ 2. Every animal has a mother and a father in the beginning. (Grade 1)

0 3. A fish egg grows to be a fish in its mother's uterus. (Grade 2)

+ 4. A dog's egg is fertilized inside the mother dog's body. (Grade 2)

+ 5. All life comes from the same kind of life. (Grade 1)

+ 6. All animal life begins when a sperm joins an egg. (Grade 2)

0 7. In human beings the egg is fertilized in the uterus. (Grade 4)

0 8. An animal baby (puppy, kitten) needs only a mother to begin new life. (Grade 2)

0 9. If an egg that is bought at a grocery store is placed in an incubator it will grow into a chick. (Grade 3)

+ 10. A fertilized human egg grows in the mother's uterus. (Grade 3)

Part II. Animal development

Below are listed eight steps necessary in the fertilization and growth of an egg to a chick. Arrange these sentences in order beginning with fertilization. (Grade 3)

2 The rooster sends his sperm into the hen.

7 The egg is kept warm.

   8   The egg begins to grow into a chick.

   1   The hen makes an egg.

   5   A shell covers the egg.

   3   A yolk covers the egg.

   6   The hen lays the egg.

   4   White covers the yolk of the egg.

Part III. Processes in new life

Match the words in the left-hand column with the definitions in the right-hand column.

D	fertilization	A.	The joining together of the mother's and father's body in love. (Grade 5)
C	reproduction	B.	Contains the heredity information needed to make a girl. (Grade 4)
B	X chromosome	C.	The bringing about of the birth of a new plant or animal of the same kind. (Grade 2)
E	Y chromosome	D.	The joining together of a sperm and an egg. (Grade 2)
A	intercourse	E.	Contains the heredity information needed to make a boy. (Grade 4)

Part IV. Heredity

A baby receives two genes for every trait, one gene from the baby's mother and the other gene from the baby's father. A baby has received the following genes for different traits. Which gene is dominant? (Grade 4)

brown A gene for brown skin or a gene for white skin.

tall   A gene for being tall or a gene for being short.

curly A gene for curly hair or a gene for straight hair.

brown A gene for brown eyes or a gene for blue eyes.

Part V. Male reproductive system

Fill in the sentences describing the boy's body parts using the following words:

testes	vas deferens	epididymis	semen	penis
scrotum	seminal vesicle	prostate gland	urethra	Cowper's glands

scrotum   A small sac between the boy's legs that holds the testes.

epididymis   A tube-like resting station where the sperm grow up to look like tadpoles.

scrotum   A small sac between the boy's legs that holds the testes.

epididymis _____ A tube-like resting station where the sperm grow up to look like tadpoles.

testes _____ The place where the male reproductive cells, the sperms, are made.

seminal vesicle _____ A filling station that provides the sperm with sugar energy.

vas deferens _____ A long tube that goes up into the body. It is a waiting station for the sperms.

Cowper's glands _____ Two small cleaning stations that secrete cleansing fluid to clean the urethra.

semen _____ The milky sugary fluid that contains the sperm.

prostate gland _____ A storage container for milk-water.

urethra _____ A tube inside the penis.

penis _____ Located between the boys legs. It is soft and hangs down and looks like the thumb.

Part VI. Female reproductive system

Fill in the sentences describing the girl's body parts and processes using the following words:

ovary	navel
Uterus	hymen
Fallopian tube	menstruation
placenta	sanitary pad
vagina	FSH

navel _____ A mark that is left on the baby showing where the baby was attached to its mother.

sanitary pad _____ A soft disposable pad used to absorb the menstrual flow.

Fallopian tube _____ A tube leading from the uterus to the ovary.

uterus _____ A nest in which a baby can grow inside a girl's body.

ovary _____ A storage room filled with thousands of eggs.

placenta _____ A food and garbage exchange that connects a mother to her baby.

hymen _____ A thin piece of skin that covers the opening of the vagina to the outside of the body.

menstruation _____ The unwanted egg and blood that leave the uterus each month that no baby is made.

FSH _____ A message from the pituitary gland that tells the baby eggs sleeping in the ovary to wake up and begin to grow.

vagina _____ A tunnel that leads from the uterus to the outside of the body.

UNIT ONE: THE FAMILY AS THE BASIC UNIT OF SOCIETY

Introduction: the origin of life

The family is the basic unit of society. One of its many responsibilities is to pass life on from generation to generation.

During each minute of every day, every week, every hour, a new life begins. The new life brings much joy and happiness to each family.

The many hours waited and preparations made for the arrival of a new baby are soon forgotten. The family has learned a great deal about the origin of new life.

We all belong to families that have experienced the joy of new life. In later years when we marry, we will belong to another family, and we will be concerned with the raising of another generation.

For this reason we will want to learn about life from its earliest existence and trace through its development step by step.

Life begins as a single cell

A baby begins life as a single cell, smaller than the tiniest grain of sand and barely visible to the naked eye.

The first cell

The first cell is created by the joining of two parent cells:

1. The egg or ovum from the mother.

2. The sperm from the father.

Let us trace back to the beginning of each of these parent cells. We will begin with the egg cell.

Origin of the egg cell

When a girl is born, each of her ovaries contains some 200,000 to 400,000 egg cells. These egg cells are sometimes called primary follicles.

The sleepy egg cells

These egg cells or primary follicles remain asleep or inactive until they receive a hormone message that tells them to begin to grow.

Pituitary messengers

Between the ages of 11 and 14, these hormonal messengers begin acting under the direction of the pituitary gland in the brain.

This pea sized gland sends out hormonal messengers that announce that it is time for the girl's body to undergo vast remodeling.

A vast remodeling period

This remodeling period is known as puberty. During puberty, many changes take place in a girl's body as well as in the egg cells in her ovaries. All these changes are brought about by the hormone messengers we mentioned.

Secondary sex characteristics

First, we will look at the changes in the girl's body at puberty. These changes are known as the secondary sex characteristics.

Estrogen increases organ size

During puberty the ovaries release a hormone messenger called estrogen. Estrogen causes each of the female reproductive organs to increase in size.

Anatomy review

(Review the anatomy of the female reproductive organs with the class as you discuss the increase in organ size of each. As you identify each organ point to it on a diagram or overlay.)

1. Ovaries

A woman has two ovaries situated deep in the pelvis. They are slightly below and to each side of her navel.

Each ovary is oval: 1½ inches long, 1 inch wide, and ¾ inch thick.

At birth each ovary contains between 200,000 and 400,000 primary follicles or egg cells. These egg cells remain asleep or inactive until puberty.

2. Fallopian tubes

There are two Fallopian tubes. They extend from the ovary to the uterus. Each tube is 2 to 4 inches long and is lined with tiny hairs. The outer wall of the tube is composed of muscle that contracts in a slow rhythmic manner.

3. Uterus

The uterus is a muscular organ extending from the Fallopian tubes to the vagina. It is about the size and shape of a pear. The stem end is at the vaginal end of the uterus. This part of the uterus is called the cervix. The upper part called the body connects with the Fallopian tubes.

The uterine walls are divided into walls or layers. The inner wall lining is called the endometrium. This is a soft lining, which thickens each month to provide a nest for a growing baby. The outer uterine wall is quite muscular. It has the remarkable ability of being able to grow and expand enough to hold a 20 inch, 9 pound baby.

4. Vagina

The vagina is a 4 inch muscular tube that extends from the cervix of the uterus to the outside of a woman's body. The vaginal opening is between a woman's legs. It is behind the urethra from which urine comes and in front of the rectum from which bowel movements pass.

At rest, the vaginal walls are closed and touching each other. The walls are separated during menstrual flow, intercourse, and childbirth.

5. Hymen

Just inside the vagina is a thin membrane called the hymen. This membrane has one or more openings through which the menstrual flow leaves the vagina. The size of this opening differs among girls, just as girls differ in size and height. The size of the hymen and its presence or absence mean little, if anything.

6. Labia

The labia majora or outer lips are rounded folds of skin and fatty tissue that protect the structures lying between them and the vagina. The labia majora are covered by pubic hair. Inside the larger labia majora are two smaller and thinner folds of skin called the labia minora. They are the inner lips protecting the vagina.

7. Clitoris

Where the upper folds of the labia minora join together there is a small organ the size and shape of a pea. This organ is called the clitoris. The clitoris is richly supplied with nerves and blood vessels. It is very sensitive to touch.

8. Mons veneris (mons pubis)

The mons veneris or mons pubis is a mountain of fatty tissue covering the pubic bone. This area is covered with curly hair and protects the inner female reproductive organs from a shock or blow.

Continuation of Lecture

The streamlined young woman

In addition to increasing the size of the female reproductive organs, estrogen is responsible for the more streamlined appearance of the adult female.

The breasts develop

Under estrogen influence, fat is deposited in the breasts and an elaborate duct system for the secretion of milk develops.

Rounding the figure

Fat is also deposited in the buttocks and thighs, rounding out the female figure. The pelvis broadens and changes from a narrow funnel-like outlet to a broad, oval outlet.

These bodily changes are only a part of the maturation of the female reproductive system at puberty.

A message to the egg cells

During this vast remodeling period, the pituitary gland sends a message to the immature follicles or egg cells in the ovary via FSH.

FSH's important message

FSH is short for follicle-stimulating hormone. FSH does just what its name says that it might—it stimulates the primary follicles or egg cells in the ovary to grow.

Ovulation

Each month one of the egg cells that began to grow ripens and bursts out of the ovary, a process termed ovulation. This egg cell is guided by currents and by finger-like projections within the Fallopian tube.

A short life with high aspirations

The ripened egg has a very brief life span and will soon disintegrate if a sperm cell does not meet it on the first, or at most, the second, day after its arrival in the Fallopian tube.

Origin of sperm cells

The sperm cells are produced in the testes of the father. After their production in the testes, the sperm must pass through the penis and into the female vagina to fertilize the ovum.

A carefully planned journey

The father's body plans this journey as carefully as possible. The sperm have a long journey to make up through the body and many preparations en route.

The changes in the body and the accompanying production of sperms begin at puberty, the time when a boy is approaching manhood (ten years of age).

The testosterone telegram

During puberty, the testes send out a hormonal telegram called testosterone. Testosterone alerts the boy's body to make the transition to manhood.

The telegram's message

After the body has been alerted some noticeable changes are made:

1. The voice becomes deeper.
2. The skin becomes thicker and tougher.
3. The bones become longer and the muscles larger.
4. Hair appears under the arms, on the pubic region, and on the chin and face.
5. The organs of the male reproductive system enlarge.

Accompanying these changes in a boy's body is the beginning of the production of sperms by the testes.

Alert signal to testes

At puberty the pituitary gland in the brain sends a message alerting the testes to produce many sperms.

The temperature pouch

The testes begin their work with the help of the scrotum, the small sac or pouch that holds the testes. The scrotum makes sperm production easier by maintaining the testes at an ideal temperature.

Too cold

On days when the weather is extremely cold the scrotum aids sperm production by pulling the testes close to the man's body.

Too warm

On other days the weather is so warm that sperms cannot be produced. On these days the scrotum lowers the testes away from the body.

The epididymis finishing school

After the sperms have been produced by the testes they pass into a coiled tube located right above the testes. This tube is called the epididymis. It serves as a storage house and a finishing school.

A tadpole with head and tail

The epididymis makes the finishing touches on the sperms. The sperms take on a tadpole appearance with a large head and a tail, which beats back and forth.

Wait your turn, sperm

Now that the sperms have the finishing touches, they must wait their turn to make the journey up into the body. They wait in a long tube called the vas deferens. The vas deferens winds its way up into the body.

The ejaculation journey

At last the sperms are ready to make the final preparations en route to the female vagina. The special name for the trip from the testes to the vagina is termed ejaculation.

A last minute cargo check

During ejaculation or the sperm trip, the sperms begin to journey up the vas deferens. All supplies and cargoes needed for a safe sperm trip will be supplied.

Halt for energy

Energy will be needed for the long journey ahead! The seminal vesicle, a comma shaped filling station, empties an abundant supply of sugar solution into the vas deferens.

The ejaculatory duct

After the sperms receive this extra nutrition they journey into another tube called the ejaculatory duct. As the sperms empty into the ejaculatory duct another cargo is added.

Short stop at the milk-water reservoir

Once inside the female vagina the sperms swim by beating their tails. A milky watery fluid helps them to swim. The ejaculatory duct is surrounded by a milk-water reservoir called the prostate gland. The prostate gland empties milk-water into the ejaculatory duct.

All cargoes aboard

The ejaculation journey was carefully planned indeed! The sperms are in a fluid containing milk-water and sugar cargoes vital to their survival.

Ingredients in semen

This life-giving fluid is called semen. Semen contains three important ingredients:

1. Sperms from the testes.
2. Sugar from the seminal vesicle.
3. Milk-water from the prostate gland.

The urethra—the last tube

The end of the journey is nearing. The ejaculatory duct empties the semen into a long tube inside the penis called the urethra.

Urine pathway	The urethra is the same tube through which urine passes to the outside of the body. But urine and semen never journey through the urethra at the same time.
The closing door	Between the bladder (where the urine is stored) and the urethra is a small valve or door. When semen is nearing the urethra, this door closes, keeping urine inside the bladder.
Two cleansing stations	To doublecheck to be extra sure that the urethra is free of urine, there are two cleaning stations called Cowper's glands, one on either side of the urethra.
	Each of the Cowper's glands squirts cleansing fluid down the urethra to wash away any urine that might be left.
Clear road ahead	Now the road is clear for the final stage of ejaculation—the passage of semen down the urethra and out of the penis into the female vagina to fertilize the egg.
Coming together	But before fertilization or the coming together of the sperm and the egg, there must be a coming together of the father and the mother.
Important interchange	This coming together is called intercourse, which means an interchange, as one interchanges thought, feeling, friendship, or love with another.
Desire to share	Intercourse is a special way that married husbands and wives express their love and their desire to share everything with one another.
Interchanging love	The father and the mother lie close to each other sharing kind words, embraces, and kisses—interchanging the deep love they feel for one another.
The penis erects	The father's penis, which is usually soft, becomes hard and straight as a result of this deep feeling for his wife. This is called an erection.
Two closely fitting passages	The father places his erect penis into the mother's vagina and moves it back and forth, causing the semen to be released into the vagina.
Married love	
1. Sharing each other	Intercourse is a very special part of married love, and the closeness brings much pleasure to the man and wife. Because a man and wife who love each other want to be close to each other, they will have intercourse even when they do not intend to have a baby.

2. Sharing new life

When a married couple does want to have a baby, intercourse provides another kind of sharing. It allows a married couple to share the joy of bringing new life into the world.

Timing in the life-bringing process

The sharing together in bringing about new life requires special timing. The short life span of the egg cell, 12 to 24 hours, limits the time period during each month in which a sperm and an egg can unite. This time period lasts about two days each month.

Extra sperm cells

The chance of a sperm and an egg joining together is greatly increased by the fact that the father produces millions of sperms when only one is needed.

Few reach their destination

When the semen is released, millions of sperms swim up the vagina through the uterus and into the Fallopian tube, but only a few reach the egg.

An excited sperm

When a sperm reaches the egg it becomes excited, and its tail beats more rapidly. The beating tail gives the sperm more force to push its head into the egg.

Attempted breakthrough

The sperm cell cannot get into the egg cell by force alone. To help the sperm accomplish this task there is a special fluid inside the head of the sperm.

This fluid is similar to the fluid that eats away at the food in your stomach. The sperm releases this substance as it nears the egg. This substance eats away at the covering of the egg cell and allows the sperm to enter.

Not yet complete

The union of the sperm and egg is still not complete, however. The important directions for making a new baby are contained in the nucleus of the sperm and the nucleus of the egg. The nucleus of the sperm cell is in its head. The nucleus of the egg cell is in its center.

Gene instructions

Inside the nucleus of the sperm and inside the nucleus of the egg are genes. The genes contain all the instructions necessary for the design of every part of a new baby.

Pooling of information

A design for a new baby is laid out when the sperm nucleus combines its information with the nucleus of the egg, or, to put it another way, when the genes from the sperm are joined with the genes from the egg.

Important decisions

This pooling of instructions or genes will result in such important decisions as:

1. Whether the baby will be a boy or girl.

2. What color of eyes the baby will have.

3. What color of hair the baby will have.

4. What color of skin the baby will have.

5. Whether the baby will be tall or short.

More cells needed

After the genes from the sperm cell join the genes from the egg cell, the fertilized egg begins to divide into many cells. These cells will be needed to carry out the instructions from the genes.

Drifting to destination

During the first three or four days after this union, the dividing cells drift down the Fallopian tube toward the uterus.

Preparations for a comfortable nest

Meanwhile the uterus has been busily preparing a nest for the fertilized egg. The wall of the uterus is now extra thick and is filled with rich nourishing blood.

Floating cluster of cells

When the group of dividing cells arrive at the uterus on the fourth day they don't settle into the nest. Instead, they float around in the uterus for about four days.

Nesting for nourishment

Finally, in need of food and nourishment the group of cells burrow a nest in the uterine wall and settle inside. This is called "nesting."

Carrying out the instructions

Comfortable in their new home, the dividing cells are carrying out the instructions from the genes. This group of dividing cells, called an embryo, will have a lot of growing to do before a baby is formed.

During this growth period inside the uterus the embryo will need a means of obtaining food; oxygen, water, and a means of removing waste products.

Food and garbage service

This food and garbage service is provided by the placenta. The placenta is a depot in which the transport systems of mother and baby meet to exchange cargoes.

The mother's transport system brings nutrition and oxygen to the placental depot while the baby's transport system brings waste products.

Link between mother and baby

The placenta is connected to the growing embryo by the umbilical cord. When you were growing inside your mother, you had an umbilical cord attached to the placenta. But after you were born you didn't need the umbilical cord anymore, so the doctor tied and cut it. This left a scar, which you call your navel. So you see, the umbilical cord is attached to the baby at the location of the navel.

Mother shares supplies

The growing baby needs this attachment. He is dependent upon his mother for everything.

The mother takes care of the baby by taking care of herself. The baby can only receive as much food, oxygen, calicum, and vitamins as the mother has to share. In short, the baby has to depend on its mother's health for its own health.

This may be unfortunate for a baby who is growing inside a mother who does not take care of herself. The baby may receive some special supplies from its mother that it would rather not have.

"Supplies unwanted"

Do you think that a baby needs these supplies to grow?

1. Alcohol, wine, or beer.

2. Harmful ingredients from cigarette smoke.

3. Diseases such as flu, measles, or a cold.

Smoking, drinking, disease

Because babies share all supplies there is good reason for mothers to avoid smoking and drinking during pregnancy. Pregnant mothers should also avoid coming into contact with persons carrying disease.

Lifesaving supplies

Fortunately, many drugs to wipe out sickness (such as penicillin) can be supplied to the baby if needed. These supplies can be used to keep the baby healthy.

The drug is given to the mother, and within an hour it arrives at the placenta depot to be shared with the baby.

Further supplies

A further health measure is the "bag of waters," which tightly surrounds the growing embryo in the uterus. This bag of water is called the amnion.

Comfortable environment

The amnion protects the growing embryo by cushioning it from blows. Also, the temperature of the amniotic water is ideal for the embryo's growth.

Careful clockwork

With such ideal conditions in the uterus, the embryo's growth proceeds like clockwork. The time schedule for the growth of each body part is carefully planned.

Class activity

Divide the class into nine groups representing each month of intrauterine growth. Have a section of library books and materials available in your classroom. Each group will do research on the growth that takes place during their assigned month. Each group will also prepare a report to share with the class on what they have learned. Large illustrations made by the group will be combined on one large bulletin board to show the nine-month developmental sequence.

Below is an outline, month by month, of the development of the baby. It is intended to help the teacher organize the nine groups and is not intended to be lecture material. The monthly facts were taken from *Pregnancy,* a booklet presented by the Carnation Company.[1] You will want to send for several copies to have in your classroom.

End of first month

1. About 3/16 inch long.
2. Backbone and spinal canal forming.
3. Heart pulsating and pumping blood.
4. No eyes, nose, or external ears visible.
5. Digestive system beginning to form.
6. Small buds, which will eventually become arms and legs, are present.

End of second month

1. About 1 1/8 inches long.
2. Weighs about 1/30 of an ounce.
3. Face and features forming: eyelids fused.
4. Limbs beginning to show distinct divisions into arms, elbows, forearm and hand, thigh, knee, lower leg, and foot.
5. Distinct umbilical cord formed.
6. Long bones and internal organs developing.
7. Tail-like process disappears.

End of third month

1. About 3 inches long.
2. Weighs about 1 ounce.
3. Arms, hands, fingers, legs, feet, and toes fully formed.
4. Nails on digits beginning to develop.
5. External ears are present.
6. Tooth sockets and buds forming in the jawbones.
7. Eyes almost fully developed but lids still fused.
8. Heartbeat can be detected with special instruments.
9. Baby's hands are fully formed with fingers and nails all distinctly present.
10. The uterus begins to enlarge with the growing fetus and can now be felt extending about half-way up to the umbilicus.

---

[1] Address the Medical Department, Carnation Company, 5045 Wilshire Boulevard, Los Angeles, California 90036.

End of fourth month

1. The baby is now about 6 1/2 to 7 inches long and weighs about 4 ounces.

2. It has a strong heartbeat, fair digestion, and active muscles.

3. Its skin is bright pink and transparent and is covered with a fine, down-like hair.

4. Most bones are distinctly visible throughout the body.

5. The head is disproportionately large at this stage.

6. The eyes, ears, nose, and mouth approach typical appearance.

7. Eyebrows appear.

End of fifth month

1. The baby measures about 10 to 12 inches long and weighs 1/2 to 1 pound.

2. It is still bright red.

3. Its increased size now brings the dome of the uterus to the level of the umbilicus.

4. The internal organs are maturing at astonishing speed, but the lungs are insufficiently developed to cope with conditions outside the uterus.

5. The eyelids are still completely fused at the end of five months.

6. Some hair may be present on the head.

End of sixth month

1. At the end of the sixth month the baby measures 11 to 14 inches and may weigh 1 1/4 to 1 1/2 pounds.

2. The skin is quite wrinkled and still somewhat red and is covered with a heavy protective, creamy coating.

3. The eyelids are finally separated and eyelashes are formed.

4. Fingernails now extend to the ends of the fingers.

End of seventh month

1. The baby's weight has almost doubled since last month, and it is about 3 inches longer.

2. However, it still looks quite red and is covered with wrinkles, which will eventually be erased by fat.

3. At seven months the premature baby has a fair chance for survival in nurseries cared for by skilled physicians and nurses.

4. The seven-month baby is wrinkled and red.

End of eighth month

1. In the absence of premature labor the growth and maturation of the baby in the last two months are extremely valuable.

2. From the 2 1/2 to 3 pounds at the beginning of the month, it will add 2 to 2 1/2 more pounds and will lengthen to 16 1/2 to 18 inches by the end of the eighth month.

    3. The bones of the head are soft and flexible.

    4. If born now its chances for survival are much greater than those of a seven-month fetus, although there is a popular fallacy to the contrary.

    5. Ossification of all bones of the hand and wrist is not complete until the child is nearly 17 years old.

End of ninth month

    1. At birth or at full term the baby weighs, on an average, about 7 pounds if a girl and 7 1/2 if a boy.

    2. Its length is about 20 inches.

    3. The fine, downy hair has largely disappeared.

    4. Fingernails may protrude beyond the ends of the fingers.

    5. The size of the soft spot between the bones of the skull varies considerably from one child to another, but generally will close within 12 to 18 months.

Birth begins

As birth nears, the uterus becomes narrow. This straightens the baby's body so that the head is pressed against the closed cervix.

Vigorous contractions by the muscles of the upper uterus begin the birth process by pushing the baby through the cervix and into the vagina.

These muscles contract and relax in periodic rhythm. They break the protective bag of waters or amnion.

Trickling water

The water from the amnionic sac spurts out into the vagina. This water lubricates the birth passage.

First stage over

As the baby's head slips down through the cervix, the first stage of birth is completed.

The second stage of birth begins. This stage of birth is shorter but requires added force.

The mother labors

During this second stage, a great deal of effort is required by the mother. This is why the birth process is appropriately called labor.

Special muscles

Special muscles in the mother's body are geared to begin expelling the baby from the uterus through the vagina.

Stretching

At the same time the muscles of the vagina stretch to allow the baby to pass through to the outside of the body.

Crowning

At last the baby's head peeps through the opening. The birth of the baby's head is called crowning.

A gentle hand	When the head appears the doctor gently assists in the removal of the baby from the birth canal.
Unneeded cord	After the baby is removed from the birth canal the doctor ties the umbilical cord and cuts it close to the body.
No more than a haircut	This cutting cannot be felt any more than you feel your hair being cut off at the beauty parlor or barbershop. This cutting of the cord leaves a scar that we call the belly button or navel.
Baby is through	The baby's birth is now complete. On the average, a baby will weigh 7 pounds at birth and be approximately 19 to 21 inches in length.
	The baby may be covered with water, fluid, and downy hair from its stay in the uterus. The nurse or doctor will clean these away.
The mother works on	Meanwhile, the mother's job is not yet complete. The uterus is still contracting and expelling after the baby is born.
Afterbirth	The remainder of the umbilical cord and the placenta are expelled through the vagina. Together they are called the afterbirth.
Food again	Three days after the mother and baby have completed the birth process, the baby turns to its mother again for food.
Breastfeeding	The mother will put the baby to her breast and the baby will suck on her nipples to get milk. This is what we know as breastfeeding the baby.
Bottle feeding	Some mothers prefer not to breastfeed their babies. Carefully prepared milk formulas are fed to the baby by bottle. Both breastfed and bottle-fed babies receive ample nourishment.
Helpless infant	Babies require a lot of care. They are born helpless and depend upon their family for survival. The family is indeed important.
The family plan	Families must plan carefully for each baby. Each family has a responsibility to the helpless new being to care for it and love it so that it may grow up happily and healthfully. As long as there are families who share and love one another there will be more babies . . . more families . . . more babies.

SUGGESTED BIBLIOGRAPHY FOR THE SIXTH GRADE

Adler, Irving, and Adler, Ruth, *Evolution*. New York: The John Day Co., 1965.
    An excellent book to explain in detail the DNA molecule, chromosomes, and genetic infor-

mation. The book explains the division of cells and the process by which DNA replicates itself.

Clare, June, *The Stuff of Life.* New York: Roy Publishers, 1964.

A book that describes the miraculous process by which living things make copies of themselves over and over again. Shows the process by which genes carry the original message into the living thing, whether it be flower or man.

Gruenberg, Benjamin C., and Sidonie M., *The Wonderful Story of You.* New York: Garden City Books, 1960.

A book that discusses the entire person—the relationship between one's development and one's everyday living. It explains the different feelings and emotions during different growth periods.

Hutchins, Carleen May, *Life's Key.* New York: Coward-McCann, Inc., 1961.

The key facts about DNA and the role it plays in heredity are clearly explained. It offers a clear picture of the cell and its control by DNA. Directions are given for having the children construct their own DNA model.

Ingelman-Sundberg, Axel, and Wirsen, Claes, *A Child Is Born, The Drama of Life Before Birth.* New York: Delacorte Press, 1966.

A photographic depiction of the processes involved in human reproduction. Includes the first photograph taken of a live child within a womb.

Lerrigo, Marion C., and Southard, Helen, *What's Happening to Me?* New York: E. P. Dutton & Co., 1955.

A good transitional book from the biological process of reproduction to the social aspects of understanding boy-girl relationships at this age.

Levine, Milton, and Seligman, Jean H., *Human Reproduction.* New York: Harper & Row, Publishers, 1967.

A discussion of the structure and function of the reproductive systems, the development of the fetus, and the fertilization of twins. Includes a detailed discussion of the bodily and emotional changes accompanying adolescence.

Levine, Milton I., and Seligman, Jean H., *The Wonder of Life.* New York: Golden Press, 1952.

A book that discusses the beginning of life quite scientifically. Repeats concepts taught in grades one to five but goes into greater detail.

May, Julian, *Man and Woman,* Chicago: Follett, 1969.

A discussion of the changes that take place during adolescence and the implications of being a man or a woman.

Pilkington, Roger, *Human Sex and Heredity.* New York: Franklin Watts, Inc., 1961.

An up-to-date treatment of the story of the ingenious mechanisms of fertilization, heredity, the determination of the sex of children, and other aspects of reproduction. Emphasis is placed on the inheritance of family characteristics.

SUGGESTED FILMS FOR THE SIXTH GRADE

Especially for Boys. Henk Newenhouse, Inc., 1826 Willow Road, Northfield, Illinois 60093.

A color filmstrip explaining the growth process as boys mature.

Especially for Girls. Henk Newenhouse, Inc., 1826 Willow Road, Northfield, Illinois 60093.

A color filmstrip explaining the growth process as girls mature.

Human Growth. E. C. Brown Trust, 220 S.W. Alder Street, Portland, Oregon 97204.

Shows growth changes in boys and girls from ages 3 to 21. Deals especially with the changes at puberty in preparation for parenthood. The film may be used as a summary of the male and female reproductive systems and an introduction to pregnancy. The film depicts the different stages in pregnancy quite clearly, keeping the facts at a level that is easy for the sixth grade child to digest.

Personal Hygiene for Boys. Coronet Films, 65 E. South Water Street, Chicago, Illinois 60601.
During adolescence, boys require guidance in practical health habits. Why and how to shower, to shave, to guard against athlete's foot, to care for one's complexion, and to eat a balanced diet are straightforwardly discussed in this film. For boys only.

Personal Health for Girls. Coronet Films, 65 E. South Water Street, Chicago, Illinois 60601.
We watch Peggy's routine daily health habits that are so necessary to social poise and self-confidence. Cleanliness, proper complexion care, moderate exercises, and the importance of a balanced diet are some of the features that will be meaningful to young girls. For girls only.

Physical Aspects of Puberty. McGraw-Hill Films, 330 West 42nd Street, New York, New York 10017.
Diagrams of the normal development of the sex organs and the secondary sex characteristics help to explain the physical and emotional changes of adolescence. The social and emotional growth of the adolescent and his need for sympathetic understanding by parents are also shown.

Human Heredity. E. C. Brown Trust, 220 S. W. Alder Street, Portland, Oregon 97204.
A film in the series "Understanding Ourselves," which helps the child to understand the basic principles of heredity and environment. Clearly explains sex cells, chromosomes, and dominant and recessive genes. Ends by asking the film audience if they have any questions they would like to ask their teacher.

Heredity and Environment. Coronet Films, 65 E. South Water Street, Chicago, Illinois 60601.
Audience learns that heredity gives us certain basic capabilities and that the environment determines the extent and direction of our use of those capabilities. An overview of cultural inheritances, genetics, environmental influences, and their interrelationships is presented accurately.

CHAPTER NINETEEN

Sex Education in the Junior and Senior High School

Sex education in the elementary grades emphasizes the fact that sexuality exists and that it is the basis for all family life. Junior and senior high school sex education curricula emphasize the fact that sexuality exists and that it is good *when used wisely*.

The wise use of sexuality is dependent upon a careful synthesis of information relative to the biological, psychological, and sociological aspects of human sexual behavior. But presenting this information is rendered difficult by the fact that junior and senior high school curricula in the United States do not demonstrate any consistent pattern of sex education. Thus, this chapter was planned around specific topics rather than by grade level.

Resource information for each of the units in this chapter is found in Sections One, Two, and Three of this book. The Atlas at the end of this book contains illustrations especially designed to accompany the various teaching units. The basic purpose of this chapter is to suggest methods whereby this resource information can be organized into a meaningful learning experience for junior and senior high school students.

The units are:

1. Education for Love, Chapter 1

2. The Biological Male, Chapter 2.

3. The Biological Female, Chapter 3.

4. Human Sexual Response, Chapter 4.

5. Pregnancy, Childbirth, and Lactation, Chapter 5

6. Contraception and Population Stabilization, Chapter 6

7. Abortion, Chapter 7.

8. Venereal Diseases, Chapter 8.

9. Intelligent Choice of a Sexual Life Style, Chapter 9

10. Masturbation, Chapter 10.

11. Homosexuality, Chapter 11.

The units included here are coordinated into a meaningful whole by the use of a notebook on human sexuality. The student records his class notes and outside materials from each unit in this notebook. In addition, the student develops a vocabulary of terms through the use of unit vocabulary sheets. This compiling of information and vocabulary is an ongoing project throughout the program.

In addition to these methods, which provide for unity between topics, there are a variety of teaching techniques and procedures dealing with each topic individually. Open-ended questions are completed by the class and then discussed to measure attitudes. Parental interviews and questionnaires are completed to keep the line of communication open between parent and child. Classroom debates are employed to develop critical thinking. Diagrams are labeled to reinforce biological and anatomical knowledge. Models are constructed to clarify information. Visitations to slum areas broaden the realm of experience of the class. Research is examined and conducted by the class to distinguish fact from hearsay. Cartoons are used to depict the humor and ambiguity that attend man's sexuality. School and community campaigns are organized to develop responsibility and community concern. Patterns of living and problem-solving techniques are analyzed to give insight into a successful code of ethics.

UNIT ONE: EDUCATION FOR LOVE

Introduction

One of the outcomes of a successful sex education program is that the student will have real concern for others.

Practicing this concern in relationships with others can begin in the classroom. Thus, a series of activities "to get to know others" is probably the best way to begin a sex education class.

Several activities to promote learning about others are explained below.

"The Person Next To You"

As an opening lesson, hand out a copy of "The Person Next To You" to each student.

The Person Next to You[1]

Who is the person next to you?

You might say a name, and describe how tall he is, and the color of eyes and hair.

But none of these things are what the person is. A person is invisible activities.

The person nearest to you is an inexhaustible sort of existence. Nine-tenths of his possibility has not yet been touched off. There is all kinds of good that is struggling to be born from way within that person. There are also worries, fears, hates that are struggling to get themselves expressed. At the core of every man are these inexhaustible energies.

Deep within this person is a great toughness for his own integrity—a great tenacity in the face of adversity. Human nature is the most indestructible thing that we know. It has almost unlimited ability to take whatever comes—to go on surviving in the midst of un-believable difficulties and persecutions. A person is an over-powering will to survive, to arrive at destinations. To blossom and be—with all the spontaneity of a rose at seven o'clock on a June morning.

The person sitting next to you is an urge to become manifest. To become something in particular . . . .

He is a pain to be authentic. To experience a moment of truth. To have a story, and a song.

He is a need to be known even as he knows himself and at a level deeper than words.

The person sitting next to you is a unique world of experience. Within him is constantly going on a world premiere of experiences that no person has ever had, will ever have.

He is a cluster of memories of the past and expectations of the future.

He is a whole colony of persons, people met all during his life who have become inner inhabitants. Something of these people has entered into his person forever, so that the person sitting next to you is really a community. In that community live still the father and mother of this person, the boys and girls with whom he played most, the people with whom he went to school, the persons with whom he competed; the enemies he met; all the bad things of this world that came and interacted with him. They are still deep within . . . .

The person sitting next to you is a right to choose and decide, to run himself, to show responsibility in situations of life. He may greaten in the act of choice.

He has things he can do well. There are some things that he can do better than anybody else in the whole world . . . .

There is something his one life on earth means and cares for. But does he dare speak of it to you? . . .

[1] Ross Snyder, "The Ministry of Meaning," *Risk*. 3:3 and 4, pp. 171-173, World Council of Churches, Geneva, 1965.

The person sitting next to you is suffering.

He is working away at problems. He has fears. He wonders how he is doing. Often he doesn't feel too good about how he is doing; and finds that he can't respect or be a good friend of himself. When he feels that way about himself, he has a hard time loving others. When he dosen't feel good about himself and finds it hard to love others, he suffers.

He also suffers when two desires try to lead him in different directions. They clash against each other. He is indecision, he is disorganized. And in indecision and disorganization he is so close to chaos that pain becomes intense. For it is only when energy is in motion and in pattern that we are really happy.

The person sitting next to you is suffering partly because he keeps repeating patterns of solving problems and of relating himself to other people that never worked too well. But he learned them in a situation where he was very tense and somewhat fearful. Because of that he over-learned them; they tend to be the only ways which he can use. And so he goes on trying to solve his personal problems by using ways of feeling and attacking problems that don't work well, but were the means that he found when he was in a state of desperate need . . . .

In the fast darkness of the nonpersonal world, each of us is but a faint flow, hoping desperately to find light and warmth.

In the vastness of vibrant space which is galaxy beyond galaxy of continuous creation, we are an aliveness that savors its own existence . . . . and often finds it repellent.

Born of micro-patterned energy, we seek to be a link in the evolution of some stream of life, but suspect that we will be forgotten by the third generation.

Kin of the shrub and of the animal, alive only by the grace of our immersion in an ocean of air that so far is life-giving, we aspire to cover the earth with a network of thinking man's reverence for life, yet perhaps it will be of sick destruction.

Let us appear to each other before we are ended.

After the class has read the handout have them react to its contents. In particular, have them react to the end statement "Let us appear to each other before we are ended."

Explain to the class, that during the next few days the class will be doing activities "to appear to each other."

Advertisement

Part of loving is self-love. To love others, a person must feel worthy and he must find himself lovable. What is it your students love about themselves?

Have the students bring to class several magazines, glue and scissors. Give each student a sheet of poster board. Have each student make a poster to advertise himself.

If you were going to advertise yourself, what things would you want someone else to know?

After the students have completed their posters, place them around the room. Have the class guess what poster belongs to whom.

Each student can explain his poster and can answer questions that the class might have.

"Self-image"

The preceding activity was shared with the class. It would help the students to know each other better and it would also help you as the teacher to identify positive reinforcements in your pupils.

The following activity is aimed at examining the student's self-image. Why? Self-image is very much related to behavior, particularly sexual behavior.

Have your students examine their self-image by writing a paper to answer the following questions. (The questions are from the Columbus YWCA *Youth Outreach Rap Session*, 1-10, 73.)

1. Have you recently looked at yourself through your mirror?
   a) What did or do you see?
   b) Do you like what you see?
   c) What changes would you make in your appearance?

2. What do you like best about yourself?
   a) What do you like least about yourself?

3. What "bugs" you the most about the way you behave?
   a) What do you consider are your good points?

4. Who could influence you the most to change?

5. Who would you most like to pattern yourself after?
   a) In what way?
   b) Why?

6. What do your friends like best or least about you?

7. Do you have any enemies?
   a) Why do some people dislike you?

8. Is it important to you for kids your age to like you?
   If yes, why?
   If no, why?

9. What about adults, is it important that you be liked by them or be able to get along with them (parents, teachers, etc.)?

10. Is it difficult or easy for you to apologize or admit your mistakes?

11. Does change begin with you or someone else?
    Why?

12. How, when and where do you think that you can begin to make changes in yourself?

Brown bag

In dealing with our sexual behavior, we test our values. The "brown bag" activity can be used at the onset of our sex education program to lead into a discussion of value formation.

Have each student select one of his personal belongings that is very meaningful to him. Have the student put the belonging in a paper bag and bring it to class.

Place all the bags in a pile. (Fragile might be written on bags with breakables.)

The teacher can open the bag and show the class the item. After looking at the item, the class can identify reasons why the item is valued by someone. For example, a necklace could be valued because a loved person gave it as a gift.

After each item is discussed, have the students claim their item and explain why they cherish it.

Learning about others

Learning about others and sharing experiences is also a part of developing good personal relationships.

The following activity is designed to help students talk to others about their experiences. This strategy is taken from Sidney B. Simon et al., *Values Clarification*, New York: Hart Publishing Co., 1972. The directions are part of the handout.

My Name _____

The object of this little exercise is to keep you busy and give the teacher a rest, as well as to help you get slightly acquainted with each other. The winner gets, well, maybe, a package of orange tapicoa pudding mix. Find someone to fit each category below; the person who gets people for the greatest number of different categories wins. Use each person's name only twice, except that you can use the name of the teacher only once, and your own name only once (besides the name at the top of the page so I can tell whose this is). Use only one name for each category; if you use two and one of them is wrong in any way you get no credit for that one. Get both the first and the last name—spelled right, please. Now, find someone who

1. has mixed up his own mint tea.

2. has a dog, a cat, and a bird, all at once.

3. is wearing a handmade article of clothing.

4. has milked a goat.

5. has built a tree house.

6. is a surfer.

7. has drunk two brands of European beer.

8. has won a prize in a state or county fair.

9. has been out of the U.S. for six months at a time.

10. plays rugby.

11. plays pinochle.

12. plays chess.

13. plays guitar.

14. has climbed a 10,000 foot mountain.

15. is a radio ham.

16. has a frisbee at school.

17. has written a letter to a newspaper or a public official.

18. has made orange tapioca pudding in the last month.

19. has participated in a greased pig contest.

20. has been dunked in a carnival dunk tank.

Summary activity

To end the introductory activities, relate them all to love. That is, relate them to self-love as well as love of others.

Discuss Erich Fromm's[2] statement:

> What does one person give to another? He gives of himself, of the most precious he has, he gives of his life. This does not mean that he sacrifices his life for the other—but that he gives him of that which is alive in him; he gives him of his joy, of his interest, of his humor, of his sadness—of all expressions and manifestations of that which is alive in him.

UNIT TWO: THE BIOLOGICAL MALE

Introduction

Prior to this discussion, have the boys in the class make a list of things they don't understand about themselves.

Then have the girls make a list of things that they don't understand about boys.

This activity provides a good introduction for the class.

Vocabulary sheet

Distribute the list of words pertaining to the biological male. This list is found at the end of this unit.

The word list will be a valuable aid to the student in his note taking.

It will also assist him in the proper pronunciation and spelling of terms.

Human sexuality notebook

During the discussion of the biological male, students should be encouraged to compile interesting facts in their notebooks. Outside reading and materials should also be considered for the notebook.

The teacher may wish to provide some class time to work on the notebooks.

[2] Eric Fromm, *The Art of Loving,* Bantam Books, Inc., New York, 1963, p. 20.

Dictionary of terms

The students may also develop a human sexuality dictionary to include the meanings of new words.

This dictionary may be included as a separate section in the human sexuality notebook.

Anatomical diagram

An unlabeled diagram of the male anatomy may be distributed to the students prior to class. As the lesson is presented, the teacher may locate the male reproductive organs for the student, using the male anatomical drawing on the overhead projector (Figure 15 in the Atlas). As each reproductive organ is located, the student should label the diagram that he has received.

For quick review have the students turn the diagram over to the blank side and list in chronological order the successive structures the sperms pass through during ejaculation.

Illustrations

Students can make illustrations for their notebooks or for the classroom bulletin board to visualize their understanding of male physiology.

An illustration can be used to depict the various glands involved in reproduction. Each gland can be carefully drawn on a silhouette drawing of a male. The glands should be carefully labeled. Arrows can be drawn from each gland to the side margin where the names of the hormones secreted by the glands should be listed.

An illustration can be prepared to depict the maturation and development of the male secondary sex characteristics at puberty. The seconary sex characteristics which are difficult to depict in an illustration are as follows:

1. Longer and heavier bones.
2. Larger muscles.
3. Thicker and tougher skin.
4. Deep voice.
5. Baldness in later life.
6. Characteristic distribution of body hair.
7. Increased metabolism.

Physiological observations

It has been known for years that a castrated animal is less vigorous, aggressive, ambitious, impatient, exploitative, and violent. The following classroom activity can be used to demonstrate that in terms of energy, sex hormones must unquestionably be the most powerful substance known to man. Obtain a castrated rat and a normal rat and place each one in a separate cage with an exercise wheel. The normal rat will run 73 times the distance of the castrated rat on a daily basis.

Classroom reports

Outside reports may be used in a variety of ways to enhance the learning experience. Topics may be assigned for group discussion, for outside reading, or for term papers.

An alternate method of using the outside report is to allow students to volunteer in advance to prepare a report to present to the class. The student's report can be used to enrich the classroom material when the teacher covers the appropriate subject matter.

The following topics can be dealt with in the variety of ways mentioned:

1. Cancer of the prostate.
2. Cryptorchidism.
3. Inguinal hernia.
4. Artificial insemination.
5. Biological evolution of the male.
6. Role of the endocrine glands.
7. Male aggression.

Classroom debate

The teacher can organize a classroom debate to encourage the student to delve into the available literature on human sexuality. Critical analysis of a topic on human sexuality will help the student to develop the responsibility needed to make decisions regarding male sexuality.

For example, the students can explore the available pros and cons of circumcision. They should be careful to quote authorities and sources. This exercise will not only be valuable in learning to analyze a topic but will provide a classroom situation for discussion of the validity of medical arguments. What criteria can we use to distinguish fact from hearsay?

Other topics for debate might include:

1. Are males or females more healthy?
2. Are males or females more aggressive?

WORDS PERTAINING TO THE BIOLOGICAL MALE[3]

1. Abdomen (ab-do'men)
2. Acrosome (ak'ro-sōm)
3. Bulbo-urethral glands (bul-bo-u-re'thral)
4. Castration (kas-tra'shun)
5. Circumcision (ser-kum-sizh'un)

---

[3] Definitions of these terms can be found in the glossary at the end of this book.

6. Climacteric (kli-mak-ter'ik)

7. Cowper's glands (kow'perz)

8. Cryptorchidism (krip-tor'ki-dizm)

9. Ejaculation (e-jak-u-la'shun)

10. Ejaculatory duct (e-jak'u-lah-to-re)

11. Epididymis (ep-i-did'i-mis)

12. Erection (e-rek'shun)

13. Eunuch (u'nuk)

14. Follicle stimulation hormone (fol'li-k'l)

15. Foreskin (fōr'skin)

16. Glans (glanz)

17. Gonad (gon'ad)

18. Hernia (her'ne-ah)

19. Hormone (hor'mōn)

20. Hyaluronidase (hi-ah-lu-ron'i-dās)

21. Hypothalamus (hi-po-thal'ah-mus)

22. Inguinal hernia (ing'gwi-nal)

23. Interstitial cell stimulating hormone (in-ter-stish'al)

24. Luteinizing hormone (lu'tin-i-zing)

25. Milliliter (mil'li-leter)

26. Orgasm (or'gazm)

27. Penis (pe'nis)

28. Pituitary gland (pi-tu'i-tār'e)

29. Prepuce (pre'pūs)

30. Prostate gland (pros'tāt)

31. Retrograde ejaculation (ret'ro-grād)

32. Scrotum (skro'tum)

33. Semen (se'men)

34. Seminal vesicle (sem'i-nal ves'i-k'l)

35. Seminiferous tubules (se-mi-nif'er-us tu-būlz)

36. Silicone (sil'i-kōn)

37. Smegma (smeg'mah)

38. Spermatogenesis (sper-mah-to-jen'e-sis)

39. Spermatozoa (sper-mah-to-zo'ah)

40. Testes (tes'tez)

41. Testosterone (tes-tos'ter-ōn)

42. Uretha (u-re-thrah)

43. Vas deferens (vas def'er-enz)

44. Vasectomy (vas-ek'to-me)

SUGGESTED FILMS FOR USE WITH THE UNIT ON THE PHYSIOLOGY OF MALENESS

About Men (For Girls). Rose and Abraham Dyck, Family Life Publications, Box 6725, Durham, North Carolina 27708.

A 45-minute tape that answers questions from 3000 high school and college girls about male biology and psychology.

As Boys Grow. Medical Arts Production, P.O. Box 4042, Stockton, California 95203.

A coach deals with junior high school boys in different setting—locker room, field, and so forth. Explains the many changes that occur at adolescence, including secondary sexual characteristics, masturbation, and seminal emission. The film can also be used prior to discussing the relationship between the sexes.

Boy to Man. Churchill Films, 6671 Sunset Boulevard, Hollywood, California. 90028.

All the signs of male adolescent maturity—secondary sex characteristics, wet dreams, masturbation—are covered in this film as well as a discussion of the male role in reproduction. Helps boys to understand their changes in feelings as well as the changes in their bodies.

Human Reproduction. McGraw-Hill Films, 330 West 42nd Street, New York, New York 10036.

An excellent film showing the structure and function of the male and female reproductive systems and the miracle of human birth. The birth process is followed from conception to birth, ending with a live scene in a delivery room where a mother is observed seeing her newborn child for the first time.

Physical Aspects of Puberty. McGraw-Hill Films, 330 West 42nd Street, New York, New York 10036.

This animated film describes the development of primary and secondary sex characteristics in boys and girls and helps them to understand and accept their own body changes during adolescence.

Reproduction in Animals. Coronet Films, 65 E. South Water Street, Chicago, Illinois 60601.

This film introduces the fundamental principles of the process of reproduction among animals. With the emphasis on reproduction in mammals, we observe various animals. The function of each parent, the three main types of sexual reproduction, the development of the embryo, and birth processes are illustrated.

The Human Body: Reproductive System. Coronet Films, 65 E. South Water Street, Chicago, Illinois 60601.

Reviews the anatomy of the male and female reproductive systems as well as discussing fertilization. A good film for review of the physiology and anatomy learned in grades one through six.

UNIT THREE: THE BIOLOGICAL FEMALE

Introduction

Prior to this discussion have the girls in the class make a list of things that they don't understand about themselves.

Then have the boys make a list of things that they don't understand about girls.

This activity provides a good introduction for the class discussion.

Vocabulary sheet

Distribute the list of words pertaining to the biological female. This list can be found at the end of this unit.

The word list will be a valuable asset to the student in his note-taking.

It will also assist him in the proper pronunciation and spelling of terms.

Human sexuality notebook

During the discussion of the biological female, students should be encouraged to compile interesting facts in their notebook.

The teacher may wish to provide some class time to work on the notebooks.

Dictionary of terms

Students may also develop a human sexuality dictionary to include the meanings of new words.

This dictionary may be included as a separate section in the human sexuality notebook.

Anatomical diagram

An unlabeled diagram of the female anatomy may be distributed to the students prior to class. As the material is presented, the teacher may locate the female reproductive organs for the student, using the female anatomical drawing on the overhead projector (Figure 22 in the Atlas). As each reproductive organ is located, the student should label the diagram that he has received.

For review have the students turn over the diagram to the blank side and list in chronological order the itinerary of the egg from ovulation to disintegration during the menses.

Illustrations

Students can make illustrations for their notebooks or for the classroom bulletin board to visualize the female physiology.

For example, an illustration can be used to show the secondary sex characteristics caused by the release of estrogen. These changes can be listed somewhere on the poster or bulletin board:

1. Deposition of fat in the breasts accompanied by development of an elaborate duct system.

2. Broadening of the pelvis which changes from a narrow, funnel-like outlet to a broad, oval outlet.

3. Development of soft and smooth skin.

4. Deposition of fat in the buttocks and thighs.

5. Development of pubic hair with a flat upper border.

6. Early uniting of the growing end of long bones with the bone shaft.

Observations

Ask for girl volunteers to conduct a study in their physical education classes on physical performance during the menses. Have the girls decide upon certain skills to be measured in their physical education class. The girls should measure these same skills daily, comparing the level of performance from day to day. The study should reveal that there is no significant difference in performance during the menses.

Compare the results of your students' study with a study done at the Tokyo Olympics including 66 women athletes:

1. 70 per cent retained normal performance.
2. 15 per cent did better.
3. 15 per cent did worse.

Projects

Allow students to work in groups on classroom projects to clarify their understanding of the biology of femaleness. The following activities are suggested to supplement the learning experiences in this unit.

A group of students can construct a model of a primary follicle. Their model should clearly show the thin layer of follicular cells surrounding the immature ova. After the model is constructed the group can explain to the class the process of ovulation.

A group of students can construct a model of the uterus. Different models can be used to depict the corpus or body, isthmus, cervix, myometrium, and endometrium. The group can explain through their models the changes in the endometrium throughout the menstrual cycle. They can also compare the sizes of the uterus at birth, at puberty, during pregnancy, and at menopause (see Figure 23 in the Atlas).

Another group of students can supplement the uterine model project by constructing graphs to explain the menstrual cycle. These graphs should focus on the level of hormonal secretion during different phases of the menstrual cycle. These hormonal phases should be related graphically to the phases of the menstrual cycle: proliferative, secretory or progestational, and menstrual phases (see Figure 27 in the Atlas).

Research

Appoint two groups of students to discuss the safety of the sanitary tampon. One group can gather a list of common misconceptions and old wives' tales. The other group will gather available research articles on the topic. (This group can write to Tampax, Inc., for information.)

Debate   Present the foregoing material in a classroom discussion. The first group will represent housewives. The second group will represent medical authorities. The first group will present one of the old wives' tales listed in their findings. The second group, the medical authorities, will present medical research findings to clarify the point made.

WORDS PERTAINING TO THE BIOLOGICAL FEMALE[4]

1. Amenorrhea (ah-men-o-re'ah)
2. Anemia (ah-ne'me-ah)
3. Bartholin's glands (bar'to-linz)
4. Cervix (ser'viks)
5. Cilia (sil'e-ah)
6. Climacteric (kli-mak-ter'ik)
7. Clitoris (kli'to-ris)
8. Corpus (kor'pus)
9. Corpus luteum (kor'pus lu'te-um)
10. Cumulus cells (ku'mu-lus)
11. Dysmenorrhea (dis-men-o-re'ah)
12. Ectopic pregnancy (ek-top'ik preg'nan-se)
13. Endometrium (en-do-me'tre-um)
14. Estrogen (es'tro-jen)
15. Fallopian tube (fal-lo'pe-an)
16. Fertilization (fer-ti-li-za'shun)
17. Follicle stimulating hormone (fol'li-k'l)
18. Follicular cells (fo-lik'u-lar)
19. Genitalia (jen-i-ta'le-ah)
20. Gonad (gon'ad)
21. Graafian follicle (graf'e-an fol'li-k'l)
22. Hymen (hi'men)
23. Isthmus (is-mus)
24. Labia majora (la'be-ah)
25. Labia minora (la'be-ah)
26. Luteinizing hormone (lu'tin-i-zing)
27. Menarche (me-nar'ke)
28. Menopause (men'o-pawz)
29. Menorrhagia (men-o-ra'je-ah)
30. Menstruation (men-stroo-a'shun)
31. Mittelschmerz (mit'el-shmarts)
32. Mons veneris (monz ven'er-is)
33. Myometrium (mi-o-me'tre-um)
34. Ovary (o'vah-re)
35. Ovulation (ov-u-la'shun)
36. Papanicolaou smear (pap-ah-nik-o-la'oo)
37. Pelvis (pel'vis)

---

[4] Definitions of these terms can be found in the glossary at the end of this book.

38. Pituitary gland (pi-tu'i-ta-re)
39. Placenta (plah-sen'tah)
40. Primary follicle (fol'li-k'l)
41. Progesterone (pro-jes'ter-on)
42. Proliferation (pro-lif-er-a'shun)
43. Puberty (pu'ber-te)
44. Pudendum (pu-den'dum)
45. Stigma (stig-mah)
46. Stratum vascularis (stra'tum vas'ku-lar-is)
47. Tampon (tam'pon)
48. Uterus (u'ter-us)
49. Vagina (vah-ji'nah)
50. Vestibule (ves'ti-bul)
51. Vulva (vul'vah)

SUGGESTED FILMS FOR USE WITH THE UNIT ON THE PHYSIOLOGY OF FEMALENESS

About Girls (*For Boys*). Rose and Abraham Dyck, Family Life Publications, Inc., Durham, North Carolina 27708.
   A 45-minute tape that tells boys what they need to know about female physiology and psychology.
Girl to Woman. Churchill Films, 6671 Sunset Boulevard, Hollywood, California 90028.
   An excellent movie presenting the changes from girlhood to womanhood—both physiological and sociological. The movie is up to date, and girls depicted discuss topics of common concern to the growing adolescent—physical development, menstruation, kissing, and dating.
Human Reproduction. McGraw-Hill Films, 330 West 42nd Street, New York, New York 10036.
   An excellent film showing the structure and function of the male and female reproductive systems and the miracle of human birth. The birth process is followed from conception to birth, ending with a live scene in a delivery room where a mother is observed seeing her newborn child for the first time.
Physical Aspects of Puberty. Coronet Films, 65 East South Water Street, Chicago, Illinois 60601.
   This film introduces fundamental principles of the process of reproduction among animals. With the emphasis on reproduction in mammals, we observe various animals. The function of each parent, the three main types of sexual reproduction, the development of the embryo, and birth processes are illustrated.
The Human Body: Reproductive System. Coronet Films, 65 E. South Water Street, Chicago, Illinois 60601.
   Reviews the anatomy of the male and female reproductive systems as well as discussing fertilization. A good film for review of the physiology and anatomy learned in grades one through six.
The Importance of Mother. Graphic Curriculum, Inc., P.O. Box 565, Lenox Hill Station, New York, New York 10021.
   Originally seen on NBC-TV, this film stresses the importance of the early relationship between mother and child. This relationship is demonstrated when a monkey is deprived of this relationship and then is awkward in forming social relations, care-eliciting behavior, play, curiosity, and sexual relationships.

UNIT FOUR: HUMAN SEXUAL RESPONSE

Introduction

Prior to the lecture on the human sexual response, pretest the students on the following questions:

1. Are males or females more sexually aggressive?

2. Do males and females respond differently in the sexual situation?

3. For what purposes is the sex act performed? Rank in order these purposes.

4. Which factor is more important in affecting female sexual response: the amount of love the female has for her male sex partner, or the sex technique the male uses to arouse the female?

Vocabulary sheet

The human sexual response vocabulary sheet should be distributed to the students prior to the lecture. This sheet will aid the student in note taking. It will also assist him in the proper pronunciation and spelling of terms. (This sheet can be found at the end of the suggested methods and activities.)

Discussion of the four phases of sexual response

The discussion of the four phases of sexual response can be related to jumping off a diving board. To utilize this approach, draw a diving board on the blackboard.

There will be four phases of diving that you will discuss. Discuss the simple task of jumping off a diving board—do not relate this to sexual behavior at first.

Your discussion should include all the conditions that surround this activity. For example:

Phase I (Climbing the board).

1. Excitement begins.

2. Person may be trying something new.

3. Person might be frightened if he has never done this before.

4. Person may turn back out of fear.

5. Person may be coaxed to try something when he really would rather not.

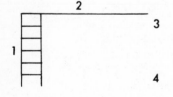

Phase II (Walking out on the board).

1. The excitement is now building.

2. There is less chance that the person will turn back.

3. It is more difficult to turn back.

4. As the person reaches the end of the board, he is very involved.

5. The person may fall off the board accidentally.

Phase III (Diving).

1. The dive may be very successful.

2. The dive most likely will be awkward, since it is a first attempt.

3. The person may hit the water very awkwardly and not enjoy the dive at all.

Phase IV (Getting out of the water).

1. The person has a new attitude about diving; he has formed some feelings.

2. He may decide from this one experience that he does not like to dive.

3. He may decide from this experience that he enjoys diving.

4. If he enjoys diving, it will become easier and easier to jump off the board.

After your class has discussed all possibilities for the initial experience of diving, relate this to human sexual response and sexual behavior.

Below are listed the phases of response, definitions, and possible discussion ideas.

Phase I—Excitement. The excitement phase begins with the initial sexual stimulation, ranges from a few minutes to as long as several hours, and ends by passage into the plateau phase.

> Discussion: relate the early part of excitement, kissing, petting, to climbing the diving board. Examine first apprehensions, new feelings that occur, and building tensions.

Phase II—Plateau. During the plateau phase tension builds up for the leap into orgasm.

> Discussion: relate building sexual tensions to the diving board. Once sexual tension builds up it is difficult to turn back. Also, a person may lose control (fall off the board) as he becomes more involved.

Phase III—Orgasmic. The orgasmic phase in both male and female consists of rapid muscular contractions that release accumulating tensions.

> Discussion: the commitment to jump is made, and the

person is involved in the peak of the activity. What will the first attempt be like? How will it affect the person?

Phase IV—Resolution. During the resolution phase, biological structures return to their pre-excitement state.

Discussion: this can be related to the "cooling off" period in the water when talking biologically. Relating this to psychology or a person's real experience, we can consider his feelings after the activity. Have his fears and anxieties increased because of a bad experience? Because he has committed himself once, will it be easier to jump again and again?

The purpose of discussing the diving board first was to get lots of students to talk. Many will explain their own thoughts about the first time they jumped into the water. Some very interesting comments will be made. Write these on the blackboard and then when you shift the topic to sexual behavior see how they apply.

Human sexuality notebook

The students should take notes on the discussion and carefully organize them into separate units to compile a notebook on human sexuality. Encourage outside reading and the inclusion of additional materials in the notebook. (The high school teacher may want to allow class time for the student to work on his notebook.)

Dictionary of terms

The students should include the meanings of technical terms from the human sexual response lecture in the dictionary section of their notebooks on human sexuality.

Classroom discussion

List examples of pleasure seeking. Why is pleasure seeking one of the most difficult activities man has ever undertaken? What benefits does man receive from pleasure seeking? What dangers are there in pleasure seeking?

Diagram of the brain

The students should diagram the brain and label the cerebral cortex and the hypothalamus. On the left side of the brain list the functions of the cerebral cortex. On the right side of the brain diagram list the functions of the hypothalamus.

Report

A student or group of students can volunteer to do some research and report to the class on the differences between human sexuality and the sexuality of lower animals.

Classroom discussion

Have the class analyze the following list, differentiating the effect of each on the sex drive of the male and of the female.

Touch
Smell

Sight
Personality
Pornography
Alcohol
Affection
Love
Physical attractiveness
Intelligence
Sense of humor
Compatibility
Commitment to partner

Diagram of the sex drive

The students can include in their notebook on human sexuality the following diagram summarizing the factors influencing the sex drive:[5]

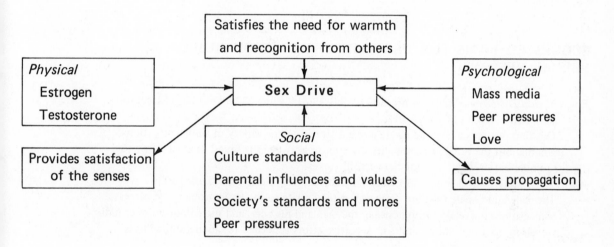

WORDS PERTAINING TO THE HUMAN SEXUAL RESPONSE[6]

1. Androgen (an'dro-jen)
2. Bartholin's glands (bar'to-linz)
3. Brain (brān)
4. Castrate (kas'trat)
5. Central nervous system (sen'tral ner'vus sis'tem)
6. Cerebral cortex (ser-e'bral kor'teks)
7. Cervix (ser'viks)
8. Clitoris (kli'to-ris)
9. Cowper's gland (kow'perz)
10. Ejaculation (e-jak-u-la'shun)
11. Erection (e-rek'shun)
12. Erectile tissue (e-rek'til)
13. Erogenous (e-ro'je-nus)

---

[5] Adapted from Florence Benell, *Behavioral Dynamics in Sex Education.*
[6] Definitions of these terms can be found in the glossary at the end of this book.

14. Excitement
15. Frigidity (fri-gi′di-tee)
16. Glans (glanz)
17. Hypogonadism (hi-po-go′nad-izm)
18. Hypothalamus (hi-po-thal′ah-mus)
19. Impotence (im′po-tens)
20. Masturbation (mas-tur-ba′shun)
21. Menopause (men′o-pawz)
22. Orgasm (or′gazm)
23. Orgasmic phase (or′gaz-mic)
24. Penis (pe′nis)
25. Plateau phase (plah-to′)
26. Resolution phase (rez-o-lu′shun)
27. Sexual response (seks′u-al)
28. Spinal cord (spi′nal)
29. Testicle (tes′ti-k′l)
30. Uterus (u′ter-us)
31. Vagina (vah-ji′nah)

SUGGESTED FILMS FOR USE WITH THE UNIT ON HUMAN SEXUAL RESPONSE

Psychological Differences Between the Sexes. McGraw-Hill Films, 330 West 42nd Street, New York, New York 10036.
 This film portrays a boy and girl reacting differently to a variety of similar situations, pointing out the primary personality differences between the sexes. Suggests ways to promote better understanding between the sexes.

Who's Boss? McGraw-Hill Films, 330 West 42nd Street, New York, New York 10036.
 The male and female roles are discussed as they relate to the basic problems of careers, competition, the relationship between the man and his wife, and the compromise of individuals in marriage. Shows that a cooperative effort is needed to eliminate the "boss" concept in a marriage relationship.

UNIT FIVE: PREGNANCY, CHILDBIRTH, AND LACTATION

Question box

Prior to the lecture on pregnancy, childbirth, and lactation, have the students write questions on 3 by 5 inch cards and place them in a question box.

Vocabulary sheet

The pregnancy, childbirth, and lactation vocabulary sheet should be passed out to the students prior to the lecture. This sheet will be a valuable asset in helping the students to take notes. It will assist them in the proper pronunciation and spelling of terms.

Human sexuality notebook

The students should take notes on the pregnancy, childbirth, and lactation discussion and carefully organize them into a unit for their notebook on human sexuality. Encourage the use of outside reading and materials in the organization and development of this unit.

Dictionary of terms

The students should include meanings of the technical terms from the pregnancy, childbirth, and lactation lecture in the dictionary section of their notebook of human sexuality.

Reports

Individually or in groups, students benefit from independent study, which expands beyond the classroom learning experience. The following report assignments supplement the learning spiral developed in this unit:

1. Preparation of a report on what constitutes a healthy diet for a mother during her nine-month pregnancy.

2. Development of a complete list of all the dominant and recessive genes known to man.

3. Preparation of a report to be shared with the class on the story of the Dionne quintuplets.

Projects

The teacher can allot class time for the development of projects to supplement the unit. Students may have many ideas for worthwhile activities. The following projects supplement this unit:

Students can study heredity by working out a family tree chart that encompasses the previous three generations. The students can use class time to write relatives for information. This information can be written with India ink on antiqued or smoked paper to indicate the historical content. Encourage the students to share the finished product with their families.

The students can develop a study of the development of the embryo during each of the nine intrauterine months. For this project the class can be divided into nine separate groups, each representing one of the months of pregnancy. Each group can report on the growth of the embryo during one month. Large illustrations can be made by each group to supplement their project.

An understanding of the Rh factor and of blood types is difficult to explain without a project to facilitate the learning experience. Obtain the help of the school nurse and science teacher and take blood samples from the students to determine blood types and Rh factors. Chart the findings to show which blood types will mix and how the Rh factor will influence the blood of the baby.

Illustrations, charts, and graphs

Illustrations, charts, and graphs are especially important in supplementing an organized sequential learning experience. The passage of time involved in the process of pregnancy can be depicted in a series of charts.

Develop charts that show the movement of the ovum beginning with ovulation and ending with implantation.

Develop charts that show the expansion of the mother's uterus during her nine-month pregnancy.

Make a graph that shows the life span of the egg and the life span of the sperm. Indicate on the graph when pregnancy can occur.

Make charts to illustrate the inheritance of hemophilia, color blindness, and other sex-linked diseases.

Draw a placenta on a large poster. On the left side of the poster, list the cargoes that cannot be exchanged between the mother and the baby. On the right side of the poster, list the cargoes that can be exchanged between the mother and the baby. On the poster show the specially constructed compartments within the placenta that store various products until they are needed. List the names of these stored cargoes adjacent to the compartments.

Debates

The classroom debate is a valuable tool, which can be used to bring additional material into the learning experience. The following debates can be used to highlight research information, although neither side of the debate teams should "win."

1. Environment vs. heredity.

2. Breast-feeding vs. bottle-feeding.

Models

Construct models of the cell, sperm, and ova, including the nucleus, chromosomes, genes, DNA, RNA, protein, and cellular enzymes.

Construct the following model of the DNA molecule:[7]

> Here are the directions for making your own DNA model to a scale that is about two hundred million times larger than the actual DNA coiled within each chromosome of a cell nucleus. The DNA in one chromosome would reach from New York to Rome, Italy, if it were enlarged to this scale!

---

[7] From Carleen M. Hutchins, *Life's Key-DNA*, Coward-McCann, Inc., New York, 1961. Reprinted by permission of Coward-McCann, Inc. Copyright 1961 by the National Foundation.

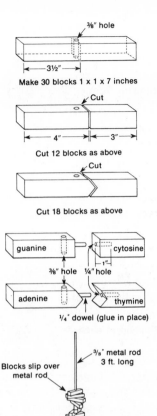

⅜" hole

←——— 3½" ———→

Make 30 blocks 1 x 1 x 7 inches

←Cut

←— 4" —→←— 3" —→

Cut 12 blocks as above

←Cut

Cut 18 blocks as above

guanine   cytosine

⅜" hole   ¼" hole

adenine   thymine

¼" dowel (glue in place)

⅜" metal rod
3 ft. long

Blocks slip over
metal rod

10" x 10" base

FIGURE 173

Materials: About 20 feet of clear soft wood that is a full inch square. (Many lumber yards carry a standard 1 1/16 × 1 1/16 inch clear pine called baluster that is excellent for this purpose.) Three feet of metal (preferably aluminum) rod 3/8 of an inch in diameter. Six feet of 1/4 inch hardwood dowel rod. A 10 inch square of wood or metal heavy enough to support the metal rod in a vertical position.

The work of making the model can be done by hand with simple woodworking tools. However, it is advisable to use a drill press for drilling accurate holes in the blocks.

Cut 30 pieces of the baluster (1″ × 1″) exactly 7 inches long. Round the ends of each block slightly. Lay these blocks out in a row, turning them so that any variation in grain or size is in the same direction. Then mark the center line on the upper face of each block (3 1/2 inches from either end if the cuts are accurate). On this center line locate a point one-third the width of the block from one side. Using this point as the center for the drill bore a 3/8 inch hole in each block so that it can be slipped over the metal rod. Fasten the rod into the 10 inch square support so that it will hold the blocks in a vertical pile.

With the blocks piled on the rod so that the same side of each is facing you, draw a line on the blocks where they will be cut later, as shown in the diagram: 12 blocks to represent the guanine-cytosine pairs and 18 blocks to represent the adenine-thymine pairs. This gives about the right proportion of the two types of base pairs in human DNA.

The position of the mark for the cut in both sets should be seven twelfths of the total length, or approximately 4 inches from the longer end. Take the blocks off the rod and cut them with a right angle cut on these lines as indicated.

Using a drill press and a proper jig, drill a 1/4 inch hole into the exact center of the end of each piece where it has just been cut. Be careful not to go into the holes already in the longer pieces or they will have to be cleaned out to fit on the metal rod. In the long blocks drill to a depth of 3/8 of an inch; in the short blocks, 1 inch.

Glue a short length of the 1/4 inch dowel rod into the end of each of the longer pieces, the ones with the vertical holes. The vertical rod will give trouble if you glue them into the shorter ones by mistake. Leave about an inch of the dowel sticking out of the longer pieces so that they will fit snugly but easily into the opposite short pieces. If the holes are accurate, all of the straight-cut pieces will fit into each other, and all of the angle-cut pieces will be interchangeable. In this way the blocks can be used to illustrate the specific pairing of the nitrogen bases as well as the DNA code or key.

Put all of the pieces together, each with its proper opposite, and slip the blocks onto the vertical rod in any order. The more mixed up the better.

In this way the blocks represent a few of the types of paired chemical bases that lie with the coils of the double helix of a DNA molecule. The cuts, where they are doweled together, represent the weak hydrogen bonds that are easily broken by chemical and physical changes in the surrounding medium.

For good demonstration purposes, each of the four bases can be labeled and painted a different color; for example, adenine-yellow; thymine-blue; guanine-orange; cytosine-green.

To represent one configuration of the bases within the double helix of DNA, each base pair is turned at an angel of 35 degrees to the next one. This means that there will be 10 pairs of blocks in one complete rotation (360°). Remember that the blocks can be placed in any order, as well as flipped end to end as they are piled on the vertical rod.

With this arrangement of base pairs, a long strip of clear plastic can be fastened to each end of the bottom block and wound upward so as to touch the ends of succeeding blocks in the form of a double helix. A white spot representing a sugar group can be painted on the plastic helix where it touches the end of each block. (The base pairs are joined to the sugar groups in the double helix.) In between the sugar groups can be painted a black spot to represent the phosphate groups alternating with the sugar along the two chains of the coiled helix. These sugar and phosphate groups make the backbone of the long chain polymer, the DNA molecule.

WORDS PERTAINING TO PREGNANCY, CHILDBIRTH, AND LACTATION[8]

1. Abortion (a-bor'shun)
2. Afterbirth (af'ter-berth)
3. Amniotic fluid (am-ne-ot'ik)
4. Breech birth
5. Cervix (ser'viks)
6. Chorionic gonadotropin (ko-re-on'ik)
7. Chromosome (kro'mo-sōm)
8. Conception (kon-sep'shun)
9. Corpus luteum (kor'pus lu'teum)
10. Deoxyribonucleic acid (de-ok-se-ri-bo-nu-kle'ik)
11. Endocrine gland (en'do-krin)
12. Endometrium (en-do-me'tre-um)
13. Enzyme (en'zim)
14. Estrogen (es'tro-jen)
15. Fallopian tube (fal-lo'pe-an)
16. Fertilization (fer'ti-li-za-shun)
17. Fetus (fe'tus)
18. Follicle stimulating hormone (fol'li-k'l)

---

[8] Definitions of these terms can be found in the glossary at the end of this book.

19. Genes (jēnz)
20. Gonadotropin (gon-ah-do-tro'pin)
21. Hormone (hor'mōn)
22. Implantation (im-plan-ta'shun)
23. Intrauterine (in-trah-u'ter-in)
24. Labor (la'bor)
25. Lactation (lak-ta'shun)
26. Luteinizing hormone (lu'tin-i-zing)
27. Metabolism (me-tab'o-lizm)
28. Nucleus (nu'kle-us)
29. Obstetrician (ob-ste-trish'un)
30. Oxytocin (ok-se-to'sin)
31. Parturition (par-tu-rish'un)
32. Pituitary gland (pi-tu'i-tar-e)
33. Placenta (plah-sen'tah)
34. Pore (por)
35. Pregnancy (preg'nan-se)
36. Progesterone (pro-jes'ter-on)
37. Protein (pro'tēn)
38. Testosterone (tes-tos'ter-on)
39. Umbilical (um-bil'i-kal)
40. Uterus (u'ter-us)

SUGGESTED FILMS FOR USE WITH THE UNIT ON PREGNANCY, CHILDBIRTH, AND LACTATION

A Normal Birth. Medical Arts Productions, P.O. Box 4042, Stockton, California 95203.
    An actual delivery designed to be shown in controlled group settings where the discussion can relate the content to the needs of the group.
Biography of the Unborn. Encyclopedia Britannica Educational Corporation, 425 North Michigan Avenue, Chicago, Illinois 60611.
    The film begins with the wandering female ovum during the ovulation period, pictures the sperm swimming to meet the ovum, and the moment of conception. Week by week development in the mother's womb then follows.
Cell Biology: Mitosis and DNA. Coronet Films, 65 E. South Water Street, Chicago, Illinois 60601.
    The nearly endless number of arrangements of nucleotides within the DNA molecule account for the differences among individuals as well as those between species. Models illustrate the structure of the DNA molecule and its duplication prior to cell division. Cinemicroscopy of the division of a living cell, supplemented by animation, illustrates step by step the five stages of the meiotic processes. Included is a short explanation of meiosis.
Childbirth: The Great Adventure. Childbirth Education League, P.O. Box 188, Lynnwood, Washington 98306.
    An excellent film stressing the importance of the father in his supportive role throughout the process of childbirth. In addition to clarifying and giving meaning to the role of the father, the film emphasizes the biology of pregnancy and childbirth.
DNA: Molecule and Heredity. Encyclopedia Britannica Educational Corporation, 425 North Michigan Avenue, Chicago, Illinois 60611.
    Nobel Prize winner and discoverer of DNA, Dr. George Beadle, explains why DNA is the basis of growth and reproduction and the mechanism for transporting heredity specifications from one generation to the next.

From Generation to Generation. McGraw-Hill Films, 330 West 42nd Street, New York, New York 10036.

The physiological facts from conception to the birth of a child. Special emphasis is placed upon childbirth as an emotional and a spiritual experience as well as a biological one.

Gene Action. Encyclopedia Britannica Educational Corporation, 425 North Michigan Avenue, Chicago, Illinois 60611.

This film shows the structure of DNA, how DNA replicates itself, and how the DNA code determines the structure of a cell's proteins.

Genetics: Chromosomes and Genes. McGraw-Hill Films, 330 West 42nd Street, New York, New York 10036.

Specially constructed models show that differences in individuals of every plant or animal species are traceable to the sperm and the egg cells, and produced through the process of meiosis. These cells contain only half the number of chromosomes present in other body cells. The chromosomes are randomly assorted, thus accounting for individual differences. Other causes demonstrated in this film are crossing over and mutation.

Genetics: Functions of DNA and RNA. Coronet Films, 65 E. South Water Street, Chicago, Illinois 60601.

"In all living things—simple or complex, one celled or many celled—heredity means the transmission of characteristics from cell to cell. This film shows cellular mechanisms that make heredity possible: DNA in the nucleus and messenger RNA and transfer RNA in the cytoplasm. The film illustrates not only how specific DNA codes result in specific proteins, but how mutation and differentiation may occur."

Genetics: Mendel's Laws. Coronet Films, 65 E. South Water Street, Chicago, Illinois 60601.

Scientists study human inheritance from three viewpoints: biochemical genetics, which deals with the chemistry of DNA and the chemical changes caused in the body by genes; nature nurture studies, which compare the effects of heredity and environment; and population genetics, which is concerned with the frequencies of occurrence of certain genes in whole populations. The film illustrates with specific examples some findings of the three approaches.

Genetics: Mendel's Laws. Coronet Instructional Films, 65 E. South Water Street, Chicago, Illinois 60601.

"Scenes photographed in Gregor Mendel's own garden in Bruno, Czechoslovakia, add authenticity to this presentation of the original work with pea plants, which has become the basis of the present science of genetics. The film duplicates some of Mendel's experiments, and clearly explains his laws of dominance, segregation, and independent assortment."

Heredity and Prenatal Development. McGraw-Hill Films, 330 West 42nd Street, New York, New York 10036.

Describes the growth, subdivision, and union of male and female sex cells, the fertilization of the ovum by the sperm cell, and the prenatal development of an offspring. The development of the basic physiological actions in a newborn infant and the connection between physical and emotional sensitivity in children are also discussed.

Laws of Heredity. Encyclopedia Britannica Educational Corporation, 425 North Michigan Avenue, Chicago, Illinois 60611.

Demonstrates how inheritance is determined in statistically predictable ways. Presents the insights and conclusions about inheritance that were first achieved by Gregor Mendel.

Life with Baby. McGraw-Hill Films, 330 West 42nd Street, New York, New York 10036.

With the use of candid camera sequences photographed through a one-way vision dome, this film shows how children grow. Observing youngsters of different ages, the patterns of normal child development are revealed and examined.

UNIT SIX: CONTRACEPTION AND POPULATION STABILIZATION

Note to the teacher

Contraception is a highly inflammatory topic in many communities, and some teachers will be forced to omit the topic or to treat it in only a superficial way.

The authors feel, however, that contraception is an essential part of sex education and for many high school students will provide the last opportunity to discuss contraception in a formal and meaningful way.

Thus this unit is presented in a very open manner. The teacher may wish to modify the approach or present the information only in answer to student questions.

Combining the two topics of the population explosion and contraception should serve as the stimulus for the required questions.

Introduction

Prior to the lectures on the population explosion and contraception, pretest the class on the following questions:

1. Is there a population explosion?
2. If so, what threats to life does the population explosion pose?
3. What means do we have to curb the population?

Class discussion of the answers to the pretest question will help to introduce the discussion on the population explosion to be followed by the discussion of contraception.

Vocabulary sheet

The contraception vocabulary sheet should be distributed to the students prior to the lecture. This sheet will aid the student in taking notes on the discussion. It will also assist him in the proper pronunciation and spelling of terms.

Human sexuality notebook

The students should take notes and carefully organize them into separate units to compile a notebook on human sexuality. Encourage outside reading and additional materials for inclusion in the notebook. (The high school teacher may want to allow class time for the student to work on his notebook.)

Classroom presentation

To enhance the presentation of the contraception discussion, bring various contraceptive devices to class to show the students. If this is not possible, use the drawings of contraceptive devices provided in the Atlas.

Values Clarification

The following exercise is used to have the students identify factors which would perpetuate the human race. In addition to examining personal values, it will help the teacher to evaluate student perceptions about fertility and genetics.

Fallout Shelter[9]

Your group is given the responsibility of selecting six persons from the list of candidates below who are to be placed in the fallout shelter in order to *perpetuate the human race*. In all probability there will be no other survivors, and you may not accompany the candidates. You have fifteen minutes to reach consensus on this matter. (No copping out by voting or drawing straws.)

The Candidates Are

1. High school dropout, sixteen, has a dubious I.Q., is pregnant.

2. Ex-policeman, twenty-eight; always wears a gun, thrown off the force for brutality. The gun goes with him.

3. Rabbi, or priest, seventy-five years old.

4. Female physician, thirty-six, has had hysterectomy.

5. Male violin player, forty-five: suspected of homosexual activity.

6. Male black militant, has no skills, has never worked.

7. Retired prostitute, thirty-nine.

8. Law student, twenty-six, and his wife twenty-nine; she has had a hereditary form of leukemia, and he won't go without her.

9. Male architect, thirty-six: ex-convict, convicted of pushing heroin.

It would be helpful if there were more information available on each of the candidates, but you must remember that in the real world we are continually forced to make judgments based on incomplete data.

After your committee has reached its decision, then it should discuss what four or five values you have been trying to protect.

Span plan

One of the goals of family planning is to plan a family so that both parents can also meet individual goals other than those of producing offspring. The technique used to get students to look at long range goal setting is called the "span plan." This technique was developed by Barbara Watts, Assistant Dean of Students at The Ohio State University.

Give a copy of *Span Plan* to each student in the class.

---

[9] Reprinted by permission of Hart Publishing Company, Inc., from its copyrighted volume, *Values Clarification: A Handbook of Practical Strategies for Teachers and Students* by Sidney B. Simon, Leland W. Howe, and Howard Kirschenbaum.

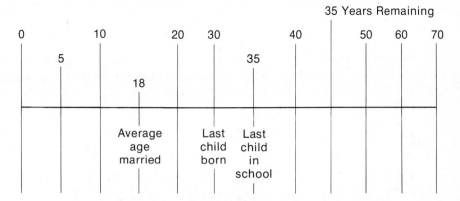

The averages used on span plan are from 1972. Explain to the class that these averages are not meant to influence them but to provide them with some information.

The task at hand is to: 1) identify age of marriage predicted for yourself; 2) place offspring on chart; 3) block in years planned for a career. In giving the directions, remember to explain to the students that marriage is not necessary for this activity, i.e., one-parent families. Also, childless marriages are perfectly acceptable and many women chose to have a career throughout marriage. The important message is that young people do some planning for the future and that this goal setting should be discussed with any future mate prior to marriage.

Selecting a contraceptive

A handout which might be useful is "Selecting a Contraceptive" from *Go To Health.* New York: Dell Publishing Company, 1972.[10] In utilizing this handout ask the students why the questions on the chart were used.

Charts, illustrations, and graphs

Use of charts and graphs will help clarify the subject matter presented in this lesson. The students can work individually or in groups on the following projects:

Make a chart showing the pregnancy rate (the frequency with which conception occurs among women participating in normal sexual intercourse) for each of the birth control methods. Rank order the methods on the chart, beginning with the method that has the lowest pregnancy rate and ending with the method that has the highest.

Make a calendar of a 30-day menstrual cycle, indicating the order for taking the sequential oral contraceptives:

1. No pills for the first five days.

2. Estrogen pills for the next 20 days.

3. Estrogen pills with progestogen added for the next five days.

[10] Adapted from "Contraception: When the Pill Isn't the Answer," *PATIENT CARE.* May 1969. Copyright © Miller and Fink Publishing Corporation. All rights reserved.

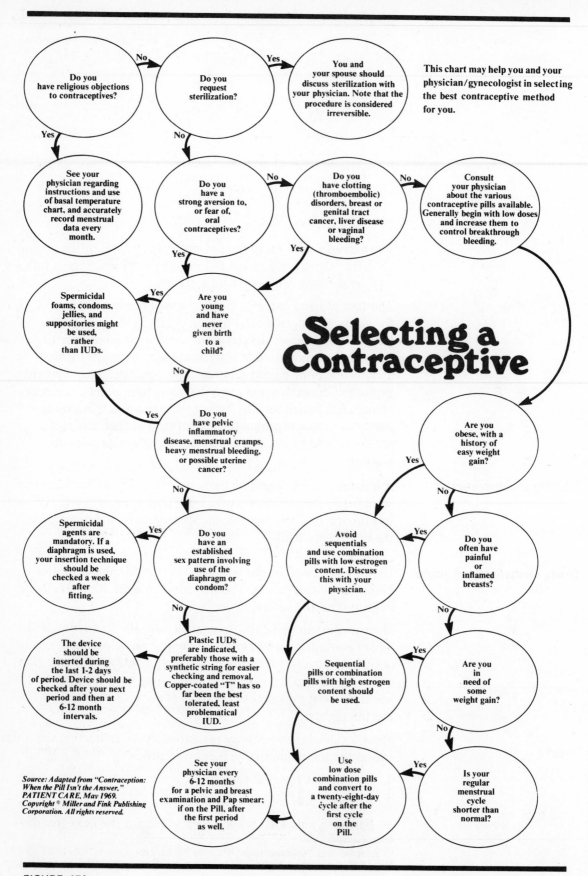

Selecting a Contraceptive

This chart may help you and your physician/gynecologist in selecting the best contraceptive method for you.

Do you have religious objections to contraceptives? — No → Do you request sterilization? — Yes → You and your spouse should discuss sterilization with your physician. Note that the procedure is considered irreversible.

Yes ↓ (from religious objections) See your physician regarding instructions and use of basal temperature chart, and accurately record menstrual data every month.

No ↓ (from sterilization) Do you have a strong aversion to, or fear of, oral contraceptives? — No → Do you have clotting (thromboembolic) disorders, breast or genital tract cancer, liver disease or vaginal bleeding? — No → Consult your physician about the various contraceptive pills available. Generally begin with low doses and increase them to control breakthrough bleeding.

Yes (from aversion) and Yes (from clotting) → Are you young and have never given birth to a child? — Yes → Spermicidal foams, condoms, jellies, and suppositories might be used, rather than IUDs.

No ↓ Do you have pelvic inflammatory disease, menstrual cramps, heavy menstrual bleeding, or possible uterine cancer? — Yes → (to Spermicidal foams, condoms...)

No ↓ Do you have an established sex pattern involving use of the diaphragm or condom? — Yes → Spermicidal agents are mandatory. If a diaphragm is used, your insertion technique should be checked a week after fitting.

No ↓ Plastic IUDs are indicated, preferably those with a synthetic string for easier checking and removal. Copper-coated "T" has so far been the best tolerated, least problematical IUD. → The device should be inserted during the last 1-2 days of period. Device should be checked after your next period and then at 6-12 month intervals.

Are you obese, with a history of easy weight gain? — Yes → Avoid sequentials and use combination pills with low estrogen content. Discuss this with your physician.

No ↓ Do you often have painful or inflamed breasts? — Yes → Sequential pills or combination pills with high estrogen content should be used.

No ↓ Are you in need of some weight gain? — Yes → (to Sequential pills or combination pills with high estrogen content should be used.)

No ↓ Is your regular menstrual cycle shorter than normal? — Yes → Use low dose combination pills and convert to a twenty-eight-day cycle after the first cycle on the Pill.

Plastic IUDs → See your physician every 6-12 months for a pelvic and breast examination and Pap smear; if on the Pill, after the first period as well.

Source: Adapted from "Contraception: When the Pill Isn't the Answer," PATIENT CARE, May 1969. Copyright © Miller and Fink Publishing Corporation. All rights reserved.

FIGURE 174

Plot the following increase in birth rate by year on a graph:

Year	World Population
Time of Christ	250 million
1650	500 million
1850	1 billion
1925	2 billion
1969	3.5 billion
1980	4 billion
1990	5 billion
2000	6.5 billion

Cartoons

Have the class draw humorous cartoons depicting the serious population problems of our times. The following description of a cartoon can be used as an example:

> A recent cartoon depicts a stork flying with a baby over a large city. As the stork reaches the city he sees a large sign projecting in the sky that reads "Sorry, Full."

Debates

In the future the students will be responsible for making intelligent decisions regarding contraceptive methods and the population explosion. To expose them to the kinds of decisions they will be faced with, hold the following class debates:

1. The use of the birth control pill—pro and con. (You may wish to use the "pill scale" found in the Appendix.)

2. The pros and cons of legalized abortion.

3. The pros and cons of tax deduction benefits for limiting family size.

Visitation

Have the class visit a slum area or an orphanage to gain a better understanding of the lives of the poverty striken or the unwanted child. The students can then discuss what the necessities are for a "quality" life.

Discussion

Examine the following statement, drawing insights and implications:

> There is a high correlation between the food supply and the incidence of political violence both within and between countries.

Reports

The following reports can be written to familiarize the student with the population explosion on an international level:

A study of the family planning programs instituted in India, Pakistan, South Korea, and Taiwan.

A study of the sources of the world's food supply. What countries export food? Kind of food? Quantity? What countries import food? Kind of food? Quantity? Amount of food surplus 100 years ago as compared to food surplus today.

WORDS PERTAINING TO CONTRACEPTION[11]

1. Abortion (ah-bor'shun)
2. Asynchrony (ah-sin'kro-ne)
3. Basal body temperature (ba'sal)
4. Calendar
5. Cancer (kan'ser)
6. Carcinogenic (kar-si-no-jen'ik)
7. Cervical mucus (ser'vi-kal mu'kus)
8. Cervix (ser'viks)
9. Coitus interruptus (koi'tus in-ter-rup'tus)
10. Conception (kon-sep'shun)
11. Condom (kon'dum)
12. Contraception (kon-trah-sep'shun)
13. Contraindicated (kon-trah-in'di-ka-ted)
14. Corpus luteum (kor-pus lu'te-um)
15. Diaphragm (di'ah-fram)
16. Douche (doosh)
17. Ejaculation (e-jak-u-la'shun)
18. Endometrium (en-do-me'tre-um)
19. Enovid (e'no-vid)
20. Estrogen (es'tro-jen)
21. Fallopian tube (fal-lo'pe-an)
22. Fertile (fer'til)
23. Fertilization (fer-til-li-za'shun)
24. Gastrointestinal disburbance (gas-tro-in-tes'ti-nal)
25. Gynecology (jin-e-kol'o-je)
26. Implantation (im-plan-ta'shun)
27. Intercourse (in'ter-kors)
28. Intrauterine (in-trah-u'ter-in)
29. Metabolism (me-tab'o-li-zim)
30. Nausea (naw'se-ah)
31. Obstetrics (ob-steh'triks)
32. Ossification (os-i-fi-ka'shun)
33. Ovulation (ov-u-la'shun)
34. Population (pop-u-la'shun)
35. Pregnancy rate (preg'nan-se)
36. Progestogen (pro-jes'to-jen)
37. Progesterone (pro-jes'ter-on)
38. Promiscuity (pro-mis-cu'ity)
39. Prostheses (pros-the'sis)
40. Rhythm (rith'm)
41. Sequential oral contraceptives
42. Sterilization (ster-i-li-za'shun)
43. Suppository (su-poz'i-to-re)
44. Surgical (sur'je-kal)
45. Thromboembolism (throm'bo-em'bo-lizm)
46. Tubular ligation (tu'bu-lar li-ga'shun)
47. Vaginal jelly (vaj'i-nal jel'e)

---

[11] Definitions of these terms can be found in the glossary at the end of this book.

48. Vas deferens (vas def′erens)
49. Vasectomy (vas-ek′to-me)

SUGGESTED FILMS FOR USE WITH THE UNITS ON CONTRACEPTION AND THE POPULATION EXPLOSION

Beyond Conception. Henk Newenhouse, 1825 Willow Road, Northfield, Illinois 60093.
   An excellent film discussing birth control techniques, the population problem, and man's personal responsibility. The film can be used to introduce discussion of the human being and his environment.

Can the Earth Provide? McGraw-Hill Films, 330 West 42nd Street, New York, New York 10036.
   Examines the state of world agriculture and discusses the role that science may play in future world food production.

Challenge to Mankind. McGraw-Hill Films, 330 West 42nd Street, New York, New York 10036.
   Five world-known authorities express their views on the threat of overpopulation to mankind and offer some possible solutions.

Contraception. John Wiley and Sons, Inc., One Wiley Drive, Somerset, New Jersey 08873.
   An up-to-date coverage of available contraceptives. Sociological as well as factual.

Night Children. National Film Board of Canada, 680 Fifth Avenue, New York, New York 10019.
   Typical of the social situations that exist in the dark inner city are those portrayed by Children's Aid Society caseworkers. Special emphasis is placed on neglected, abused, and deprived children. Good material for use in classroom discussion.

Nobody's Children. McGraw-Hill Films, 330 West 42nd Street, New York, New York 10036.
   This film can be used with a discussion of fertility and childless families. It deals with the procedure of adoption, the problems of the "black market" adoptions, and the responsibilities of adoption.

People by the Billions. McGraw-Hill Films, 330 West 42nd Street, New York, New York 10036.
   Examines the implications for the future of a rapidly growing population—overcrowding, hunger, insufficient natural resources.

The Global Struggle for Food. McGraw-Hill Films, 330 West 42nd Street, New York, New York 10036.
   A report on the progress being made in efforts to increase world food production.

To Plan Your Family. Henk Newenhouse, 1825 Willow Road, Northfield, Illinois 60093.
   A family planning film for women of limited education. Persuasive reasons for limiting the size of families is presented, as well as a discussion of the different birth control methods. Emphasis is placed upon the pill and the IUD.

UNIT SEVEN: ABORTION

Introduction

Introduce the unit on abortion by handing out a sheet with the following terms:

1. Spontaneous abortion

2. Induced abortion

3. Threatened abortion

4. Imminent abortion

5. Inevitable abortion

6. Incomplete abortion

7. Complete abortion

8. Missed abortion

9. Septic abortion

10. Habitual abortion

11. Therapeutic abortion

12. Criminal abortion

13. Embryonic abortion

14. Fetal abortion

Explain each term and then have the student put the sheet in his notebook.

Identifying community attitudes, laws, and services

Have the class divide into three groups to study and report to the class on the following:

1. Community Attitudes—what different attitudes prevail in the community regarding the abortion issue? What position do different religious groups take? Doctors? What abortion groups, such as Birthright, exist in the community? What positions are held among these various groups?

2. Laws—copy the Supreme Court ruling and all state rulings to put the issue into effect.

3. Services—examine the community's services for abortion counselling and for carrying out the abortion process. What psychological services are available? What is the cost of the different types of abortions in your locality?

Paper

For examination, have each student explain when the following method for abortion is used, how safe the method is, and what possible side effects may result:

1. Vacuum or suction curettage

2. Dilation and curettage (D & C)

3. Saline injection

4. Hysterotomy (abdominal surgery)

WORDS PERTAINING TO ABORTION[12]

1. Abortion (a'bor-shun)
2. Amniotic sac (am-ne'ot-ik sac)

---

[12] Definitions of these terms can be found in the glossary at the end of this book.

3. Aspiration (as-pi-ra′shun)
4. Cervix (ser′viks)
5. Curettage (kyur-e′tazh)
6. Fetus (fe′tus)
7. Forceps (for′seps)
8. Hysterotomy (his-ter-ot′o-me)
9. Miscarriage (mis-kar′ij)
10. Prostaglandin (pros-tah-glan′din)
11. Saline injection (sa′len)

UNIT EIGHT: VENEREAL DISEASES

Introduction

Introduce the unit on venereal diseases by emphasizing responsibility as an important component in living. Have the students react to this idea.

Vocabulary sheet

The venereal disease vocabulary sheet should be distributed to the students prior to the lective. This sheet will be a valuable asset in students' note taking. It will also assist them in the proper pronunciation and spelling of terms.

Human sexuality notebook

The students should take notes on the discussion and carefully organize them into separate units to compile a notebook on human sexuality. Encourage outside reading and the inclusion of additional venereal disease literature in the notebook.

Dictionary of terms

The students should include meanings of the technical terms in the dictionary of terms section of their notebook on human sexuality.

Classroom presentation

To enhance the presentation of the venereal disease unit show pictures of the gonococcus and spirochete under the microscope (Figures 55 and 57). The students can observe them carefully and draw them for their notebooks.

Report

Have the students write to their congressmen to learn what legislation is being proposed for the control of venereal disease in this country and in their specific locality.

Resource person

Invite a public health nurse or public health educator to discuss the control of venereal disease in the immediate area. The resource person can be called upon to discuss the following topics:

1. What is the incidence of venereal disease in our community?

2. Where do persons with VD in our community go for help?

3. Can teenagers in our community report that they may have contacted syphilis or gonorrhea and remain anonymous?

4. Will the public health authority tell their families?

5. How can venereal diseases be controlled in our community?

Class project

The class can work together on a campaign to educate the rest of the school or the community regarding the knowledge an informed citizen should have of venereal diseases. The students can collaborate on a pamphlet or on a series of articles for the school newspaper or perhaps a school assembly.

The students can plan the materials that should be included in their program. Suggested topics:

I. Information
    1. What are venereal diseases?

    2. Transmission of venereal diseases.

    3. Signs and symptoms of venereal diseases.

    4. Diagnosis of venereal diseases.

    5. Treatment of venereal diseases.

II. Responsibility

    1. The role of the schools in VD education.

    2. The role of the public health department.

    3. The role of the family doctor.

    4. The role of the citizens.

WORDS PERTAINING TO VENEREAL DISEASE[13]

1. Abdomen (ab-do'men)
2. Antibiotic (an-ti-bi-ot'ik)
3. Antibody (an'ti-bod-e)
4. Antiseptic (an-ti-sep'tik)
5. Anus (a'nus)
6. Arthritis (ar-thri'tis)
7. Bacteria (bak-te're-ah)
8. Cervix (ser'viks)
9. Chancre (shang'ker)
10. Chancroid (shang'kroid)
11. Chronic (kron'ik)
12. Conjunctivitis (kon-junk-ti-vi'tis)

---

[13] Definitions of these terms can be found in the glossary at the end of this book.

13. Contagious (kon-ta'jus)
14. Diagnosis (di-ag-no'sis)
15. Erythromycin (e-rith-ro-mi'sin)
16. Fetus (fe'tus)
17. Genital organs (jen'i-tal)
18. Gonococcus (gon-o-kok'us)
19. Gonorrhea (gon-o-re'ah)
20. Granuloma inguinale (gran-u-lo'mah ing'gwi-nal-e)
21. Groin
22. Homosexual (ho-mo-seks'u-al)
23. Incubation (in-ku-ba'shun)
24. Infectious (in-fek'shus)
25. Inoculate (in-ok'u-lat)
26. Immunity (i-mu'ni-te)
27. Latent (la'tent)
28. Lesion (le'shun)
29. Lymph (limf)
30. Lymphogranuloma venereum (lim-fo-gran-u-lo'mah ve-ne're-um)
31. Mucous membrane (mu'kus)
32. Nongonococcal urethritis (non-gon-o-kok'al u-re-thri'tis)
33. Organism (or'gan-izm)
34. Pelvic (pel'vik)
35. Penicillin (pen-i-sil'lin)
36. Placenta (pla-sen'tah)
37. Promiscuous (pro-mis'ku-us)
38. Rectum (rek'tum)
39. Residual (re-zid'u-al)
40. Silver nitrate (sil'ver ni'trat)
41. Sterility (ste-ril'i-te)
42. Streptomycin (strep-to-mi'sin)
43. Sulfanilamide (sul-fah-nil'ah-mid)
44. Syphilis (sif'i-lis)
45. Tetracycline (tet-rah-si'klen)
46. Treponema pallidum (trep-o-ne'mah pal'li-dum)
47. Ulcer (ul'ser)
48. Urethra (u-re'thrah)
49. Urethritis (u-re-thri'tis)
50. Urination (u-ri-na'shun)

SUGGESTED FILMS FOR USE WITH THE UNIT ON VENERAL DISEASE

A Quarter of a Million Teenagers. Churchill Films, 662 N. Robertson Boulevard, Los Angeles, California 90069.
    The increasing problem of teenage veneral disease is handled in good taste. This film covers the sociological as well as the biological problems in the control of veneral disease.
Dance Little Children. Calvin Productions, Inc., 1105 Truman Road, Kansas City, Missouri 64106
    A suburban setting is the location for the emergence of a syphilis epidemic. A good illustration of the attitudes of parents and teenagers. This film is an excellent supplement for *A Quarter of a Million Teenagers.*
Her Name Was Ellie, His Name Was Lyle. Louis de Rochemont Associates, 18 East 48th Street, New York, New York 10017.

A veneral disease epidemic threatens until those involved report contacts and have treatment themselves. In revealing sexual contacts many social implications are made. An excellent film to stress the emotional and physical effects of the problems associated with veneral disease.

The Innocent Party. Calvin Productions Inc., 1105 Truman Road, Kansas City, Missouri 64106. A teenage boy contracts syphilis from a pickup and transmits it to his girl friend. A doctor helps the boy to realize that he has a responsibility to himself as well as to his infected girl friend. The film deals with the nature, recognition, cure, and control of syphilis as well as the social implications.

VD: Epidemic. McGraw-Hill Films, 330 West 42nd Street, New York, New York 10036. Discusses all the aspects of this national health problem—its rapid increase, the importance of early treatment to the individual, the significance of the proper action by public health officials, and the high cost of the disease to the nation in dollars and health. Includes interviews with people who have been infected, treated, and cured.

VD: Name Your Contacts. Coronet Films, 65 E. South Water Street, Chicago, Illinois 60601. Presented are seven case histories of people with gonorrhea who are convinced by public health authorities of the necessity to name their contacts in confidence. Only in this way, the victims learn, can they help stop the spread of infection and give those who are infected a chance of certain cure before irreparable damage is done. This film opens the eyes of young people to the dangers of complacency and irresponsibility.

Venereal Diseases. John Wiley and Sons, Inc., One Wiley Drive, Somerset, New Jersey 08873. A very frank, detailed explanation of venereal disease. Excellent for teens.

UNIT NINE: INTELLIGENT CHOICE OF A SEXUAL LIFE STYLE

Introduction

This is one of the most important units in the sex education curriculum.

Thus, it should be very carefully planned prior to its introduction.

The authors have found that completion of a sexual behavior chart provides an excellent introduction to this topic.

This chart, which is found at the end of the unit, is introduced through an analogy to a basketball game.

Distribute copies of "The Rules of the Game" to the class.

Have the students read the introduction and the directions for completing the chart.

Before the students begin to fill out the chart, you may need to explain the following terms:

French kissing is a deep kiss accompanied by a close embrace and caressing. French kissing involves mutual exploration of tongue, mouth, and lips.

Necking is generally understood to include putting your arms around a person's neck or waist, holding hands, sitting close or cheek to cheek, and French kissing. It expresses your affection for that person, but it does not try to arouse him or her to readiness for intercourse.

Petting goes much further and involves caressing the most sensitive parts of the body, such as the breasts or genitals, and deep kissing. It is the kind of lovemaking that prepares a person for intercourse.

Sexual intercourse consists of inserting the erect penis into the vagina and a series of thrusting motions of the penis inside the vagina. Usually the act terminates after ejaculation.

The students can complete the chart, keeping their answers to themselves, if they so desire. Their own commitment should be a personal one.

Human sexuality notebook

The students should take notes on the discussion of an intelligent choice of a sexual code and carefully organize them into a unit for their notebook on human sexuality. Encourage the use of original ideas and logical development of thought in this unit. The sexual commitment chart filled out previously should be included in the notebook.

Analyzing intimacy

A discussion of sexual life style would be incomplete without a discussion of intimacy, very close personal contact. To stimulate discussion and personal evaluation use the survey "What Is Your Intimacy Quotient?" *Go To Health.* New York: Dell Publishing Company, 1972. This survey can be found in the Atlas of this book. Included is a discussion of intimacy, the survey, and a means of evaluating the survey.

Values continuum

A technique found in Sidney B. Simon, Leland W. Howe, and Howard Kirschenbaum's *Values Clarification.* New York: Hart Publishing Company, 1972, can be used to discuss premarital sex. The technique is to construct a value continuum.

Draw the following continuum on the blackboard:

Gloves   Mattress
Glenda   Millie

The continuum is designed to depict extreme opposite viewpoints regarding premarital sexual activity. Gloves Glenda is opposed to all premarital contact in every circumstance. Mattress Millie approves of premarital sexual activity with no restrictions or limitations. Have the class place all of the other alternatives they can think of on the continuum.

Moral problem solving

Distribute to each member of the class a 3 by 5 inch card. On the card each student should record and describe one of the moral decisions faced by teenagers. The students do not sign their names on the cards. Collect the cards.

The teacher reads the cards to the class, and the class votes on the moral decision to be made in the case of each problem. The tabulation of votes can be recorded by a student on the blackboard.

After the teacher has read at least five cards, which the students have voted upon, ask the students what criteria they used to make the moral decision in each problem. Several students can explain the rationale behind the criteria they used.

Then, each student should write a short paper for his notebook, explaining the criteria he uses in making decisions involving moral judgments.

Peer group tape recordings

A group of girls can develop a script to be recorded on a tape recorder in which they discuss their reactions to various types of boys and their conduct on a date. A group of boys will record a locker room discussion of girls and their conduct on a date. Play the tapes to the mixed group and discuss the expectations that boys and girls have of each other. To complete this session have each student write a brief composition, "The Kind of Reputation I Want to Have With Boys (Girls)."

Parent questionnaire

Distribute to the class a mimeographed sheet with the following open-ended questions written on it:

1. Parents never _____

2. Parents always _____

3. Parents should _____

The students will complete the sentences on the cards. Collect the cards. Divide the students into groups of five, giving each group five cards.

Each group reads and discusses the cards. Then the students make a list of items concerning the behavior of teenagers in their parents' generation.

The students can use these items to develop a questionnaire to learn more about the dating activities and behavior of the previous generation.

After the interviews the class can discuss the topic, "Were dating activities and behavior vastly different a generation ago?"

Mass media analysis

Have the students analyze the attitudes on dating, sex appeal, popularity, heterosexual relationships, and marriage advanced by mass media. Separate committees can be formed to report to the class on:

1. Television advertisements.
2. Family television shows.
3. Radio advertisements.
4. Newspaper articles.
5. Newspaper advertisements.
6. Magazine articles.
7. Magazine advertisements.

THE RULES OF THE GAME

Every basketball player learns early in his career to abide by the rules of the game. He knows that if he does, the game will move along more smoothly, and he'll get more chances to play. He also knows that his opponents have learned the same rules. Because basketball players are all committed to play by rules, each basketball player can predict and evaluate his behavior and the behavior of others in the game. There is much value to be gained from abiding by the rules; it makes the game more meaningful and gives direction to its outcome.

Direction and meaning are essential to all human experience if the outcome is to be favorable. Rules or standards are essential to guide behavior according to the purpose of the game. Male-female dating is not meant to be a game, but it does possess some of the same ingredients. The first common ingredient is purpose. The purpose of male-female dating is to prepare oneself and one's companion for the deepest relationship known to man—married love. The depth of genuine married love is not reached haphazardly. It begins in much the same way that a coach approaches the team for the first time. First, the rules of the game are set for the players. In the preparation for love, first, we set standards for ourselves. These standards are called commitments—commitment to what we believe is the appropriate type of sexual behavior for a particular human relationship. Neither the basketball game nor the human relationship should begin without commitment and a sense of direction.

After a commitment has been made to a given set of standards, the game can begin, the players always abiding by the rules. Of course at times it's most difficult to abide by the sexual standards to which one commits himself. It's difficult to keep from fouling in a basketball game, too. But what happens when we break the rules? Let us suppose that a basketball player fouls his opponent, and his opponent is badly injured as a result of this infraction of the rules. Can the consequences of rule breaking be brushed off lightly? Certainly not. The player who was injured suffers unnecessary injury. And what about the player who committed the foul? If he has compassion for his fellow man he aches inside from his mistake. This aching is a form of guilt—we have guilt feelings when we deviate from our standards. The effects of the mistake do not end with the two players involved; rarely does any mistake affect just the individual. There is what we call a "social mistake," a mistake that affects the members of society. In this case, the entire team of the injured player was hurt; his friends were hurt and his family. So you see one person's action can have quite an effect on society.

Sexual mistakes have the same consequences. When we deviate from a standard of behavior we have set for ourselves, and when we cause another person to deviate from his standards, who is hurt? Both persons; each person has deviated from set standards and each person will suffer guilt feelings. Society, or the so-called social team, suffers too. The social team in this case is composed of your friends, your family, his or her friends, and his or her family.

How can a social mistake be avoided? Suppose that there is a basketball player standing under the basketball hoop. Another basketball player, not looking ahead, drives hard under the basket. He sees the player he is about to crash into, but it's too late to stop. BAM! Now we both know that the basketball player would like to have avoided the painful crash. If only he had stopped to look and to think ahead. But it was just too late.

Sexual behavior works much in the same way. Teenagers can begin their dating years without looking and thinking ahead. Soon they become engaged in sexual activity that leads to full sexual activity quite different from what they had originally intended. For this reason it is necessary for young people to do some thinking and to adopt some personal standards, limits, or guidelines to assist them in disciplining their sexual activity.

The chart that follows has been designed to help you make some preparation for the future. (Look at the chart.) It will help you to set standards for yourself concerning your sexual behavior as it relates to another person. This relationship of yourself to another person is in the form of a commitment. When you make a commitment, you agree to take personal responsibility for your sexual behavior and for the rights and feelings of another individual.

In the center of the chart is an inverted triangle listing sexual behavior beginning with "light embracing or fond holding of hands" and ending with "sexual intercourse." It is represented by an inverted triangle to show that as we progress in sexual behavior, our relationship becomes more meaningful and we are more selective in choosing a partner. At the bottom of the chart is a code for indicating the depth of the relationship. "A" symbolizes casual attraction. "B" symbolizes good friends. "C" symbolizes going steady. "D" symbolizes tentative engagement (engagement that has not been formally announced). "E" symbolizes official or announced engagement. "F" symbolizes marriage.

On the left side of the triangle is a column entitled "Male Commitment"; males will fill in this column. On the right side of the triangle is a column entitled "Female Commitment"; females will fill in this column. You are ready to begin filling in your personal commitments. Begin on the line that says "light embracing or fond holding of hands." Decide what type of relationship is appropriate for this type of sexual behavior—this will be your commitment. Remember that whenever you decide upon this commitment it means that each time you engage in this behavior this is how you feel about the other person—you are committed to him on the relationship level you indicate. Find the proper code (A, B, C, D, E, F) and mark it in the code box. There is a column to indicate any additional meaning this relationship might have to you. Now move down to the item "casual goodnight kissing." Find and record the proper code letter for the relationship and any additional criteria you feel and appropriate for the relationship. Continue these steps throughout the entire range of sexual behavior.

When you have completed half of the chart, you are ready to begin the other

SEXUAL BEHAVIOR CHART

Male Commitment				Female Commitment	
Code	Additional Criteria			Additional Criteria	Code
		light embracing or fond holding of hands			
		casual good-night kissing			
		intense (French) kissing			
		horizontal embrace with some petting but not undressed			
		petting of female's breast from outside her clothing			
		petting of female's breast without clothes intervening			
		petting below the waist of the female under her clothing			
		petting below the waist of both male and female under clothing			
		nude embrace			
		sexual inter-course			

Personal Commitment	Code
casually attracted	A
good friends	B
going steady	C
tentatively engaged	D
officially engaged	E
married	F

379

half. Males should now fill in the female half of the chart and females the male half. Begin again at "light embracing and fond holding of hands." This time decide the commitment you would like the other person who is dating you to have. Think to yourself, if this boy or girl embraces me or holds my hand, how should he or she feel about me in our relationship? Look at the code and choose a relationship (A, B, C, D, E, F), and mark it in the code box. Add any additional criteria you want. Continue these steps throughout the entire triangle of sexual behavior.

After you have completed both sides, male commitment as well as female commitment, read through your commitments carefully. You may want to discuss these commitments with your friends, your parents, or your teacher. Although you discuss them with others, they are still personal. They are your personal standards of behavior which have great meaning to you and will guide your sexual behavior.

SUGGESTED FILMS FOR USE WITH THE UNIT ON SEXUAL STANDARDS

A Basis for Sex Morality. Stephen Bosustow Sound Filmstrips, Classroom Film Distribution, 5610 Hollywood Boulevard, Hollywood, California 90028.

A complete set of six educational sound filmstrips, records, study guides, and projectionist scripts designed to meet the urgent demand for guidelines for sex behavior in today's society. The first three filmstrips in this series of six deal with love and sexuality, while the last three deal with ethical sex behavior.

"Love-Friendship-Marriage"—the importance of personal relationships to physical, mental, and spiritual health.

"The Nature of Sex"—the need for understanding the truer and deeper dimensions of sex.

"The Man-Woman Relationship"—the growth of sexual activity through successive periods of life.

"Premarital Relationships"—responsibility to self, lover, and society.

"Rationalizing Sex Behavior"—arguments used to rationalize illicit premarital sex behavior and why abstinence is the wiser choice.

"Guidelines for Sex Behavior"—guidelines for evaluating sex behavior, plotting a course through friendship, engagement, marriage.

Bertrand Russell Discusses Happiness. Coronet Films, 65 E. South Water Street, Chicago, Illinois 60601.

In this film, Lord Russell describes the factors he considers necessary for happiness: health, sufficient means to keep one from want, happy personal relations, and successful work. In addition, he discusses what he considers to be sources of unhappiness—worry, envy, and boredom.

Date Behavior. Society for Visual Education, 1345 Diversey Parkway, Chicago, Illinois 60614.

Filmstrip and guide or a filmstrip and record, which discuss qualities that boys and girls want in each other.

Going Steady. Coronet Films, 65 E. South Water Street, Chicago, Illinois 60601.

The question of going steady is discussed in terms of advantages and disadvantages from the boy's point of view and from the girl's point of view. A couple solves the problem of going steady to their mutual satisfaction. The film leaves the class prepared to debate the topic.

How Do You Know It's Love? Coronet Films, 65 E. South Water Street, Chicago, Illinois 60601.
   A high school boy and girl, a mother, and an engaged couple view love quite differently. Love evolves through many stages before it gains all the characteristics of maturity. The film contains a helpful set of questions for analysis of the depth of love between two people.

How Do I Love Thee? Brigham Young University, 290 HRCB, Provo, Utah 84601. Two college roommates find themselves forced by social and peer pressures to take a stand on pre-marital intercourse. One of the roommates takes the traditional stand while the other roommate questions the moral standards of the past. The question of whether the moral standards of the past have become outdated is debated back and forth.

How Much Affection? McGraw-Hill Films, 330 West 42nd Street, New York, New York 10036.
   "How far should we go?" The question of sexual behavior between steady couples is discussed with respect to how much affection and petting can be allowed within the bounds of social mores and personal standards.

How to Say No. Coronet Films, 65 E. South Water Street, Chicago, Illinois 60601.
   Moral maturity implies that a teenager has learned to say "no" when necessary and is definite about his decision. The skills and principle of saying "no" without losing friends or being regarded as "chicken" are depicted in this film.

Love and the Facts of Life. Evelyn Millis Duvall, Cathedral Films, 2921 Alameda Avenue, Burbank, California 91505.
   Based upon the book of the same title, these filmstrips are available with accompanying study guides in a five-part educational edition or a six-part religious edition.
   "Learning about Sex and Love"
   "Growing Up, from Childhood to Maturity"
   "Having a Baby—Miracle of Creation"
   "Understanding Your Love Feelings"
   "Who Am I? The Search for Self"
   "Sex and Your Religious Faith"

Merry-Go-Round. McGraw-Hill Films, 330 West 42nd Street, New York, New York 10036.
   Psychotherapist Albert Ellis, columnist Ann Landers, and educator Mary Winspear present three divergent views on teenage sexual behavior. The film dramatizes a dating situation in which a boy and a girl are considering premarital sexual experience.

Phoebe: A Story of Premarital Pregnancy. McGraw-Hill Films, 330 West 42nd Street, New York, New York 10036.
   A day in the life of an unwed pregnant girl reveals the emotional turmoil she must cope with.

Popularity Comes to You. McGraw-Hill Films, 330 West 42nd Street, New York, New York 10036.
   Popularity comes to you by your showing a genuine interest in friends, considering another viewpoint, being generous with praise and encouragement, and seeing another's good qualities rather than faults.

Premarital Sex Behavior. David R. Mace and Walter Stokes, National Council on Family Relations, 1219 University Avenue S.E., Minneapolis, Minnesota 55414.
   A taped dialogue between David Mace and Walter Stokes containing statements of the philosophies of sex of each and discussion of the implications of premarital sex, sexual freedom, responsible sex acts, and the meaning and purpose of marriage.

The Game. McGraw-Hill Films, 330 West 42nd Street, New York, New York 10036.
   The dramatization of the mental and emotional consequences—for both boy and girl—of a boy's casual seduction of a girl. An open-ended film to stimulate discussion of what is responsible sex behavior.

The Use of Sex in Human Life. David Mace and Albert Ellis, National Council on Family Relations, 1219 University Avenue S.E., Minneapolis, Minnesota 55414.

A taped dialogue of sexual philosophies presented by David Mace and Albert Ellis. The tape deals with the use of sex in human life.

Ready for Dating. Society for Visual Education, 1345 Diversey Parkway, Chicago, Illinois 60614.

A filmstrip accompanied by a record or guide that helps young teenagers develop the basic skills of dating, self-confidence in boy-girl relationships, and acceptable standards of thought and conduct.

Right or Wrong? Coronet Films, 65 E. South Water Street, Chicago, Illinois 60601.

The film deals with a gang of high school boys who break a warehouse window. One of the boys is caught. The moral decisions of the watchman, the boy's mother, the property owner, the police sergeant, and the boy are presented. Excellent film for discussion of the relationship of our own moral decisions to the community. Develops a sense of moral responsibility to others.

Sex Ethics, Sex Acts, and Human Need. David Mace and Walter Stokes, National Council on Family Relations, 1219 University Avenue, S.E., Minneapolis, Minnesota 55414.

A taped dialogue between David Mace and Walter Stokes concerning the ethics of sexuality, sex acts, and their relationship to human need.

Values for Teenagers: The Choice Is Yours. Guidance Associates, 23 Washington Avenue, Pleasantville, New York 10570.

UNIT TEN: MASTURBATION

Introduction

The basic material to be presented in this unit might include a discussion of Dr. Evans' article, "What Do You Tell Parents Who Are Concerned About Their Children's Masturbation?"

Prior to presenting this information, however, it is important to assess the current attitudes of your class.

To accomplish this, the teacher may wish to begin with a general discussion, explaining what masturbation is and something about its frequency.

Then the teacher might outline the four philosophical positions on masturbation defined by the Sex Education Information and Educational Council of the United States:[14]

A. The traditional view, which regards masturbation as always gravely sinful and as harmful to health with some modification of its severity and rigidity in light of new scientific knowledge.
B. The view of many religionists, which sees masturbation often as an imperfect egocentric eroticism that deflects the individual from the Christian concept of sexuality as being ideally an essential relation with another.

[14] Warren R. Johnson, *Masturbation* (Study Guide No. 3), Sex Education Information and Education Council of the United States.

C. An attitude of neutrality, which accepts masturbation [and] recognizes that further study of its various patterns is required, but is not prepared to encourage it among young people as an aid to more mature psychosexual growth.

D. And a more radical position, which views masturbation as not only harmless, but positively good and healthy, and therefore encourages it among young people as an aid to more mature psychosexual growth.

After you have outlined the preceding positions ask each student to take a stand on one of these philosophical positions. Ask the students to list reasons to justify their position. Follow the individual thought process with group discussion.

Note: It is important that in the early development of the unit the students be allowed to explore the outlined positions and arrive at their own stand without any indication as to the position of the teacher.

WORDS PERTAINING TO MASTURBATION[15]

1. Autoeroticism (aw-to-e-rot'i-sizm)
2. Cerebral cortex (ser-e'bral kor'teks)
3. Clitoridectomy (kli-to-rid-ek'to-me)
4. Clitoris (kli'to-ris)
5. Creative
6. Egocentric
7. Eroticism (e-rot'i-sizm)
8. Genitals (jen'i-tals)
9. Labia (la'be-ah)
10. Manipulation (ma-nip-u-la'shun)
11. Masturbation (mas-tur-ba'shun)
12. Mons pubus (monz pu'bis)
13. Penis (pe'nis)
14. Psychosexual (si-ko-seks'u-al)
15. Rectum (rek'tum)
16. Repression (re-presh'un)
17. Sanity (san'i-te)
18. Self-concept
19. Stimulus (stim'u-lus)
20. Transient psychosis
21. Tolerance (tol'er-ans)

SUGGESTED FILMS FOR USE WITH THE UNIT ON MASTURBATION

Achieving Sexual Maturity. John Wiley and Sons, Inc., One Wiley Drive, Somerset, New Jersey 08873.

---

[15] Definitions of these terms can be found in the glossary at the end of this book.

Deals with biological and social growth. Especially good discussion of masturbation. Film should be reviewed by teacher before showing it to a class. It shows different sexual behaviors very tastefully.

As Boys Grow. Medical Arts Productions, P.O. Box 4042, Stockton, California 95203.

A coach deals with junior and senior high school boys in different settings—locker room, field and so on. Explains the many changes that occur at adolescence, including secondary sexual characteristics, masturbation, and seminal emission. The film can also be used prior to discussing the relationship between the sexes.

UNIT ELEVEN: HOMOSEXUALITY

Pretest

Prior to the discussion of homosexuality pretest the class on the following questions:

1. What is a homosexual?
2. How many homosexuals are there in the United States?
3. What causes homosexuality?
4. Can homosexuality be changed?
5. Can someone be a homosexual and a heterosexual at the same time?

Vocabulary sheet

The homosexuality vocabulary sheet should be distributed to the students prior to the discussion. This sheet will aid in note taking. It will assist the student in the proper pronunciation and spelling of terms.

Human sexuality notebook

The students should take notes during class and carefully organize them into separate units to compile a notebook on human sexuality. Encourage students to do outside reading and gather outside materials for their unit on homosexuality.

Dictionary of terms

The students should include the meanings of technical and slang terms from the homosexuality lecture in the dictionary section of their notebook on human sexuality.

Classroom legislation

The Wolfender Committee in England, and in the United States the American Law Institute (a high level body of scholars that concerns itself with theoretical law) have recommended that private sexual behavior between consenting adults should be removed from the list of crimes, regardless of how it is morally considered. Although church opinion is divided, a number of churchmen support these recommendations. Such a revision has been made in Illinois law and is under consideration in other states.[16]

Have the class examine the laws governing homosexuality in your state. Does the class support the legislation governing this behavior? If not, have the students discuss and adopt laws that they feel are adequate. A group of students can be appointed by the class to send a letter to their congressman expressing the views of the class.

Research questions

Have students research the following questions:

1. Is homosexuality inherited?

2. Is homosexuality an illness?

3. What are the chances of a homosexual's being happy?

Definitions

The class can write definitions distinguishing between the following terms:

Masculinity vs. maleness

Femininity vs. femaleness

(Maleness and femaleness refer to biological characteristics that are unique for each individual. Masculinity and femininity refer to patterns of behavior that are characteristic of males or of females in a particular culture.)

Resource speaker

Invite a cultural anthropologist or sociologist to speak to the class on masculine and feminine roles.

Reports

After the speaker's visit, the discussion of masculine and femine roles can be followed by a class project. The class can study the role changes of males and females throughout history:

1. Clothing fads

2. Hair styles

3. Dances

4. Educational opportunities

5. Family responsibilities

6. Community responsibilities

7. Sexual responsibilities

Analysis and evaluation

After the class has identified changes in the masculine and feminine roles they can analyze each change:

1. Has this change improved society?

---

[16] Isadore Rubin, *Homosexuality,* SIECUS Publication No. G02, 1965.

2. Has this change resulted in any problems or complications in the functions of males and females in society?

3. Are the sexes becoming more alike?

4. Are "sameness" and "equality" in the sexes synonymous?

5. Differentiate between "sameness" and "equality."

Have the students make three lists to identify:

1. Patterns of behavior and traits that are characteristic of males in our culture.

2. Patterns of behavior and traits that are characteristic of females in our culture.

3. Patterns of behavior and traits that are characteristic of both males and females in our culture.

Have each student draw the chart shown below on a separate sheet of paper. Begin at the left-hand side of the chart which represents patterns of behavior and traits exclusively characteristic of males in our culture. List characteristics exclusive to males in this area.

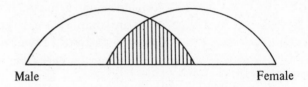

Male   Female

Begin at the right-hand side of the chart. This side represents patterns of behavior and traits exclusively characteristic of females in our culture. List characteristics exclusive to females in this area.

In the middle of the chart, the male and female characteristics overlap. List patterns of behavior and traits that are characteristic of both males and females in this area.

This chart can be used to show that although men are mostly masculine and girls are mostly feminine, no person is entirely masculine or feminine. There is some degree of femininity in all men and some degree of masculinity in all women.

Role playing

Role playing situations in which actions more typical of females are appropriate for males, such as "being a sissy," "crying," or "deep sensitivity." Role playing situations in which actions more typical of males are appropriate for females, such as "athletic prowess," or "dedication to an occupation."

In addition to this activity, the students can collect magazine and newspaper articles, and pictures of famous persons who possess attributes of the opposite sex.

WORDS PERTAINING TO HOMOSEXUALITY[17]

1. Abortion (a-bor'shun)
2. Autosexual (au-to-sex'u-al)
3. Bestiality (bes-ti-al'i-ty)
4. Contrasexuality (con-tra-sex-u-al'i-ty)
5. Cunnilingus (cun-ni-ling'us)
6. Fellatio (fel-la'she-o)
7. Fetish (fe'tish)
8. Genetic (ge-net'ic)
9. Homosexual (ho-mo-sex'u-al)
10. Homosexuality (ho-mo-sex-u-al'i-ty)
11. Katasexual (kat-a-sex'u-al)
12. Lesbianism (les'bi-an-izm)
13. Narcissism (nar'sis-sizm)
14. Pederasty (ped'er-as-ty)
15. Prostitution (pros-ti-tu'tion)
16. Sapphism (saf'fizm)
17. Sodomy (sod'om-y)
18. Uranism (u'ran-izm)

SUGGESTED FILM FOR USE WITH THE UNIT ON HOMOSEXUALITY

The Homosexuals. Carousel Films, Inc., 1501 Broadway, New York, New York 10036.
    The psychological and sociological implications of homosexuality are discussed. This
    discussion originally appeared on CBS Reports.

SUGGESTED READING LIST FOR JUNIOR AND SENIOR HIGH SCHOOL STUDENTS

Bauer, W.W., *Moving into Manhood*. New York: Doubleday & Co., Inc., 1964.
    Dr. Bauer has written an excellent book for the young boy who is moving into manhood.
    His book includes a frank discussion of both biological and emotional growth. First, he
    outlines the changes that take place in the boy's body and in the girl's body. Next, he
    discusses the change in feelings boys and girls have for each other as a result of these
    physical changes. He goes further to discuss the beginning of new life and how to choose
    a marriage partner.
Bell, Robert, *Premarital Sex in a Changing Society*. New Jersey: Prentice-Hall, Inc., 1966.
    Presents the effect of social changes on premarital sex through historical perspective.
    Discusses the influence of social class, race, and religion on sexual attitudes and behavior
    and deals with issues of marital, extramarital, and postmarital sex.
Belliveau, Fred and Richter, Lin., *Understanding Human Sexual Inadequacy*. New York:
    Bantam, 1970.
Belshaw, Michael, *The Economics of Underdeveloped Countries*. Minneapolis: Lerner Publica-
    tions Co., 1973.
Bergler, Edmund, *Homosexuality: Disease or Way of Life?* New York: Hill & Wang, Inc., 1956.
    An excellent discussion of homosexuality intended to clarify the reader's understanding

---

[17] Definitions of these terms can be found in the glossary at the end of this book.

of the nature of this behavior. In addition to this information, Dr. Bergler presents his position on the topic, Homosexuality: Disease or Way of Life?

Bertocci, Peter, *Sex, Love and the Person.* New York: Sheed & Ward, 1967.

Dr. Bertocci's main thesis is that all life centers around a basic set of values. Values that we find desirable and worth sharing are called "value claims." In evaluating our value claims and disvalue claims we, with the help of others, must think out the connection of each value claim in light of other value claims. We must know certain facts about ourselves. We need to go beyond the surface glitter to value experiences that are not only immediately desired but also dependably desired because they support more of the other claims we want, for ourselves and in relation to others.

Bracher, Marjory L., *SRO—Overpopulation and You.* Philadelphia: Fortress Press, 1966.

Population trends and pressure points, methods of control, criteria for family planning, human values, responsibilities of government, and the conscience of the individual are highlighted as vital issues of private and public concern.

Brecher, Ruth, and Brecher, Edward, (eds.) *An Analysis of Human Sexual Response.* New York: New American Library, 1966.

Bullis, Edmund, *Human Relations in Action.* New York: G. P. Putnam's Sons, 1954.

Dr. Bullis attempts to help the reader grasp a better understanding of what constitutes good human relations and how one goes about forming such relationships. His book was originally intended for nurses in their associations and relationships with others. However, this is indeed restricting the book. His book applies to all situations in which people come into contact with other people. Several of the points he makes are worth mentioning in a unit on interpersonal relationships.

Bundensen, Herman, *Toward Manhood.* Philadelphia: J. B. Lippincott Co., 1951.

A straightforward discussion for boys and young men of the many problems and questions relating to sex. Contains frank, unstilted consideration of such subjects as human reproduction, the process of physical maturation, boy-girl relationships, and many others.

Cain, Arthur, *Young People and Sex.* New York: The John Day Co., 1967.

Young people today are bombarded with sex, whether it be in movies, discussion, or current literature. This has left today's generation in a state of confusion. Dr. Cain's book has a dual purpose: clarification and control. The book is written to help young people help themselves and to know what they are doing, when they are doing it, and why.

Callahan, Daniel, *Abortion: Law, Choice and Morality.* New York: The Macmillan Co., 1970.

Characteristics of Male and Female Sexual Response. Siecus Publications, 1855 Broadway, New York, New York 10023.

Many of the problems that married people have and many adolescent dating problems are discussed in the light of male-female sex differences. A better understanding of these male-female differences should be of help in reducing frustrations and unhappiness in man-woman relationships.

Cory, Donald W., *The Lesbian in America.* New York: Citadel Press, Inc., 1964.

One of the limited number of books examining female homosexuality (lesbianism) in depth.

Crawley, Lawrence, *Reproduction, Sex and Preparation for Marriage.* New York: Prentice-Hall, Inc., 1964.

An excellent book dealing with the biological facts necessary for a sound education. A discussion of birth control methods is included.

Davis, M., *Sex and the Adolescent.* New York: Permabooks, 1968.

A guide for young people and their parents. Written with the realization that attitudes toward sex have changed and that rules and ideas suited to past generations no longer apply to today's youth.

Duvall, Evelyn, *Facts of Life and Love*. New York: Association Press, 1967.
   This book is an honest effort to answer questions young people ask about what it means
   to grow up, how to understand themselves and each other, and how to get along together
   satisfactorily. The book is divided into four sections: "Becoming Men and Women,"
   "Getting and Keeping Dates," "Loving and Being Loved," and "Heading Toward
   Marriage."

Duvall, Evelyn, *Why Wait Till Marriage?* New York: Association Press, 1968.
   An excellent and thorough discussion of premarital sex. The arguments in favor of
   premarital sex are examined carefully.

Duvall, Sylvanus M., *Before You Marry*. New York: Association Press, 1968.
   Answers to 101 common questions young people ask prior to marriage. The discussion is
   oriented toward the total personality adjustment as the deciding factor in marital success.

Ellis, Albert and Abarbanel, Albert (eds.), *Encyclopedia of Sexual Behavior*. New York:
   Hawthorn Books, 1967.

Fast, Julius, *What You Should Know About Human Sexual Response*. New York: G. P.
   Putnam's Sons, 1966.

Frank, Lawrence, *The Conduct of Sex*. New York: William Morrow & Co., Inc., 1961.
   The main theme is the role of sexuality in human life. The problem with sexuality is
   not one of enforcing morals but one of exercising ethics. The author discusses sexuality
   as it relates to the population explosion, the sex act, the family, the emergence of
   women, the personality, and the future.

Friedenberg, Edgar, *The Vanishing Adolescent*. New York: Dell Publishing Co., 1959.
   Mr. Friedenberg writes, "understanding . . . is more sustaining than cheerfulness." This
   book with its argument that adolescence, and the kind of selfhood it may in the best
   cases bring, is disappearing in our society, exhibits great understanding, much passion
   and compassion, a leavening of irony, and precious little cheerfulness. In this book an
   aggressive-hostile approach to homosexuality is attacked.

Fromm, Erich, *The Art of Loving*. New York: Harper & Row, Publishers, 1967.
   Learning to love, like other arts, demands practice and concentration. More than any
   other art it demands genuine insight and understanding. In this startling book, Dr.
   Fromm discusses love in all aspects, not only romantic love, so surrounded by false
   conceptions, but also love of parents for children, brotherly love, erotic love, self
   love, and love of God.

Fromme, Allan, *The Ability to Love*. New York: Farrar, Straus & Giroux, Inc., 1965.
   According to Allan Fromme, "No one admits even to himself that he is less than a good
   lover, or merely an average lover." Yet an examination of the human and interpersonal
   relationships of people often reveals a lack of understanding of what love is and how one
   goes about loving. The purpose of the book is to describe the effects we have—through
   the strengths and weaknesses of our personality—on love.

Glassberg, Bert Y., *Teenage Sex Counselor*. Barron's Educational Series, Inc., 1970.
   Written for the perplexed teenager who is reluctant to seek "in person" advice. A doctor
   psychologist gives sympathetic, warmly human counsel on how to channel all aspects
   of growing up into well adjusted maturity.

Goldstein, Martin and Haeberle, Erwin, *The Sex Book: A Modern Pictorial Encyclopedia*.
   New York: Herdu and Herdu, Inc., 1971.

Guttmacher, Alan F., *Pregnancy and Birth: A Book for Two Expectant Parents*. New York:
   Viking Press, 1962.

Harden, G., *Birth Control*. New York: Pegasus, 1970.

Homosexuality. Siecus Publications, 1855 Broadway, New York, New York 10023.
   The extent of homosexual behavior has not been fully established, but the figures given,
   although they are to be considered as estimates, make it clear that it is not a rare phe-

nomenon but is widespread in our society. This pamphlet substitutes understanding based on available scientific evidence for condemnation based on ignorance and fear.

Hooker, E., "Homosexuality—Summary of Studies." In Duvall, E.M. and Duvall, S.M., *Sex Ways—In Fact and Faith: Basis for Christian Family Policy*. New York: Association Press, 1961, pp. 166-183.

A comprehensive summary of knowledge designed to answer the questions young people may have concerning homosexuality.

Johnson, Eric, *Love and Sex in Plain Language*. Philadelphia: J.B. Lippincott Co., 1967.

A book based upon three assumptions: first, that sex is a part of life; second, that the power of sex for good and evil is so great that we must make every effort to see that it is used responsibly; third, that to act responsibly a person needs all the relevant knowledge that he can understnad. The content in Dr. Johnson's book indicates his attempt to treat each assumption in detail.

Jones, Claire, Gadler, Steven J., and Engstrom, Paul H., *Population: The Population Explosion*. Minneapolis: Lerner Publications Co., 1973.

Karen, A., *Sexuality and Homosexuality*. New York: Norton, 1971.

Katchadourian, Herant A. and Lundt, Donald T., *Fundamentals of Human Sexuality*. New York: Holt, Rinehart and Winston, Inc., 1972.

Landers, Ann, *Ann Landers Talks to Teenagers About Sex*. Greenwich, Connecticut: Fawcett Publications, Inc., 1968.

Straight talk about love and sex with answers to questions every teenager asks. Included in the list of topics: premarital sex, venereal disease, homosexuality.

Levinsohn, Florence, *What Teenagers Want to Know*. Chicago: Budlong Press, 1967.

An excellent booklet answering questions teenagers have about physiological development, dating, premarital sex, venereal disease, and marriage.

Lipke, Jean Coryllel, *Conception and Contraception*. Minneapolis: Lerner Publications Co., 1973.

Lipke, Jean Coryllel, *Loving and Dating*. Minneapolis: Lerner Publications Co., 1973.

Lipke, Jean Coryllel, *Sex Outside of Marriage*. Minneapolis: Lerner Publications Co., 1973.

Maccoby, Eleanor, *The Development of Sex Differences*. Stanford, California: Stanford University Press, 1966.

This book deals with differences between the sexes in behavior other than specifically sexual behavior. The focus is on sex differences. Eight contributors discuss special areas of the subject. The "afterword" raises the question, Why are myths about masculinity and femininity believed and sustained—even in the face of evidence to the contrary?

Marmor, J., *Sexual Inversion*. New York: Basic Books, Inc., Publisher, 1965.

A collection of articles by experts on homosexuality. This book presents the varied points of view attending this behavior.

Menninger, William, *How to Understand the Opposite Sex*. New York: Cornerstone Library, 1965.

Dr. Menninger's book is based upon a survey in which 3000 teenage boys and girls were asked to write on the topic, "What I can't understand about the opposite sex." In his book written for junior high school students, he attempts to give the teenage reader insight into the problems he has in dealing with the opposite sex.

Ashley Montagu, M. F., *Life Before Birth*. New York: New American Library, 1964.

Morris, Desmond, *The Naked Ape*. New York: McGraw-Hill Book Co., 1967.

Nilsson, A. L., et al., *A Child Is Born*. Boston: Seymour Lawrence, Inc., 1965.

Premarital Sex Standards. Siecus Publications, 1855 Broadway, New York, New York 10023.

There is a good deal of premarital sexual permissiveness, but it is largely regulated, particularly for females, by the amount of affection of the participant. It is the objective of this pamphlet to spell out in greater detail what this means and to examine some of the research data in this area.

Scheinfield, Amram, *You and Heredity*. Philadelphia: J. B. Lippincott Co., 1965.

Schultz, Gladys, *Letters to Jane*. Philadelphia: J. B. Lippincott Co., 1960.

A frank, helpful discussion of the emotional aspects of sex that perplex and disturb young people who are growing into maturity. It presents some of the problems of early dating, adjustment, and sex life in the form of a charming exchange of letters between a mother and her daughter.

Spock, Benjamin, *Baby and Child Care*. New York: Pocket Books, 1970.

Taylor, Gordon, *The Biological Time Bomb*. New York: The World Publishing Co., 1968.

Vincent, Clark E., *Unmarried Mothers*. New York: The Free Press of Glencoe, Inc., 1961.

Weinberg, George, *Society and the Healthy Homosexual*. New York: St. Martins Press, 1972.

Westoff, Leslie A., and Westoff, Charles F., *From Now to Zero: Fertility, Contraception and Abortion in America*. Boston: Little, Brown, 1971.

Winter, Gibson, *Love and Conflict*. New York: Doubleday & Co., Inc., 1961.

Modern man finds himself living a double life. He is preoccupied with the achievement of intimate relationships in the home. He is entangled in a multiplicity of impersonal dealings outside the home. This cleavage is reflected in strains within the family. An attempt to understand these strains is the fundamental concern of the book.

Witt, Elmer, *Life Can Be Sexual*. St. Louis: Concordia Publishing House, 1967.

This is a book on how to think about sex and sexuality, written from a Christian perspective. An excellent book to assist the student in the formation of values and attitudes.

Wolfenden, J., *Report of the Committee on Homosexual Offenses and Prostitution*. London: Her Majesty's Stationery Office, 1957 (United States: Stein and Day)

The authoritative report written by Parliament to recommend changes in the British laws governing homosexuality. An excellent report to analyze and discuss.

Glossary of Terms

Abortion	The termination of pregnancy prior to the 28th week of gestation.
Induced abortion	Expulsion or removal of an embryo resulting from an intentional act by the mother or another person.
"AC-DC"	A person who has sexual relations with members of either sex.
Adultery	Sexual intercourse wherein at least one partner is married to another person.
Afterbirth	The placenta that is discharged at the third stage of labor. All nonhuman mammals eat the afterbirth.
Amenorrhea	The absence of menstruation.
Amniotic sac	A fluid-filled sac that serves to protect the embryo.
Androgen	Hormonal substances that produce masculine characteristics.
Androphobia	An abnormal fear of men.
Annulment	A legal proceeding that renders a marriage void.
Aphrodisiac	A drug or other substance that increases sexual drive.
Autoeroticism	Another term for masturbation or self-stimulation.
Bartholin's glands	Two secreting glands found at either side of the vaginal entrance.
Bestiality	Having sexual intercourse with animals.
Bisexual	*Anatomy:* having sexual organs of both sexes. *Behavior:* having sexual relations with both sexes.
Breech birth	Childbirth in which the baby is presented buttocks first.
Bulbourethral (Cowper's) glands	Tubular glands that secrete into the male urethra.
"Butch"	A very masculine appearing female homosexual.

393

Cantharides	A dangerous substance (obtained from a South European beetle) that irritates the bladder, urethra, and digestive system; also called "Spanish fly."
Castration	Removal of the gonads.
Celibacy	A way of life in which the individual abstains from any sexual activity.
Cervix	The neck of the uterus.
Cesarean birth	A method of childbirth in which a surgical incision is made through the abdominal wall and uterus. The name comes from Julius Caesar, who was thought to have been born in this manner.
Chancre	An ulcer or sore caused by the syphilis bacterium. It usually is the first sign of syphilis.
Chancroid	An infection of the genitalia, usually venereal. Painful lesions develop and local lymph nodes are generally enlarged.
Circumcision	A surgical procedure in which the foreskin of the penis is removed.
"Clap"	A slang expression for gonorrhea.
Clitoris	The female organ devoted entirely to increasing sexual tension; located just above the urinary opening.
Coitus	Another term for sexual intercourse.
Coitus interruptus	Withdrawal of the penis prior to ejaculation in an attempt to avoid pregnancy.
Colostrum	The portion of milk first secreted following pregnancy.
Conception	The physiological uniting of sperm and egg.
Condom	Rubber sheath worn over male penis to prevent pregnancy or venereal disease.
Congenital	Being present at birth but not hereditary.
Continence	Refraining from sexual activity.
Contraceptive	Something used to prevent pregnancy.
Copulation	Sexual intercourse.

Corpus luteum	Temporary endocrine gland formed in the ovary after ovulation; it secretes estrogen and progesterone.
Couvade	Sympathetic pregnancy among husbands. A psychological reaction in which men experience many of the symptoms of pregnancy.
"Crabs"	Pubic lice.
Cryptorchidism	Undescended testes. In this condition the male is sterile until the testes descend or are surgically relocated.
Cul-de-sac	A closed pouch located between the anterior surface of the rectum and the posterior surface of the uterus.
Cunnilingus	Oral stimulation of the female genitals.
Detumescence	Loss of male erection secondary to a loss of blood from erectile tissue.
Diaphragm	A dome-shaped device worn over the cervix to prevent pregnancy.
Douche	Cleansing the vagina with a liquid.
Dysmenorrhea	Painful menstruation.
Dyspareunia	Painful intercourse; may be caused by physical or psychological factors.
Ectopic pregnancy	Extrauterine pregnancy; pregnancy that occurs outside the uterus (e.g., in the Fallopian tube).
Ejaculation	Male discharge of semen.
Ejaculatory duct	Anatomical junction of the vas deferens and the duct of the seminal vesicle with the male urethra. It is embedded in the prostate gland.
Emasculate	To deprive of manliness; to castrate.
Endometrium	The lining of the uterus.
Epididymis	Anatomical structure connecting the testis with the vas deferens.
Estrogen	Female sex hormone produced by the ovaries.
Eugenics	The science concerned with improving genetic constitution.

Eunuch	A term for the castrated male.
Fallopian (uterine) tubes	A tube-like extension of the uterus whereby eggs from the ovaries may pass to the uterus.
Fellatio	Oral stimulation of the penis.
"Femme"	Feminine appearing lesbian.
Fetish	An inanimate object that arouses erotic feelings.
Follicle stimulating hormone (FSH)	A hormonal substance released by the pituitary gland to stimulate the gonads.
Foreplay	Any form of sexual behavior preliminary to sexual intercourse.
Foreskin	A retractable fold of skin found over the head of an uncircumcised penis; also termed the prepuce.
Fornication	A term used to describe sexual intercourse outside marriage; in many states fornication is illegal.
Frattuier	One who gains sexual satisfaction by rubbing against women in crowds.
French kiss	Kiss that includes tongue contact.
Frenulum	Anatomical attachment of the penis to the foreskin.
Frigidity	A general term for female sexual unresponsiveness.
Gamete	Sperm or ovum; a reproductive cell.
"Gay"	Another term for homosexual.
Genitalia	External sexual organs.
Gestation	That period of time extending from conception to childbirth; pregnancy.
Gonadotropic hormones	Pituitary secretions that stimulate the sex glands.
Gonads	Testes or ovaries; sex glands.
Gonococcus	The bacterium that causes gonorrhea.
Gonorrhea	A venereal disease caused by the gonococcus.

Gravid	The state of being pregnant.
Gynecology	The medical science that deals with the treatment of disorders of the female reproductive system.
Hermaphrodite	A person possessing both testes and ovaries.
Heterosexual	One whose sexual interests are directed toward a member of the opposite sex.
Hirsutism	A condition in which an unusual growth of hair is exhibited.
Homosexual	One whose sexual interests are directed toward a member of the same sex.
"Honeymoon" cystitis	Irritation of the female bladder wall from sexual intercourse.
Hustler	A male homosexual prostitute or a female prostitute.
Hyaluronidase	An enzyme found in the head of the sperm that is thought to aid in penetration of the egg.
Hydrocele	A condition in which fluid accumulates in the scrotum.
Hymen	A membrane that partially guards the entrance to the vagina.
Hysterectomy	The surgical removal of the uterus.
Impotence	Inability of the male to have an erection.
Incest	Sexual relations that occur between closely related individuals; incest is universally taboo.
Inguinal hernia	Hernia is an abnormal protrusion of the contents of some anatomical cavity. In inguinal hernia the protrusion is through the inguinal canal, that is, the canal through which the testes normally descend.
Insemination	Artificial or natural deposition of semen into the vagina.
Interstitial cells	Cells in the testicles that produce male sex hormones.
Intromission	Insertion of the penis into the vagina.
IUD (intrauterine contraceptive device)	A small plastic device inserted into the uterus to prevent pregnancy.
Katasexual	Sexual behavior with a nonhuman partner.

Lecherous — Being very lustful.

Lesbian — A female homosexual.

Leukorrhea — A whitish vaginal discharge containing mucus and pus.

Luteinizing hormone (LH) — Pituitary hormone that stimulates the gonads.

Libido — Sex drive.

Lymphogranuloma venereum — A venereal disease of viral nature. Lesions develop on the genitalia and are usually followed by enlargement of the lymph nodes.

Maidenhead — Another term for hymen.

Masochism — A condition in which pain or humiliation is necessary for sexual satisfaction. The word comes from the name, Leopold von Sacher-Masoch, author of the nineteenth century masochistic novel "Venus in Furs."

Mastectomy — Removal of a breast.

Mastitis — Inflammation of the breast.

Menarche — The first menstrual flow; usually occurs between 12 and 14 years of age.

Menopause — The last menstrual flow; usually occurs between 45 and 50 years of age.

Menorrhagia — Excessive bleeding at the time of menstrual flow.

Miscarriage — An occurrence in which the fetus is expelled for reasons beyond the control of the mother.

Miscegenation — Marriage or sexual intercourse between persons of different races.

Mons veneris — Mound covered with hair and found in the female pubic region.

Myometrium — Muscles of the uterus.

Narcissism — Excessive love of one's self.

Nocturnal emission — Involuntary ejaculation occurring during sleep.

Nulliparous (Nonparous) — Describes a woman who has never borne a child.

Nymphomania   A condition in which the female physiologically or psychologically has an insatiable sexual desire.

Obstetrician   A physician specializing in the care of pregnant women and in the delivery of babies.

Onanism   Ejaculation of semen outside the vagina. The term applies only to the situation in which the penis is withdrawn from the vagina during intercourse. It is not a synonym for masturbation.

Oral contraceptive Hormonal substances taken to prevent pregnancy; in most cases estrogen and progesterone are taken to prevent ovulation.

Orchitis   Inflammation of the testes; frequently following mumps.

Orgasm   A series of muscular contractions that occur at the peak of sexual activity. In the male, these contractions are responsible for ejaculation. In the female, they promote relief of congestion in the pelvic area.

Ovary   The female reproductive gland. It releases eggs and produces estrogen and progesterone.

Panhysterectomy Removal of uterus, ovaries, and Fallopian tubes.

Parthenogenesis Reproduction without male fertilization.

Parturition   The act of giving birth.

Pederasty   Sexual intercourse by means of the anal canal; also refers to male sexual relations with a young boy.

Pedophilia   An abnormal interest in a child on the part of an adult.

Penis   Male organ for copulation and urination.

Penis captivus   A condition in which the penis becomes trapped in the vagina, as occurs in copulation among dogs. It does not occur with humans.

Pervert   One who departs from accepted standards of sexual conduct; often used to describe the homosexual.

Phallus   The penis.

Phimosis   In this condition the foreskin is too narrow to allow it to be retracted over the head of the penis.

Pimp	A person who solicits for a prostitute.
Polyandry	Having more than one husband.
Polygamy	Having more than one wife.
Pornography	Literature or art serving only for the purpose of sexual arousal in the beholder.
Potent	Able to perform sexual intercourse; able to have an erection.
Primigravida	One who is pregnant for the first time.
Progesterone	A hormonal substance produced by the corpus luteum; it prepares the uterus for implantation and maintains pregnancy.
Prostrate gland	Anatomical structure that surrounds the neck of the urinary bladder and the beginning of the male urethra.
Prostatectomy	Surgical removal of part or all of the prostate gland.
Psychosexual	Refers to the psychological or emotional aspects of sexuality.
Rhythm method	A method of contraception in which the partners attempt to schedule sexual intercourse in such a way that no sperms are present during the short life span of the egg.
Ridgling	A term describing a male with one testicle.
Sadism	A condition in which a person is sexually stimulated by inflicting pain upon another.
Salpingectomy	A surgical procedure in which the Fallopian tubes are removed.
Sapphism	Female homosexuality or lesbianism; the term comes from the name of the Greek poetess, Sappho.
Satyriasis	An insatiable sex desire in men.
Scrotum	Sac-like container that encloses the testicles. A major function of the scrotum is temperature regulation.
Semen	Fluid ejaculated at male orgasm.
Seminal vesicles	Glands that connect with the ejaculatory duct and secrete, among other substances, fructose.
Seminiferous tubules	Tubules in the testes that produce sperm.

Sexology	The science of sex.
Sexuality	A term that includes all aspects of maleness and femaleness: sociological, philosophical, psychological as well as biological aspects.
SIECUS	Sex Information and Education Council of the United States. Publishes study guides on sex education. (Address: 1855 Broadway, New York, N.Y. 10023.)
"Sixty-nine"	A slang term describing mutual oral-genital relations.
Smegma	A wax-like secretion that accumulates under the foreskin.
Sodomy	Illegal sexual behavior; most often anal intercourse.
"Soixante-neuf"	French for 69; used to described two sexual partners, both of whom are providing oral-genital stimulation.
Spanish fly	See Cantharides.
Spermatogenesis	The physiological process whereby sperms are produced.
Spermicide	Chemical substance that kills sperms.
Statutory rape	Sexual intercourse with a girl under the age of statutory consent.
Sterility	The inability to have children.
"Straight"	Another term for heterosexual.
Syphilis	A bacteria-caused venereal disease; the disease may cripple or kill.
Tampon	Absorbent type material that is inserted into the vagina to absorb the menstrual flow.
Teat	The nipple of the breast.
Testes	Male gonads; testicles.
Testosterone	Male sex hormone produced by the testes.
Transsexual	A person who thinks that he was "meant" to be a member of the sex other than the one indicated by his sexual organs.
Transvestite	A person with a compulsive desire to wear the clothes of the opposite sex.

Treponema pallidum	The bacterium that causes syphilis.
Tubal pregnancy	Implantation of a fertilized egg in the Fallopian tube.
Tumescence	Increased size of the penis or other anatomical structures secondary to the accumulation of blood.
Umbilical cord	An anatomical connection between the unborn baby and the placenta.
Urethra	A canal extending from the bladder to the external urethral orifice. In the male it extends approximately 9 inches; the female length is about 1 1/2 inches. In the male the canal serves as a passageway for urine and ejaculate.
Urethritis	An inflammation of the urethra.
Uterus	The womb; the organ that receives the fertilized ovum, supports it during pregnancy, and contracts to aid in expulsion at the time of childbirth.
Vagina	Female birth canal and organ for sexual intercourse.
Vaginismus	A condition in which the muscles of the vagina involuntarily contract and prevent entry of the penis.
Vaginitis	An inflammation of the vagina.
Vasectomy	Male sterilization in which the sperm duct is cut and tied off.
Vas (ductus) deferens	Anatomical structure connecting the epididymis with the ejaculatory duct.
Virginity	A term to describe the state of never having participated in sexual intercourse.
Virilism	Masculinization of the female.
Voyeur	A "Peeping Tom," a person who obtains pleasure from observing the reproductive anatomy or behavior of others.
Vulva	External female anatomy; includes the labia majora, labia minora, and clitoris.
Whore	A prostitute or a disparaging term for a promiscuous woman.
Womb	Another term for uterus.

X chromosome   Female sex chromosome.

Y chromosome   Male sex chromosome.

Yohimbine   Substance obtained from the yohimbe tree; some think
                              yohimbine has aphrodisiac properties.

Zooerastia   Bestiality; sexual intercourse with nonhuman partners.

A Speech to Introduce Sex Education to the Community

A successful sex education program requires the support of the community. Thus an early step in introducing sex education should be open communication with parents. Parent-teacher meetings are excellent opportunities for such a discussion. In planning a presentation for parents, a review of the speech that follows may be of some value. This speech was given by one of the authors in introducing sex education to an Ohio community.[1] It includes many of the basic concepts presented in this book. A suggested program format follows:

1. Have a speaker outline the problems that attend human sexuality at the current time.

2. Disseminate a brief statement of the philosophy of your sex education program and some specific objectives for each grade level. This is very important because the parent will have no idea of what might be included in a sex education curriculum.

3. Provide a panel to discuss the curriculum in the local school district: an elementary teacher, a junior high school teacher, a high school teacher, and a school administrator.

SEX EDUCATION IN SYLVANIA
(Text of a Speech)

Sex education as a part of education

Education is dedicated to the proposition that each new generation deserves the right to profit from the mistakes and compromises of their parents, their grandparents, and, indeed, all previous generations.

We say of those who have no respect for the knowledge accumulated by older generations: "You are disrespectful, foolish, immature, and perhaps egotistical."

---

[1] The speech was recently revised and updated.

404

But despite statements to the contrary, I sincerely feel that to-day's youngsters are very appreciative of the worthwhile activities of previous generations.

For example, I feel that they are appreciative of the knowledge in medical science that enables them to avoid smallpox or polio.

And I think that they are equally impressed by the recommendations of teachers in the humanities against human exploitation.

The young appreciate real wisdom

Thus I feel that we can proceed under the assumption that young people are very much interested in any wisdom that we have to pass along.

On the other hand, it is becoming increasingly difficult to sell personal bias on the wisdom market.

In view of this, we are meeting together tonight as adults to ask and discuss the question: Has our generation or any generation before us accumulated and organized any wisdom relative to human sexuality that should be passed on to our children?

What's worth telling

Put another way, what do you know about sexuality that is worth telling?

And if there is some wisdom available, how, when, where, and by whom should it be passed on?

A dissection of life in twentieth century United States might bring us to one of two conclusions: either that we don't know anything worth telling, or that we have decided that the younger generation does not have the right to profit by the sexual mistakes and compromises of history.

Until the recent emphasis on sex education, the schools or churches did not discuss the topic and only one in 20 parents ever mentioned it to his child.

No formal sex education

Being very sensitive to the criticism that new programs in education are often initiated without good reason, I think that we should first examine the consequences of continuing in the current "no formal education" approach.

This week, in a large midwestern university not too far from here, there were 40 unwanted pregnancies by 40 unmarried girls.

The pregnancy problem

Next week there will be 40 more. Each week since October there has been an average of approximately 40.

These girls come from homes not very different from those in this community.

And they were impregnated by young men not very different from those in our community.

It is very likely that they attended schools and churches very similar to those in our community.

Do you and I possess any wisdom to prevent this from happening to our daughters or sons?

I would like to suggest that we do.

And I would further suggest that the background values for proper sexual behavior are best developed in elementary school.

Old concepts for young people

Relative to participation in the sex act, I give my students at the university this advice:

Before you engage in sexual relations, both partners should meet five criteria:

1. Each should have a blood test for venereal diseases. It is degrading to humanity to pass on an infectious disease that easily could be prevented.

2. Both should agree to love, educate, and care for any offspring, or carefully evaluate the effect of an abortion. An unwanted, unloved child begins life without the human dignity that should be everyone's birthright.

3. Prior to participation in sexual intercourse the two people involved should have some notion of direction and goals in life and be able to answer the question: How does participation in sexual intercourse fit into the goals that I have set for myself and the goals of my partner?

    Put another way, a person should find himself before entering into sexual intercourse.

4. The act should be for the mutual improvement of both, and one should not be exploited at the expense of the other. The most degrading of all human acts is to use another person as a means to a selfish end.

5. Prior to participation in sexual intercourse, both partners should agree upon the desirability or undesirability of having children. If children are not wanted, a mutually acceptable and effective form of contraception should be planned.

Reasonable criteria

In the experience of the authors, most young people agree that these are reasonable criteria. Many, however, do not feel that their private agreement to these criteria necessitates marriage.

But the notion that today's young person is less moral than those of previous generations is a myth.

For example, they are far less likely to visit a prostitute than the youth of previous generations.

And they do not tolerate exploitation when they are able to discern it.

Homosexuality

A beautiful and intelligent college girl recently told me that she could never go home again—her father had learned that she was homosexual and had let it be known that he would shoot her if he ever saw her again.

Are you that type of parent? How do you feel about the fact that approximately 6 to 8 per cent of all the youngsters in our schools are homosexuals?

Should we shoot them? Send them to jail? Send their parents to jail? Pretend that they don't exist?

The American Psychiatric Association has recently removed homosexuality from its list of mental disorders. In view of this, doesn't it seem reasonable to discuss the problem at least?

A problem of ignorance

Since 7:30 P.M. yesterday, thousands of teenagers in the United States have contracted V.D.

But this is more a condemnation of the adult than of the teen-age population.

We have not allowed them to profit by the accumulated wisdom.

You see, we know the cause of these diseases, we know the method of transmission, and we have effective cures.

What then is the problem?

An example is perhaps the best illustration.

Last week I talked to a group of high school seniors about sexuality. At one point a girl raised her hand to ask: "This may sound silly, but what is a venereal disease?"

Indeed, a recent survey indicated that some 90 per cent of high school seniors thought syphilis could be inherited.

And there are many adults who claim that theirs is really a case of doorknob syphilis.

But you don't contract it from doorknobs or toilet seats.

You can contract a venereal disease in the bathroom, but as Dr. Eugene Schoenfield puts it: ". . . the floors are usually very cold and hard."[2]

Nor do the southwestern winds blow it down from Detroit. If you want a Detroit strain you have to go to Detroit or meet someone who is visiting from there.

"Sorry, full"

A recent cartoon depicts a stork flying with a baby over a large city. As the stork reaches the city he sees a large sign projecting in the sky that reads "Sorry, full."

---

[2] *Time*, March 7, 1969.

This bit of humor renders clear the major problem of our times.

Most people in this country are aware of the population explosion, but few really understand what it means.

Perhaps this is because the birth rate in the United States has decreased in recent years, with the exception of the East Coast blackout and the Midwest snow storm a few years back. These were followed nine months later by a baby boom, proving that human beings confined to close quarters revert to cuddly primates with one track minds.

But let's see what the population explosion really means.

250 to 500 million

It is estimated that the world population at the time of Christ was approximately 250 million.

It required 1650 years for this figure to double to 500 million.

500 million to one billion

Then by the year 1850, just 200 years later, we had reached the one billion mark.

One billion to two billion

The population doubled again by 1925, i.e., 75 years later. At this date there were approximately two billion people in the world.

The present estimates are as follows:

1969	3.5 billion
1980	4.0 billion
1990	5.0 billion
2000	6.5 billion

70 per cent hungry

It is currently estimated that among the world's children under six years of age, 70 per cent are already malnourished.

This is rendered tragic by the fact that the world population is increasing at a rate of 2 per cent per year whereas the food supply is increasing at a rate of 1 per cent per year.

The average daily intake in the world today is 2100 calories per day. By 2000 it is estimated to be 1340 whereas 1350 per day is starvation level.

Science will save

But the typical attitude is: We don't have to worry about population explosion—science will take care of that.

And it is indeed true that much can be done to increase the food supply.

For example, it is estimated that one female green turtle could produce 7200 pounds of meat per year if the baby mortality were reduced.

But the difficulty is that the underdeveloped countries don't have the "know-how" to increase the food supply.

Preoccupied with space ships

And the countries with more advanced technology are entertaining themselves with space ships.

It might be well to remember that underdeveloped countries are usually more impressed with food than with flashes of power.

The problem within the United States is not quite so drastic.

Our technology is very advanced; and our rate of growth is relatively low; hence, it is very likely that our food supply will more than keep pace.

Quantity vs. quality

So it is the quality of life that will be most affected in this country.

On a personal basis, you have perhaps encountered the problem in some of the following ways:

1. Trying to find room to ski on the weekend.
2. Waiting your turn to play golf.
3. Looking for a clear spot to swim in a public pool.
4. Attempting to get a bowling alley.
5. Trying to get a seat for an athletic contest.
6. Looking for a place to hunt, fish, or camp.

These are but a few examples of the problem that attends a population increase in an affluent society.

They are less important by comparison with the following list:

1. Not enough doctors for medical care.
2. Diminished resources and energy.
3. The feeling of being just a number or a face in a large crowd.
4. Unemployment.

How do we solve the greatest problem in the world today? By refusing to discuss birth control!

Those who are concerned about the quality of life in the United States must also be concerned about the quantity of life.

Sexual inadequacy

Another problem of sexuality frequently occurs for people who have never had a venereal disease, have never had tendencies toward homosexuality, are well educated and married:

It is the inability to establish a happy sexual relationship in marriage.

Such sexual inadequacy stems primarily from a poor understanding or attitude toward sexuality.

May I suggest, Ladies and Gentlemen, that healthy attitudes toward sexuality are best developed in elementary school.

How the schools get involved

The schools were prompted to start sex education programs for three reasons:

1. They believed that a body of knowledge relative to sexuality exists.
2. They believed that young people deserve to profit by the mistakes and compromises of previous generations.
3. Finally, no one else was willing to tackle the problem.

It is very important that you understand the spirit in which schools all over the country are initiating programs of sex education.

It is out of a sincere feeling that it is what is best for the student.

If you think it is hard to talk to your child about sexuality, consider the possibility of talking to 35 at once.

Don't complain

This means a lot of extra work on the part of teachers and not all of them are happy with the extra duty.

So if you don't support them or if you speak out against them, don't be surprised if they say, "Fine, do it yourself."

But in this case it is the child who loses.

Your child's values

I think that it is well to remember that the values your child holds are likely to be nearer to those of his close friends than those of his parents.

Thus you and I have a real interest in the community in general and not just our own children.

And I am happy to report that sex education is being introduced throughout the country with full support of parents.

There are a few who protest.

A protest group

In New Jersey there is a group who call themselves Parents Against Undemocratic Sex Education.

They claim that sex education is a communist plot.

When I heard about this group, I was reminded of a note received from a parent in this part of the state:

It read: "Please excuse Mary from physical education for the next three days as she is in heat."

Prepoverty?

A friend of mine, on reading in the news that a group in New Jersey were protesting sex education for prepoverty students, called the newspaper to find out what it was all about.

The girl who had written the article confessed that she didn't really understand what sex education for prepoverty students meant but she would ask the editor.

The editor was heard over the phone to say:

"That's not prepoverty; it's prepuberty, you idiot."

I guess the state could use some sex education.

The Soviet experience

At the risk of being called a communist, I would like to tell you about the experiences of the Soviet Union with sex education.

In the early 1930's, the Soviet Union advocated free love.

But as it happened, such a practice was soon to destroy the family system and the Soviets quickly reversed their position.

Their publication, *Soviet Education,* concedes the mistake in these words:

"Practices such as free love lead to relationships unworthy of man, cause personality problems, unhappiness and disruption of the family, making orphans of children."

Having identified this problem they are now trying to correct it.

The Soviet approach

The Soviet approach is very candid:

"Every parent must work toward training the future citizens to be happy only in family love and to seek the joys of sex life only in marriage. If parents do not set such a goal for themselves and do not reach it, their children will lead a promiscuous sex life full of dramas, unhappiness, misery and injury to society."

Their primary objective is unequivocal:

Education for love

"Sex education is and should be education for love—that is, great and profound feeling enhanced by unity of life, yearning and hopes."

I totally agree that sex education should be education for love.

So let's examine the nature of love.

Eric Fromm has skillfully dissected love into four constituent parts:

Labor—meaning that one is willing to work for and give of one's self for those whom he loves.

Responsibility—meaning that one constantly evaluates the consequences of his behavior as it relates to others and stands prepared to help when needed by those he loves.

Respect—meaning that one refrains from the exploitation of others.

Understanding—meaning that one tries to place himself in the shoes of another.

Sex education as education for love attempts to render clear these four constituents of love as they relate to sexual behavior:

Labor

With respect to labor, the sex educator attempts to point out again and again the inconsistency in the behavior of those who say they love but are unwilling to give of themselves for the person they profess to love.

Responsibility

To provide the knowledge that will enable the individual to evaluate and effectively handle the consequences of his sexual behavior is another role of the sex educator.

Understanding the biological, sociocultural, psychological, and health consequences of various types of sexual behavior is a part of one's responsibility.

Respect

In the total realm of personal relationship there is probably no greater temptation to exploit another human being than in the area of sexual behavior.

Sex education points out the danger to human happiness.

Understanding

Understanding means becoming aware of the motivations that underlie the wishes and desires of others.

It means putting yourself in the shoes of another.

Sex education does not excite curiosity

Some of you who still have reservations about sex education might be comforted by a statement from Dr. Milton I. Levine, a physician and Professor of Clinical Pediatrics at Cornell University Medical College in New York City:

"There is no evidence whatsoever that sex education is harmful, that it excites curiosity or stimulates sex urges and desires. On the contrary, there is ample evidence that it aids children in gaining a wholesome attitude toward sex and an understanding of the normal sex attitudes, roles and relationships.

"Sex education, however, is not offered as a panacea, a preventive or a cure for sex delinquency, illegitimacy, marital discord or homosexuality.

"But if may aid our boys and girls to learn to direct and channel their sex impulses with more knowledge and intelligence, to make a correct choice between operating codes of heterosexuality and homosexuality, and to recognize and understand those men and women with sex desires and urges which are deviant."

What Is
Your
Intimacy
Quotient?*

Psychologists have gloomily diagnosed our society as neurotic, emotionally plagued, armored, flattened, one-dimensional, contactless, repressed. These are ways of saying that intimacy is lacking in human relationships—it is the societal "missing link." Without a sense of intimacy, interpersonal contact becomes a worrisome job of guarding our psychic territory against invaders. Both male supremacy and women's lib are products of this rupture in our consciousness, which can turn love into infantile dependency, and sex into a track-and-field event.

Intimacy is the venturous encounter between two equally vulnerable people. It is so soft that many men fear it as a threat to their masculinity, yet it is incredibly hard in the quantity of sheer courage required to risk the possibility of a surprise attack with one's defenses down. Beyond ideas of softness or hardness, intimacy is—psychologists are beginning to suspect—a biological necessity. Behavioral scientists have discovered that without close emotional contact, even well-fed babies and animals can die—from sensory starvation.

This quiz is designed to measure your capacity for intimacy—how well you have fared in (and what you have learned from) your interpersonal relationships from infancy through adulthood. In a general way, it helps measure your sense of security and self-acceptance, which gives you the courage to open yourself to the ego hazards of intimacy—to risk the embarrassment of proffering love or friendship or respect and getting no response. Some are blessed with this ability; some acquire it through experience and maturity; others, not even comprehending it, or too fearful of it, survive behind a facade they continually seek to strengthen but can never quite make shatterproof. The insight this test should provide can alert you to weaknesses that may be reducing your performance in everything from business, meeting and interacting with potential mates to ordering food in a restaurant.

If it is convenient, try taking it with someone you feel intimate with—afterward compare and discuss your answers. It may indicate how potentially compatible you are, socially or sexually. This is one area of interpersonal relationships in which opposites do not necessarily attract. A person of high intimacy capacity

---

can intimidate someone of low capacity who is fearful to respond. But those of similar capacities whether high or low, will tend to make no excessive demands on each other and, for that reason, will find themselves capable of an increasingly intimate and mutually fulfilling relationship.

The questions can be answered easily. If your response is yes or mostly yes, place a plus (+) in the square preceding the question. If your response is no or mostly no, place a minus (−) in the square. If you honestly can't decide, place a zero in the square; but try to enter as few zeros as possible. Even if a particular question doesn't apply to you, try to imagine yourself in the situation described and answer accordingly. Don't look for any significance in the number or the frequency of plus and minus answers. Simply be honest when answering the questions.

Each section will be discussed in terms of the different areas of attitudes and behavior and of how the answers provide an index to your potential for intimacy.

☐   1. Do you have more than your share of colds?

☐   2. Do you believe that emotions have very little to do with physical ills?

☐   3. Do you often have indigestion?

☐   4. Do you frequently worry about your health?

☐   5. Would a nutritionist be appalled by your diet?

☐   6. Do you usually watch sports rather than participate in them?

☐   7. Do you often feel depressed or in a bad mood?

☐   8. Are you irritable when things go wrong?

☐   9. Were you happier in the past than you are right now?

☐   10. Do you believe it possible that a person's character can be read or his future foretold by means of astrology, *I Ching*, tarot cards or some other means?

☐   11. Do you worry about the future?

☐   12. Do you try to hold in your anger as long as possible and then sometimes explode in a rage?

☐   13. Do people you care about often make you feel jealous?

☐   14. If your intimate partner were unfaithful one time, would you be unable to forgive and forget?

☐   15. Do you have difficulty making important decisions?

☐   16. Would you abandon a goal rather than take risks to reach it?

☐   17. When you go on a vacation, do you take some work along?

☐   18. Do you usually wear clothes that are dark or neutral in color?

☐   19. Do you usually do what you feel like doing, regardless of social pressures or criticism?

20. Does a beautiful speaking voice turn you on?

21. Do you always take an interest in where you are and what's happening around you?

22. Do you find most odors interesting rather than offensive?

23. Do you enjoy trying new and different foods?

24. Do you like to touch and be touched?

25. Are you easily amused?

26. Do you often do things spontaneously or impulsively?

27. Can you sit still through a long committee meeting or lecture without twiddling your thumbs or wriggling in your chair?

28. Can you usually fall asleep and stay asleep without the use of sleeping pills or tranquilizers?

29. Are you a moderate drinker rather than either a heavy drinker or a teetotaler?

30. Do you smoke not at all or very little?

31. Can you put yourself in another person's place and experience his emotions?

32. Are you seriously concerned about social problems even when they don't affect you personally?

33. Do you think most people can be trusted?

34. Can you talk to a celebrity or a stranger as easily as you talk to your neighbor?

35. Do you get along well with salesclerks, waiters, service-station attendants and cabdrivers?

36. Can you easily discuss sex in mixed company without feeling uncomfortable?

37. Can you express appreciation for a gift or a favor without feeling uneasy?

38. When you feel affection for someone, can you express it physically as well as verbally?

39. Do you sometimes feel that you have extrasensory perception?

40. Do you like yourself?

41. Do you like others of your own sex?

42. Do you enjoy an evening alone?

43. Do you vary your schedule to avoid doing the same things at the same times each day?

44. Is love more important to you than money or status?

45. Do you place a higher premium on kindness than on truthfulness?

□   46. Do you think it is possible to be too rational?

□   47. Have you attended or would you like to attend a sensitivity or encounter-group session?

□   48. Do you discourage friends from dropping in unannounced?

□   49. Would you feel it a sign of weakness to seek help for a sexual problem?

□   50. Are you upset when a homosexual seems attracted to you?

□   51. Do you have difficulty communicating with someone of the opposite sex?

□   52. Do you believe that men who write poetry are less masculine than men who drive trucks?

□   53. Do most women prefer men with well-developed muscles to men with well-developed emotions?

□   54. Are you generally indifferent to the kind of place in which you live?

□   55. Do you consider it a waste of money to buy flowers for yourself or for others?

□   56. When you see an art object you like, do you pass it up if the cost would mean cutting back on your food budget?

□   57. Do you think it pretentious and extravagant to have an elegant dinner when alone or with members of your immediate family?

□   58. Are you often bored?

□   59. Do Sundays depress you?

□   60. Do you frequently feel nervous?

□   61. Do you dislike the work you do to earn a living?

□   62. Do you think a carefree hippie life style would have no delights for you?

□   63. Do you watch TV selectively rather than simply to kill time?

□   64. Have you read any good books recently?

□   65. Do you often daydream?

□   66. Do you like to fondle pets?

□   67. Do you like many different forms and styles of art?

□   68. Do you enjoy watching an attractive person of the opposite sex?

□   69. Can you describe how your date or mate looked the last time you went out together?

□   70. Do you find it easy to talk to new acquaintances?

□   71. Do you communicate with others through touch as well as through words?

□   72. Do you enjoy pleasing members of your family?

□   73. Do you avoid joining clubs or organizations?

74. Do you worry more about how you present yourself to prospective dates than about how you treat them?

75. Are you afraid that if people knew you too well they wouldn't like you?

76. Do you fall in love at first sight?

77. Do you always fall in love with someone who reminds you of your parent of the opposite sex?

78. Do you think love is all you presently need to be happy?

79. Do you feel a sense of rejection if a person you love tries to preserve his or her independence?

80. Can you accept your loved one's anger and still believe in his or her love?

81. Can you express your innermost thoughts and feelings to the person you love?

82. Do you talk over disagreements with your partner rather than silently worry about them?

83. Can you easily accept the fact that your partner has loved others before you and not worry about how you compare with them?

84. Can you accept a partner's disinterest in sex without feeling rejected?

85. Can you accept occasional sessions of unsatisfactory sex without blaming yourself or your partner?

86. Should unmarried adolescents be denied contraceptives?

87. Do you believe that even for adults in private, there are some sexual acts that should remain illegal?

88. Do you think that hippie communes and Israeli kibbutzim have nothing useful to teach the average American?

89. Should a couple put up with an unhappy marriage for the sake of their children?

90. Do you think that mate swappers necessarily have unhappy marriages?

91. Should older men and women be content not to have sex?

92. Do you believe that pornography contributes to sex crimes?

93. Is sexual abstinence beneficial to a person's health, strength, wisdom or character?

94. Can a truly loving wife or husband sometimes be sexually unreceptive?

95. Can intercourse during a women's menstrual period be as appealing or as appropriate as at any other time?

96. Should a woman concentrate on her own sensual pleasure during intercourse rather than pretend enjoyment to increase her partner's pleasure?

97. Can a man's efforts to bring his partner to orgasm reduce his own pleasure?

☐ 98. Should fun and sensual pleasure be the principal goals in sexual relations?

☐ 99. Is pressure to perform well a common cause of sexual incapacity?

☐ 100. Is sexual intercourse for you an uninhibited romp rather than a demonstration of your sexual ability?

Mood and Psychosomatics—(Questions 1-8)

Because the mind is part of the body, anything that affects one also affects the other. Questions 1 through 8 deal with those aspects of your feelings and physiology that most reflect your degree of emotional adjustment and your ability to cope with stress. In this section, the more minus answers, the better.

Studies carried out at the Chicago Institute for Psychoanalysis found that psychosomatic afflictions occur most often in people whose dependencies and ego needs come into conflict with their adult desire to be independent and self-sufficient. These psychosomatic symptoms or ailments demonstrate an inability to express emotions and to willingly accept certain needs and conflicts as normal and inevitable.

Even when illnesses are genuinely organic in origin or the result of bad nutrition and health habits, the effect still is to dull a person's ability to cope with stress, to interact with others and to enjoy his surroundings. Sometimes these "real" health problems are themselves a defense against intimacy. A person who has little love for himself may use health neglect as a form of self-punishment; the consequent health problems—being chronically run-down, overweight or whatever—make him unattractive to others and thereby spare him the anxieties of close interpersonal interaction.

The interdependence of mental and physical well-being is experienced by everyone during periods of depression. The best cure for the blues is activity. A brisk walk or a game of tennis gives the body and, with it, the mind, a quick pick-me-up. But the blues can also produce such physical lethargy that a depressed person can't even force himself to physical exertion. In some, a mild, unrecognized depression, with its accompanying sluggishness, becomes a way of life.

The Burden of Being Independent—(Questions 9-19)

Questions 9 through 19 deal with the conflict between the wish to remain a dependent child with no responsibilities and the need to mature into a self-sufficent, independent adult, and, except for question 19, minus answers suggest a favorable resolution of the conflict.

The person who has not adequately resolved his adult-child conflict often sees the past as a happier time than the present; he also tries to derive a sense of strength and security from any number of sources outside himself—booze, drugs, astrology, religion, a spouse, sympathetic friends. By indulging his dependencies, he also evades assuming personal responsibility when things go wrong—as they invariably do, simply because those people or things he has put in charge of his life can't really run it for him.

A person so dependent on others tends toward jealousy and possessiveness, which often causes the smothered one to seek relief through solitude or even infidelity, which is never forgiven nor forgotten but used to stoke the fires of resentment that the betrayed calls love. Though he constantly professes love, he has not enough even for himself, much less for anyone else, and his possessiveness eventually strangles any love that others have for him.

In general, the truly independent person is secure enough to dress as he likes, live as he likes, and shrug off criticism that his own code or conscience tells him is unwarranted. Most important, he is secure enough to respect the rights and differences of others and not feel threatened.

Awareness: Those Who Have Eyes to See—(Questions 20-30)

"Lose your mind—come to your senses," Fritz Perls used to tell his students. Questions 20 through 30 explore your capacity to not just see and hear but to perceive and feel and respond to others as well as to your surroundings. Here, hopefully, your answers are pluses.

If you turn on to all kinds of sights, sounds, feels, tastes, odors and places, you probably have a high capacity for intimacy simply because your senses are so highly tuned.

Take, for example, the sense of smell. Most humans left it behind when our species stopped navigating on all fours, using our noses to warn us of danger or lead us to food and water and sex. Uptight people may have a highly developed sense of smell, but it's likely to be one that rejects most human and organic odors because of personal inhibitions against the intimacy these suggest. And if the sense of smell is deficient, the sense of taste usually suffers: either from disuse of that sense or from suppression of it through inhibitions. Such people are rarely sexually adventurous and find it difficult to engage in intimate relationships that may expose their inhibitions to sensory stimuli that cause them anxiety.

Sensuous people also, within reasonable limits, don't take anything too seriously—especially themselves. They are amused by unexpected happenings that would be threatening to others. They can laugh when a joke is on *them*. Because they find it so easy to relate to the moment in which they are living, they can turn boredom into relaxation and fatigue into pleasant drowsiness the minute they fall into bed.

Sensuous people distinguish themselves by their lack of need for artificial stimulants or drugs to free them of their inhibitions. They are stimulated by reality; they are by nature uninhibited. And this capacity to enjoy other people, things, and themselves gives them a high potential for intimacy.

Empathy Versus Sympathy—(Questions 31-39)

Sympathy is cheap. Anyone who drives past a serious car accident and sees injured people being cared for can sympathize with their misfortune. But the far greater accomplishment is to encounter another human being under less spectacular circumstances and be able to literally feel his distress in such a way that you are genuinely able to understand what he's saying, what he's doing, how he is trying to cope with his emotional crisis. Questions 31 through 39 test your ability to put yourself in another person's place—emotionally, not just intellectually—and honestly share whatever feelings are affecting him at a given moment. Here, the plus answers count.

Ordinary sympathy includes strong elements of superiority or judgment on the part of the sympathizer. Empathy does not; it is simple understanding and sharing. It is, moreover, a prerequisite to intimacy, creating the ability to accept strangers trustingly, to understand problems one has never personally faced and to withhold judgment out of simple respect for other people's differences and weaknesses. This has nothing to do with extra-sensory perception—if anything, it should be called supersensory perception—but the person capable of deep empathy may wonder at times if he *is* picking up some kind of telepathic communications, because he's so perceptive to the unexpressed thoughts, feelings, and needs of family, friends, and lovers.

Self-Image and Self-Esteem—(Questions 40-42)

These three questions should provide good clues to your real feelings about yourself and the way you view life in general. Hopefully, the view is positive—and your answers are pluses.

If you find yourself unlovable, you can expect others to find you that way, too. For the most part, people will accept your evaluation of yourself and react to you accordingly. That may make them unloving in your eyes, so you build more barriers against them—an activity they view as hostile. Perceiving their reactions, you likewise find them hostile and decide the world is a cold, unfriendly place. An entirely different cycle of interactions is set in motion if you are able to love yourself. Then others see you as lovable and offer you affection. Surrounded by love instead of barriers, you find the world a warm, accepting place.

Do you enjoy the company of your own sex? Can you spend a pleasant evening alone? It's not love but dependency when someone needs another simply to escape feelings of loneliness.

Child, Parent, and Adult—(Questions 43-50)

Questions 43 through 50 give some indication of whether an individual is primarily controlled by his inhibited, critical "parent," who represents parental and social conditioning; by his insecure but satisfaction-seeking "child," who demands both pleasure and support; or by his "adult," the sensibly rational element in his personality that tries to mediate between his immediate desires and his long-range best interests. Ideally, the adult, mature by virtue of experience and good judgment, dominates the other elements of personality *most of the time* but still gives each other element its due. Your degree of maturity, or "adultness," is indicated in this section by the number of plus answers to questions 43 through 47 and minus answers to questions 48 through 50.

When the parent is in charge, a person may appear to be functioning efficiently, but there is little joy or spontaneity in his life. The rise in popularity of sensitivity or encounter groups in recent years is a sign that we realize this and that we're looking for ways to strengthen the adult-oriented child within us. At his best, the child in our natures is spontaneous, feeling and outgoing. At his worst, he is dedicated to instant gratification, regardless of the effects on other people or of the long-range consequences to himself.

Since the child, conditioned by the parent, may feel that sex is a forbidden pleasure, people are often beset by sexual problems; it is the adult in a person that recognizes these for what they are and seeks professional help, since the child may think that unsatisfactory sex, or none at all, is an appropriate punishment for unquenchable sexuality.

Nowhere is the child in our sexual attitudes more evident than in a fear of homosexuals, for few of use have learned to handle our own personality components that we associate with the other sex—and with homosexuality. Women are frightened of their aggressive impulses, men of their desires for dependence. Both wonder if these secret, hidden feelings are abnormal and can be detected by other people they've been taught to believe are abnormal also. To keep such fears controlled, we ostracize those who arouse them—and thereby diminish our capacity to love.

Games People Play—(Questions 51-53)

We shortchange our love lives when we try to relate to each other as actors playing traditional masculine and feminine roles instead of interacting as real, live, distinctive individuals. Questions 51 through 53 attempt to gauge the extent to which you communicate openly and honestly without assuming or assigning protective roles that can only prevent intimacy in relationships. Here, the more minus answers, the better.

Roles are not conducive to communication and without communication, there can be no intimacy. Sex is a type of communication, and partners who can't talk or touch or express their fears and feelings to each other are almost certain to experience sexual difficulties sooner or later. For this reason, the first effort by most sex therapists is to re-establish, or strengthen, a couple's capacity to communicate.

Fortunately, there are indications, verified by surveys, that the traditional sex roles are on their way out. Men now often tell researchers that they are looking for women who are intelligent, athletic, adventurous, and independent— qualities that weren't considered very feminine just a few years ago. And women, more and more, are looking for men who are communicative, sensitive, educated, and intelligent—not the aggressive "strong, silent type" of olden days.

What You Do is What You Are—(Questions 54-62)

A person's day-to-day behavior is largely predetermined by childhood training, psychological experiences, and acquired attitudes. It is the you that other people know. Questions 54 through 62 give some indication of how uptight you are in certain areas that later portions of this analysis will deal with more specifically. Plus answers here suggest that your behavior is not working very well as a problem-solving device but is being dictated by your problems.

Behavior manipulation and behavioral response are major elements in daily living. Parents manipulate children by rewarding desired behavior and by withholding rewards to discourage behavior they consider bad. Adults use similar tactics on each other, but usually in an unconscious way that too often backfires. When a woman suspects her husband of infidelity, she may shower him with attention in an effort to keep his love—and find that she has only aggravated the problem. He probably feels a sense of guilt already and her increased affection increases his guilt. Because he doesn't like feeling guilty, he resents all the more her implicit demands for a response that he will not or cannot provide voluntarily. Or we have the woman who simply feels neglected, gives up trying to win love and approval with constructive behavior, and settles for the angry attention elicited by nagging. If her husband tries to deal with this phenomenon by ignoring it, the nagging increases in volume and duration until a response—any response—has been obtained.

We also reinforce our *own* behavior, sometimes consciously, sometimes not. At the end of the day, we take a drink because we've worked hard and earned it or because everything has gone wrong and we deserve it. In this way, habits are built, day by day, that both reflect and affect the personality of the individual. For instance, if a person lives in disorder, it can mean he habitually ignores his surroundings by way of surviving in them—to the point where this has become his style of life.

Quite different is the person who guiltlessly pampers himself. He buys flowers, or whatever, because they delight him; occasionally he treats himself to luxuries at the expense of necessities, and he will likely accord the same treatment to others simply to please them—not to impress them. The key word here is guiltlessly; it distinguishes between self-pampering for pleasure and self-indulgence out of need.

A person can escape boredom even when alone for long periods if he has developed the habit of pleasing himself. He's not dependent on others to amuse him nor to structure his time. He looks forward to Sundays, not as dull days when he has difficulty finding something to do but as weekly gifts of time to spend for his own satisfaction. Opposite is the Sunday neurotic who works weekends at home mainly to escape the guilt of relaxation, which he equates with sloth and laziness.

He is wrathful toward welfare recipients and angry toward ambitionless street people and hippies. Far from occasionally envying those who enjoy an apparently carefree life, he is psychologically threatened by their very existence. Compulsive workers who cannot enjoy periods of complete nonproductivity feel like martyrs to their careers, families or other obligations. The chief differences is that their kind of martyrdom demands equivalent suffering from everyone else. To say the least, such people are not sufficiently satisfied with themselves to make good intimate partners, except, possibly, for other masochists.

Playfulness and Creativity—(Questions 63-69)

"All work and no play makes Jack a dull boy," as the old saying goes. But it's probably more accurate to say that Jack was a dull boy to begin with and, lacking imagination and creativity, he finds it easier to work than to let himself go in what his work ethic tells him would be a wasteful orgy of conversation, creativity, and imaginative flights of fancy. If he is to permit himself any relaxation, it must be passive receptivity to some form of entertainment that demands no active participation and permits him, temporarily, to simply turn his mind off for the purposes of recharging his physical and mental batteries. Questions 63 through 69 measure your ability to indulge in things that should, at least, be pleasurable relaxation and pleasantly intimate encounters. In this section, plus answers are good signs.

In general, creative people are curious, cognizant, and adventurous. They fondle pets, marvel at the ordinary, and accept the unusual. In short, they explore and search for novelty and uniqueness and refuse to categorize people simply as rich, poor, liberal, conservative, male, female. As a result, they have a wide variety of enthusiasms as well as friends, and their success with the opposite sex often astounds their associates. "What does she see in him?" envious males ask one another as he leaves with the girl the rest were watching. But it wasn't what she saw in him, it was what he saw in her that made the difference. For he didn't see her as "a cute chick" or "a great bod" but as a unique and appealing person, and this feeling was successfully communicated. This is such an unusual and flattering way for a woman to be approached that her response is almost always warm. The same goes for men, whom most women treat initially as just another representative of the male sex.

This kind of creative seeing is even more important after 20 years of looking at each other. That's because partners imprint each other when they fall in love, and if a couple never bothers to update the original impression, except critically, the original imprint is lost over the years.

Such disillusionment doesn't occur between creative, intimate partners. In the beginning, their imprints on each other were more than skin deep. And because they never expected themselves to stay the same forever, they kept seeing and communicating with each other and renewing the imprint. They never wake up to find themselves well-acquainted strangers. Rather, for them, the original intimacy and love remain and serve to continuously strengthen their relationship.

Good-Neighbor Policies–(Questions 70-75)

Because life, at least a full life, requires close and frequent contact with other human beings, the ability to comfortably interact with casual acquaintances and total strangers is an important trait in anyone's character. Questions 70 through 75 provide clues to the positive or negative behavior patterns you have cultivated in dealing with others. The first three answers are, hopefully, pluses; the second three, minuses.

The person who feels he has no talent for playing the piano usually doesn't try; he can still enjoy music by listening to records or attending a concert. But the person who feels he has no talent for interpersonal relationships doesn't have such options, because the quality of his life depends heavily on his ability to interact with others. Too many individuals experience difficulty meeting new people or feel uncomfortable around strangers and conclude that sociality is a gift bestowed on some people but not on others. They make the best of the situation by adopting standardized and safe (which usually means agreeable but distant) behavior responses toward others. They avoid meeting new people, dislike shaking hands—touching or being touched—and keep interpersonal contacts to a minimum simply to minimize the chance of being caught with their "responses down."

What the socially inept person most needs is practice. That's what the socially adept person has been doing, intentionally or not, all his life, He began learning to please members of the opposite sex by pleasing those in his own family. He has practiced relating to store clerks, people at bus stops, cabdrivers and waitresses, observing that they may be having a particularly harried day and allowing for this, or that they seem in unusually good spirits and would welcome letting someone know. In short, he *works* at interpersonal relationships, rejecting the propaganda that advises him constantly that all he needs to be popular is the right deodorant, mouthwash, automobile, or clothing. He knows that he can't compensate for personality deficiencies with either chemicals or possessions, but he can overcome them with personal insight put into constant practice.

Love Versus Need—(Questions 76-85)

That pleasant tingling sensation and feeling of warmth and euphoria that rushes through the body when one receives an enthusiastically romantic response may be love; but too often it is nothing more than a feeling of great psychological relief that a strong need is being or is about to be satisfied. Thus, the feeling of love is easily confused with the *need* for love. Questions 76 through 85 attempt to determine your real motives when you feel that you love someone. The first four questions should have minus answers; on the others, plus answers are a good sign that your feelings are expressive, not exploitative.

People who fall in love at first sight are rarely interested in establishing an emotionally intimate relationship. More likely, they have just laid eyes on a person who conforms closely enough to their physical ideal and who seems malleable enough to be changed, with a little effort, into Miss or Mr. Right. In many cases, Miss or Mr. Right reminds this person of a childhood love—an older sister or brother or a parent—someone so thoroughly known and predictable that he or she represents no threat of displaying individuality for which one might have to make allowances. In almost every case, however, Miss or Mr. Right will not and cannot make the changes this kind of love demands; and if, to retain affection or secure a wedding band, the loved one tries to fake it, soon enough the facade will collapse of its own weight and leave standing there Miss or Mr. Wrong.

People without parental hang-ups or illusions of changing someone, who marry out of a genuine mutual attraction, can still come to grief if they expect too much of love and of their loved one and abdicate responsibility for their own happiness. Any two people who think that love conquers all are in for an unpleasant surprise. Love is a complex combination of emotions that includes hostility, hate, envy, anger, and other feelings we've been taught to deplore. Only when we understand that all these feelings are components of love can we handle the situation when a stress symptom surfaces. If we don't understand this, then we leap to the conclusion that love is dead in the face of anger or rejection and bury it prematurely or repress the unacceptable emotion.

Partners who never fight aren't really intimate; those who are intimate constantly make adjustments and only the most minor of these are made without some conflict and compromise. But they resolve these conflicts immediately and honestly, without silently waiting for one or the other to capitulate or for time to simply bury the problem.

Sex is always fertile ground for conflict. Even with the best-matched partners, desire for sex doesn't always coincide, any more than does desire for food, recreation, or sleep. In a secure relationship, neither feels the need to project blame for sexual disappointments on the other nor feels that occasional sexual incapacity or disinterest means anything more than tiredness, too much partying, or too many emotional distractions left over from the day. These are problems only when chronic, because sex, like everything else in life, has its routine ups and downs. Indeed, it's when sex seems unappealing that the truly intimate couple can give each other the psychological support and nondemanding physical caresses that permit sex to blossom again.

Sex Behavior: Good and Bad—(Questions 86-100)

In some ways, this is the most important section of the quiz, for personality strengths and weaknesses tend to reveal themselves more acutely in sexual attitudes than in any other area of life. Questions 86 through 100 measure your sexual inhibitions and the extent to which you allow your sexuality to give you (and others) pleasure, not just fulfillment of physiological and psychological needs. Minus answers to questions 86 through 93 mean your sexual attitudes are liberal; plus answers from question 94 on indicate that you use sex in a productive way not only to enjoy yourself but to enhance the intimacy of a mature and loving relationship.

Significantly, sex is the only natural physiological function surrounded by legal taboos, which illustrates the extent to which our culture has viewed sexuality as something dangerous and menacing. Implicit in these laws is the idea of preventing people from engaging in certain sexual relations, as though sex, in itself, were a national peril.

Though various experiments in communal living show the traditional nuclear family to be more of an old rural and agrarian survival device than a modern-day necessity, law and social pressure try to preserve the concept of the patriarchal family unit. But, at the same time, the evidence is virtually indisputable that children fare better either in a communal environment or with a single parent than when unhappy partners in an unworkable marriage attempt to preserve their union at all costs because they think they owe it to their offspring.

Even for the congenially married, advancing age can be a frustrating time because of the myth that people should—and usually do—retire from sex the minute they go on Social Security. The myth of a sexless old age is one reason divorce after twenty years or more of marriage is so common and so often brought about by anxieties rather than actual incompatibility.

Other harmful myths are that pornography leads to sex crimes, that sexual self-restraint either is healthful or preserves sexual ability longer, that intercourse during menstruation is either unhealthy or inappropriate.

Orgasm is considered a necessity for men, but continues to be regarded by many as a luxury for women, whose greatest pleasure is supposed to come from giving pleasure to their partners. Such selflessness may seem commendable, but Masters and Johnson learned in their research that the woman who tries to give pleasure "by the numbers" cannot become immersed in the sensuous stimuli that should also bring her complete sexual satisfaction. This not only limits her own sexual pleasure but can be disturbing to her partner if he happens also to be acting the part of a noninvolved spectator.

Why would a woman try to fake an orgasm and a man try to find her out? Because for too many people, performance means more than pleasure. The man's role in sexual athletics demands that *he* bring *her* to orgasm; and if she fakes it, he must conclude he wasn't "good" enough and the show was hers. Similarly, if a man doesn't become wildly aroused and reach a stupefying climax, some women regard this as evidence that they lack sexual virtuosity.

Rather a competitive picture of what should be the most intimate of human involvements, isn't it? Orgasm that happens as a part of physical communication between intimate partners is an ecstatic experience, but it loses much of its magic and luster, and sometimes becomes impossible to achieve, when it is the sole goal of sexual activity.

The pressure to *perform* well is a factor in almost every case of sexual inadequacy. It is such an important factor that Masters and Johnson find the elimination of the pressure to perform an important first step in treating all sexual incapacity.

Couples who would avoid sexual troubles and keep the joy in their love-making would do well to concentrate on pleasure rather than performance—the moment-by-moment sensual delights that their physical closeness brings. Orgasm can be a high point in that pleasure. But since orgasm cannot be forced nor willed, it can become an elusive goal.

Questions 1-18, count your minuses_____
Questions 19-47, count your pluses _____
Questions 48-62, count your minuses_____
Questions 63-72, count your pluses _____
Questions 73-79, count your minuses_____
Questions 80-85, count your pluses _____
Questions 86-93, count your minuses_____
Questions 94-100, count your pluses _____
Total_____

Subtract from this total *half* the number of zero answers to obtain your corrected total.

If your corrected total score is under 30, you have a shell like a tortoise and tend to draw your head in at the first sign of psychological danger. Probably life handed you some bad blows when you were too young to fight back, so you've erected strong defenses against the kind of intimacy that could leave you vulnerable to ego injury. If you scored between 30 and 60, you're about average, which shows you have potential. You've erected some strong defenses, but you've matured enough, and have had enough good experiences, that you're willing to take a few chances with other human beings, confident that you'll survive regardless. Any score over 60 means you possess the self-confidence and sense of security not only to run the risks of intimacy but to enjoy it. This could be a little discomforting to another person who doesn't have your capacity or potential for close interpersonal relationships, but you're definitely ahead in the game and you can make the right person extremely happy just by being yourself. If your score approaches 100, you're either an intimate Superman or you are worried too much about giving right answers, which puts you back in the under-30 category.

ATLAS OF TEACHING ILLUSTRATIONS

[This Atlas is made up of the more important illustrations used in the body of the text. It is our thought that teachers may wish to remove these for overhead projection or for other kinds of reproduction to facilitate discussion of the material with their students.]

Figure 1   **431**

Descent of Testes

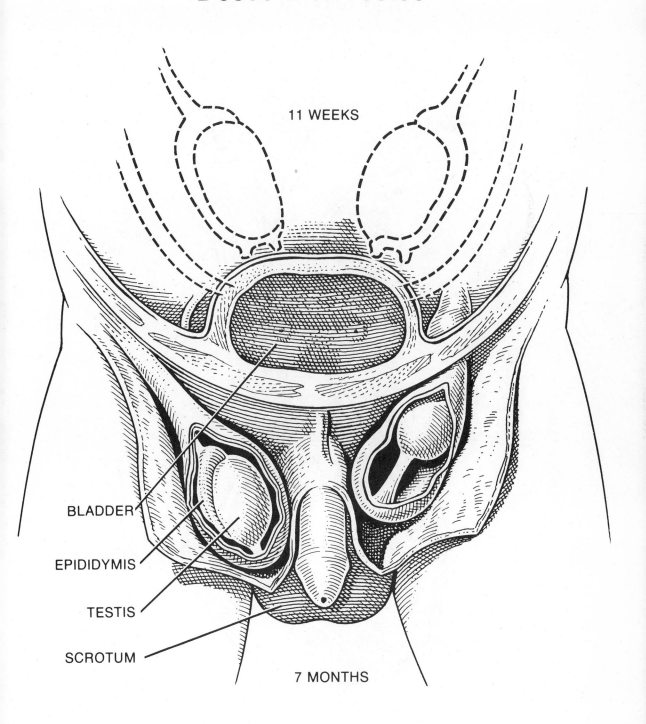

11 WEEKS

BLADDER

EPIDIDYMIS

TESTIS

SCROTUM

7 MONTHS

Hernia

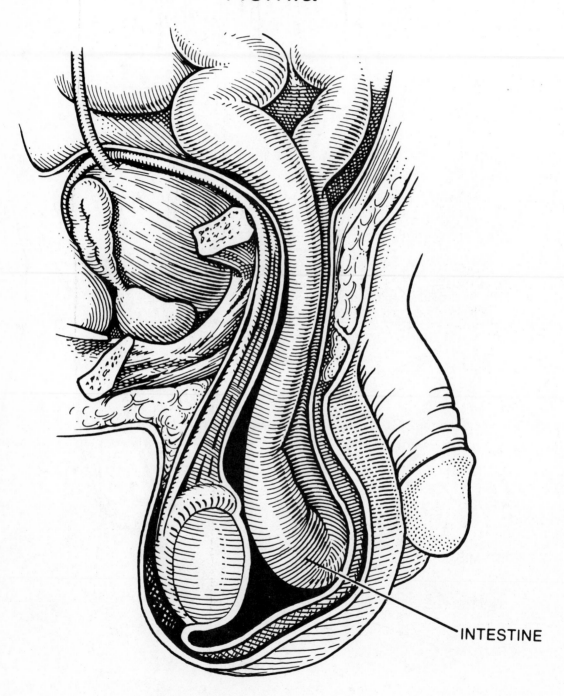

INTESTINE

Figure 3   **433**

Cremasteric Muscles

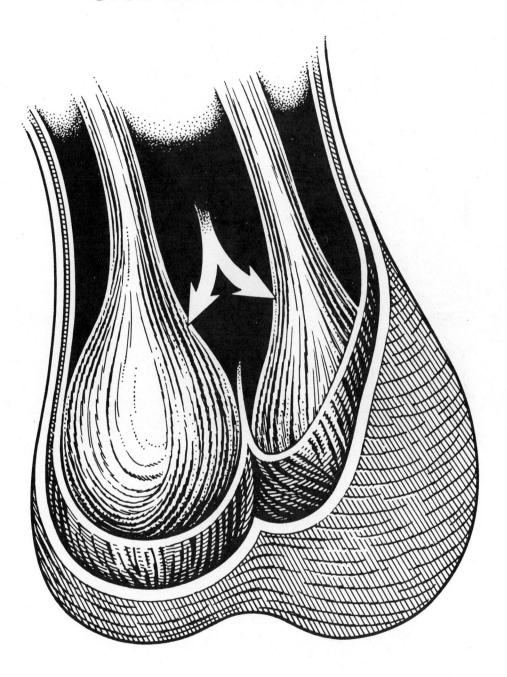

Seminiferous Tubules
and Interstitial Cells

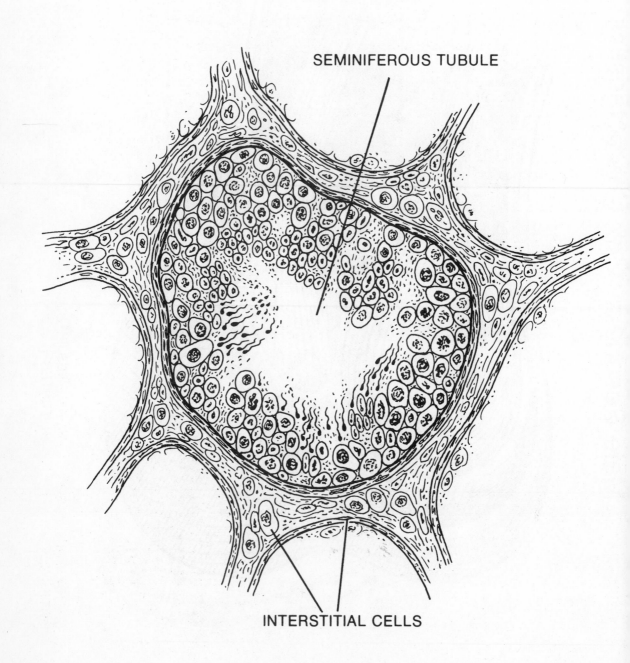

SEMINIFEROUS TUBULE

INTERSTITIAL CELLS

Figure 5   **435**

Male Secondary Sex Characteristics

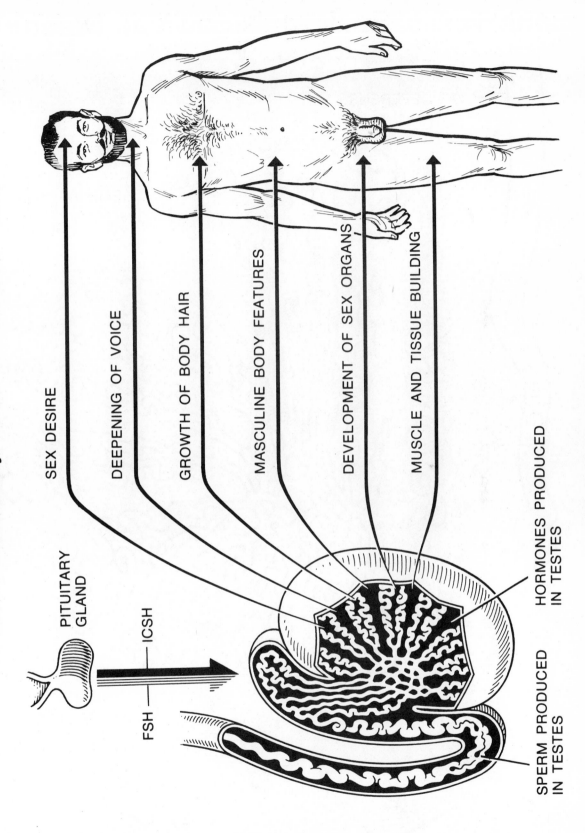

SEX DESIRE

DEEPENING OF VOICE

GROWTH OF BODY HAIR

MASCULINE BODY FEATURES

DEVELOPMENT OF SEX ORGANS

MUSCLE AND TISSUE BUILDING

PITUITARY GLAND

ICSH

FSH

HORMONES PRODUCED IN TESTES

SPERM PRODUCED IN TESTES

The Testis, Epididymis, and Vas Deferens

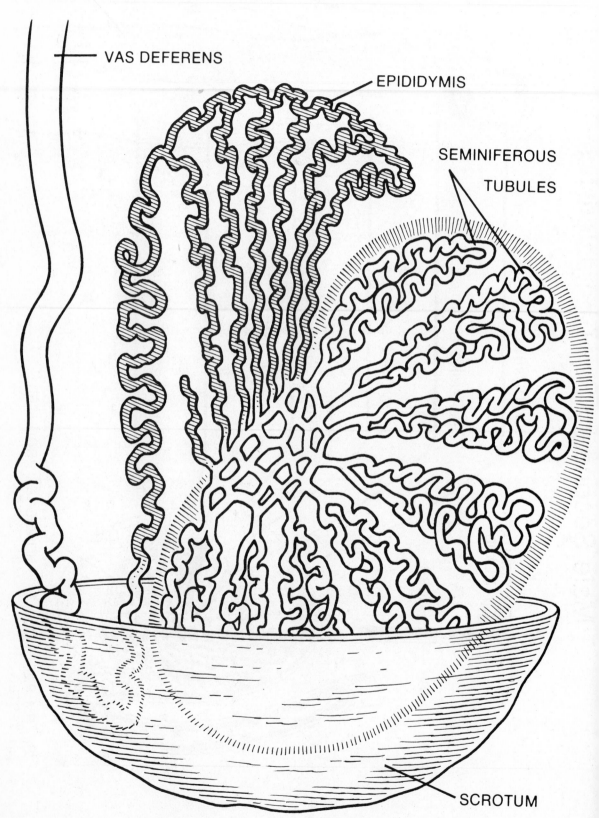

VAS DEFERENS

EPIDIDYMIS

SEMINIFEROUS
TUBULES

SCROTUM

Sperm Development

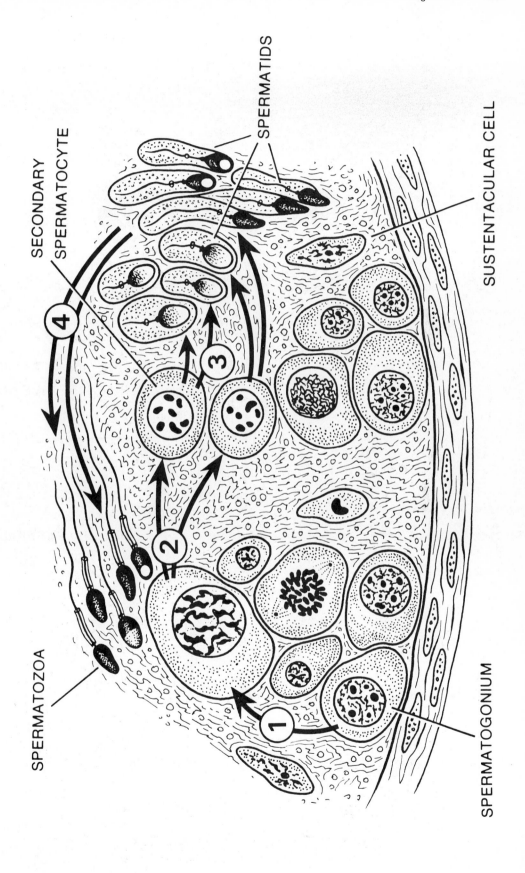

Figure 7   **437**

SPERMATIDS

SECONDARY
SPERMATOCYTE

SUSTENTACULAR CELL

SPERMATOZOA

SPERMATOGONIUM

Seminal Vesicle

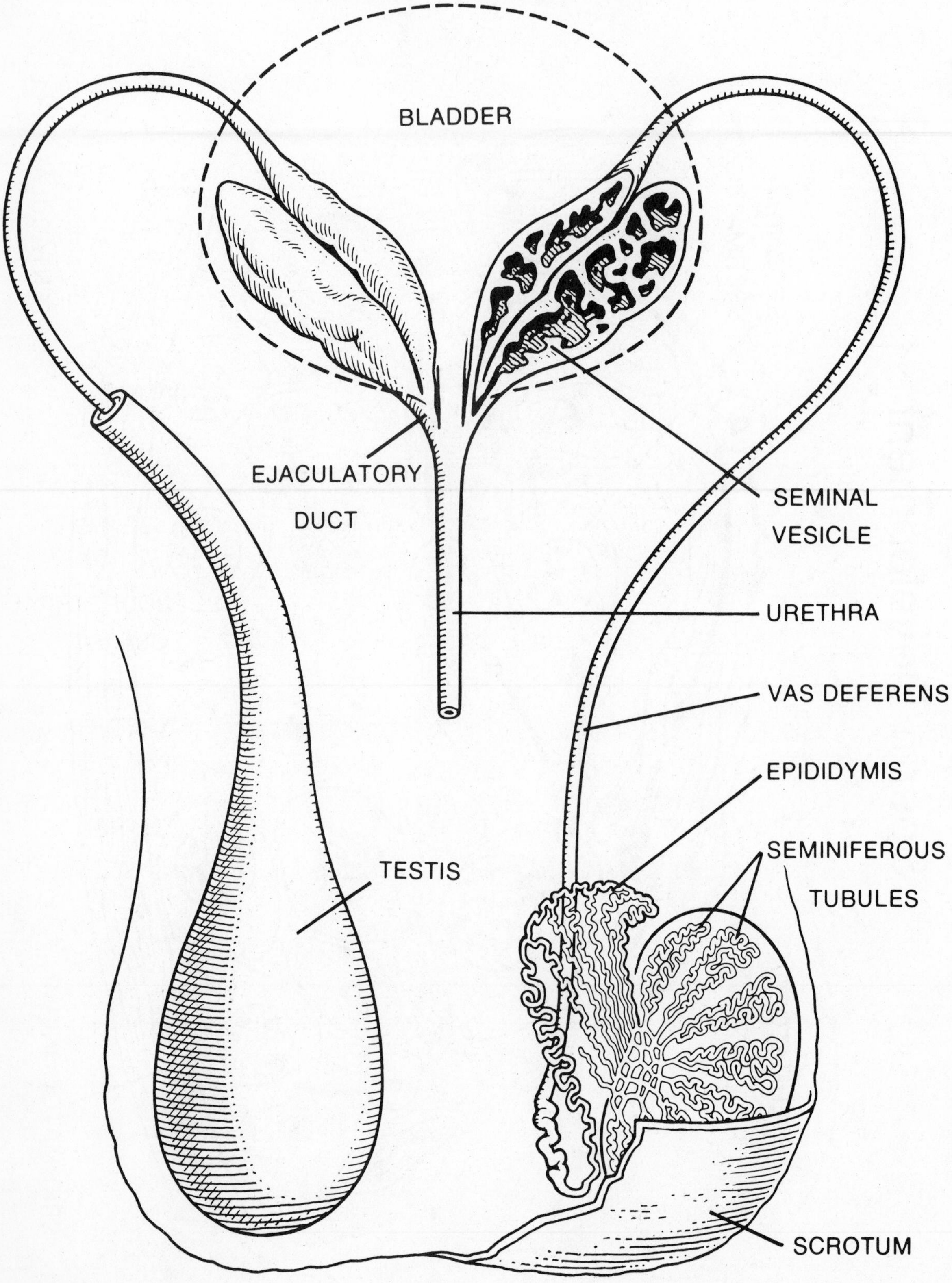

BLADDER

EJACULATORY

DUCT

SEMINAL

VESICLE

URETHRA

VAS DEFERENS

EPIDIDYMIS

SEMINIFEROUS

TUBULES

TESTIS

SCROTUM

Figure 9   **439**

Prostate and Bulbourethral Glands

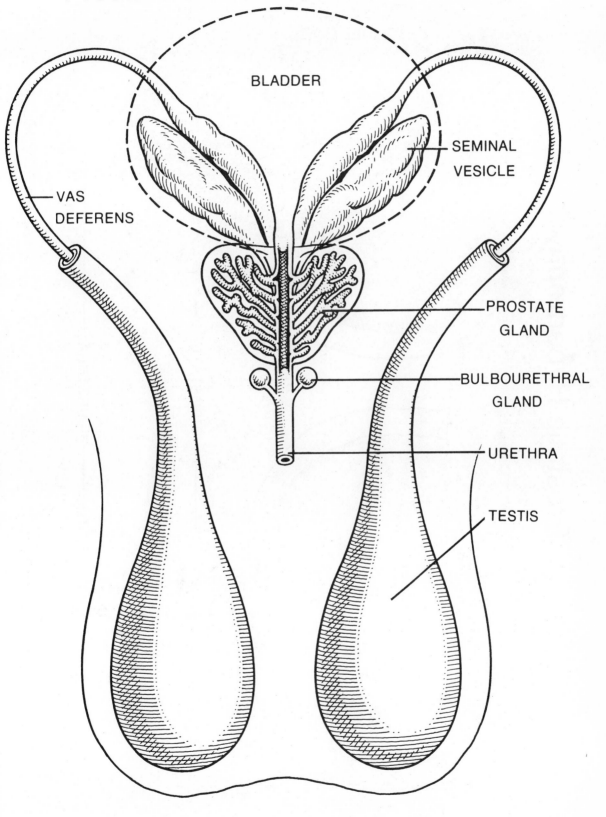

BLADDER

VAS
DEFERENS

SEMINAL
VESICLE

PROSTATE
GLAND

BULBOURETHRAL
GLAND

URETHRA

TESTIS

Prostatic Hypertrophy

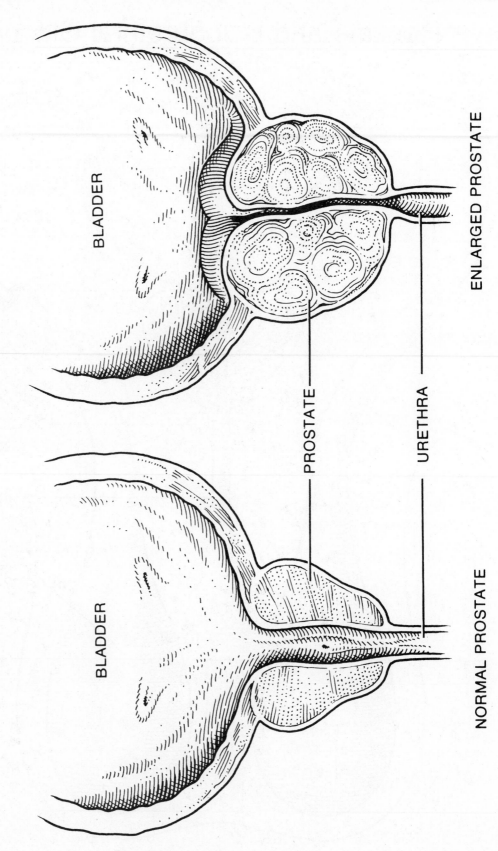

BLADDER

BLADDER

PROSTATE

URETHRA

ENLARGED PROSTATE

NORMAL PROSTATE

Figure 11   **441**

Rectal Examination of the Prostate

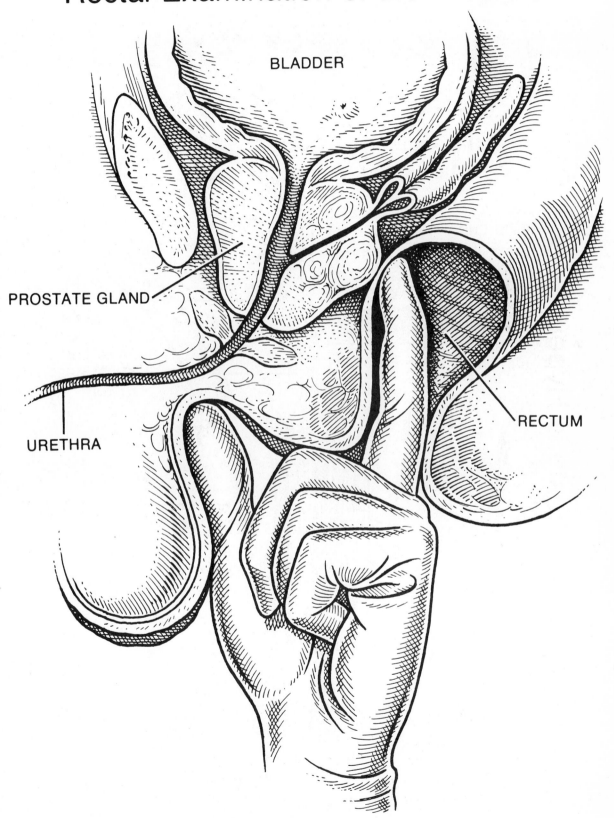

BLADDER

PROSTATE GLAND

URETHRA

RECTUM

Bulbourethral Glands and Penis

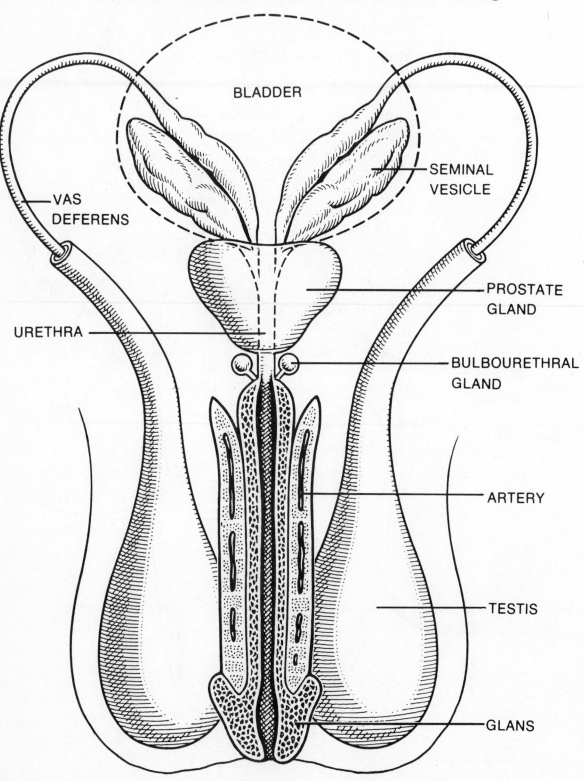

BLADDER

VAS
DEFERENS

SEMINAL
VESICLE

PROSTATE
GLAND

URETHRA

BULBOURETHRAL
GLAND

ARTERY

TESTIS

GLANS

Figure 13   **443**

Smegma Secretion

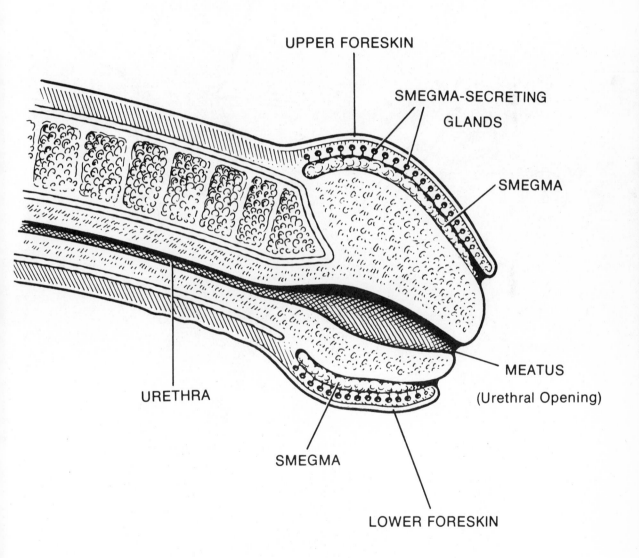

Circumcision

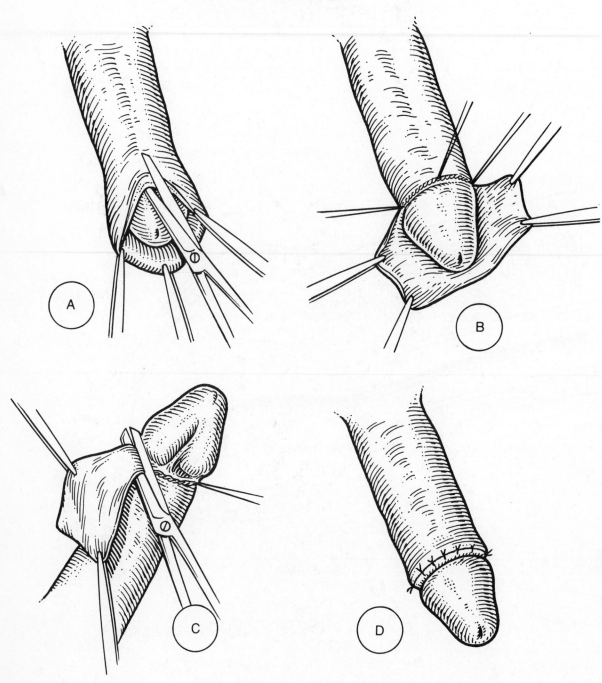

Figure 15   **445**

Male Reproductive System (Side View)

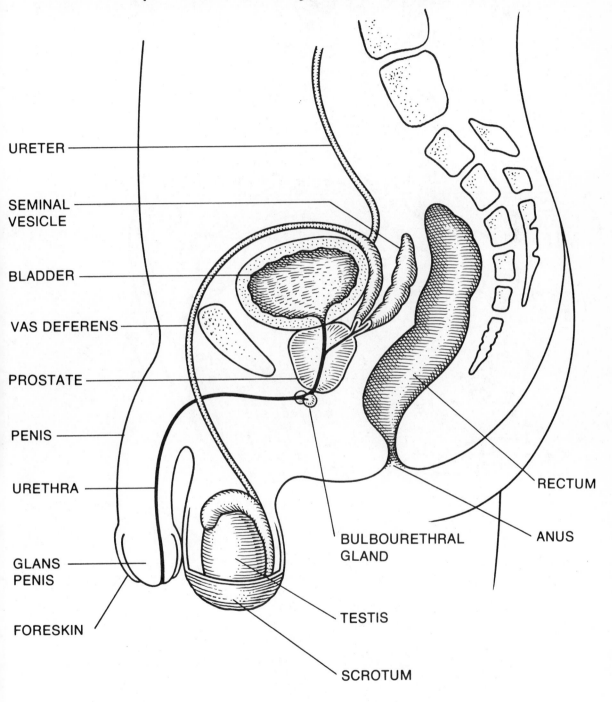

URETER

SEMINAL
VESICLE

BLADDER

VAS DEFERENS

PROSTATE

PENIS

URETHRA

GLANS
PENIS

FORESKIN

BULBOURETHRAL
GLAND

TESTIS

SCROTUM

RECTUM

ANUS

Fertilization

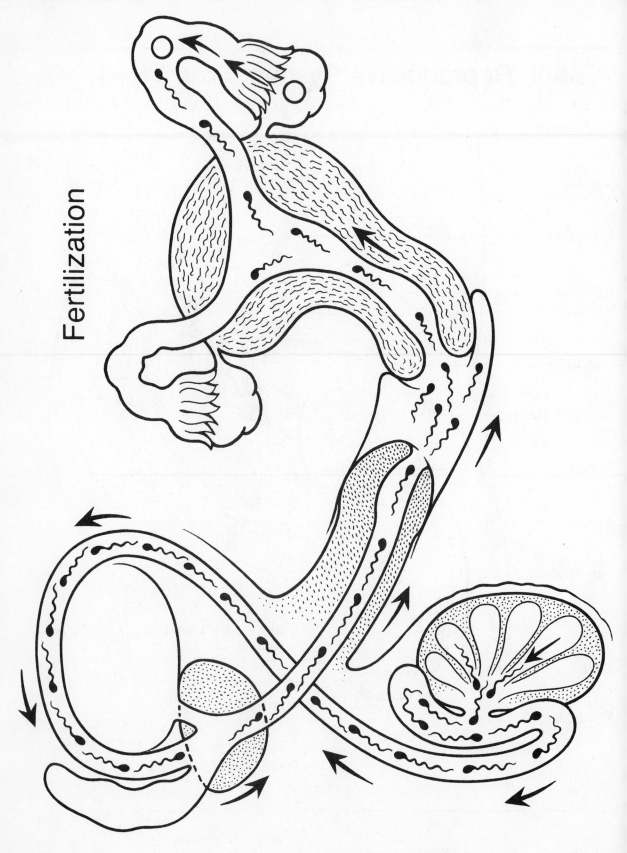

Figure 17   **447**

Erectile Tissue

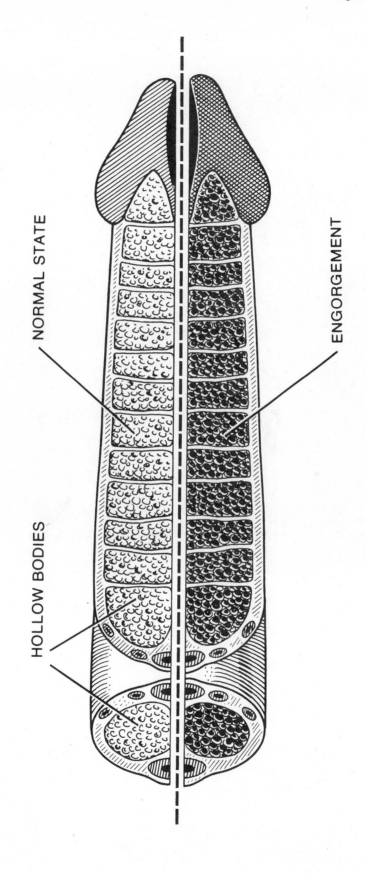

NORMAL STATE

ENGORGEMENT

HOLLOW BODIES

Structure of a Sperm

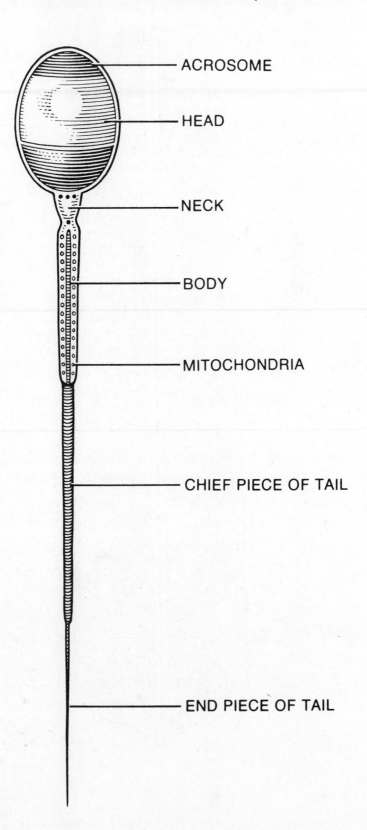

ACROSOME

HEAD

NECK

BODY

MITOCHONDRIA

CHIEF PIECE OF TAIL

END PIECE OF TAIL

Figure 19   **449**

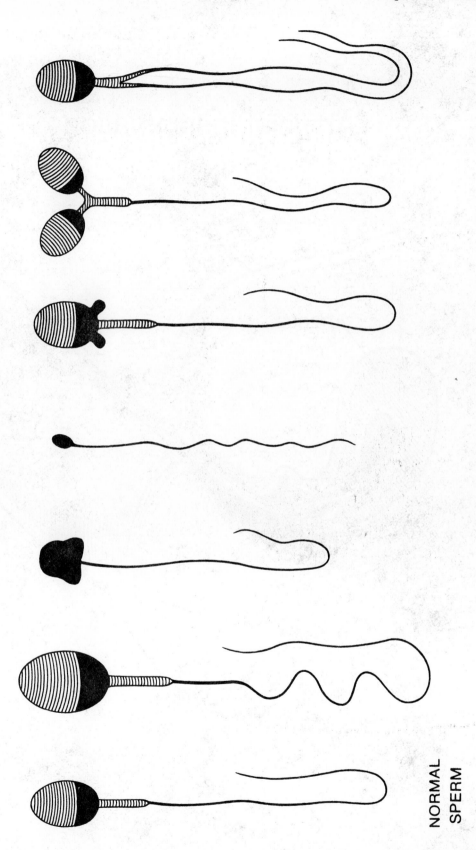

Abnormal Sperm

NORMAL
SPERM

Artificial Insemination

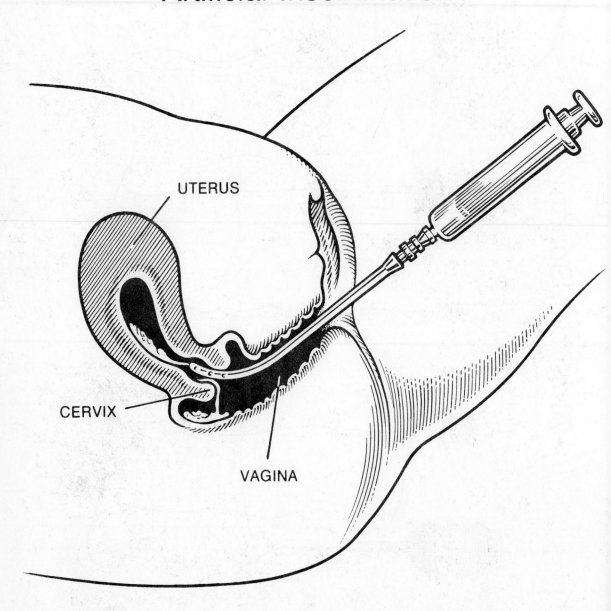

Figure 21   451

Vasectomy

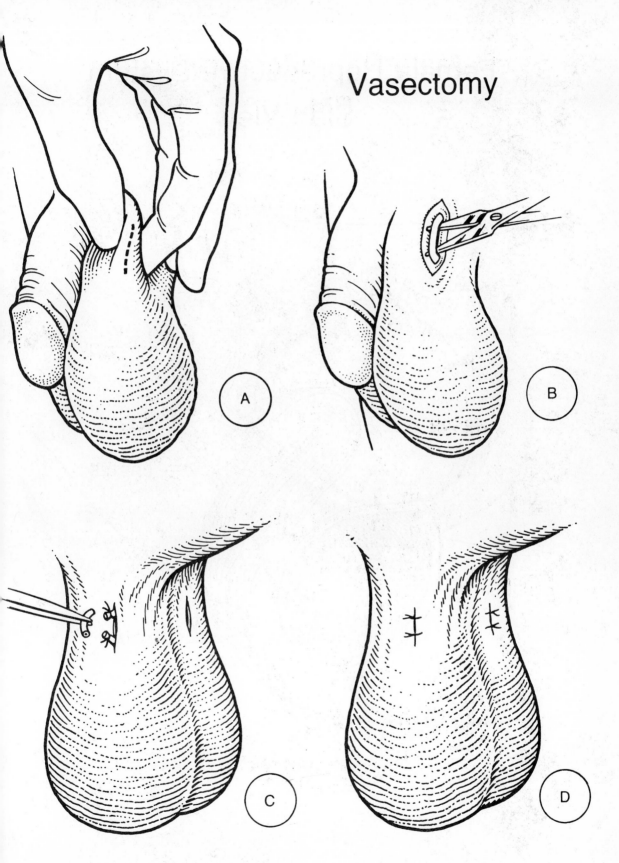

Female Reproductive System
Side View

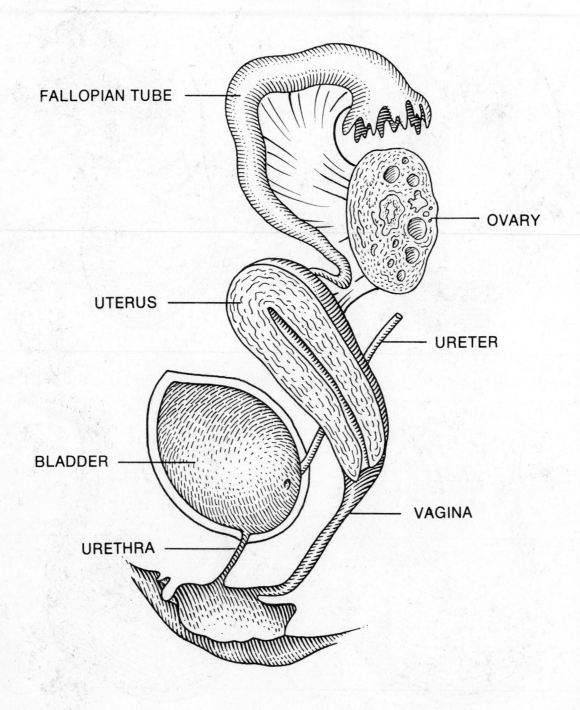

FALLOPIAN TUBE

OVARY

UTERUS

URETER

BLADDER

VAGINA

URETHRA

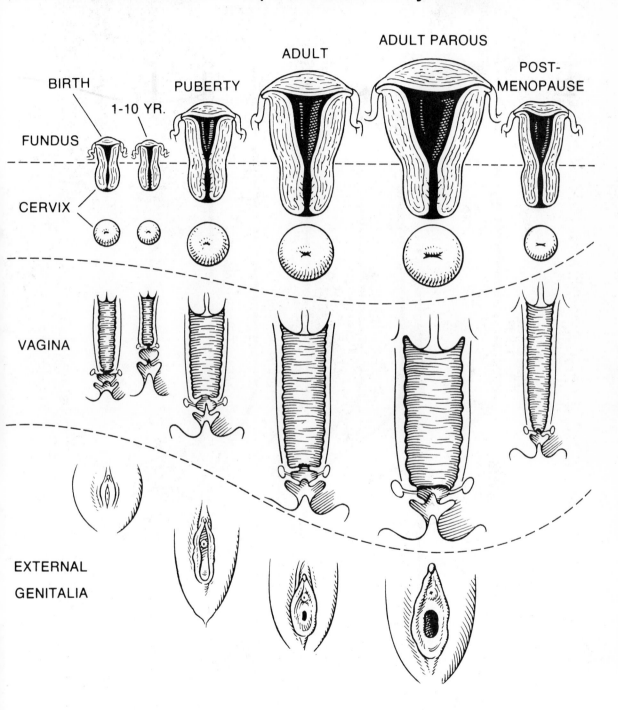

Figure 23   **453**

Growth of the
Female Reproductive System

Female Secondary Sex Characteristics

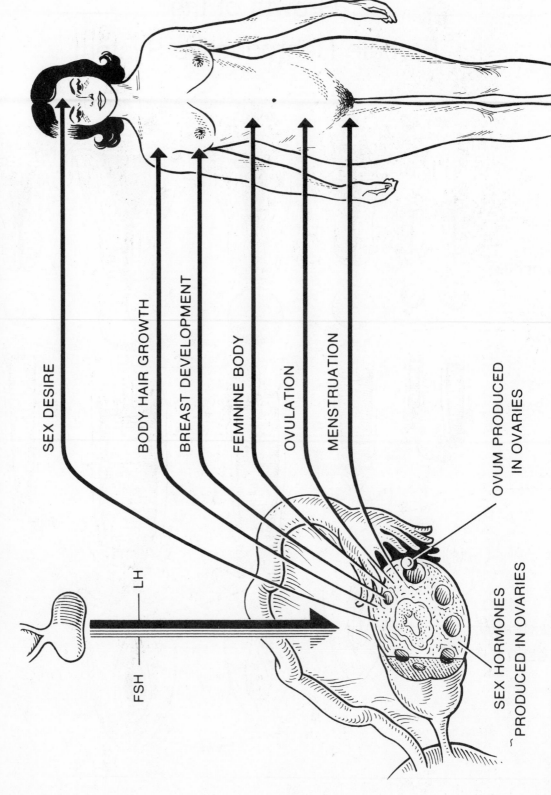

SEX DESIRE

BODY HAIR GROWTH

BREAST DEVELOPMENT

FEMININE BODY

OVULATION

MENSTRUATION

LH

FSH

OVUM PRODUCED
IN OVARIES

SEX HORMONES
PRODUCED IN OVARIES

Figure 25   **455**

Breast Development and Alteration

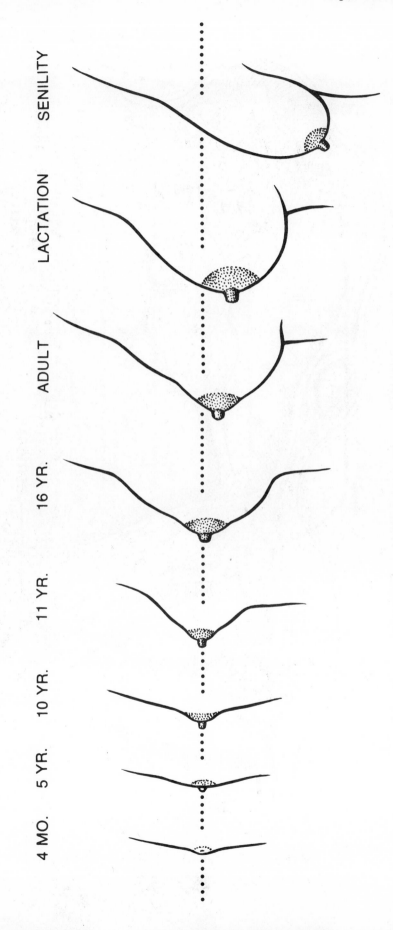

4 MO.   5 YR.   10 YR.   11 YR.   16 YR.   ADULT   LACTATION   SENILITY

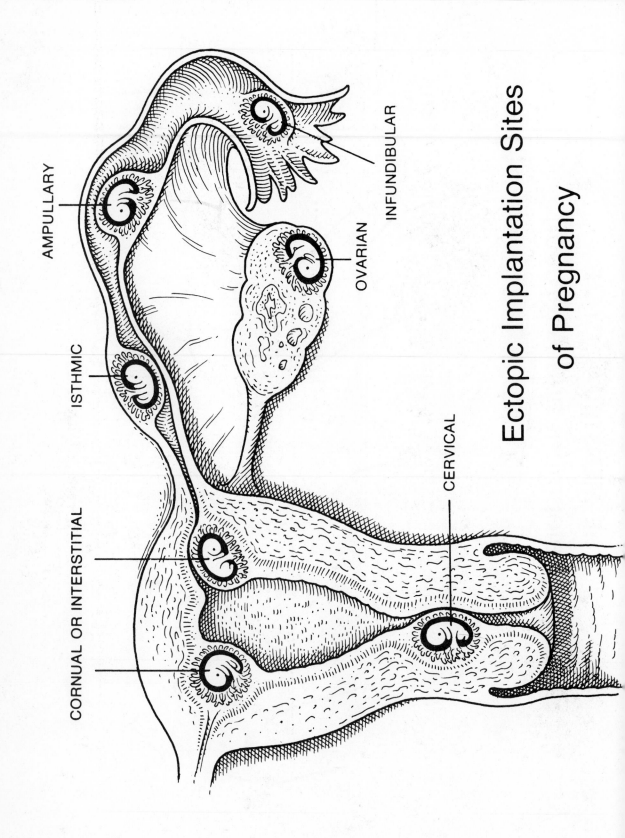

AMPULLARY

ISTHMIC

CORNUAL OR INTERSTITIAL

INFUNDIBULAR

OVARIAN

CERVICAL

Ectopic Implantation Sites
of Pregnancy

Figure 27   457

THE MENSTRUAL CYCLE

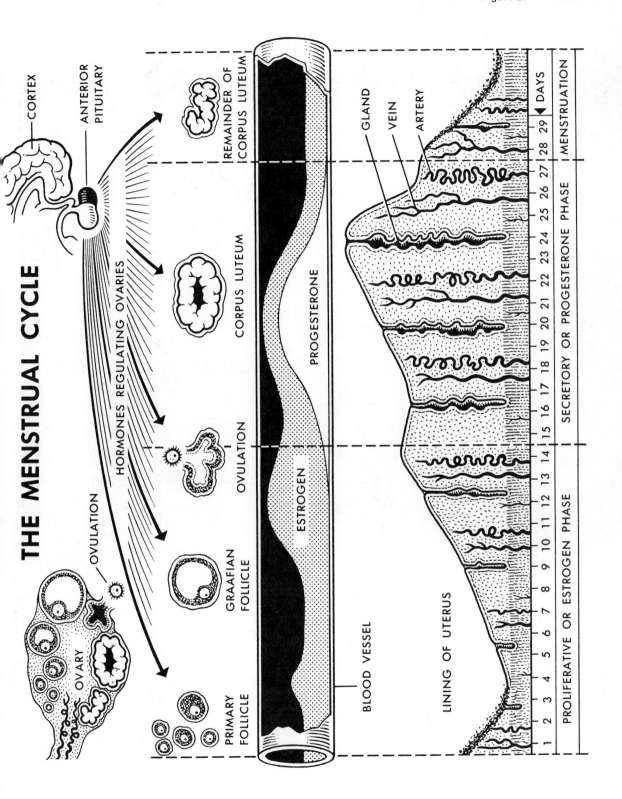

CORTEX

ANTERIOR PITUITARY

OVULATION

OVARY

HORMONES REGULATING OVARIES

REMAINDER OF CORPUS LUTEUM

CORPUS LUTEUM

OVULATION

GRAAFIAN FOLLICLE

PRIMARY FOLLICLE

PROGESTERONE

ESTROGEN

BLOOD VESSEL

GLAND

VEIN

ARTERY

LINING OF UTERUS

DAYS

1 2 3 4 5 6 7 8 9 10 11 12 13 14 15 16 17 18 19 20 21 22 23 24 25 26 27 28 29

PROLIFERATIVE OR ESTROGEN PHASE

SECRETORY OR PROGESTERONE PHASE

MENSTRUATION

Lining of the Uterus in Three Stages

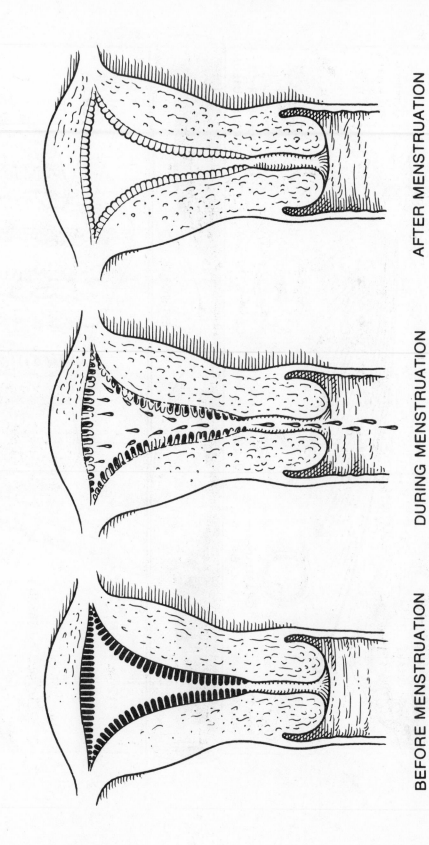

BEFORE MENSTRUATION DURING MENSTRUATION AFTER MENSTRUATION

Figure 29   **459**

Vaginal Muscles

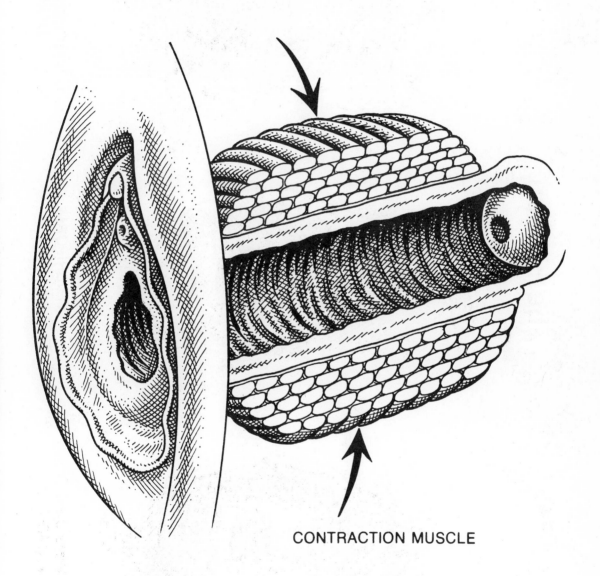

CONTRACTION MUSCLE

The Hymen

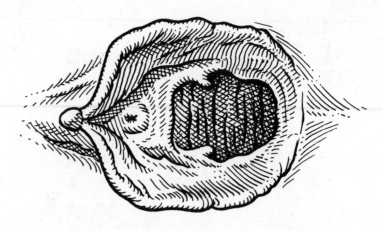

PAROUS
INTROITUS

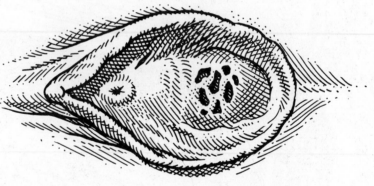

CRIBRIFORM
HYMEN

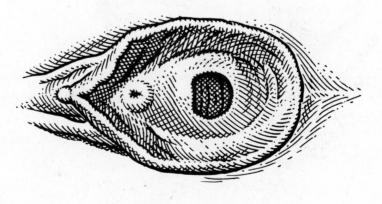

ANNULAR
HYMEN

Figure 31   **461**

Virginal Pregnancy

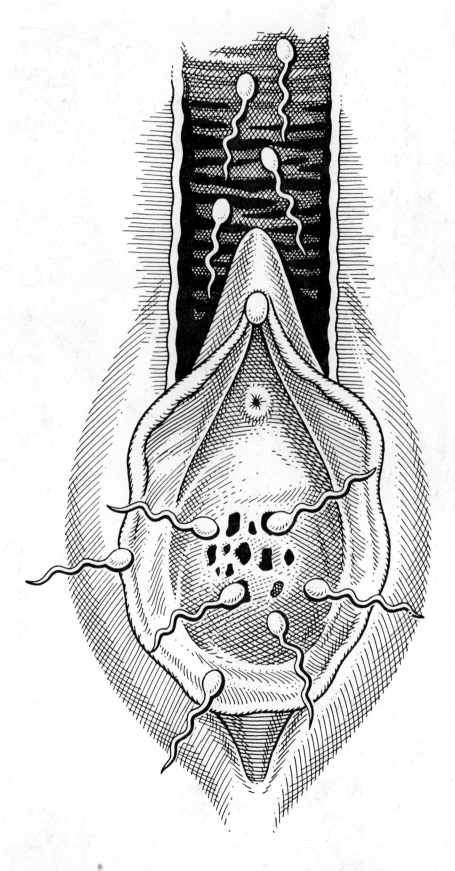

The Female Reproductive System

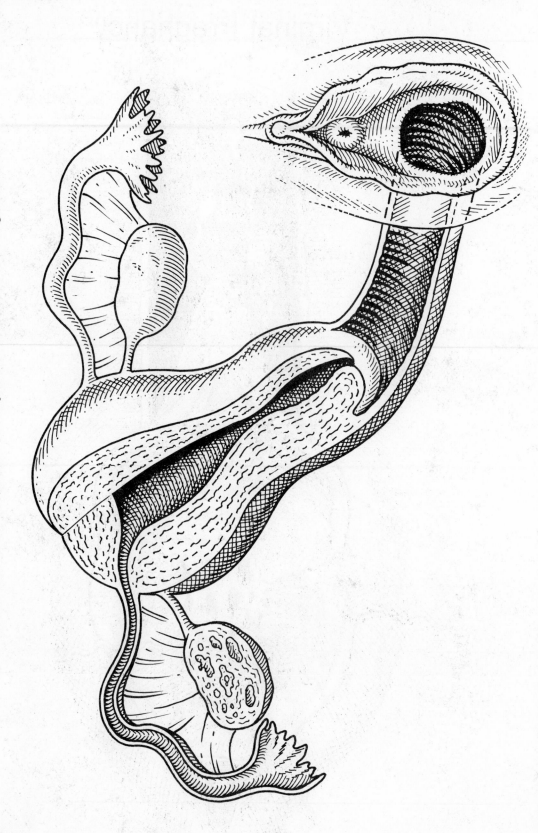

Figure 33   **463**

Female External Genitalia

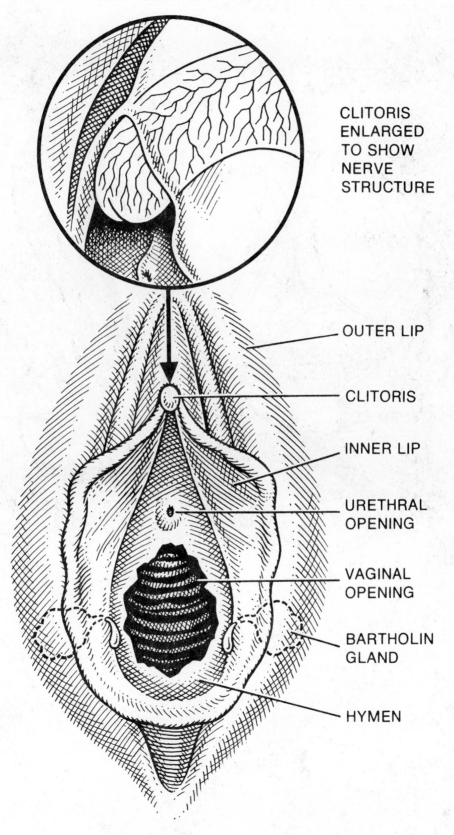

CLITORIS
ENLARGED
TO SHOW
NERVE
STRUCTURE

OUTER LIP

CLITORIS

INNER LIP

URETHRAL
OPENING

VAGINAL
OPENING

BARTHOLIN
GLAND

HYMEN

Orgasmic Platform, Seminal Pool

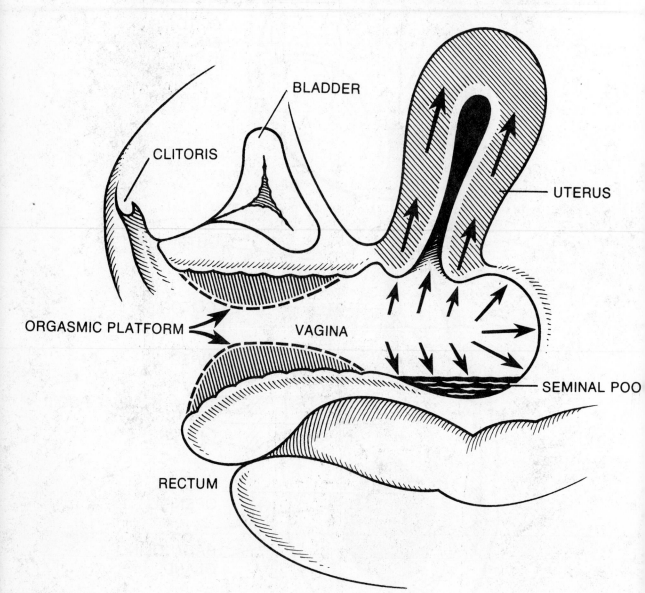

Figure 35   **465**

Immersion of Cervix in Seminal Pool

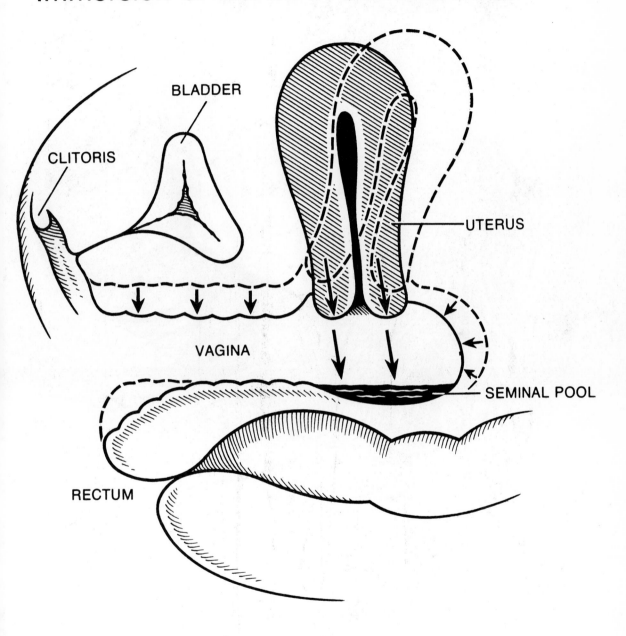

Nerve Endings Sensitive to
Sexual Stimulation

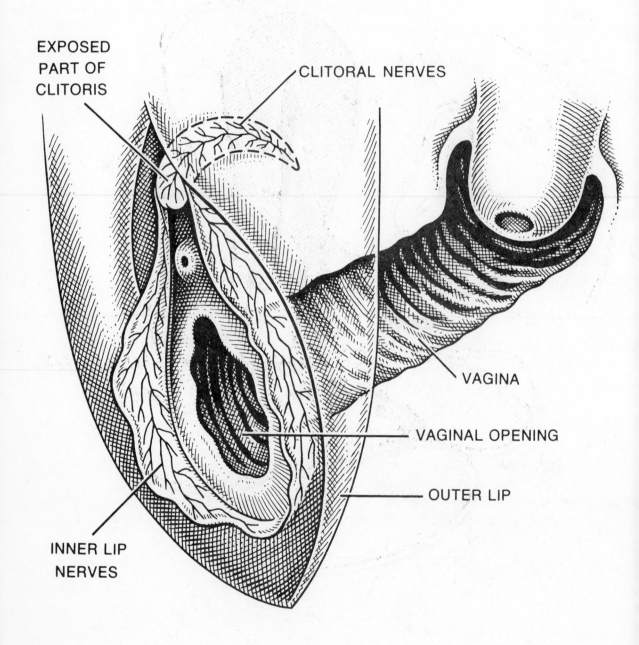

EXPOSED PART OF CLITORIS

CLITORAL NERVES

VAGINA

VAGINAL OPENING

OUTER LIP

INNER LIP NERVES

Figure 37   **467**

Amniotic Sac

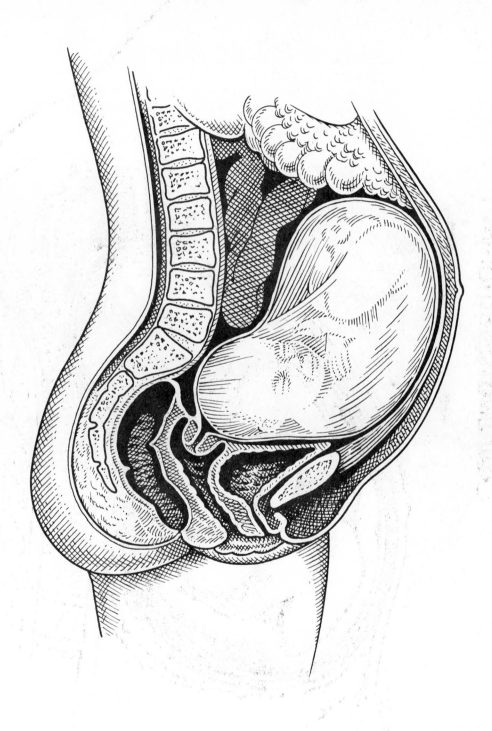

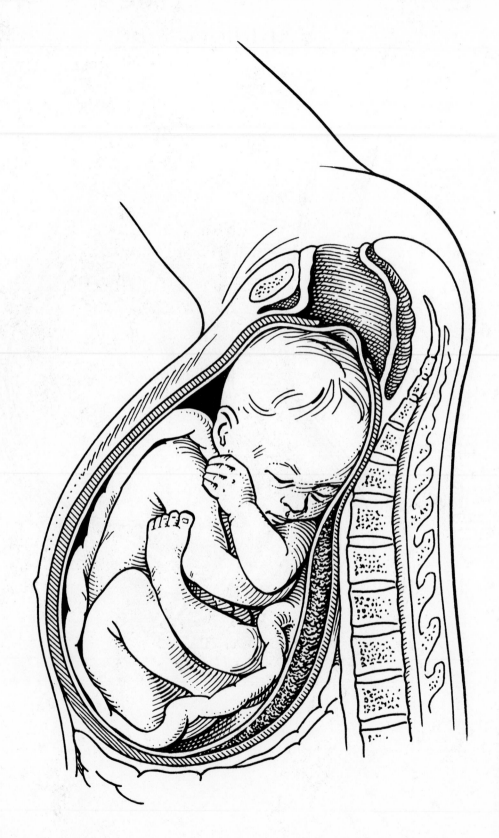

Childbirth Sequence I

Figure 39   **469**

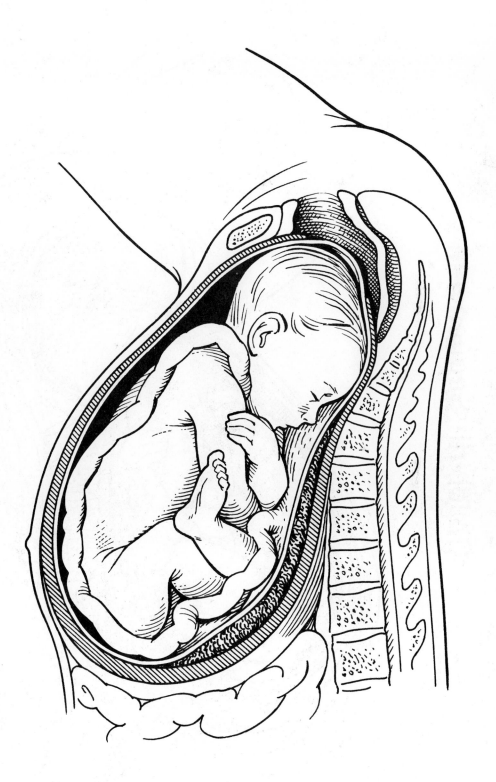

Childbirth Sequence II

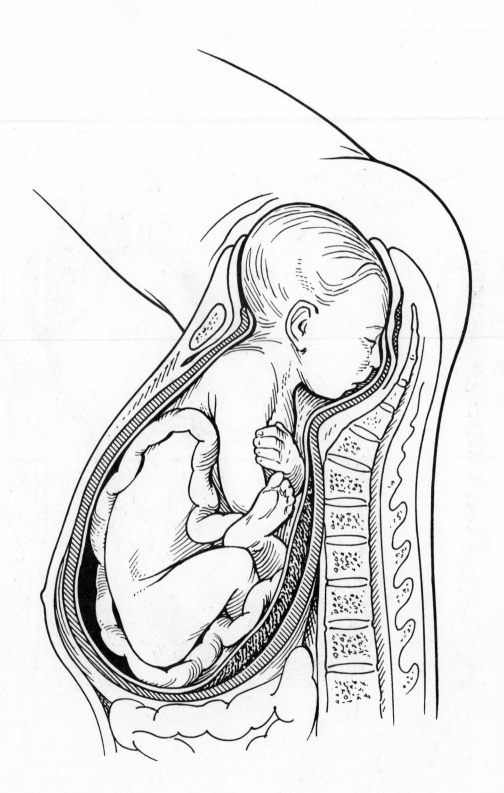

Childbirth Sequence III

Figure 41   471

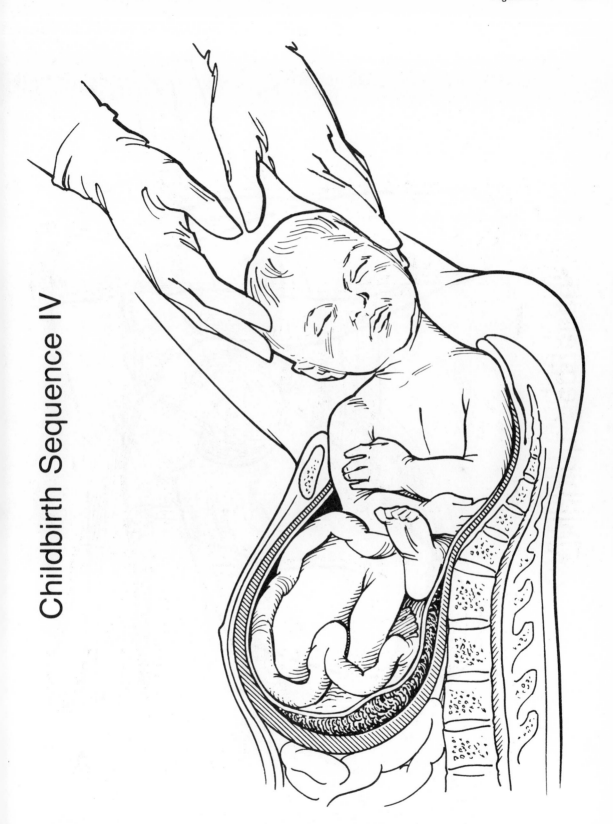

Childbirth Sequence IV

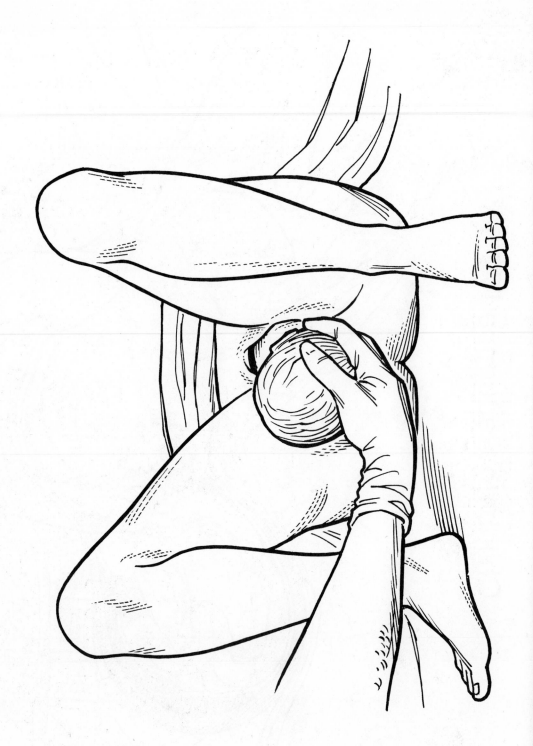

Childbirth Sequence V

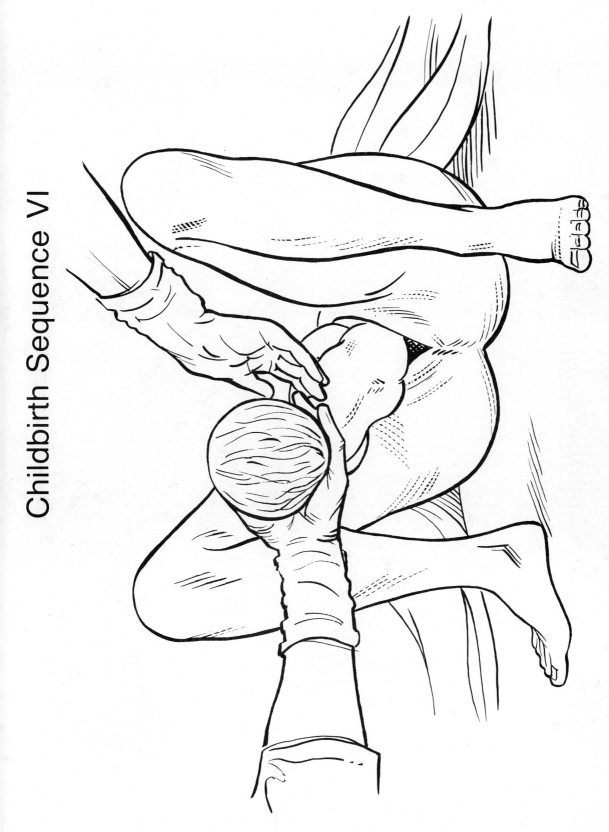

Figure 43   **473**

Childbirth Sequence VI

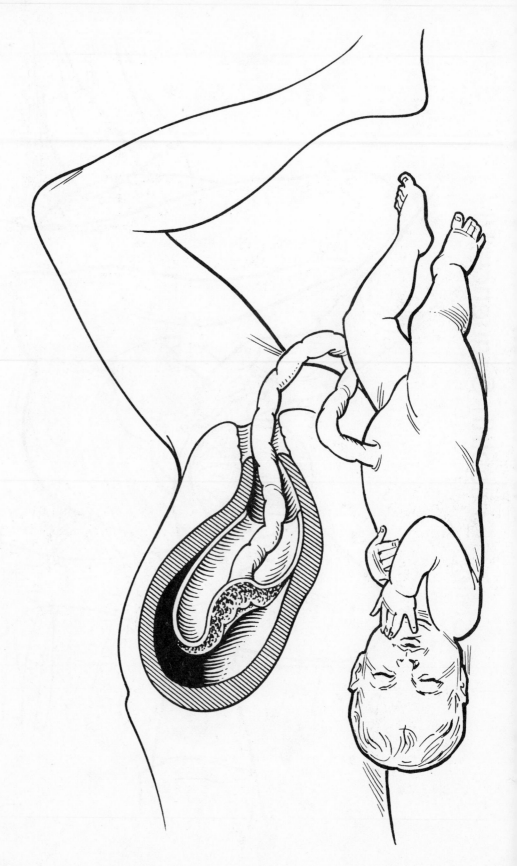

Childbirth Sequence VII

Figure 45   **475**

Childbirth Sequence VIII

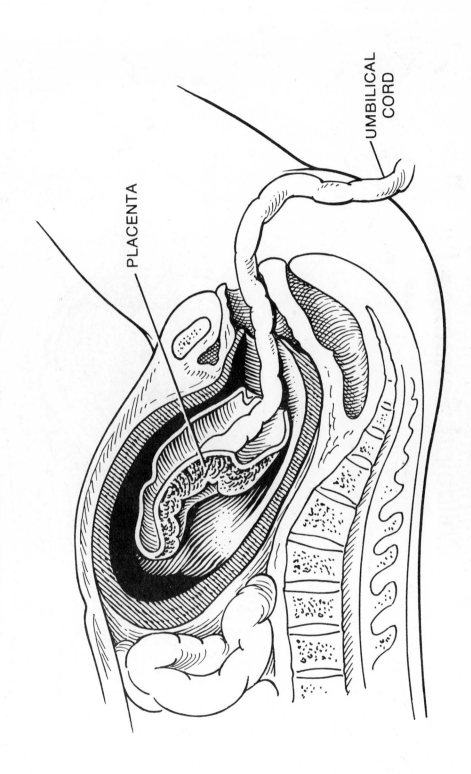

PLACENTA

UMBILICAL CORD

Childbirth Sequence IX

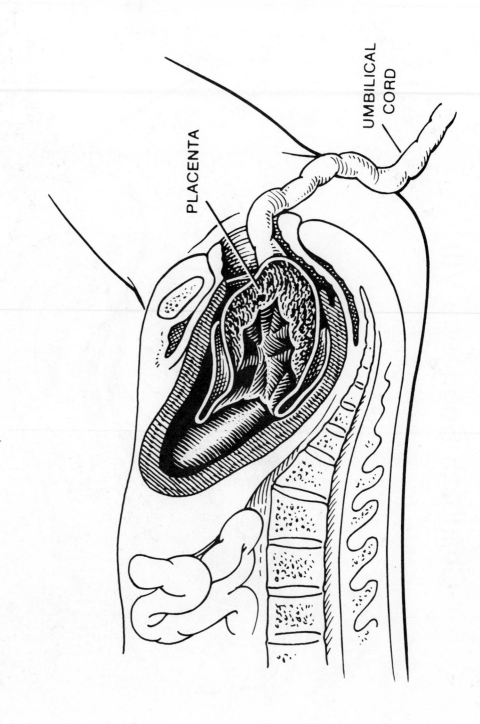

UMBILICAL CORD

PLACENTA

Figure 47 **477**

Vaginal Ring for Progestin Administration

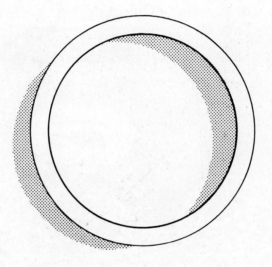

Progestin Implant

Figure 49   **479**

Female Sterilization

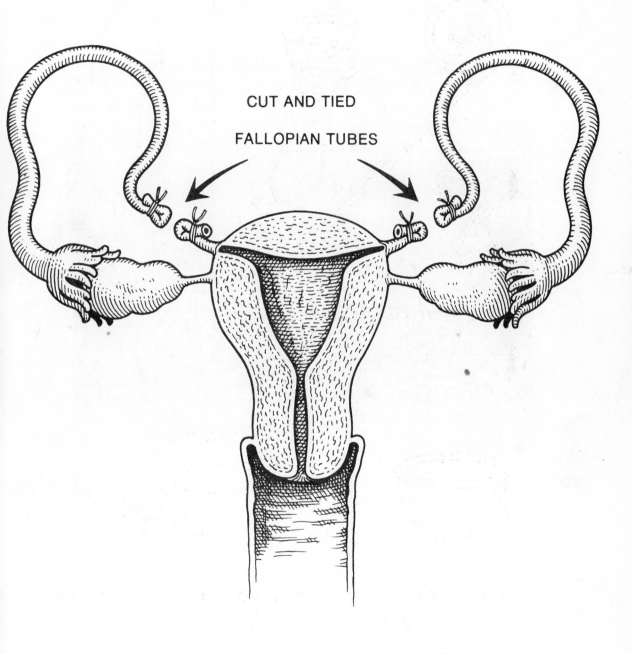

CUT AND TIED

FALLOPIAN TUBES

Mechanical Contraception

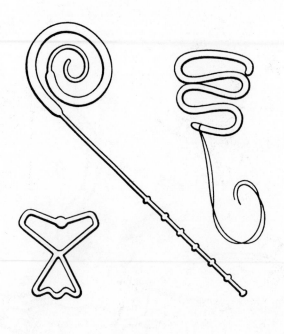

INTRAUTERINE DEVICES

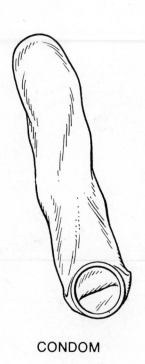

CONDOM

CERVICAL CAP

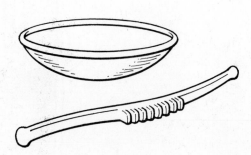

DIAPHRAGM AND INSERTION DEVICE

Figure 51   **481**

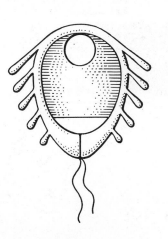

DALCON SHIELD

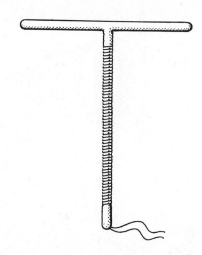

COPPER-"T"

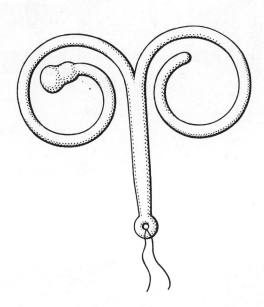

SAF-T-COIL

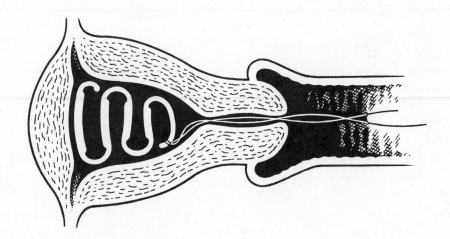

Insertion of IUD

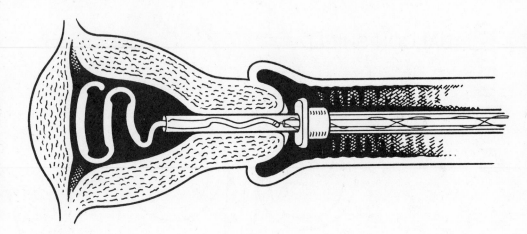

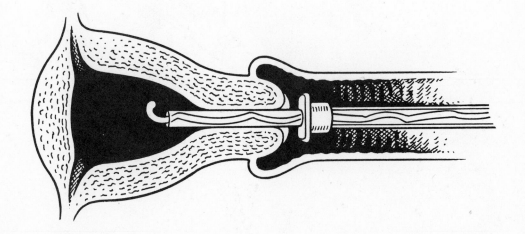

Figure 53   **483**

Diaphragm

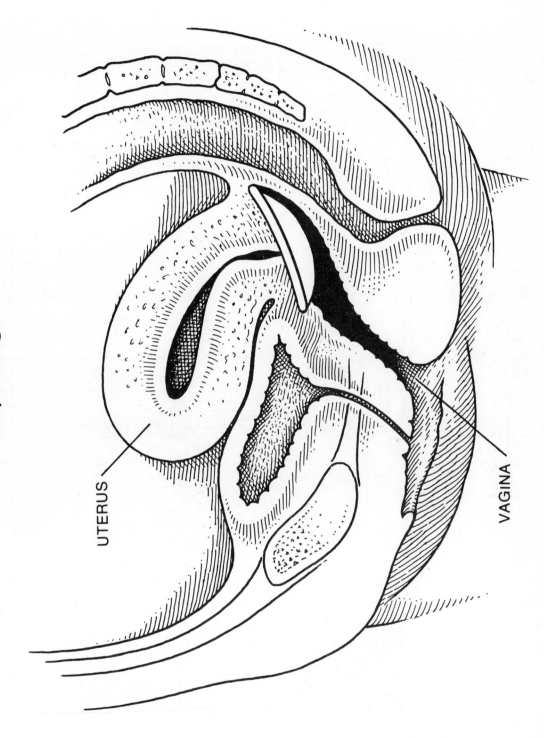

UTERUS

VAGINA

Rhythm Method by Basal Body Temperature

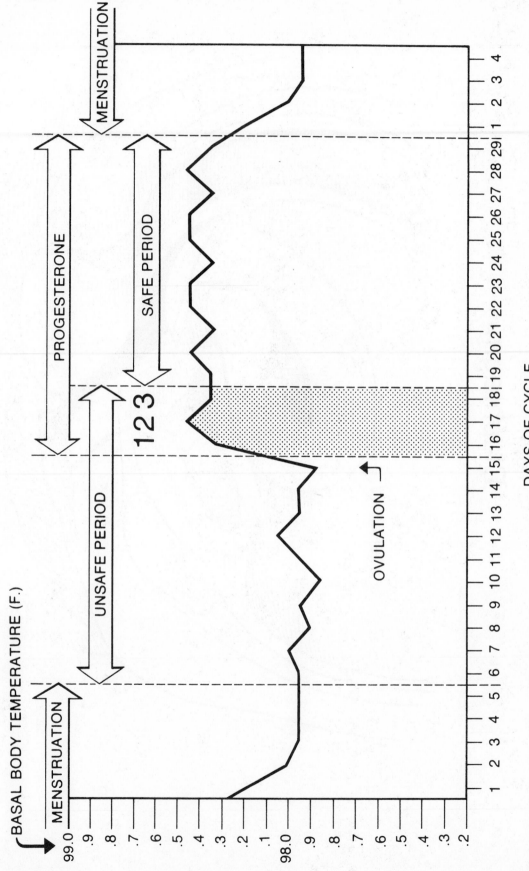

Figure 55　**485**

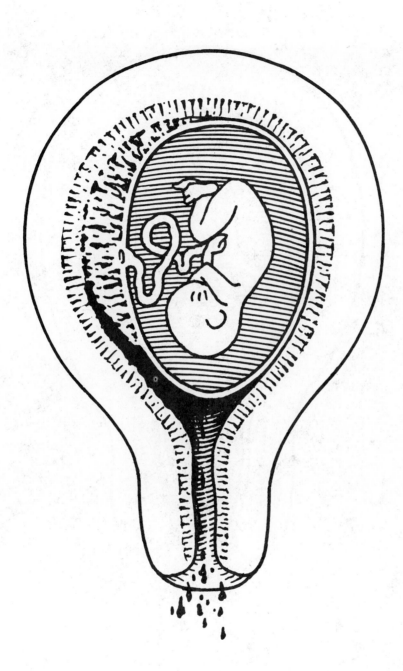

Threatened Abortion

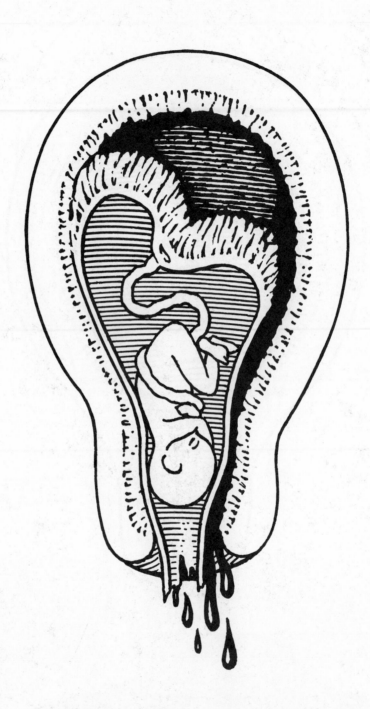

Inevitable Abortion

Figure 57 **487**

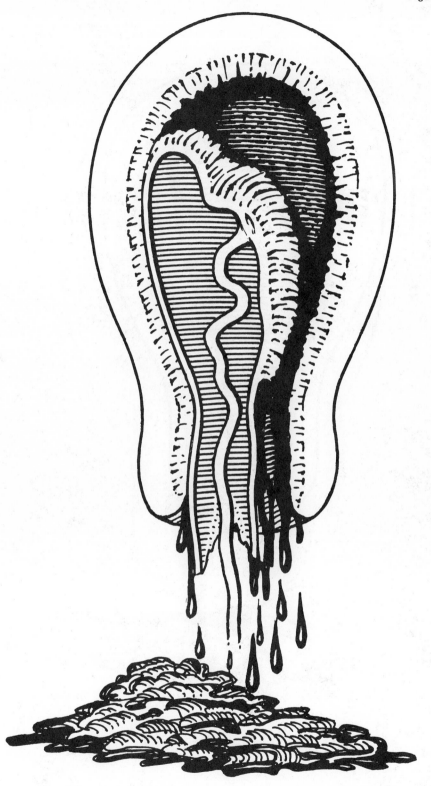

Incomplete Abortion

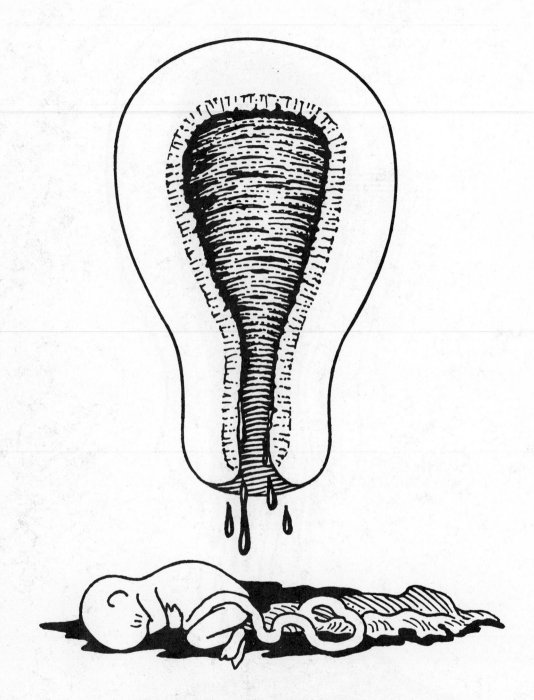

Complete Abortion

Figure 59   **489**

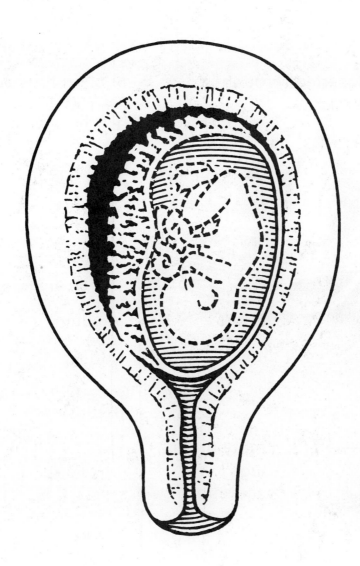

Missed Abortion

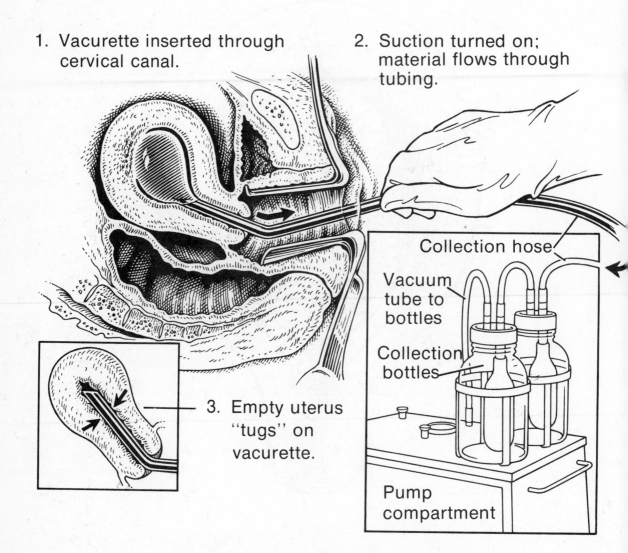

1. Vacurette inserted through cervical canal.

2. Suction turned on; material flows through tubing.

Collection hose

Vacuum tube to bottles

Collection bottles

3. Empty uterus "tugs" on vacurette.

Pump compartment

Vacuum Curettage

Figure 61   **491**

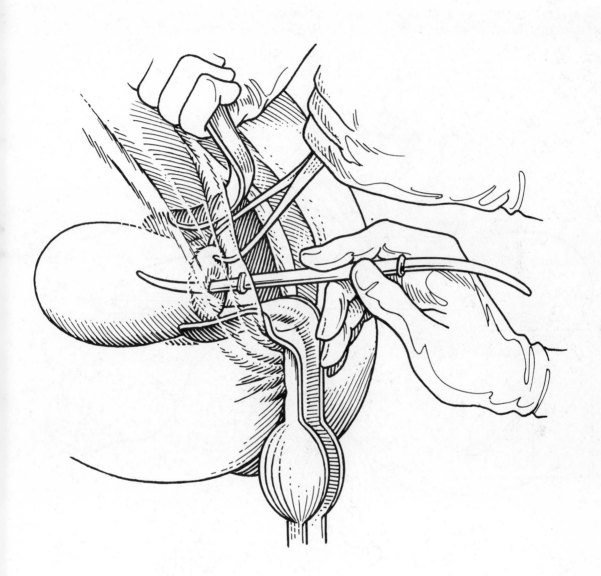

Dilatation of Cervix

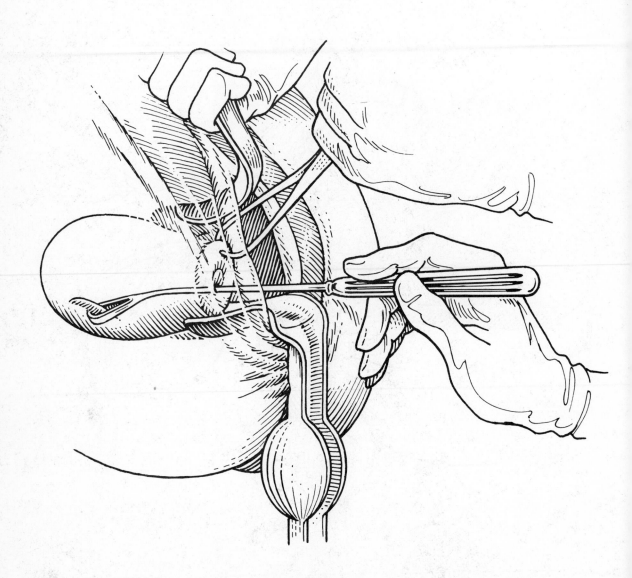

Curettage

Figure 63　　**493**

Application of Silver Nitrate
at Birth

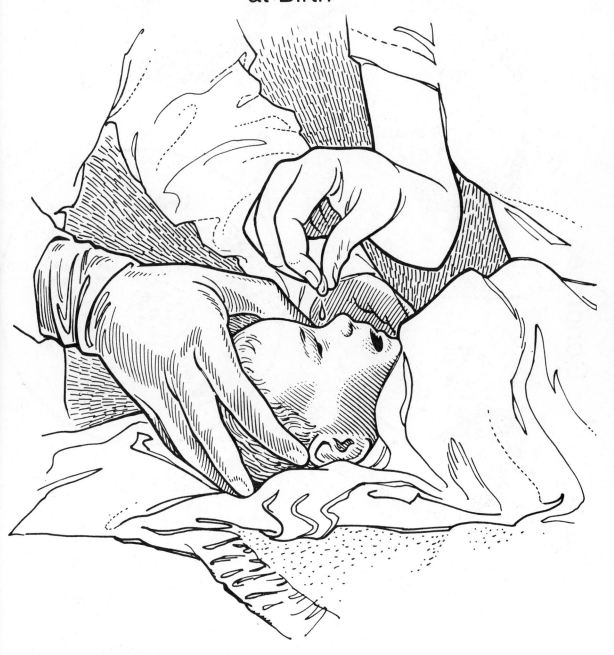

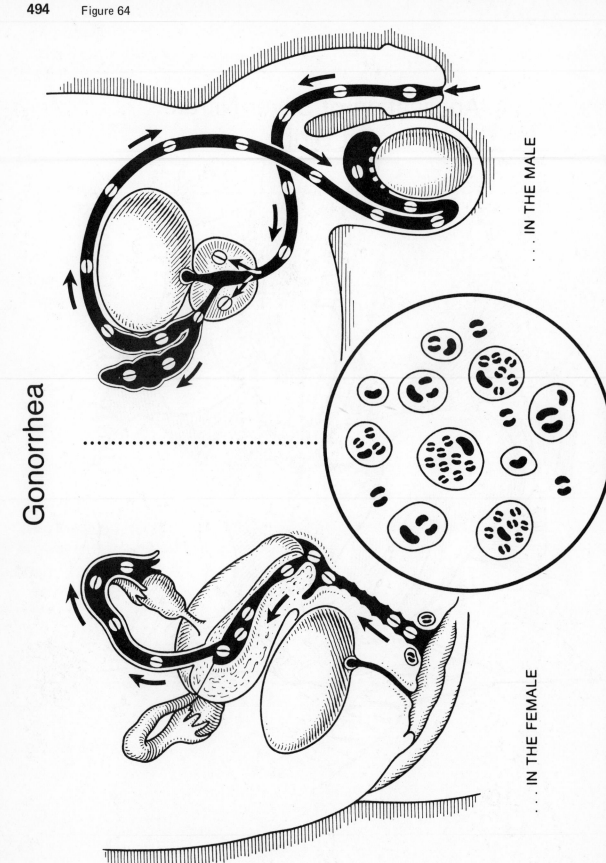

Gonorrhea

... IN THE MALE

... IN THE FEMALE

Figure 65   **495**

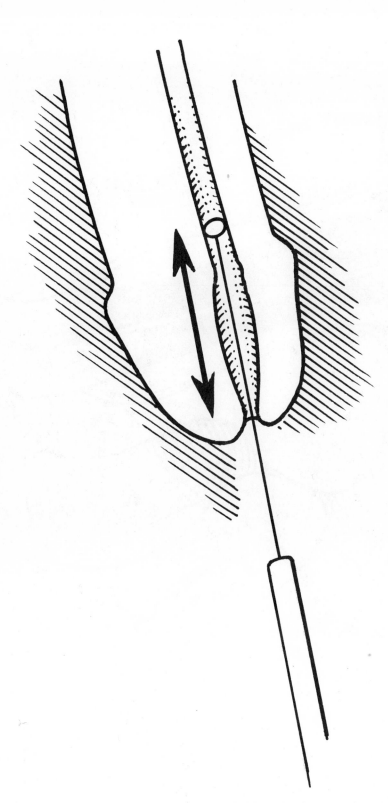

Urethral Culture

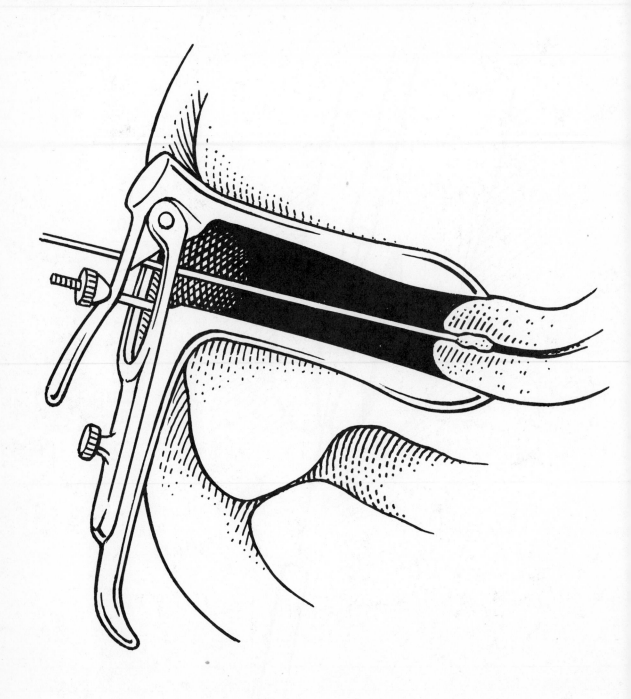

Endocervical Culture

Figure 67   497

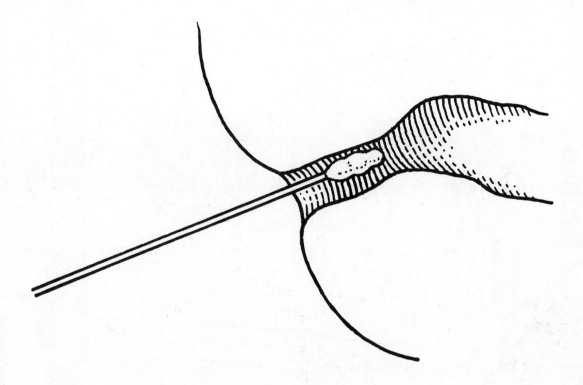

Anal Culture

The Stages of Syphilis

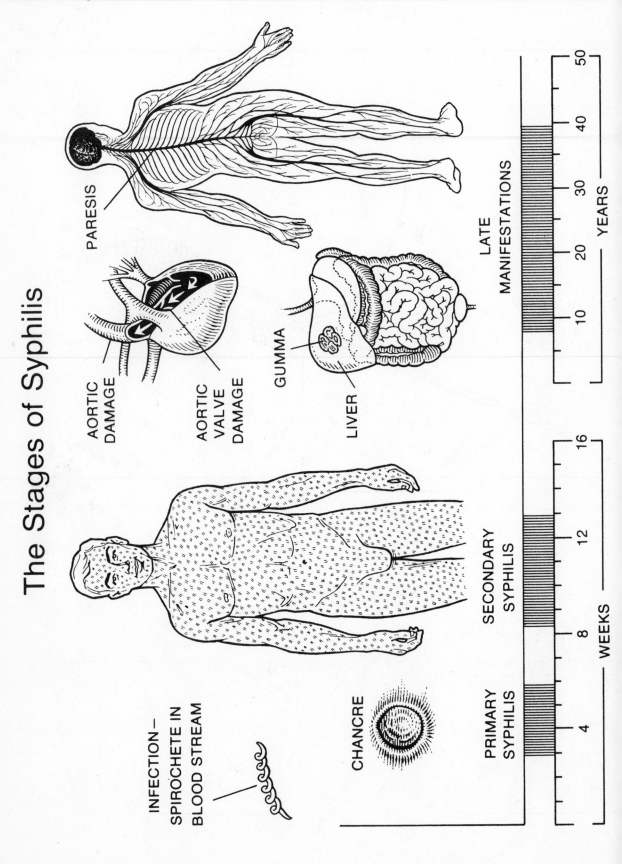

INFECTION—SPIROCHETE IN BLOOD STREAM

CHANCRE

PARESIS

AORTIC DAMAGE

AORTIC VALVE DAMAGE

GUMMA

LIVER

PRIMARY SYPHILIS

SECONDARY SYPHILIS

LATE MANIFESTATIONS

WEEKS

YEARS

4   8   12   16

10   20   30   40   50

Figure 69   **499**

Chancroid

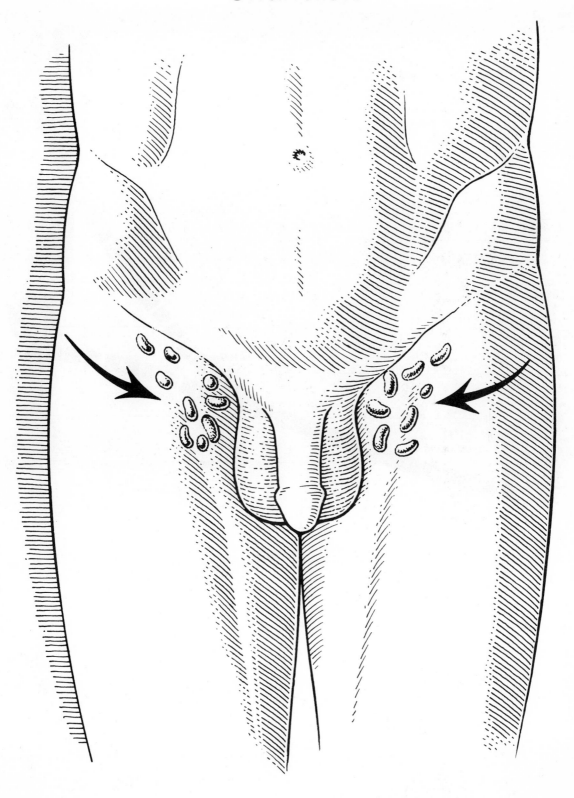

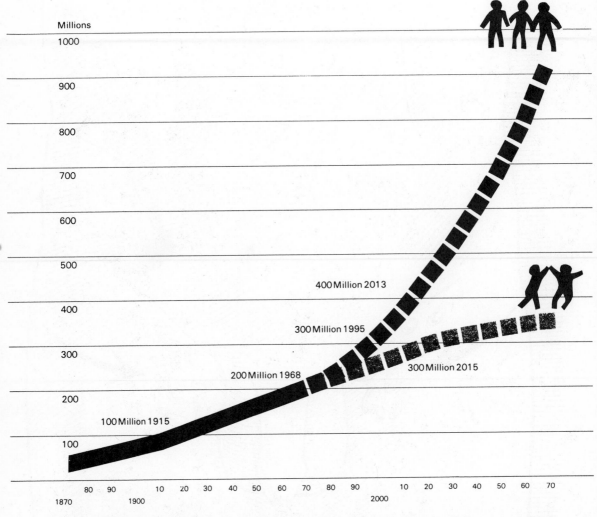

Millions

1000

900

800

700

600

500

400 Million 2013

400

300 Million 1995

300

200 Million 1968

300 Million 2015

200

100 Million 1915

100

80 90 10 20 30 40 50 60 70 80 90 10 20 30 40 50 60 70
1870 1900 2000

The population of the United States passed the 100-million mark in 1915 and reached 200 million in 1968. If families average two children in the future, growth rates will slow, and the population will reach 300 million in the year 2015. At the 3-child rate, the population would reach 300 million in this century and 400 million in the year 2013. (Projections assume small future reductions in mortality, and assume future immigration at present levels.)

Sources: Prior to 1900—U.S. Bureau of the Census. Historical Statistics of the United States, Colonial Times to 1957, 1961. 1900 to 2020—U.S. Bureau of the Census. Current Population Reports, Series P-25. 2021 to 2050—unpublished Census Bureau projections. Beyond 2050—extrapolation.

Figure 71   **501**

Male Child

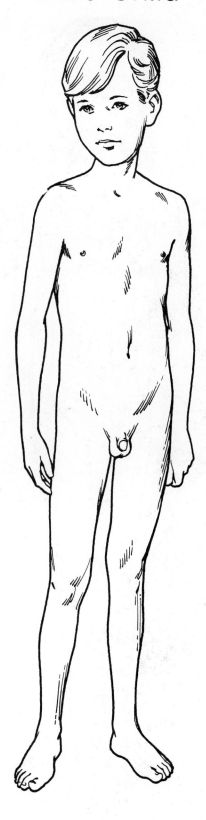

Female Child

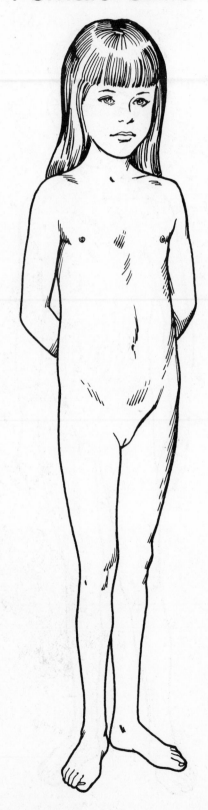

Figure 87   **503**

Let's Look at a Flower

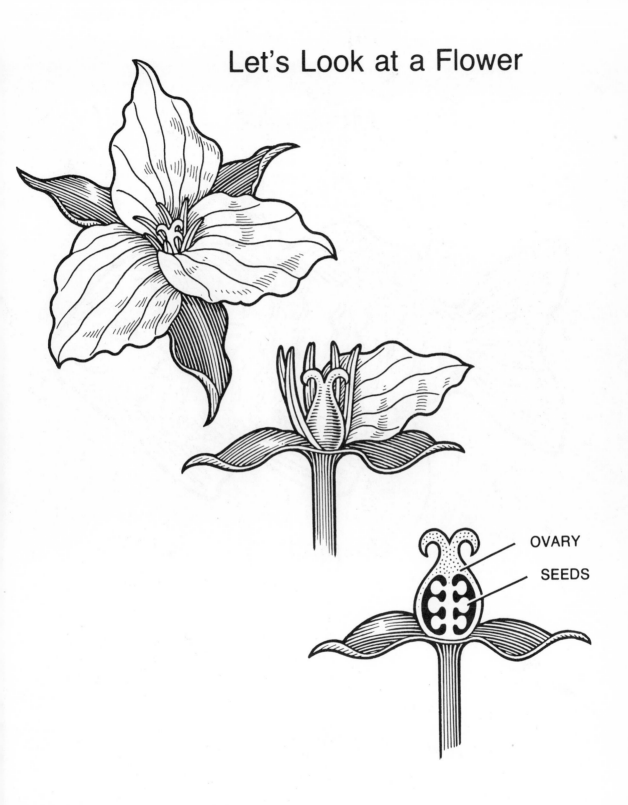

OVARY

SEEDS

Model Fish

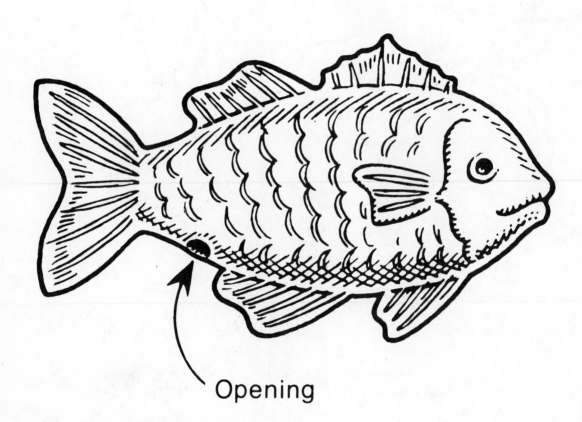

Opening

Figure 89   **505**

Frog

Fertilized Frog Eggs

Figure 93   **507**

Male Dog

Female Dog

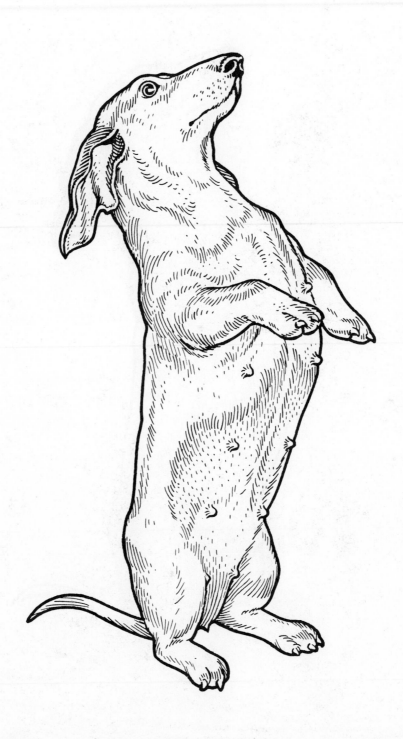

Figure 96   **509**

Pregnant Cow

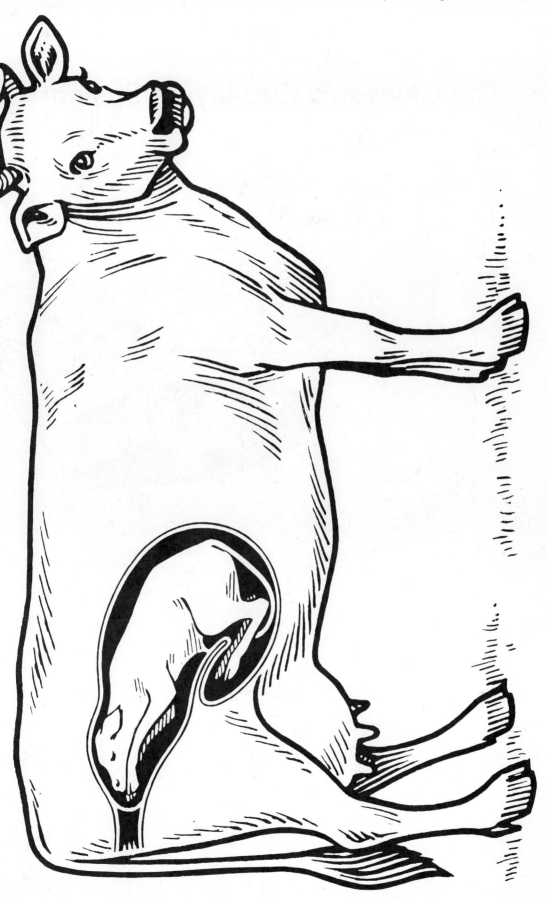

The Chicken's Egg-laying System

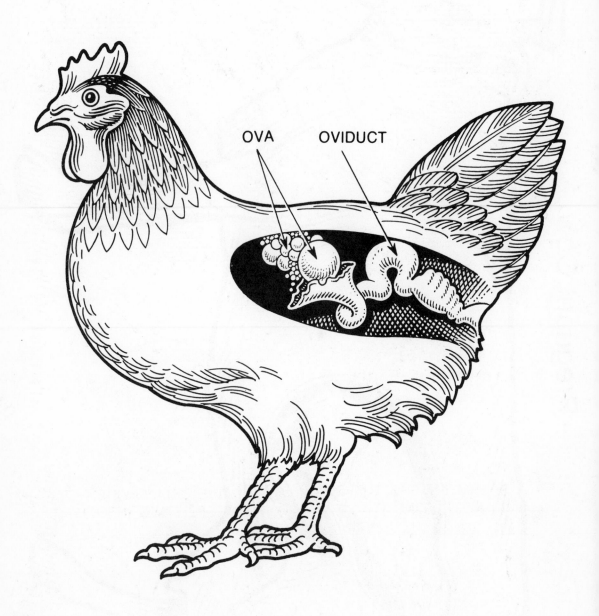

Figure 106 **511**

How Fertilization Begins

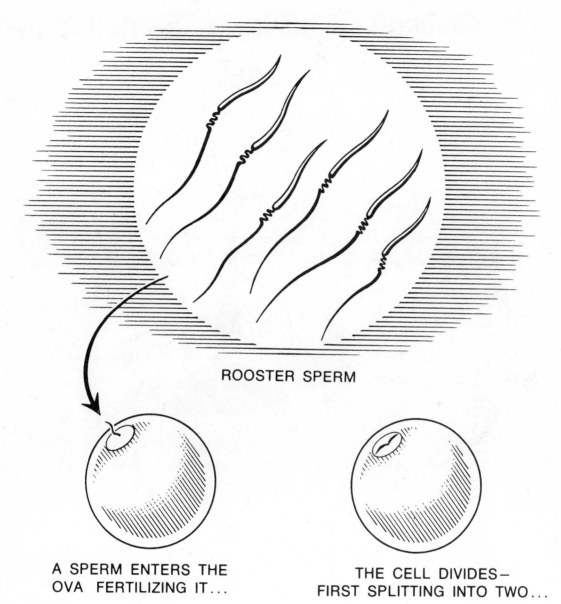

ROOSTER SPERM

A SPERM ENTERS THE
OVA FERTILIZING IT...

THE CELL DIVIDES—
FIRST SPLITTING INTO TWO...

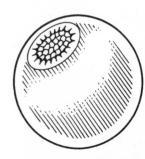

THEN INTO FOUR...

THEN EIGHT...

AND ON AND ON

Development of an Egg

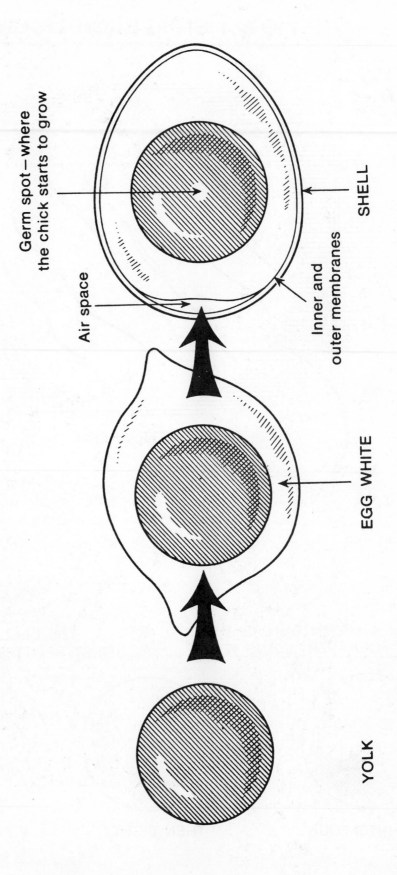

Germ spot—where the chick starts to grow

Air space

SHELL

Inner and outer membranes

EGG WHITE

YOLK

Figure 109 513

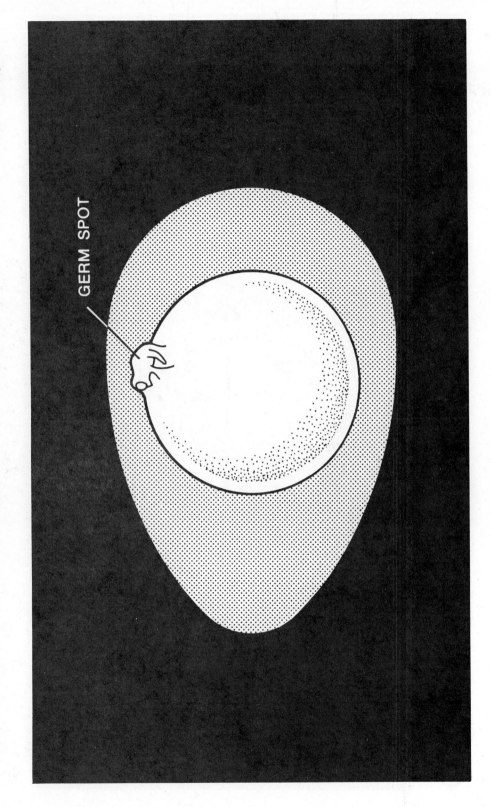

Growth of a Chick

Day 1

GERM SPOT

Growth of a Chick

Day 2

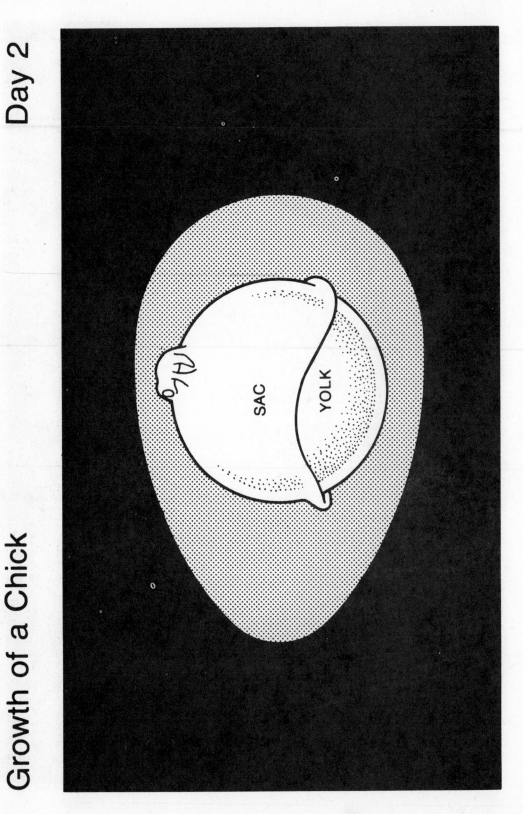

Figure 111   **515**

Growth of a Chick   Day 3

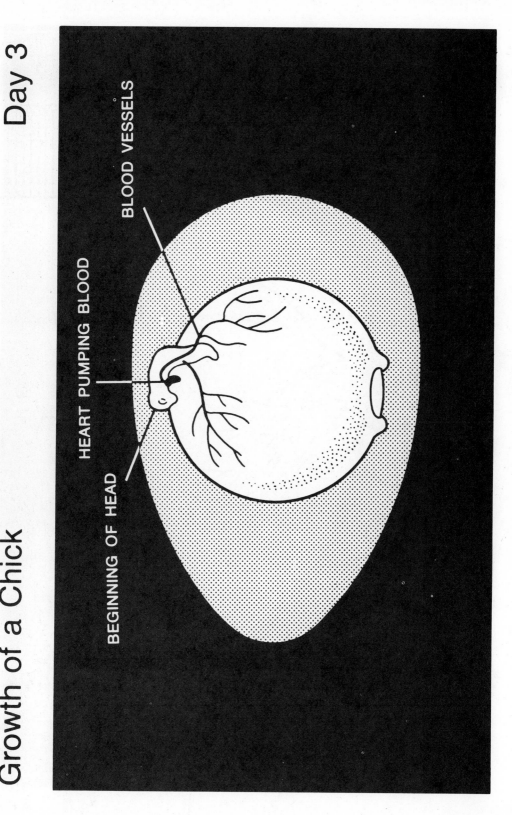

BLOOD VESSELS

HEART PUMPING BLOOD

BEGINNING OF HEAD

Growth of a Chick

Day 6

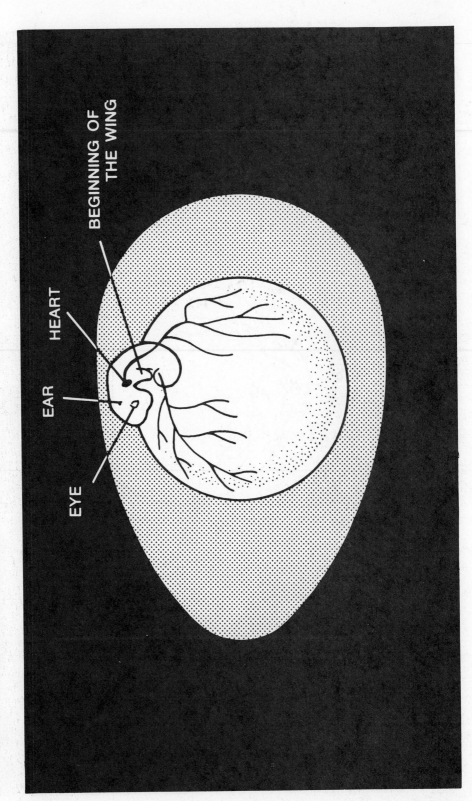

Figure 113   **517**

Candling
an Egg

6 DAYS

20-21 DAYS

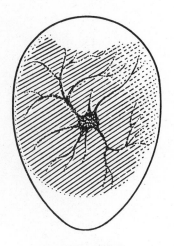

GOOD EGG

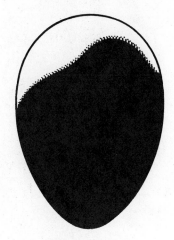

GOOD EGG

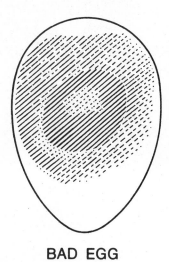

BAD EGG

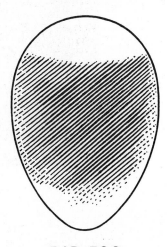

BAD EGG

Growth of a Chick

Day 7

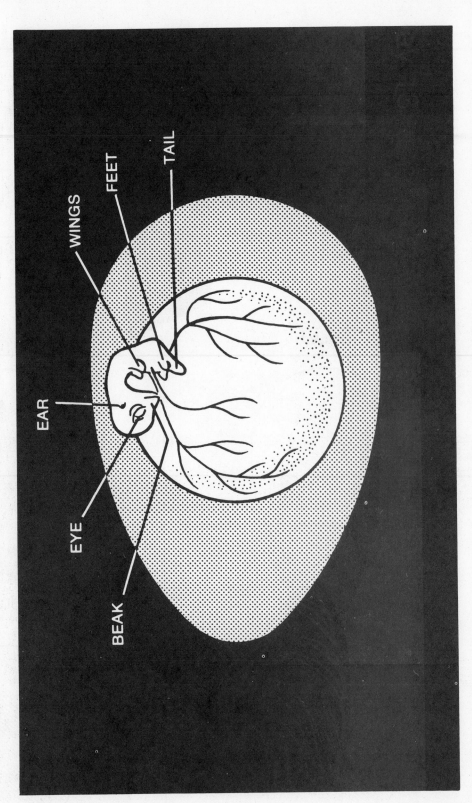

EAR

EYE

BEAK

WINGS

FEET

TAIL

Figure 115   519

Day 13

Growth of a Chick

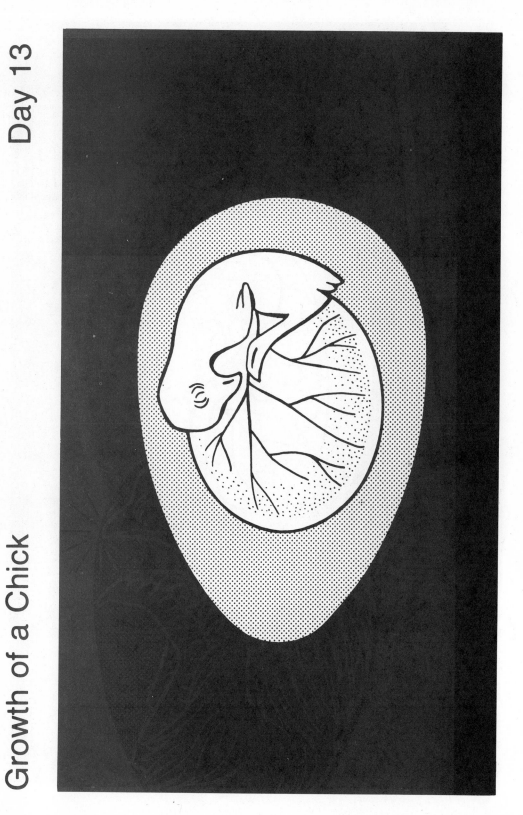

Day 16

Growth of a Chick

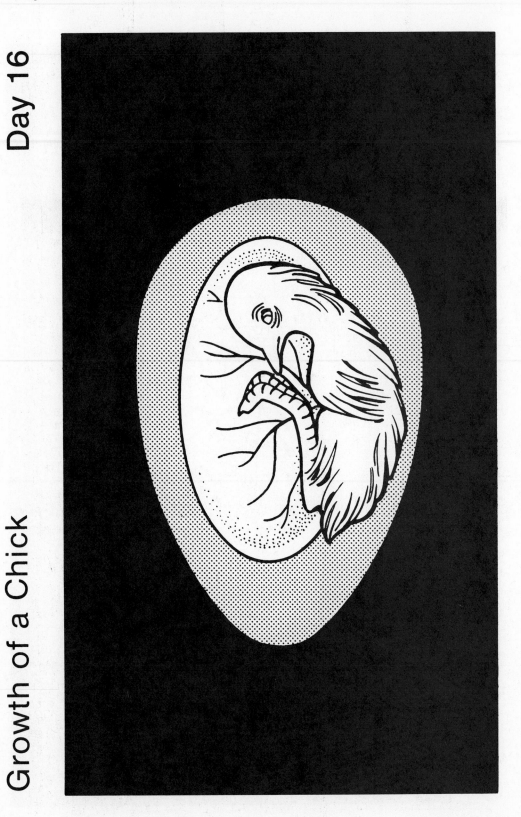

Figure 120   521

Day 19

Growth of a Chick

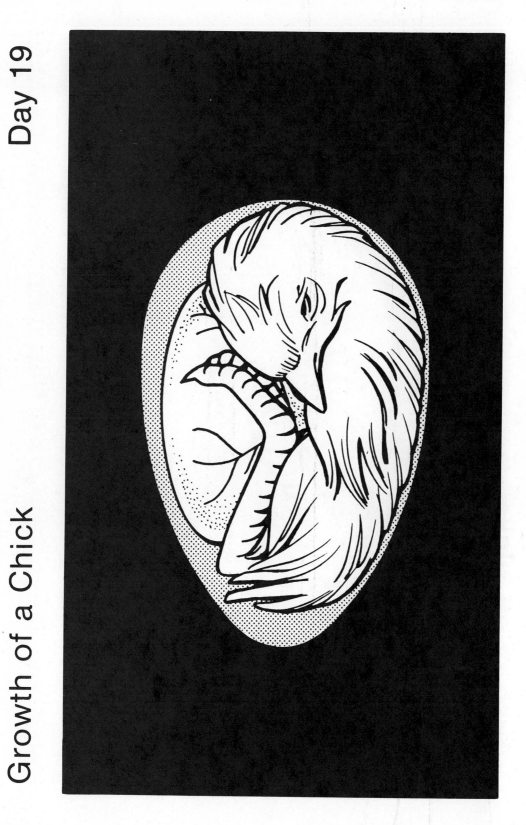

Day 20

Growth of a Chick

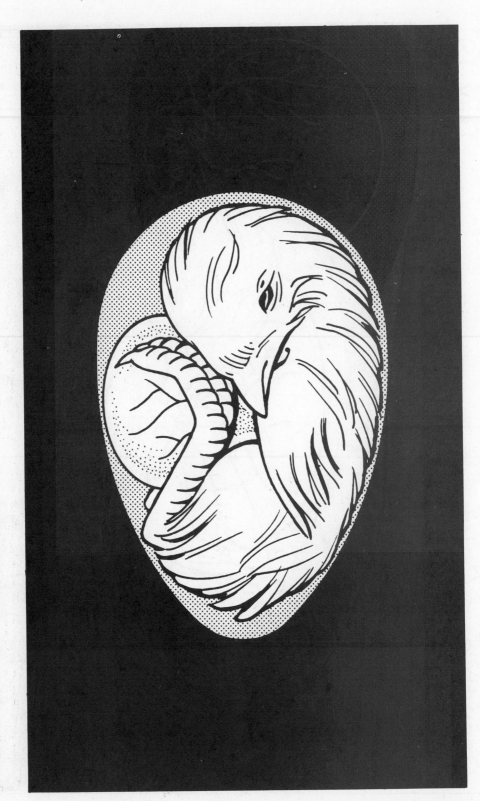

Figure 122   **523**

Day 21

Growth of a Chick

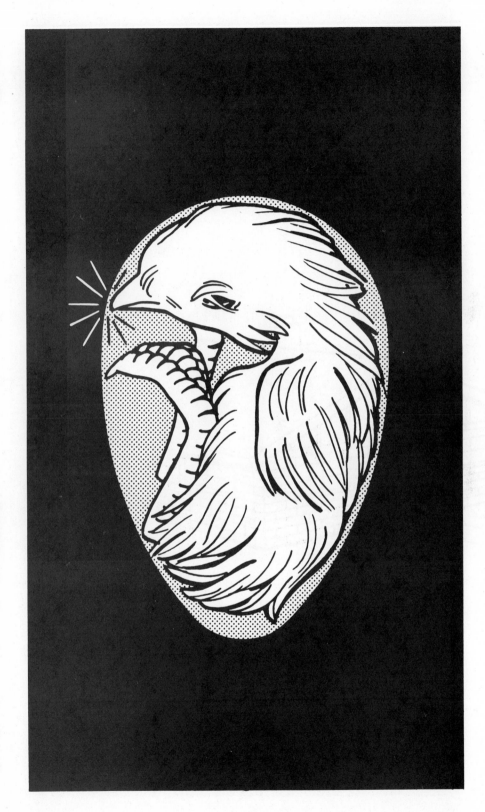

The Parts of a House

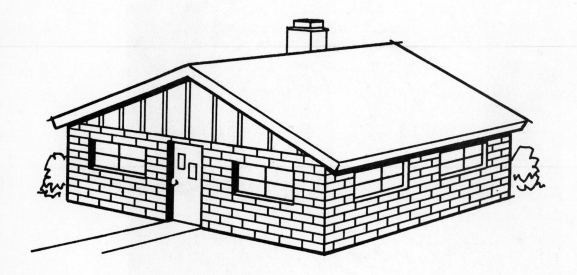

Figure 124   **525**

The Parts of a Muscle

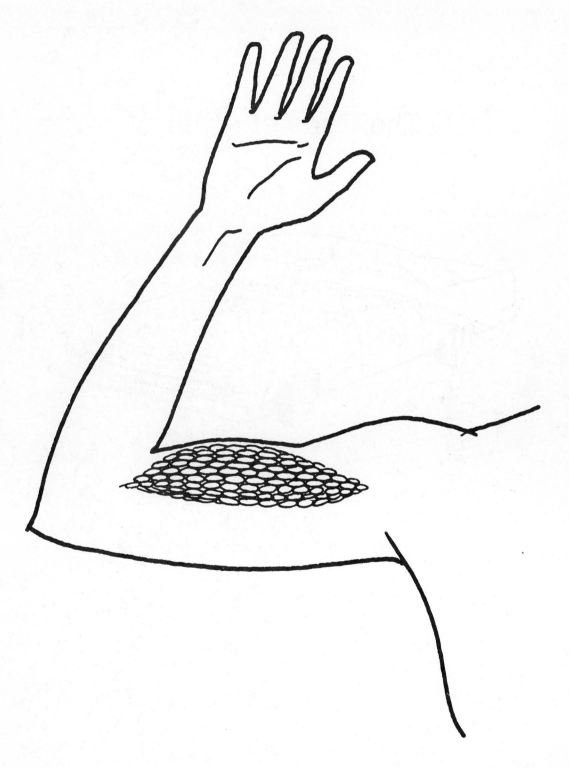

The Parts of a Car

Figure 126   **527**

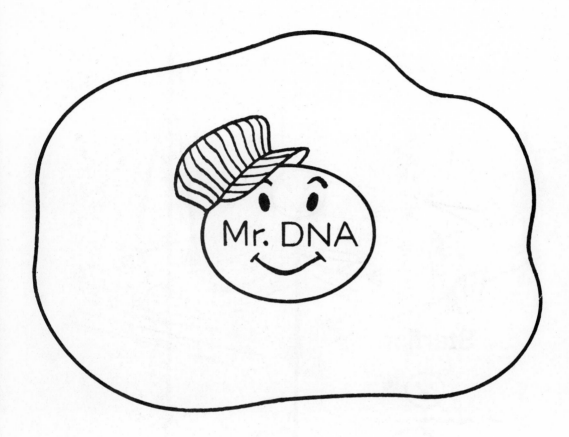

Cell

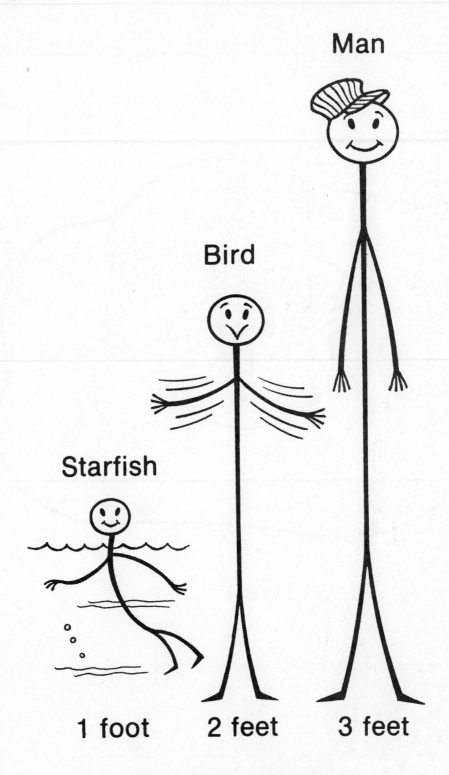

Man

Bird

Starfish

1 foot   2 feet   3 feet

Mr. DNA's length

Figure 128   **529**

The Two Halves of Mr. DNA

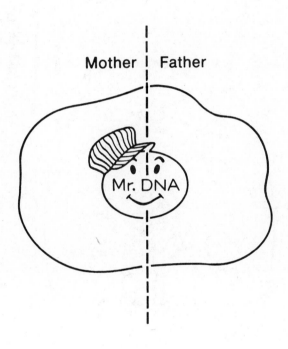

The Mother's Uterus

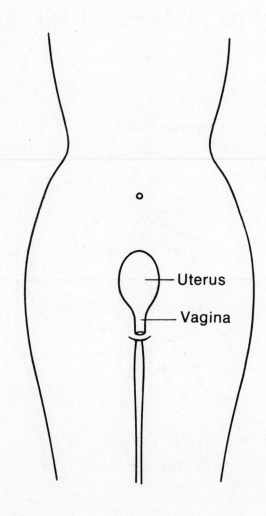

Uterus

Vagina

Figure 130   **531**

The Mother's Ovaries

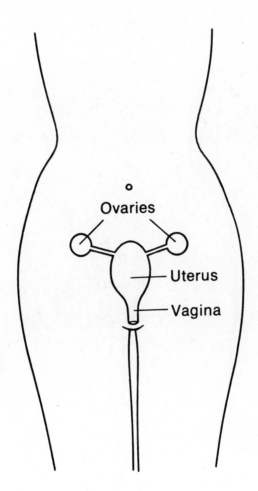

The Father's Sperm Factory

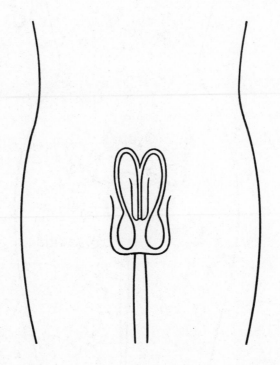

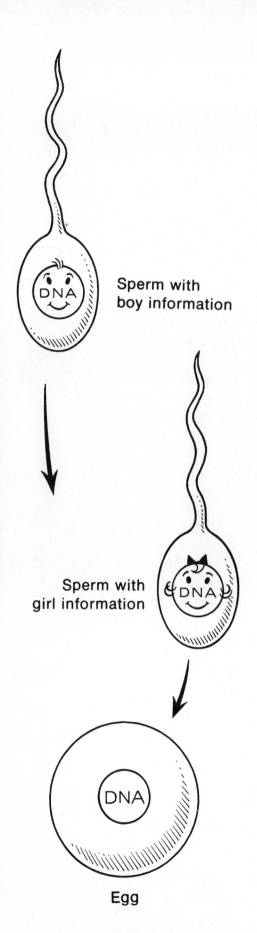

Sperm with
boy information

Sperm with
girl information

The Sperm with

Hereditary Information

Egg

The Fertilized Cell Implants Itself

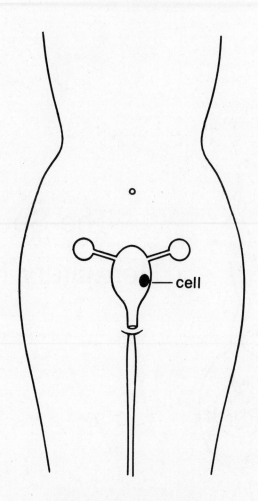

cell

New cell will grow
into full grown baby
in about 9 months

Figure 168   **535**

Inserting the Tampon

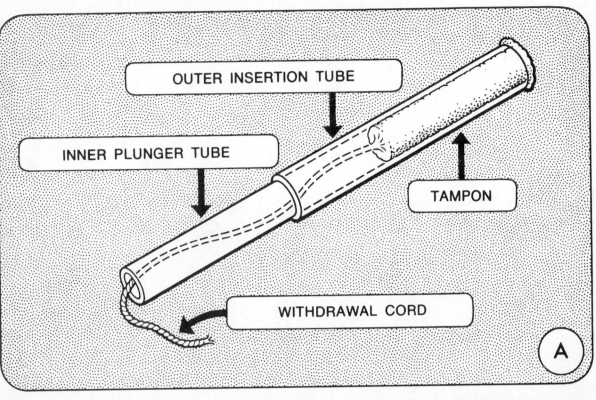

OUTER INSERTION TUBE

INNER PLUNGER TUBE

TAMPON

WITHDRAWAL CORD

A

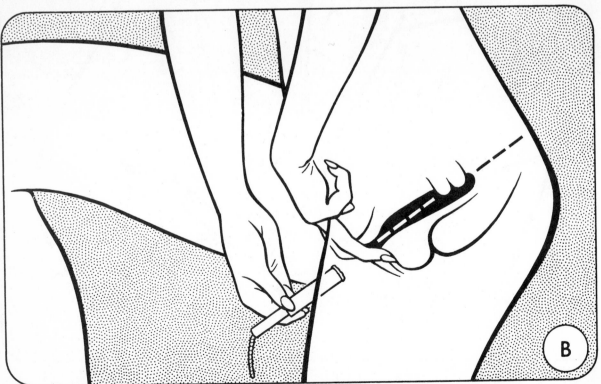

B

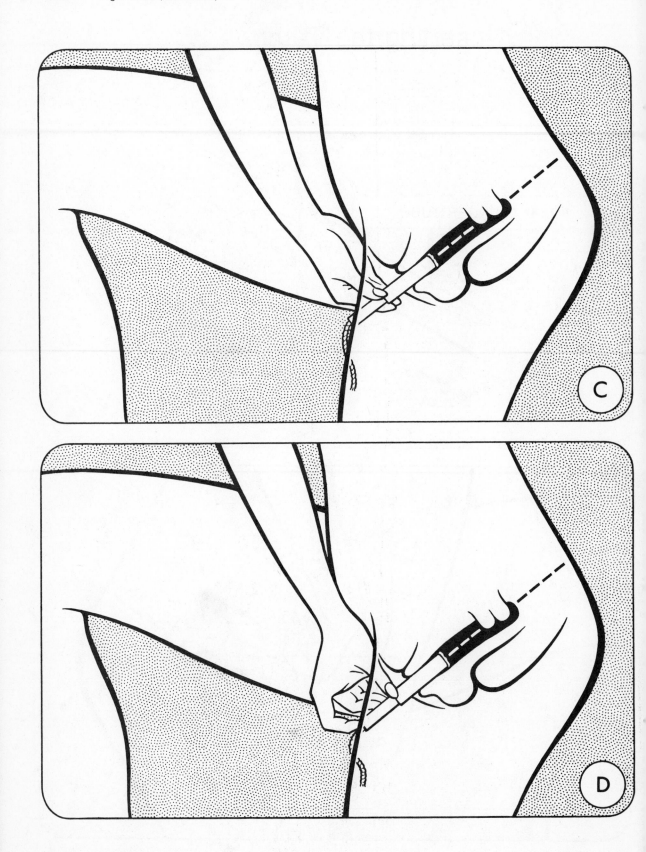

Figure 168 (continued)   **537**

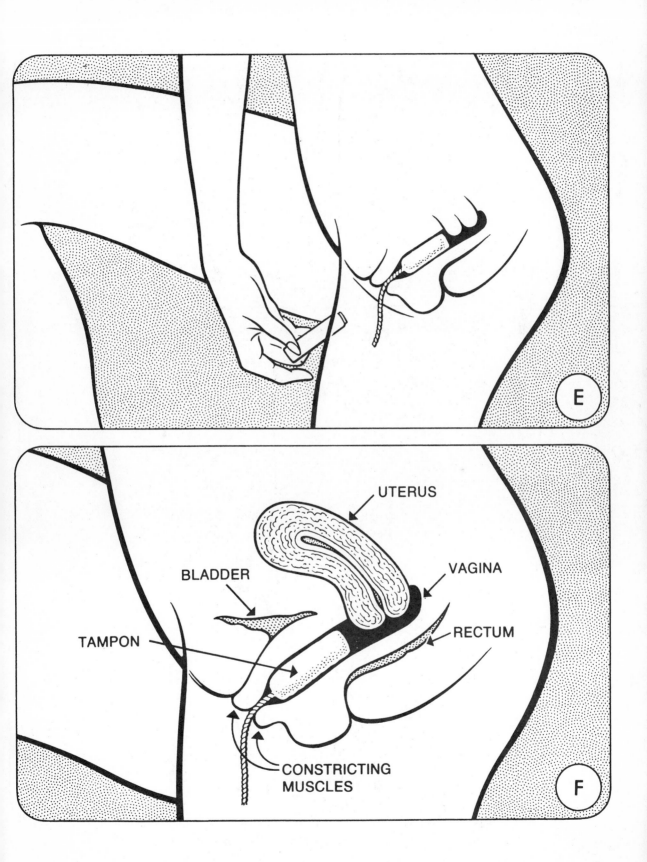

E

UTERUS

BLADDER

VAGINA

TAMPON

RECTUM

CONSTRICTING
MUSCLES

F